EXPLORERS

*From Ancient Times
to the Space Age*

EXPLORERS

From Ancient Times to the Space Age

Volume 1

Consulting Editors

John Logan Allen
Professor of Geography
University of Connecticut

E. Julius Dasch
Manager/Scientist
NASA National Space Grant Program

Barry M. Gough
Professor of History
Wilfrid Laurier University

Macmillan Library Reference USA

Simon & Schuster Macmillan
New York

Simon & Schuster and Prentice Hall International
London Mexico City New Delhi Singapore Sydney Toronto

EDITORIAL CREDITS

Developed for Simon & Schuster Macmillan by Visual Education Corporation, Princeton, N.J.

For Macmillan
Editor: Hélène G. Potter
Cover Designer: Judy Kahn

For Visual Education
DIRECTOR OF REFERENCE: Darryl Kestler
PROJECT EDITOR: Guy Austrian
ASSOCIATE EDITOR: Doriann Markey
WRITERS: Michael Burgan, John Haley, Rebecca Stefoff, Elizabeth Trundle
RESEARCH ASSISTANT: Christopher Binkley
COPYEDITING SUPERVISOR: Maureen Pancza
COPY EDITOR: Joanna Foster
INTERIOR DESIGN: Maxson Crandall
PHOTO RESEARCH: Sara Matthews
CARTOGRAPHER: Gyula Pauer
PRODUCTION SUPERVISORS: Ellen Foos, Christine Osborne
PRODUCTION ASSISTANT: Rob Ehlers
ELECTRONIC PREPARATION: Cynthia C. Feldner, Fiona Torphy
ELECTRONIC PRODUCTION: Elise Dodeles, Lisa Evans-Skopas, Deirdre Sheean, Isabelle Verret

Simon & Schuster Macmillan
1633 Broadway
New York, NY 10019

Library of Congress Catalog Card Number: 98-8809
PRINTED IN THE UNITED STATES OF AMERICA
Printing Number
1 2 3 4 5 6 7 8 9 10

Library of Congress Cataloging-in-Publication Data

Explorers and discoverers: from ancient times to the space age/consulting editors,
    John Logan Allen, E. Julius Dasch, Barry Gough.
        p. cm.
    Includes bibliographical references and index.
    ISBN 0-02-864893-5 (set).—ISBN 0-02-864890-0 (v. 1).—ISBN 0-02-864891-9 (v. 2).—
ISBN 0-02-864892-7 (v. 3)
    1. Explorers—Biography—Dictionaries.   I. Allen, John Logan. 1941–   .
II. Dasch, E. Julius.   III. Gough, Barry M.
G200.E877   1998
910´.92´2—dc21   98-8809
[B]   CIP

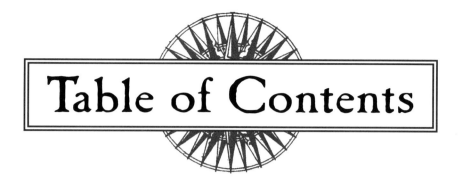

Table of Contents

Volume 1

A section of color plates, *Ancient Times and Middle Ages,* appears between pages 116 and 117.

C

D

Volume 2

A section of color plates, *The Renaissance,* appears between pages 124 and 125.

D *(continued)*

E

F

Volume 3

A section of color plates, *Modern Times,* appears
between pages 124 and 125.

List of Maps

Volume 1

Volume 2

Volume 3

Preface

This encyclopedia of *Explorers and Discoverers* contains profiles of 333 men and women who expanded our knowledge of the world and beyond. These individuals made difficult—even fatal—journeys, discovered unknown lands, mapped unfamiliar regions, and described the peoples, flora, and fauna that they encountered in their travels.

A board of distinguished consultants—experts in history, geography, and space science—selected the subjects of these profiles. The choices reflect the range of interests, skills, and professions that lead people to abandon their established lives for the uncertainty of an expedition into uncharted territory. Among the explorers profiled, readers will find geographers, merchants, navigators, botanists, archaeologists, and treasure hunters. Also profiled are people who made essential contributions to the process of discovery by working in their own countries as cartographers, inventors, and historians.

The pioneers of space exploration have carried the spirit of discovery into our own time, and some of those men and women are included in these volumes. However, the full story of the exploits of the individuals who have blazed the way in mountaineering, aviation, and undersea exploration will have to be the subject of another work.

Introductory Essays

Volume 1 of *Explorers and Discoverers* begins with three essays: "The Technology of Exploration," "Causes and Effects of Exploration," and "The History of Exploration." These three summaries provide some technical and historical background and help students to understand how each explorer's efforts were a part of the long and complex process of discovery.

Within the text, Small Caps call attention to the names by which profiled individuals are alphabetized in these volumes. Words in **boldface** are defined in the margin. Some of these terms are given fuller explanations in the Glossary at the end of Volume 3.

Biographical Profiles

The biographical profiles, which follow the essays, are arranged in alphabetical order and run through all three volumes. Each profile begins with a headnote that lists the explorer's nationality, dates of birth and death, and main activities. The text of a profile usually begins with a brief summary of the individual's accomplishments, followed by an account of the person's life before, during, and after the events that earned him or her a place in the history of discovery. Each article ends with a short list of books about the profiled individual. Students may also refer to the Bibliography at the end of Volume 3 for works that deal more generally with the topic of exploration.

The text is accompanied by over 250 photographs, paintings, drawings, and etchings. These illustrate the men and women profiled, as well as vessels, equipment, and historical events. In addition, 50 maps show the routes taken by explorers across oceans and continents.

Appendices

At the end of Volume 3, students will find four additional resources—a Glossary, a List of Explorers by Nationality, a List of Explorers by Area of Exploration, and a Bibliography.

The Glossary presents detailed information about some of the key terms used in the profiles. The two lists of explorers will help readers to study the efforts of individuals and their countries to explore the world's geographical regions. The Bibliography contains further references that are organized in two sections: General Works and Works by Region.

Acknowledgments

This reference work represents the collaboration of many people, including researchers, writers, editors, designers, layout artists, consultants, and publishers. We invite you to share the great adventures of exploration and discovery that are recounted in the following pages.

The Technology of Exploration

Christopher COLUMBUS spent eight years trying to win support for his first voyage of discovery. He studied ancient maps and made calculations to prove that he could reach Asia from Europe by sailing across the Atlantic Ocean. His wait ended in 1492, when the king and queen of Spain gave him money for three ships. For 33 days, Columbus sailed over open waters. He then landed on an island in the Caribbean Sea that he named San Salvador. However, because he had only the imprecise instruments of his time to track his course, the measurements he made were not reliable. To this day, historians who have tried to retrace his route are not sure on just which island he first landed. Eventually, Columbus returned to Spain with the information he had gathered during his voyage. Other explorers followed Columbus, and they soon realized that the ancient maps were wrong. Two unknown continents—the Americas—lay between Europe and Asia. European mapmakers began to redraw the world.

Columbus faced basic concerns that are shared by all explorers. He needed the skills of navigation that made it possible both to determine where he was going and to tell people where he had been. He needed transportation to get there and—with luck and skill—back again. Navigation and transportation are the technologies of exploration. The needs of explorers can encourage inventors to make advances in technology. New technologies, in turn, can create new opportunities for exploration.

Tools and Techniques of Navigation

The simplest way to keep track of location is by following landmarks, such as mountains or rivers. Sailors can go from one port to the next along a familiar coastline. When traveling in unknown areas or sailing on the open sea, people learned to look to the sky. From the sun by day and from the moon and stars by night, navigators could get a rough idea of time and direction. This method, known as celestial navigation, is not very precise—and is made impossible by fog and clouds.

Navigators acquired a powerful tool around the year 1000. It was discovered that lodestone, a type of magnetic iron ore, could make a needle point northward. Soon mariners were using magnetized needles that floated in bowls of water—the first compasses. These allowed people to measure direction quite accurately.

The ancient Greeks knew of another tool, the **astrolabe,** a metal disk on which navigators could measure the height of the sun or a star above the horizon. Medieval Arabs perfected this

astrolabe navigational instrument used since ancient times to determine distance north or south of the equator

---

This astrolabe had a rotating bar that a navigator could line up with the sun or stars. The angle on the rim showed the height of the sun or stars in the sky.

latitude distance north or south of the equator

quadrant navigational instrument used since the Middle Ages to determine distance north or south of the equator

sextant optical instrument used by navigators since the 1750s to determine distance north or south of the equator

longitude distance east or west of an imaginary line on the earth's surface; in 1884, most nations agreed to draw the line through Greenwich, England

chronometer clock designed to keep precise time in the rough conditions of sea travel

Inuit people of the Canadian Arctic, sometimes known as the Eskimo

For detailed descriptions of navigational tools, such as the astrolabe, quadrant, and chronometer, see the Glossary in Volume 3. Additional photographs can be found in the color sections of Volumes 1 and 2.

device, adding tables and formulas that revealed the navigator's **latitude.** By the 1500s, mariners had replaced the astrolabe with the cross-staff, a simpler tool that provided the same information. The cross-staff was an early version of the **quadrant,** which was later developed into the **sextants** and octants that are still in use today. These tools allowed mariners to determine latitude in most regions near and north of the equator. They were not as useful far south of the equator until the 1600s, when astronomers began including southern constellations in their star charts.

Mariners also needed to know their **longitude,** but for centuries they had no easy, reliable way to find this information. Using a method called dead reckoning, a navigator could estimate longitude with rough calculations of speed and direction. Dead reckoning was useful over short distances, but a small error on a long ocean voyage could lead a ship hundreds of miles off course, possibly into unknown and dangerous waters.

Mariners were making ocean crossings routinely by the 1600s, and they were desperate for an accurate way to find their longitude. The English Parliament offered a great sum of money for a solution. The prize went unclaimed for decades, until John HARRISON invented the **chronometer** in 1762. This clock kept precise time at sea despite the rough weather. The accurate measurement of time made possible an accurate calculation of longitude. As a result, explorers and mapmakers were able to determine their position at any point on the earth's surface.

Maps and Mapmaking

Maps are central to exploration. They show the boundaries of the known world, challenging adventurers to go beyond. When explorers return from unknown regions, they bring information that fills in our maps—and enlarges our understanding of the earth. Many explorers and discoverers have also been mapmakers.

The Development of Maps

The oldest known maps come from the Middle East and date from about 2500 B.C. Many cultures invented their own styles of mapmaking. The people of the Marshall Islands in the Pacific Ocean made sailing charts on stick frameworks, attaching curved sticks and seashells that represented currents and islands. The seafaring **Inuit** showed the positions of islands by stitching bits of wood or fur onto sealskin. North American Indians drew or carved maps on tree bark, skins, wood, and stone.

By A.D. 200, the Chinese were drawing maps based on square grids. Each square represented an equal area of the earth's surface, so measuring distance on the map was easy. At about the same time, the Greek scholar PTOLEMY summed up European knowledge of geography in his *Guide to Geography.* In this book, he listed the positions of 8,000 places in Europe, Africa, and Asia. He also gave instructions for using projections to create maps. Projections are ways to represent the round earth on flat paper—though only a globe can accurately represent the shape of the earth.

cartographer mapmaker

cartography the science of mapmaking

By the Middle Ages, Ptolemy's work had been lost to most Europeans. Some **cartographers** drew on Christian beliefs to create maps that were symbolic as well as geographic. These maps are often called "T-and-O" maps because they are circular in shape and show Europe, Africa, and Asia divided by a *T* that is formed by the Mediterranean Sea and various rivers. With Jerusalem at their center and imaginary monsters at the edges, these maps reflected a medieval Christian view of the world.

Medieval Arab geographers preserved knowledge of Ptolemy's work, and their maps more closely resembled Ptolemy's. Although Arab maps, like those of Europeans, contained many geographical errors, they made important advances in **cartography.** Their maps also included new information provided by Arab travelers and traders who had visited much of Africa and Asia.

The Modern Age of Mapmaking

Europeans rediscovered Ptolemy's writings in the 1400s. New world maps based on his ideas, methods, and information began the era of modern cartography. Although the Ptolemaic maps contained inaccuracies, they contributed to a new and growing interest in geography and exploration.

Meanwhile, sailors had developed another kind of map, the sea chart, to help them locate ports and avoid dangerous waters. The early charts were little more than sketches of coastlines. After magnetic compasses came into use in the Mediterranean region around 1200, mariners began to make more detailed and accurate charts called portolans. Networks of lines showed the directions of winds that would carry ships between ports. In time, cartography became a science based on precise measurements and careful calculations. Mapmakers developed hundreds of new projections that let them produce larger and more accurate maps.

European nations began to focus their efforts on exploration and mapmaking. In 1419 Prince Henry of Portugal created a center at Sagres, Portugal, for the study of maps, geography, and navigation. He sent ships on voyages of discovery that marked the beginning of the Age of Exploration. In the following centuries, opportunities for conquest, trade, and knowledge expanded. Hundreds of expeditions were organized by governments, merchants, and scientific societies. Explorers visited every part of the world, and by the early 1900s, cartographers had filled in most of the blank spots on their maps.

Smaller and easier to use than the quadrant, this sextant of the 1800s had mirrors that reflected the sun or stars along the navigator's line of sight.

For detailed descriptions of vehicles such as the caravel, sledge, and space capsule, see the Glossary in Volume 3. Additional photographs can be found in the color sections of all three volumes.

Vessels and Vehicles

Explorers needed ways to reach the places they located on maps. Naturally, the earliest travel was on foot, but people found that they could move beyond local areas more easily on rivers and seas. With the invention of aircraft, people have extended their reach into the air and even into outer space. Explorers have led the way into unknown areas, traveling by land, sea, and air. Their success—and their lives—have often depended on their transportation.

Travel over Land

Various forms of land transportation developed in different areas to fit local conditions. Wise explorers often learned the best methods from local peoples. For example, on the long, hot trade routes of North Africa, Arabia, and Asia, travelers joined camel **caravans** that might include 10,000 camels or more. In tropical central Africa, on the other hand, pack animals could not survive the humidity and the insects. Explorers of Africa's rain forests and rivers often hired (or forced) large numbers of local tribesmen to carry their supplies.

After the arrival of Europeans, horses and wagons became the most widely used form of transport on the plains and deserts of the Americas and Australia. But in some areas, small, lightly equipped groups could move more easily than huge expeditions could. Through forests, over mountains, and along rivers, trappers and scouts traveled by foot and canoe. Often they had to **portage** from one river to another. For teams of explorers in the icy polar regions, disciplined travel was even more important. Explorers had to follow precise plans, setting up supply **depots** and using dogs to pull **sledges** and **boat-sledges** over the ice and snow. Eventually, exploration of the continents was completed from the air, but for many centuries, people had to travel over land.

Ancient and Medieval Ships

Water transportation was well developed in ancient times. The people who lived around the Mediterranean Sea were skilled sailors. By 3000 B.C., the Egyptians had seagoing vessels made of short wooden planks, held together by pegs and ropes. These ships were propelled by oarsmen and a single large sail. By 2000 B.C., the Phoenicians (of what is now Lebanon) were well known in the Mediterranean region for their abilities as sailors. They eventually traveled as far west as modern-day Morocco and Spain in sturdy ships built of cedar and fir timbers.

Around 700 B.C., Greek traders began to compete with the Phoenicians. Greek cargo vessels sailed for distant ports carrying large crews to fight pirates, the seagoing bandits who attacked ships at sea. The Greeks also built oar-driven warships called **galleys.** The Romans built galleys, too, but they also developed wide, round cargo ships that could move by wind power alone.

The Norsemen of Scandinavia, Iceland, and Greenland had two main types of wooden ships powered by both oars and sails. The longships, used for fighting and raiding, may have been as long as 150 feet, with 34 pairs of oars. The *knorr,* designed for trading, was shorter and had higher sides. Norse ships could bend slightly to withstand the battering of the rough northern seas.

The Chinese sailed the western Pacific Ocean and the Indian Ocean in flat-bottomed boats called **junks.** These ships had several masts with sails made of fiber mats. In the late 1200s, Marco POLO reported seeing junks 200 to 300 feet long, with cabins for up to 60 merchants. At that time, the Arabs were the most skilled sailors in the Mediterranean Sea and the Arabian Sea. Their **dhows** may have been the first **lateen-rigged** ships.

---

caravan large group of people traveling together, often with pack animals, across a desert or other dangerous region

portage transport of boats and supplies overland between waterways

depot place where supplies are stored

sledge heavy sled, often mounted on runners, that is pulled over snow or ice

boat-sledge boat mounted on sled runners to allow travel on both ice and water

galley ship with oars and sails, used in ancient and medieval times

junk Chinese ship with sails made of fiber mats

dhow Arab vessel with triangular sails, widely used in the Mediterranean Sea and Indian Ocean

lateen-rigged having triangular sails that can catch wind from either side of a mast, making a ship easy to maneuver

This woodcut shows a caravel of the 1400s. The Portuguese began the Age of Exploration by sailing ships like this one along the west coast of Africa.

caravel small ship with three masts and both square and triangular sails

galleon large sailing ship used for war and trade

brig small, fast sailing ship with two masts and square sails

brigantine two-masted sailing ship with both square and triangular sails

schooner fast, easy-to-maneuver sailing ship with two or more masts and triangular sails

dirigible large aircraft filled with a lighter-than-air gas that keeps it aloft; similar to a blimp but with a rigid frame

satellite object launched into space to circle a planet or moon

orbit stable, circular route; one trip around; to revolve around

Modern European Ships

European shipbuilding took a great leap forward with the age of European exploration. Before that time, most voyages were short trips close to shore. But sailors were able to make longer ocean voyages as European shipyards began to produce new types of vessels. First, shipbuilders replaced the single mast, carrying a single large sail, with two or even three masts. These masts could hold a number of smaller sails, allowing a captain to position the sails at appropriate angles to catch the wind.

The Portuguese used **caravels** in their voyages along the coast of Africa in the 1400s. These ships were the workhorses of early European exploration of the seas. They had both triangular sails, which could catch shifting coastal winds, and square sails, which caught more wind on the open sea. Two of Columbus's ships, the *Niña* and the *Pinta,* were caravels. The **galleon** was the main warship of the 1500s, but like the later **brig, brigantine,** and **schooner,** it sometimes served for exploration. Explorers' vessels were adapted from many other uses. Between 1768 and 1771, for example, James Cook sailed around the world in a converted coal-hauling ship. In the 1800s and 1900s, ships were built from iron and steel, with engines powered by steam, gasoline, and nuclear reactors.

Some ships sail beneath the waves. The first submarines were built in the 1600s, but they were not truly useful for many years. In the 1900s, the vast ocean floors were opened to explorers such as Jacques-Yves Cousteau. A great success in undersea exploration came in 1958, when the American nuclear-powered submarine *Nautilus* reached the North Pole—under the ice cap.

Aerial Exploration

Exploration took to the air in the late 1700s. The early hot-air balloons and **dirigibles** crashed often, however, and most explorers of the 1900s preferred to use the airplane. The first attempt to fly into the Arctic failed in 1909, but in the 1920s, Richard Byrd flew over both the North and South Poles. Aerial explorers photographed and mapped huge stretches of remote territory in the continental interiors. They also provided cartographers with images of the tops of the highest mountain ranges.

The Space Age

Waves of new technology continued to open new frontiers of exploration in the second half of the 1900s. Navigators at sea and in the air benefited from loran, a system that calculates position by means of radio signals broadcast from various places around the planet. The next step was to broadcast the signals from space. Today's Global Positioning System (GPS) has 24 **satellites** in **orbit** around the earth. A handheld GPS receiver can calculate latitude and longitude for anyone from a cartographer to a polar explorer to a backwoods hiker.

Hundreds of other satellites gather up-to-the-minute information and broadcast it to earth. The familiar television weather map is a triumph of satellite mapping. In the 1990s, the United States began its Mission to Planet Earth, a program that uses satellites to study the atmosphere and ocean currents. These satellites also helped cartographers to make extremely accurate maps of the earth's surface. Other satellites aim their instruments at planets, stars, and galaxies throughout the universe.

Satellites are carried into space on **rockets.** When a rocket reaches space, it separates from the satellite and falls toward the earth. It burns up from heat caused by friction with the earth's atmosphere. The world's first satellite, named *Sputnik 1,* was launched by the **Soviet Union** in 1957. The Soviets went on to launch *Swallow,* the first spacecraft that held a person, in 1961. Like most early spacecraft, the *Swallow* was a tiny metal **capsule** with flight controls and a supply of air for its pilot, the **cosmonaut** Yuri GAGARIN. A heat shield protected the *Swallow* from burning up when it parachuted back to earth. Later that year, American **astronauts** Alan SHEPARD and John GLENN also rode capsules into space. In 1965 cosmonaut Aleksei LEONOV, wearing a **space suit,** made the first "space walk," floating while tethered outside his capsule for about 10 minutes.

The United States operated the Apollo space program from 1967 to 1972. Apollo spacecraft entered into orbit around the moon and then released a landing craft to the surface. When the astronauts had finished their work on the moon's surface, they blasted off, rejoined the spacecraft in orbit, and then flew back to the earth. Some Apollo missions carried four-wheeled vehicles called rovers, which were driven by astronauts on the moon's surface.

Astronauts and cosmonauts have done valuable scientific research while living on **space stations.** These spacecraft often have separate quarters for sleeping, exercising, and working. In the 1970s, the Soviet Salyut and American Skylab stations had varying amounts of success. The Soviet station *Mir* was launched in 1986 and remained in use into the 1990s. Meanwhile, the United States developed a spacecraft called the **space shuttle.** Two rockets—one on each side of a giant fuel tank—lift the shuttle into orbit around the earth. The shuttle can carry up to eight crew members and fly for up to three weeks. It returns to earth by landing on a runway, just like an airplane.

The space shuttle does not go farther than its orbit around the earth, but the United States and the Soviet Union have both sent spacecraft to other planets. These craft, called probes, have no human pilots. They are controlled by computers that communicate with the earth by radio. Some have gone into orbit around other planets and moons, and a few have made surface landings. A small number have flown beyond the solar system into **interstellar** space. For now, however, most scientists continue to explore space from the surface of the earth.

rocket vehicle propelled by exploding fuel

Soviet Union nation that existed from 1922 to 1991, made up of Russia and 14 other republics in eastern Europe and northern Asia

capsule small early spacecraft designed to carry a person around the earth

cosmonaut Russian term for a person who travels into space; literally, "traveler to the universe"

astronaut American term for a person who travels into space; literally, "traveler to the stars"

space suit protective gear that allows a person who wears it to survive in space

space station spacecraft that circles the earth for months or years with a human crew

space shuttle reusable spacecraft designed to transport people and cargo between the earth and space

interstellar between the stars

Atop this 363-foot-tall Saturn V rocket, the Apollo 11 astronauts escaped the earth's gravity on July 16, 1969. They reached the moon four days later.

Causes and Effects of Exploration

Exploration began when the earliest humans searched for food and better living conditions. It continued throughout the ages as people attempted to gain knowledge of their world and to initiate trade with people in other regions. In the 1400s, Europeans began to accelerate and organize the process of exploration, sending many expeditions into areas about which they knew little. Lasting 500 years, the European Age of Exploration resulted in the first complete and accurate geographic picture of the world. Like all periods of discovery, it was driven by a combination of forces.

Motives for Exploration

Although exploration was often a national effort, the people who traveled to the far corners of the globe for their countries were a diverse group. Why did they risk hunger, disease, and shipwreck—and worse—as explorers? Nations had a variety of political, economic, religious, and scientific motives for launching expeditions. Individual explorers often shared these goals and also sought adventure, fortune, and personal glory in journeys of discovery.

Politics

Spanish conquistadors—covered in metal armor and seated on horses—were a strange sight to the Indian tribes living in the Americas.

The desire to control territory drove many nations to explore new lands. In the late 1800s and early 1900s, Britain and Russia competed for control of Tibet. The two countries sent explorers, spies, and diplomats to learn about the country and its capital, Lhasa. These complex political maneuvers came to an end in 1904, when a British army fought its way into Lhasa under the command of Francis YOUNGHUSBAND. National glory was a motive for Chinese exploration in the 1400s. The Chinese emperor sent ZHENG He with large fleets to visit ports in Asia, Arabia, and eastern Africa. Zheng's goal was not to conquer but to demonstrate China's wealth and power to other nations. Glory was also an inspiration for many individual explorers. For example, in the 1800s, dozens of men and women competed to discover the source of the Nile River in Africa. The winner of this race, Britain's John Hanning SPEKE, stood to gain worldwide fame—as well as political control over the river valley for his country. However, the fierce criticism and doubt he faced in Britain was not overcome for many years, and Britain eventually had to give up the African empire Speke had helped to build.

Commerce

The desire for trade, precious metals, slaves, and natural resources lay behind many voyages and expeditions. The European Age of Exploration began with Portugal's search for a sea route to the spices and silks of southern Asia. The Portuguese hoped to avoid the overland routes controlled by merchants in the Middle East and Italian city-states such as Venice and Genoa.

In the 1500s, Portugal, Spain, and other nations began to establish colonies in Asia and the Americas that would become important sources of income. Spanish mines in the Americas produced vast quantities of gold and silver at a time when Europe's own mines could not keep up with the needs of commerce and industry. Spain used much of its new wealth to pay its debts and finance its armies, while the **conquistadors** reaped huge personal fortunes. Meanwhile, the known territory of North America expanded constantly as French, Dutch, and British explorers hunted for valuable furs. The European colonial powers tried to control the flow of trade in their empires in ways that would bring them the greatest possible profit.

conquistador Spanish or Portuguese explorer and military leader in the Americas

Religion

For some explorers, religious faith was the strongest motive of all. The quest of Xuan Zang, a Chinese Buddhist pilgrim, was a personal one. He made a difficult journey to India in the 600s in order to study ancient holy writings. In later centuries, Christians of the Society of Jesus, known as **Jesuits,** went to distant parts of the world to convert other peoples to Christianity. Their successes helped the Society of Jesus gain considerable influence in both European and colonial politics. Among these priests were the Italian Matteo Ricci in China, the Frenchman Jacques Marquette on the Mississippi River, and the Spaniard Eusebio Francisco Kino in the American Southwest.

Jesuit member of the Society of Jesus, a Roman Catholic order founded by Ignatius of Loyola in 1534

Science

Much exploration was based on the desire to know what lay beyond a mountain range or across an ocean. In the 1700s, scientists began to organize their studies into separate fields, such as **botany** and **geology.** It became common for naturalists such as England's Joseph Banks to travel with naval vessels. Other scientists, including the German Alexander von Humboldt, organized their own expeditions to observe the wonders of the natural world and collect samples of rocks, plants, and animals. Nations also mounted large, well-funded voyages to answer scientific questions. The U.S. South Seas Exploring Expedition gathered many volumes of scientific data between 1838 and 1842. But the voyage was also intended to demonstrate the strength of the young American nation and allow it to claim territory in Antarctica. The mission grew out of a complicated set of motives and goals, as had the European Age of Exploration.

botany the scientific study of plants

geology the scientific study of the earth's natural history

Europe and the Age of Exploration

By the end of the Middle Ages, highly developed civilizations had emerged in many parts of the world. The Islamic world of North Africa and the Middle East had made great achievements in science, medicine, and the arts. The Aztec and Inca Empires of the Americas had large populations ruled by stable governments, as did China and India. Asia's rich trade network stretched from the Mediterranean Sea to the Pacific Ocean. Yet only Europe set out to explore and colonize the rest of the world. Why this happened is an important question.

A Time of Transition

In the 1400s, Europe was changing. Using new methods of agriculture, farmers produced larger crops, making it possible to support cities and towns with larger populations. Craftspeople in the cities produced many more items, such as woolen cloth and iron tools, that could be traded. European merchants and trading companies wanted to sell these goods in foreign markets. They also looked for foreign goods to bring to Europe, especially Asia's rare and costly spices, fabrics, and gemstones.

At the same time, Europe was entering a new period in its centuries-old conflict with the Islamic world. Empires in central Asia were converting to the Muslim faith and preventing Christians from using the trade roads across Asia. When goods did reach Europe, trade was controlled by Italian merchants. Wanting to bypass the Muslims and the Italians, people in the western and northern parts of Europe searched for new sea routes to Asia.

Europeans were also facing Muslims on the battlefield. Christian armies began campaigns to force the Muslims out of Spain and eastern Europe, but the struggle was long and difficult. Europeans hoped to find or convert Christians in Africa and Asia and join with them against the Muslims. Many explorers were encouraged by the legend of Prester John, a Christian emperor who was thought to rule somewhere in India, central Asia, or Africa.

Europeans were looking outward. But the great civilizations of east Asia had little interest in the rest of the world. The Chinese in particular felt that their culture was superior to all others and that China could supply goods to meet all the needs of its people. Also, Asians did not place as high a value on converting others to their religions as Christians and Muslims did. For these reasons, Asians rarely traveled to foreign lands.

The Impact of Technology

Europeans' leap into world exploration got a boost from new technology—and their willingness to use it. Arab **dhows** performed well in the relatively calm waters of the Mediterranean Sea, the Persian Gulf, and the Indian Ocean. But sailors in western and northern Europe were faced with the rough and stormy Atlantic Ocean, North Sea, and Baltic Sea. European shipbuilders developed vessels with strong hulls, high sides, and multiple masts and sails that were well suited to long ocean crossings.

These European ships were also sturdy enough to carry hundreds of cannons, which overwhelmed Arab and Asian navies. Gunpowder had originated in China, where it was used mainly for fireworks. But Europeans made gunpowder into a weapon, using it first in cannons and then in handheld guns. Early firearms were too

dhow Arab vessel with triangular sails, widely used in the Mediterranean Sea and Indian Ocean

inaccurate and awkward to be truly useful. Sometimes the shock they created among people who had never seen them was more effective than the weapons themselves. In the 1800s, however, firearms were improved and became a major force in battle.

Printing was another technology that changed the world. Before the printing press was invented in the 1400s, books in Europe were usually handwritten in Latin. The printing press could produce books much more quickly. By writing and printing in the languages they spoke, such as English and French, Europeans were able to spread new information about the world more easily than before. By contrast, Muslims rejected printing and permitted only classical Arabic to be used in writing. These decisions limited the spread of information and ideas in the Islamic world.

Exploration's Effects on Europe

The Age of Exploration changed everything from the way Europeans ate to the way they thought of the world around them. It changed the fortunes of western Europe's nations and brought them new responsibilities as the rulers of distant colonial empires. It also led to new conflicts.

Wealth and Warfare

Beginning with the efforts of well-armed Portuguese and Spanish explorers in the 1400s and 1500s, Europeans won greater access to

This painting shows Christopher Columbus at the court of King Ferdinand and Queen Isabella, presenting treasure and Indians brought from the Americas.

many trade routes and opened new routes as well. New foods from around the world changed the diets of Europeans. Corn, tobacco, potatoes, squash, and chocolate came from the Americas, tea and spices from eastern Asia, coffee from the Middle East, and bananas from Africa. Other products flowed across the seas to European ports, including silk and gemstones from Asia, rare woods and dyes from Brazil, gold and ivory from Africa, and above all, gold and silver from Central and South America. Portugal and Spain—and later the Netherlands, France, and England—prospered and became the major powers of Europe and the world.

With explorers continuing to lead the way, European nations made ambitious efforts to map, claim, and conquer lands that possessed desirable resources, goods, or locations. They established settlements, trading posts, military bases, and colonial governments. Europeans gradually brought much of the world under their influence, if not always under their direct control.

But the Age of Empire, as it came to be called, was as costly as it was profitable. European governments faced conflict not only with the people they had conquered but often with their own colonists as well. The competition for empires also fueled the rivalries that existed among European nations and contributed to several wars, including the Seven Years' War (1756 to 1763) and World War I (1914 to 1918).

A New Way of Seeing

The changes in diet, wealth, and borders were accompanied by changes in the way Europeans viewed the world. Before the Age of Exploration, Europeans thought that the Bible and some ancient Greek and Roman writings contained all human knowledge. But explorers found many things that those texts did not mention—such as whole continents with strange plants and animals. They also found religions other than the Jewish, Christian, and Muslim faiths they already knew. The world turned out to be bigger and more varied than they had dreamed.

Even so, Europeans' faith in Christianity was powerful and constant. Confronted with exotic beliefs and cultures, most Europeans insisted that their own way of life was superior. However, some people began to see value in other cultures. For example, in the 1500s and 1600s, Jesuits arrived at royal courts in China and India and found lively debates among scholars of Asian religions such as Hinduism and Buddhism. The missionaries could not easily convert such men to Christianity. They first had to gain respect at court by learning the dress, language, and customs of the land. Only then would they be invited to join in the discussions. Later, in the 1700s and 1800s, some English and French sailors who visited Pacific islands such as Tahiti thought that the Tahitians enjoyed a simple, pleasant life, even without Christianity. Despite the less peaceful aspects of the islanders' culture, such as human sacrifice, some sailors chose to stay in the islands rather than return to Europe.

As they learned about new lands and peoples, some explorers made an effort to describe what they found as fully and accurately as they could. They began to rely more on evidence and science

Made in the early 1700s, this engraving depicts Christian missionaries performing a baptism ceremony in the Congo region of central Africa.

than on myth and faith when studying their surroundings. This shift occurred slowly, but it helped to shape the modern world.

Exploration's Effects on Other Continents

The arrival of Europeans brought enormous changes to Asia, Africa, Australia, and the Americas. Many societies on these continents came under the rule of Europeans. The native peoples struggled to retain their cultures while living in the colonial empires.

Conquest

Many explorers were officers in their nations' armies and navies, and they arrived in new lands with soldiers at their sides. Their willingness to use force was strengthened by the belief that it was their right—and even their duty—to control the world. Some individuals spoke out powerfully against the mistreatment of conquered peoples. One such defender was Bartolomé de LAS CASAS, a Spanish priest who worked through the Roman Catholic Church to protect the Indians of Mexico during the 1500s. Nevertheless, European armies fought and defeated many peoples in the Americas, Africa, and Asia.

Deadlier than their guns were the diseases the Europeans carried. People living in the Americas, long isolated from the rest of the world, had no resistance to certain European diseases, including measles, influenza, and smallpox. The effect was devastating. Soon after the Europeans landed, Indians began dying by the thousands. Smallpox helped Hernán CORTÉS conquer the stricken Aztecs in the 1500s. A century later, the Puritan settlers found New England almost empty. Diseases introduced earlier by European fishermen and traders had nearly wiped out the local Indian population.

Colonization

Along with conquest came colonization. In North America and elsewhere, Europeans claimed land for settlement and displaced the people who were already there. In other places, such as India and Indonesia, European officials took control of local governments. European customs, languages, and laws became standard. European commercial systems based on cash and private property replaced systems based on **barter** and tribal ownership of land. Missionaries worked to convert colonial subjects to Christianity. In some colonies, especially in Central and South America, Europeans and non-Europeans intermarried, leading to a mixing of their cultures.

barter exchange of goods without the use of money

European culture also spread new ideas that eventually led to the end of colonial practices such as slavery. The slave trade had long existed in parts of Africa, Asia, and the Americas, but Europeans expanded and organized the trade. To provide labor for their plantations in the Americas, they forcibly shipped millions of Africans across the Atlantic Ocean.

In the 1600s and 1700s, many Europeans—as well as some of their descendants in North and South America—came to believe in the right of all people to equality, liberty, and religious freedom. Europeans began to look hard at both slavery and colonial rule, and some began to feel that such practices were no longer acceptable.

In the early and mid-1800s, the fight against the slave trade was led by the British. During and after that same period, colonies in the Americas and elsewhere demanded independence from their parent

When India was ruled by the British, Indians and Britons both cooperated and clashed as fellow soldiers in the British army.

countries, as the United States had done in 1776. Europeans found it more and more difficult to refuse—especially when faced with fierce fighting in colonies such as Algeria and Vietnam. By the mid-1900s, most European countries were willing to let go of their empires.

Legacy

The long-term effects of exploration and the colonial rule that followed are still felt strongly today. Many colonies became new nations just a few decades ago, and they continue to suffer from problems that existed under their colonial rulers. Corrupt officials, as well as tensions among different groups of people, have made life in modern times difficult for these countries. Meanwhile, a few colonies still exist, such as the islands of French Polynesia. Traces of the old European empires remain in organizations such as the Commonwealth of Nations, a group of former British colonies that maintain cultural and commercial ties with Britain.

The Age of Exploration brought a diverse world closer together. Traders carried goods to and from every corner of the globe. Scientists made the entire world their laboratory. People of all cultures came into contact, and whether they learned from each other, fought with each other, or both, they knew that they shared a single planet. This interaction has created a global civilization that is still taking shape today.

The History of Exploration

Turn to the profiles of explorers to learn more about their lives and travels. Some profiles also contain maps of the explorers' routes.

No map or globe could exist without the efforts of the men and women who have explored the world. Since ancient times, people of all cultures have gathered information about their surroundings. This process entered a new phase in the late 1400s, when western Europeans launched what came to be known as the Age of Exploration. Over many years, mapmakers received reports from explorers and sketched the outlines of the world's continents and oceans. As explorers began to investigate inland areas, mapmakers drew in rivers, mountains, and cities. The story of how a region came to be known is the story of many hundreds of explorers, guides, soldiers, priests, traders, historians, and mapmakers.

North America

When mapmakers in Europe, Africa, and Asia began to describe the world they knew, they had no evidence that the Americas existed. Separated from the rest of the inhabited world by the vast waters of the Atlantic and Pacific Oceans, North and South America were inhabited by many different tribes. In all likelihood, these people had come from Asia across a land bridge that connected Siberia and Alaska thousands of years earlier, when sea levels were low.

Sturdy wooden ships carried Norse explorers, settlers, and raiders across the stormy northern seas.

The Coasts

Around A.D. 800, the Norse—seagoing warriors and traders from Scandinavia—began building ships that could sail the rough northern Atlantic. They pushed westward, settling the islands of Iceland and Greenland. In about the year 1001, Leif ERIKSON sailed west from a Norse colony in Greenland and landed on an island off the eastern coast of what is now Canada. He and his crew are the first Europeans known to have reached North America. The Norse eventually gave up their attempts to establish a permanent settlement on the island of Newfoundland (in present-day eastern Canada). Their adventures there remained largely unknown to other Europeans.

The next step in the exploration of North America did not occur until almost 500 years later, when the nations of western Europe were eagerly searching for a sea route to Asia. Christopher COLUMBUS sailed west from southern Europe in 1492 and arrived at islands in the Caribbean Sea. Five years later, John CABOT also sailed west, but in waters north of those explored by Columbus. Cabot probably landed on Newfoundland. Soon the English, French, and Dutch sent many more explorers to the Americas. French crews under Giovanni da VERRAZANO explored the coast from what is now Florida to Canada and proved that this area was a single landmass, not a string of islands. Spain's Alonso AL-VAREZ DE PINEDA charted the coast of the Gulf of Mexico and was the first European to see the Mississippi River. Jacques CARTIER sailed up the St. Lawrence River, establishing France's claims in the northeast. Henry HUDSON also followed water routes inland, investigating the Hudson River for the Dutch and Hudson Bay for the English. By the early 1600s, Samuel de CHAMPLAIN and other explorers had mapped most of the continent's east coast.

The exploration of the west coast began in the 1500s. European ships usually reached the coast by following Ferdinand MAGELLAN's sea route around the southern tip of South America and into the Pacific Ocean. After the Spanish established settlements on the west coast of the area now known as Mexico and Central America, ships sailed north from those ports. Juan Rodriguez CABRILLO and Sebastián VIZCAÍNO extended Spanish claims along the coast of what is now California. Parts of California were also claimed by Sir Francis DRAKE for England, but Spain built settlements there to ensure that the area remained in Spanish hands. Farther north, British navigators including James COOK and George VANCOUVER charted the west coast of Canada.

The northernmost stretches of the Pacific coast were under Russian control, thanks to Vitus BERING and Otto von KOTZEBUE, who had crossed the Bering Sea to what is now Alaska. Spaniards such as Alejandro MALASPINA and Juan Francisco de la BODEGA Y QUADRA sailed to Alaska from the south but did not interfere with Russian settlements.

United States

As explorers moved into the interior of North America, the land that is now the United States became a focus for rivalries among Spain, France, and Britain. After setting up colonies on the Caribbean islands and in Mexico, Spanish **conquistadors** pushed north in search of wealthy cities and empires to conquer. Juan PONCE DE LEÓN led the way, claiming Florida for Spain in 1513. Some 20 years later, Spain sent a large expedition to conquer lands along the Gulf of Mexico. The expedition ended in disaster. One survivor, Álvar Núñez CABEZA DE VACA, walked back to Spanish territory through the lands that are now Texas and New Mexico. As a result of his reports, new expeditions were sent north from Mexico.

Hernando de SOTO explored the Mississippi River and the American southeast from 1539 to 1542. During that same time, Francisco Vásquez de CORONADO entered regions farther west, and some of his men saw the Grand Canyon—but neither he nor Soto found the riches they sought. Spain focused its attention on its gold-producing colonies in Mexico, the Caribbean, and South America. Spain did

conquistador Spanish or Portuguese explorer and military leader in the Americas

THE EXPLORATION OF NORTH AMERICA

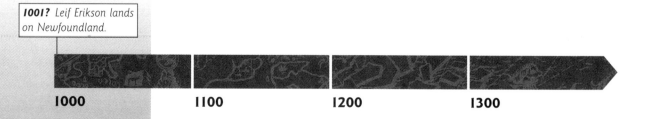

1001? Leif Erikson lands on Newfoundland.

1000   1100   1200   1300

Trade in furs and other goods brought French and British colonists into contact with Indian tribes and spurred the exploration of North America.

establish settlements to protect Mexico's northern frontier, in what became California, Arizona, New Mexico, and Texas. This area was explored by missionaries such as Eusebio Francisco KINO and governors such as Juan Bautista de ANZA.

Unlike the Spanish, who had to fight their way northward through mountains and deserts, the French controlled waterways to the heart of the continent: the St. Lawrence River and its links to the Great Lakes and the Mississippi River. The fur trade they established was extremely profitable for many years. The French were also more skilled than other Europeans at getting along with Indians, who helped them explore much of northern and central North America.

After Champlain opened a fur-trading route to the Great Lakes, Jean NICOLLET DE BELLEBORNE, Pierre Esprit RADISSON, and Médard Chouart des GROSEILLIERS further explored the lake regions. Expeditions under Louis JOLLIET and René-Robert Cavelier de LA SALLE traveled south along the Mississippi River, claiming the lands around it for France. Adventurers such as Pierre Gaultier de Varennes de LA VÉRENDRYE and his sons pushed west into the Great Plains and the fringes of the Rocky Mountains. France's efforts ended in 1763, when it lost the Seven Years' War and gave up its North American territory to Britain and Spain. But French culture has remained in North America, particularly in the present-day Canadian province of Québec.

The British concentrated on colonizing the Atlantic coast, beginning with Sir Walter RALEIGH's failed attempt to found a colony on the shores of what is now North Carolina. When Britain's American colonies became the United States in 1783, they received Britain's formerly French territory between the original colonies and the Mississippi River. The formerly French land west of the Mississippi, known as the Louisiana Territory, was given back to France by Spain in 1801. Concerned about its access to the river and the port of New Orleans, the United States purchased the western lands in 1803 in a deal known as the Louisiana Purchase. The land was bounded by the Mississippi River to the east, Canada to the north, and the Rocky Mountains to the southwest. The following American exploration

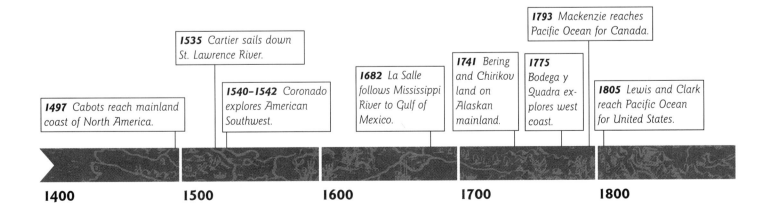

1497 Cabots reach mainland coast of North America.

1535 Cartier sails down St. Lawrence River.

1540–1542 Coronado explores American Southwest.

1682 La Salle follows Mississippi River to Gulf of Mexico.

1741 Bering and Chirikov land on Alaskan mainland.

1775 Bodega y Quadra explores west coast.

1793 Mackenzie reaches Pacific Ocean for Canada.

1805 Lewis and Clark reach Pacific Ocean for United States.

1400   1500   1600   1700   1800

The U.S. Army had a major role in the exploration and conquest of the American West, fighting bitter wars against Indians and Mexicans. This regiment of African-American cavalry won fame in the late 1800s.

of the West was a huge undertaking carried out in large part by military officers such as Meriwether LEWIS and Zebulon PIKE and fur traders such as Wilson Price HUNT and Robert STUART.

Some of the most colorful explorers were known as the Mountain Men. These trappers and traders traveled in the Rocky Mountains and the far west during the first half of the 1800s. Jedediah SMITH, James BRIDGER, Christopher "Kit" CARSON, Peter Skene OGDEN, and Joseph WALKER found routes that soon led settlers to the West. The Mountain Men were also a great help to army officers assigned to map the West, such as John Charles FRÉMONT and Benjamin Louis Eulalie de BONNEVILLE.

Canada

The exploration of inland Canada began with Champlain. He not only traveled widely but also sent men such as Etienne BRULÉ to live with the Indians, learn their languages, and explore their territory, especially around the Great Lakes. But the French were not the only Europeans active in Canada. The British wanted a share of the fur trade, too. In the late 1660s, the Frenchmen Groseilliers and Radisson helped the British launch the Hudson's Bay Company, which established many posts in the far north. After the British defeated France in the Seven Years' War and gained possession of Canada, they carried on the exploration and mapping of its northern and western reaches. Between 1770 and 1811, Samuel HEARNE, Alexander MACKENZIE, David THOMPSON, and Simon FRASER traveled through much of this rugged region of Canada. The rivers followed by Mackenzie, Thompson, and Fraser bear their names today.

Central and South America

trade winds winds that blow from east to west in the tropics

European seafarers knew that the **trade winds** blow toward the west in the tropical zones of the Atlantic Ocean for much of the year. When Christopher COLUMBUS decided to sail across the Atlantic,

This painting is one of many depicting Christopher Columbus's historic landing, which marked the beginning of the modern exploration of the Americas.

conquistador Spanish or Portuguese explorer and military leader in the Americas

Spanish Main area of the Spanish Empire including the Caribbean coasts of Central America and South America

he used these winds to propel his ships westward, arriving among the islands in the Caribbean Sea. Columbus thought that he had reached the shores of Asia. But other Europeans soon realized that the Americas were a "new world"—and a new source of wealth. Spain, having paid for Columbus's voyage, took the lead in exploring and colonizing the Caribbean islands. Using them as bases, the Spanish moved west and south into Mexico, Central America, and South America.

Mexico and Central America form a long, slender bridge between the mainlands of North America and South America. Communities of Indians existed from the coral and volcanic islands of the Caribbean to the windswept southern tip of Cape Horn. However, they were often separated by wide grasslands and deserts or by dense rain forest. Some of these Indians—especially the Aztecs of Mexico and the Inca of Peru—had built large cities and wealthy empires. The gold and silver they possessed were irresistible targets for the Spanish **conquistadors.** Despite the efforts of priests such as Bartolomé de LAS CASAS and Cristóbal de ACUÑA to protect the Indians, the history of exploration in this region is largely one of conquest.

The Caribbean

Columbus's four voyages, from 1492 to 1504, took him to the Bahamas, Cuba, Hispaniola, Guadeloupe, and other islands in the Caribbean. After founding a colony on Hispaniola, he sailed along the coasts of South America and Central America. Still determined to reach the markets of Asia, Columbus searched without success for a passage westward through the lands he had discovered.

But by the end of the 1400s, Spain was focusing less on reaching Asia and more on exploring the American islands and continents. Many of the men who completed the mapping of the Caribbean had sailed with Columbus. Among them were Vicente Yáñez PINZÓN, who visited the coast of Mexico, and Juan PONCE DE LEÓN, whose pilot discovered the powerful ocean current now known as the Gulf Stream. In 1500 Juan de LA COSA drew a world map that is believed to be the first to show the Americas. He and Rodrigo de BASTIDAS made the earliest landing on the Central American mainland, part of the area later known as the **Spanish Main.**

Central America and Mexico

Another of Columbus's former officers, the greedy and cruel Alonso de OJEDA, began the Spanish conquest of the mainland in 1499, in what later became Venezuela and Colombia. A few years later, Vasco Nuñez de BALBOA crossed Central America at its narrowest point and was the first European to see the Pacific Ocean from the Americas. Spain next turned its attention to central Mexico. Having learned from the Indians that a powerful empire existed there, Hernán CORTÉS marched boldly inland from the coast with the help of Indian guides. In 1521 he conquered the Aztec Empire and laid the foundations of the colony of New Spain. Cortés then sent some of his ambitious officers on missions of their own—partly to keep them from threatening his own control of Mexico. Pedro de AL-VARADO, Cristóbal de Olid, and Francisco de Montejo made conquests to the south, in lands that are now Guatemala, Honduras, and the Yucatán Peninsula. Once the Spanish were firmly in control of central Mexico, they expanded northward. Juan Rodriguez CABRILLO's explorations on the Pacific coast gave Spain its first claim to California.

South America

While probing the edges of the Caribbean Sea, Columbus, Ojeda, Vicente Yáñez Pinzón, and others found the northeastern shores of South America. Amerigo VESPUCCI, in the service of Spain and Portugal, sailed south along the eastern coast on two voyages between 1499 and 1502. He described the continent in letters that were published throughout Europe. The German mapmaker Martin Waldseemüller was inspired to call the continent "America" in Vespucci's honor, and the name stuck.

Portugal became more active in South America after Pedro Álvares CABRAL made an unplanned landing on the coast of Brazil in 1500. Under the **Treaty of Tordesillas,** Cabral's landfall was in Portuguese territory. The Portuguese crown soon began founding colonies in Brazil. The next milestone came in 1520, when Ferdinand MAGELLAN led Spanish ships through a strait at the continent's southern tip. He had found the passage to the Pacific Ocean that so many explorers had sought.

A few years later, Europeans entered the South American interior. Sebastian CABOT journeyed up the Río de la Plata and its **tributaries** on the continent's southeast coast. In 1533 Francisco PIZARRO, following the example of Cortés, invaded and conquered the great Inca civilization on South America's west coast. The new Spanish territory of Peru was the base for expeditions to the north, south, and east by Diego de ALMAGRO and Francisco de ORELLANA, among others. Rumors of a rich king or city called **El Dorado** drew Sebastián de BENALCÁZAR, Gonzalo JIMÉNEZ DE QUESADA, and Nikolaus FEDERMANN into the mountains of what is now Colombia.

By the middle of the 1500s, Europeans knew the general outline and geography of South America, but much of the interior remained unexplored. Several Spanish explorers, including Álvar Núñez CABEZA DE VACA, had tried and failed to travel from east to

Treaty of Tordesillas agreement between Spain and Portugal dividing the rights to discovered lands along a north-south line

tributary stream or river that flows into a larger stream or river

El Dorado mythical ruler, city, or area of South America believed to possess much gold

THE EXPLORATION OF CENTRAL AMERICA AND SOUTH AMERICA

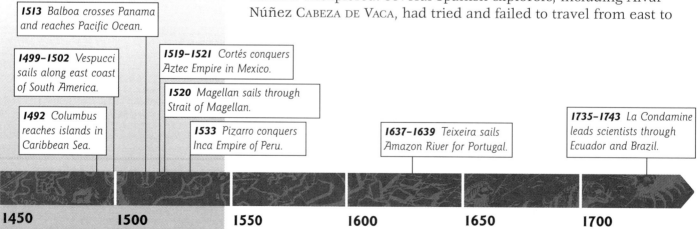

1513 *Balboa crosses Panama and reaches Pacific Ocean.*

1499–1502 *Vespucci sails along east coast of South America.*

1519–1521 *Cortés conquers Aztec Empire in Mexico.*

1520 *Magellan sails through Strait of Magellan.*

1492 *Columbus reaches islands in Caribbean Sea.*

1533 *Pizarro conquers Inca Empire of Peru.*

1637–1639 *Teixeira sails Amazon River for Portugal.*

1735–1743 *La Condamine leads scientists through Ecuador and Brazil.*

1450   1500   1550   1600   1650   1700

In 1911 an American professor named Hiram Bingham found the ruins of the Inca city of Machu Picchu, high in the mountains of Peru.

bandeirante member of a Portuguese raid into Brazil during the 1600s

latitude distance north or south of the equator

specimen sample of a plant, animal, or mineral, usually collected for scientific study or display

west across the southern part of the continent. But in the 1600s, Portuguese missionaries and adventurers began moving inward from the Brazilian coast. Pedro de TEIXEIRA's explorations gave Portugal control over most of the great Amazon River basin. In their quests for gold, gems, and slaves, **bandeirantes** such as Antonio RAPÔSO DE TAVARES crossed much ground.

South America presented scientists with many opportunities for research, especially in the Amazon rain forest. In 1735 Charles-Marie de LA CONDAMINE arrived to measure the length of one degree of **latitude** at the equator. Later, naturalists such as Alexander von HUMBOLDT, Charles DARWIN, and Alfred Russell WALLACE came to collect **specimens** and left with new scientific theories. Other scholarly explorers cast light on Indian civilizations such as the Inca, who had been conquered nearly 400 years before Hiram BINGHAM came to find the ruins they had left behind.

The Middle East and North Africa

To the ancient Greeks and Romans, the Middle East and North Africa were quite familiar. These lands are located where trade routes to Europe, Asia, and Africa meet. In its long history, this crossroads has drawn merchants and armies from all directions.

Ancient and Medieval Visitors

HERODOTUS of Halicarnassus traveled in Greece, Persia, and Egypt in the 400s B.C., and his writings summarize what the ancient Greeks knew about those lands. In the centuries that followed, military campaigns—especially those of ALEXANDER the Great—extended Greek knowledge of western Asia. But after the fall of the Roman Empire in the late A.D. 400s, much ancient knowledge was lost to the people of Europe.

Fortunately, Greek and Roman learning was preserved—and expanded—by the people of North Africa and the Middle East. The

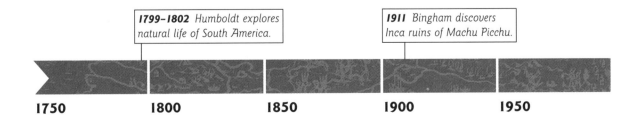

1799–1802 Humboldt explores natural life of South America.

1911 Bingham discovers Inca ruins of Machu Picchu.

1750   **1800**   **1850**   **1900**   **1950**

religion of Islam appeared in the Arabian peninsula in the 600s. In less than 200 years, it spread west to Spain and east to Persia. Unified by Islam and the Arabic language, the Islamic world became more powerful, and it once again received the attention of Europeans. The Jewish traveler BENJAMIN of Tudela and the Christian missionary ODORIC of Pordenone were among many who visited the Middle East and published accounts of their journeys. For many years, Muslims battled huge Christian armies that swept eastward in religious wars known as the **Crusades.** Meanwhile, Asians continued to travel to the region. For example, the Chinese diplomat ZHENG He commanded large fleets that visited the coast of Arabia in the 1400s.

Crusades series of Christian holy wars fought against Muslims in the Middle East, mainly between 1095 and 1270

Muslim Travelers

Islamic culture had its own tradition of travel and exploration. Trade, which took ships and **caravans** from one end of the vast Islamic empire to the other and beyond, encouraged people to make great journeys. So did the **pilgrimage** that each Muslim hoped to make to the holy city of Mecca (in what is now Saudi Arabia). Many pilgrims extended their journeys in order to visit other parts of the world. Among the Muslims who contributed to Islamic geographical knowledge were the traveler IBN FADLAN, the geographers al-MAS'UDI and IBN HAWQAL, and the mapmaker al-IDRISI. The greatest of the Muslim travelers was IBN BATTUTA, a keen observer of life in many lands from Morocco to China. Also notable was LEO AFRICANUS, a Muslim scholar who, after traveling through much of North Africa, became a Christian and wrote an important history of Africa.

caravan large group of people traveling together, often with pack animals, across a desert or other dangerous region

pilgrimage journey to a sacred place

Europeans in the Islamic World

After the Crusades failed to defeat the Muslims, Europeans began looking for new trade routes to Asia. This search was part of Europeans' growing interest in foreign lands. Some people also became more curious about the ancient world. Many ruins of ancient civilizations lay in areas that were controlled by Muslims. But since the Crusades, Christians were not welcome in Islamic countries. Those forbidden lands became all the more fascinating to Europeans. Driven by curiosity and love of adventure, travelers and scholars such as Ludovico di VARTHEMA, Johann BURCKHARDT, and Sir Richard Francis BURTON began exploring the Middle East and North Africa. They risked their lives to do so and often had to travel disguised as Arabs.

THE EXPLORATION OF THE MIDDLE EAST AND NORTH AFRICA

400s B.C. Herodotus travels to Egypt and writes Histories.

334–324 B.C. Alexander conquers Middle East and central Asia.

| 400 B.C. | 200 | A.D. 1 | 200 | 400 | 600 |

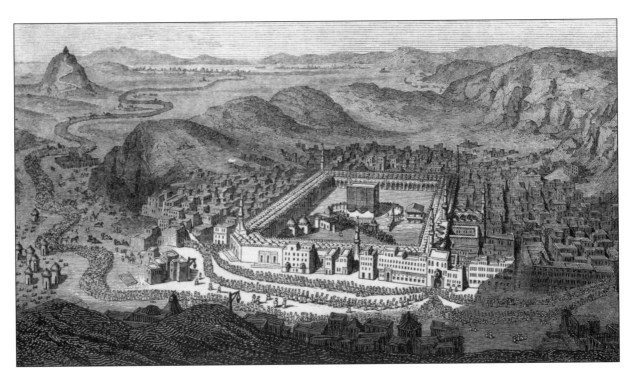

European explorers had to disguise themselves as Muslims to visit the Al-Haram mosque in Mecca, Saudi Arabia, the holiest site of Islam.

In the 1860s, George Sadlier and William Palgrave began the systematic exploration of Arabia. This task was carried on by Charles DOUGHTY, Anne Blunt, Gertrude BELL, and Freya STARK. The last blank spot on maps of Arabia was the southern desert known as the Empty Quarter. It was explored by the modern travelers Bertram Thomas, Harry St. John Philby, and Wilfred THESIGER.

Another desert, the harsh and vast Sahara, covers hundreds of thousands of square miles in North Africa. Like Arabia, it posed a challenge to Europeans. Its climate and terrain make travel difficult, and those who lived there were often hostile to non-Muslims. Muslim travelers, however, passed freely along the caravan routes that crisscrossed the Sahara. Ibn Battuta visited the Saharan kingdom of Mali at the height of its splendor.

French, Italian, and Portuguese explorers began probing the northern part of the Sahara in the Middle Ages. But modern scientific exploration did not get under way until the 1800s, when travelers such as Heinrich BARTH, Alexine TINNÉ, and Gustav NACHTIGAL embarked

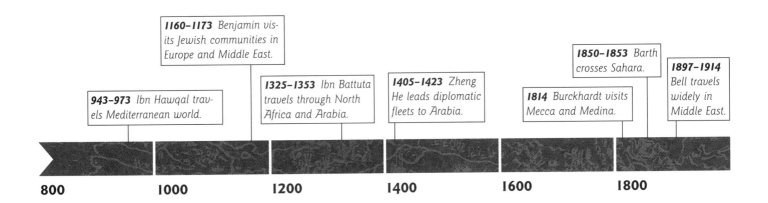

1160–1173 *Benjamin visits Jewish communities in Europe and Middle East.*

1850–1853 *Barth crosses Sahara.*

1897–1914 *Bell travels widely in Middle East.*

943–973 *Ibn Hawqal travels Mediterranean world.*

1325–1353 *Ibn Battuta travels through North Africa and Arabia.*

1405–1423 *Zheng He leads diplomatic fleets to Arabia.*

1814 *Burckhardt visits Mecca and Medina.*

800   1000   1200   1400   1600   1800

on ambitious journeys across the desert. France took the lead, and by the early 1900s, it had established its control over the region.

Africa South of the Sahara

South of the Sahara are the grasslands, forests, rivers, and lakes of the African continent. These lands remained a mystery to Europeans until the 1800s because the Sahara presented such a formidable barrier to travel from the north. Africa has no extremely high mountain ranges to block the way of explorers. However, the huge rain forests near the equator, as well as the Kalahari desert in the south, made travel difficult. Although the major rivers—the Nile, Niger, Congo, and Zambezi—seemed to offer passage to the interior, their many waterfalls and marshes prevented long-distance travel by boat. The greatest hazards were the tropical diseases that claimed the lives of many explorers.

Ancient Knowledge

The ancient Greek historian HERODOTUS relates the story of ancient Phoenicians who sailed all the way around Africa. Although there is no proof that this voyage took place, many modern historians consider it possible. Better documented is the story of HANNO, a citizen of Carthage, a city-state on the Mediterranean coast of North Africa. In the 500s B.C., he led a large expedition to establish colonies on Africa's west coast. Another Greek historian, PTOLEMY, produced the most complete geography of the ancient world. But he had little accurate knowledge of Africa south of the Sahara. He believed that it was connected to Asia and that ships could not sail around it. Europeans also remained unfamiliar with Africa's east coast, which borders the Indian Ocean. However, Arabs and Asians, including the Chinese diplomat ZHENG He, had long traded and traveled in eastern Africa.

The Portuguese Voyages

Portugal launched a new era of African exploration in the 1400s. Its explorers searched for a sea route around the Muslim lands of North Africa in order to reach the wealthy trade markets of India and eastern Asia. Over several decades, Portuguese ships cautiously sailed south, each voyage going farther than the last. Gil EANNES, Diogo CÃO, and Bartolomeu DIAS were among those who led the way for Vasco da GAMA, who reached the Indian Ocean by rounding Africa. A mapmaker at the Portuguese court, Martin Behaim, used the Portuguese discoveries to make a globe in 1492 that is the oldest still in existence.

THE EXPLORATION OF
AFRICA SOUTH OF
THE SAHARA

1488 Dias rounds Africa's Cape of Good Hope.

1486–1493 Covilhã searches for Prester John in Abyssinia.

1400

1500

1600

Traveling along Africa's Zambezi River, David Livingstone became the first European to see the falls of Mosi-oa-tunya, which he renamed Victoria Falls.

tributary stream or river that flows into a larger stream or river

The Portuguese ventured into the African interior as well, but they kept many of their findings so secret that even today we know little about their activities. Francisco ALVARES, Pedro Páez, and Pêro da COVILHĀ visited the kingdom of Abyssinia (now Ethiopia) in northeastern Africa. Abyssinia was one of several regions where Europeans hoped to find a mythical Christian ruler named Prester John. The Portuguese established gold mines and trading posts on both the west and east coasts of Africa. They also began Europe's involvement in the slave trade, capturing and enslaving Africans or buying them from Arab and African slave dealers.

The Nile and Niger Rivers

The interior remained unmapped long after Europeans had become familiar with the coasts. But in the late 1700s, Europeans began to focus on the exploration of eastern and central Africa. They were trying to solve one of the great geographical mysteries of the time: Where was the source of the Nile River? Over more than a century, Richard BURTON, Alexine TINNÉ, James BRUCE, John Hanning SPEKE, Samuel BAKER, David LIVINGSTONE, Henry Morton STANLEY, Charles CHAILLÉ-LONG, and Eduard SCHNITZER mapped the river, its **tributaries,** and the lakes of central Africa. They endured great hardships, much confusion, and bitter personal disputes.

Explorers from the late 1700s to the mid-1800s also worked to map the Niger River in western Africa and explore the lands around it. Daniel HOUGHTON, Mungo PARK, Hugh CLAPPERTON, and Alexander Gordon LAING were key figures in this effort. In 1828 René-Auguste CAILLIÉ, traveling alone, was the first European to visit the Muslim city of Timbuktu on the Niger and live to tell about it. The mapping of the river was completed by Richard Lemon LANDER.

The Continental Interior

The exploration of Africa's interior was often carried out during searches for the sources of the Nile and Niger Rivers. It was also closely linked to European nations' colonial ambitions. Baker, Livingstone, Stanley, and Verney Lovett CAMERON explored for Britain and Belgium and made the first crossings of the continent by Europeans. A new burst of exploration in the late 1800s and early 1900s helped to complete maps, advance scientific knowledge, and expand European

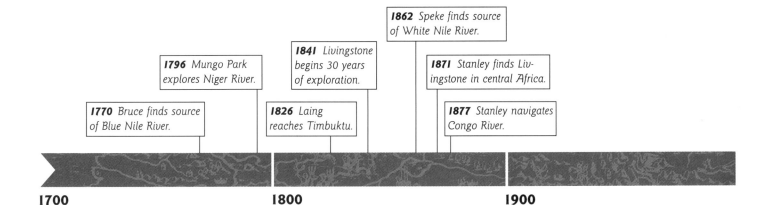

1862 Speke finds source of White Nile River.

1841 Livingstone begins 30 years of exploration.

1796 Mungo Park explores Niger River.

1871 Stanley finds Livingstone in central Africa.

1770 Bruce finds source of Blue Nile River.

1826 Laing reaches Timbuktu.

1877 Stanley navigates Congo River.

1700   **1800**   **1900**

empires. During those years, Joseph THOMSON, Paul Belloni DU CHAILLU, Pierre-Paul-François-Camille Savorgnan de BRAZZA, and many others traveled widely. Africa also drew a new generation of women explorers, such as May French SHELDON, Mary KINGSLEY, and Delia Denning AKELEY. These men and women relied heavily on the help of Africans, who worked as porters, guides, and interpreters.

Asia

Western Asia is near enough to the Mediterranean Sea to have been familiar to the ancient Greeks and Romans. But eastern lands such as India, China, and Japan were hardly known to them at all. To ancient Europeans, eastern Asia was the edge of the world. Even medieval Europeans knew these lands only as the remote sources of silk, spices, and other exotic goods.

Asia, the world's largest continent, stretches from the Mediterranean Sea to the Pacific Ocean. Its western edge merges with eastern Europe—geographers use the Ural Mountains in Russia as the border between Asia and Europe. Asia is home to a wide variety of peoples. Some of them made journeys of exploration throughout the continent well before Europeans began traveling there.

India

Separated from the rest of Asia by the Himalaya mountain range, India is a peninsula so large that it is called a subcontinent. To HERODOTUS, India was a land of marvels at the edge of the known world. ALEXANDER the Great reached the Indus River (in present-day Pakistan, northwest of modern India), and his general NEARCHUS explored part of the Indian Ocean, but the Greeks knew nothing of the rest of India. The Romans traded with India and gained somewhat broader knowledge of the region. Medieval Chinese travelers and explorers also reached India by sea and land. Among them was the admiral ZHENG He. The Chinese Buddhist monks FAXIAN, XUAN Zang, and YI Jing made pilgrimages to India, the birthplace of Buddhism.

From the 1200s on, some Europeans sought more contact between Europe and Asia. Marco POLO, Nicolò de CONTI, Pêro da COVILHÃ, Vasco da GAMA, and Ludovico di VARTHEMA were among those who visited India. Their descriptions of its spices and gems made European nations more eager than ever to trade in "the Indies"—a term that often included Southeast Asia as well as India. The British East India Company became a major force in India's politics, and by the mid-1800s, Britain had conquered and colonized the Indian subcontinent. During this time, British **surveyors** such as George EVEREST carried out the mapping of this enormous area.

surveyor one who makes precise measurements of a location's geography

Central Asia

Central Asia consists mostly of deserts and mountains. It is the region north of India and south of Russia, east of the Middle East and west of China. Though surrounded by great centers of civilization, central Asia was somewhat isolated. Travelers were often discouraged at the thought of braving the Hindu Kush Mountains, tribes of fierce horsemen, and the hostile defenders of Tibet. But as early as

Many explorers risked their lives to see the Potala, the palace of Tibet's spiritual leader, the Dalai Lama.

Jesuit member of the Society of Jesus, a Roman Catholic order founded by Ignatius of Loyola in 1534

plateau high, flat area of land

Roman times, traders passed through central Asia along the Silk Road, a caravan route linking the Middle East and China. The Silk Road was partly the result of the efforts of a Chinese diplomat and explorer named ZHANG Qian, who traveled to central Asia in the A.D. 100s. The Chinese Buddhist pilgrim Xuan Zang visited in the 600s, and Europeans, including WILLIAM of Rubruck and Marco Polo, followed in the 1200s. **Jesuits** such as Bento de GOES began making extended visits in the late 1500s.

In the 1700s, Europeans developed a great fascination with central Asia, fueled by the mystery of the city of Lhasa, located on the high Tibetan **plateau.** At that time, only a few foreigners had visited the city, which was difficult to reach and closely guarded. When European interest began to increase, Tibetan officials closed Lhasa to all foreigners.

The Europeans were not easily kept out. During the 1800s, Russia and Britain both had ambitions to control central Asia. Spies, soldiers, diplomats, and surveyors from both nations entered the region. The British writer Rudyard Kipling called these activities "the Great Game." Russians such as Nikolai PRZHEVALSKI pushed south toward Tibet, while Francis YOUNGHUSBAND and others came north from British India. Many British achievements, both in surveying and in spying, were made by Indians called "pundits." Nain SINGH, Kishen

SINGH, and KINTUP were among the Indians hired by the British to risk their lives on secret missions to the north. In 1904 Younghusband, at the head of a British army, forced his way into Lhasa, winning the "game" for Britain. Other travelers and scholars, including Sven HEDIN, Mark Aurel STEIN, Isabella Bird BISHOP, and Alexandra DAVID-NEEL, continued to explore the region well into the 1900s.

Siberia

Siberia is the immense part of northern Asia that stretches from the Ural Mountains to the Pacific Ocean. It is a land of plains, mountains, forests, rivers, and snow. The people native to Siberia were tribes of hunters and farmers scattered across the continent. Tribes in southern Siberia were related to the Mongols, an Asian people, while those in the north were related to the **Inuit** people of the North American polar region.

The exploration and conquest of Siberia was a long process carried out almost entirely by Russians. In the 1500s, the Russian state based in Moscow began looking east toward the unknown land beyond the Ural Mountains. Timofeyevich YERMAK led an early Russian attempt to conquer part of Siberia. In the following decades, Russian fur trappers and military commanders advanced eastward, exploring rivers and building forts. They insisted that the local tribes hand over furs as a sign of respect for the distant rulers in Moscow.

Almost all the great rivers of Siberia, including the Ob, the Yenisei, and the Lena, flow from south to north. As the Russians reached each of these rivers, they were frustrated to realize that they could not simply sail across the continent. But in 1639, only 60 years after Yermak's expedition, a small party of explorers led by Ivan Moskvitin became the first Russians to reach the Pacific Ocean. Later in the 1600s, Yerofei Pavlovich KHABAROV explored the Amur River along the border with China. Semyon Ivanov DEZHNEV made early progress in mapping Siberia's far northern reaches. The full outline of Siberia would not be known until the 1800s, after the explorations of Vitus BERING, Aleksei CHIRIKOV, and Gennady Ivanovich Nevelskoy.

China

China, the home of an ancient civilization, is one of Asia's largest, most varied, and most heavily populated lands. Romans knew China mainly as the source of silk fabric. A few scattered Chinese and Roman records suggest that the two empires exchanged visitors in the A.D. 100s and 200s. However, very few Europeans traveled to

Inuit people of the Canadian Arctic, sometimes known as the Eskimo

THE EXPLORATION
OF ASIA

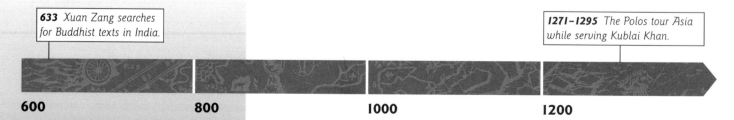

633 *Xuan Zang searches for Buddhist texts in India.*

1271–1295 *The Polos tour Asia while serving Kublai Khan.*

600   **800**   **1000**   **1200**

China before the 1200s. At that time, the Mongols gained control of China and central Asia. They maintained order along the trade routes and permitted foreigners to travel in the empire. Dozens of merchants, missionaries, and diplomats did so, and many left accounts of their journeys. Among the best known of these explorers were the Polo family, ODORIC of Pordenone, and IBN BATTUTA. XU Hongzu, one of several important Chinese explorers, roamed across China and into Tibet, seeking the sources of the Mekong and Salween rivers in the 1600s.

Soon a new wave of Europeans reached the Far East, using the sea route pioneered by the Portuguese. Matteo RICCI and Bento de Goes were among a handful of Europeans whom the Chinese permitted to enter during this period. But by the 1800s, the European powers had pressured China into allowing greater freedom to outsiders. Explorers such as Alexandra David-Neel and Ferdinand Paul Wilhelm von RICHTHOFEN traveled widely.

Japan

To medieval Europeans, Japan seemed even more remote, mysterious, and exotic than China. Marco Polo called this island kingdom Cipangu, and that name appeared on many European maps from the 1300s on. Polo did not claim to have visited the island, but he wrote that he had heard in China that Cipangu possessed "gold in the greatest abundance." Of course, this remark made Europeans very eager to go there.

At the time, Japan had little contact with the rest of the world, although it traded with Korea and China and knew of the existence of India. The arrival of Portuguese traders and missionaries such as Francis XAVIER in the mid-1500s was unsettling to some Japanese. Japan's rulers tried several times to drive out the Europeans and to limit contact between Japanese and foreigners. Explorers of the Pacific Ocean, such as Jean-François de Galaup de LA PÉROUSE and Adam Ivan von KRUSENSTERN, slowly added to Europe's knowledge of Japan. As had been the case with China, by the 1800s, travelers

This Arabic illustration from the 1500s depicts the court of Genghis Khan, the Mongol emperor whose grandson Kublai was served by Marco Polo in the 1200s.

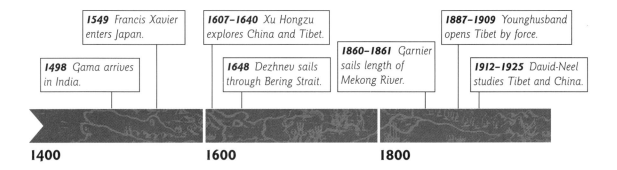

1498 *Gama arrives in India.*

1549 *Francis Xavier enters Japan.*

1607–1640 *Xu Hongzu explores China and Tibet.*

1648 *Dezhnev sails through Bering Strait.*

1860–1861 *Garnier sails length of Mekong River.*

1887–1909 *Younghusband opens Tibet by force.*

1912–1925 *David-Neel studies Tibet and China.*

1400   **1600**   **1800**

such as Isabella Bishop were visiting and traveling the country with relative freedom.

Southeast Asia

Today, Southeast Asia includes the nations of Bangladesh, Myanmar, Thailand, Cambodia, Laos, Vietnam, Malaysia, and Indonesia. It is a region of mountains, rain forests, and islands and is home to many different peoples who practice a wide variety of religions. Traders and diplomats from India and China began carrying their merchandise, culture, and politics to Southeast Asia in the A.D. 100s and 200s. The European exploration of the region began 1,000 years later, when Marco Polo and Odoric passed through it, followed by Ibn Battuta and Nicolò de Conti. The accounts of these travelers made Europeans aware that the spices of India actually came from the Spice Islands (now the Moluccas) of Indonesia.

Vasco da Gama's voyage to India opened the way for Portuguese settlement and exploration in Southeast Asia. Those activities were begun by Afonso de ALBUQUERQUE in the early 1500s. During that century, Portuguese and Spanish explorers entered dense jungles to reach the interior of the region's mainland. But their accounts of these journeys went unnoticed in their home countries. Soon the Dutch, British, and French were also active in the region, setting up trading posts and claiming territory. By the mid-1700s, Europeans had mapped the coasts of most of Southeast Asia, but many areas were still largely unknown. During the 1800s, remarkable efforts were made by explorers such as Francis GARNIER and Auguste PAVIE. They learned much about the region's geography and history, and their findings helped France gain control over much of the area that is now Vietnam, Cambodia, and Laos. Expeditions with different goals were made by scientists such as Alfred Russel WALLACE, who explored Borneo and other islands.

The Pacific Ocean and Australia

The Pacific Ocean covers one-third of the earth's surface and contains thousands of islands of all shapes and sizes. Australia is large enough to be a continent in itself, while Melanesia, Micronesia, and Polynesia are groups of thousands of tiny, widely scattered islands.

THE EXPLORATION OF
THE PACIFIC OCEAN
AND AUSTRALIA

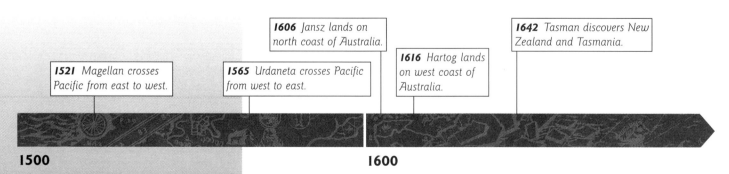

1606 Jansz lands on north coast of Australia.

1642 Tasman discovers New Zealand and Tasmania.

1521 Magellan crosses Pacific from east to west.

1565 Urdaneta crosses Pacific from west to east.

1616 Hartog lands on west coast of Australia.

1500

1600

The Dutch explorer Jacob Roggeveen was astounded to find these enormous stone statues on Easter Island, which lies in the southern Pacific Ocean.

circumnavigation journey around the world

This vast and varied world is sometimes called Oceania. Before the European Age of Exploration, the inhabitants of these islands were rarely in contact with the peoples of Asia or the Americas. But the seafaring ancestors of the Polynesians had sailed great distances to colonize tiny islands in the middle of the ocean.

The Pacific Islands

By the 1300s, Europeans knew that there was an ocean to the east of Asia, but they believed that body of water to be the same Atlantic Ocean that bordered Europe. Once Europeans realized that across the Atlantic lay the Americas, they continued to search for the ocean east of Asia. Vasco Nuñez de BALBOA sighted that body of water from a hilltop in what is now Panama, and Ferdinand MAGELLAN named it the Pacific when he sailed into it seven years later. Balboa and Magellan were right to believe that Asia would be found on the far edge of those waters—but neither of them imagined how far away that was.

Magellan made the first known crossing of the Pacific Ocean and reached what were later called the Philippine Islands. The Portuguese proceeded to explore the western Pacific from Southeast Asia. After Magellan's death in the Philippines, a member of his crew named Juan Sebastián de ELCANO led survivors back to Europe, completing the first **circumnavigation.** Soon navigators such as Miguel López de LEGAZPI, Andrés de URDANETA, Alvaro de MENDAÑA DE NEHRA, and Pedro Fernandez de QUIRÓS were crossing and recrossing the Pacific for Spain. They brought the Philippines under Spanish control and established regular sailing routes between those islands and Mexico.

The Dutch and the English were also interested in Oceania. In the early and middle 1600s, Dutch mariners Jacob Le Maire, Willem SCHOUTEN, and Abel TASMAN visited many tropical island groups, including the Tuamotu, Tonga, and Fiji Islands. Jacob ROGGEVEEN led the last major Dutch voyage in the Pacific, discovering Easter Island in 1722. English explorers of the Pacific included Francis DRAKE in the 1500s, William DAMPIER in the 1600s, and George ANSON in the early 1700s.

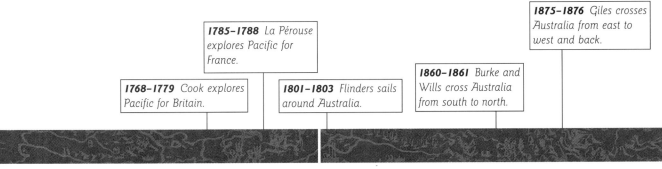

1875–1876 Giles crosses Australia from east to west and back.

1785–1788 La Pérouse explores Pacific for France.

1768–1779 Cook explores Pacific for Britain.

1801–1803 Flinders sails around Australia.

1860–1861 Burke and Wills cross Australia from south to north.

1700   **1800**

The next stage of Pacific exploration was largely scientific. John BYRON, Samuel WALLIS, and Philip CARTERET led English expeditions to chart parts of Oceania. They also searched for an enormous continent that geographers such as Alexander DALRYMPLE expected to find in the southern hemisphere. In the late 1700s, James COOK mapped much of the Pacific, proving that the huge southern continent was a myth. Around the same time, Louis-Antoine de BOUGAINVILLE, Jean François de Galaup de LA PÉROUSE, and Antoine Raymond Joseph de Bruni d'ENTRECASTEAUX sailed the Pacific for France. In the mid-1800s, Charles WILKES led a major expedition for the United States.

Australia, New Guinea, and New Zealand

Some early explorers of Southeast Asia and the Pacific Ocean caught glimpses of Australia's coast. Willem JANSZ made the first known sighting in 1605. Because he was Dutch, the land he saw was long known as New Holland. Dirck HARTOG, Abel Tasman, and William Dampier also explored parts of New Holland's coast. It was difficult to explore the dozens of islands, both large and small, that lie off the mainland's northern and eastern coasts. For years mariners did not know whether places they found were separate islands or were connected to the mainland. The work of James Cook, Entrecasteaux, Matthew FLINDERS, and Nicolas BAUDIN finally produced a complete map of the coast.

Cook's explorations gave Britain its claim to Australia, which was populated by the Aborigine people. At first the British developed Australia as a prison colony, sending only prisoners and guards to live there. But by the early 1800s, several settlements of free men and women existed on the east coast. Gregory BLAXLAND and William Charles WENTWORTH crossed the Blue Mountains in 1813, opening new areas to settlers. Hamilton HUME, Charles STURT, Edward John EYRE, John McDouall STUART, and Friedrich Wilhelm Ludwig LEICHHARDT probed the continent's harsh desert plains. Robert O'Hara BURKE and William John WILLS were the first to cross the continent from south to north. Ernest GILES made the first journey from east to west and back again. The map of Australia was largely completed by 1880, but not without many disasters.

The early explorers of Australia also investigated the large, nearby islands of New Guinea and New Zealand. New Guinea, a large, mountainous, forested island north of Australia, was first sighted in 1526 by a Portuguese sailor named Jorge de Meneses. In the early 1600s, Spain's Luis Vaez de TORRES made a survey of the island's south coast. He was followed by Willem Schouten, Abel Tasman, William Dampier, Philip Carteret, and James Cook. In the mid-1800s, Germany, the Netherlands, and Great Britain competed for the island, which is now divided between the nations of Indonesia and Papua New Guinea.

New Zealand's two main islands lie to the southeast of Australia. Europeans found them populated by a Polynesian people called the Maori. Tasman made the first recorded European sighting of the islands in 1642, and more than a century later, Cook circled and mapped them. After Cook's voyage, the British claimed New Zealand. For a time part of the Australian colony, it is now an independent nation.

The Polar Regions

The frozen Arctic Ocean around the North Pole and the continent of Antarctica around the South Pole were among the last of the earth's regions to be explored. The Arctic is bordered by populated lands: northern Europe, Russia, North America, and Greenland. Peoples such as the Inuit and the Chukchi have lived in Arctic territory for thousands of years. But Antarctica is far from other continents and has never had a human population until explorers found it in the early 1800s. At each end of the globe, travelers in these regions must overcome extreme cold, long winters, and sea ice that can trap or wreck ships.

The Northwest Passage

Northwest Passage water route connecting the Atlantic Ocean and Pacific Ocean through the Arctic islands of northern Canada

Around 1500 the English began the epic, four-century search for the **Northwest Passage.** What they sought was a waterway, far from the southern ocean routes controlled by Spain and Portugal, that would allow ships to cut across North America and sail to Asia. In the late 1500s, the English mariners Martin FROBISHER and John DAVIS searched for the passage in the far north, among ice-choked waterways and snow-covered islands. For the next 350 years, the dream of a Northwest Passage lured hundreds of explorers into the Arctic.

Henry HUDSON thought that he had found the passage, but Hudson Bay proved to be a dead end. William BAFFIN and Robert BYLOT sailed farther north than anyone else had up to that point, but they found no westward route. The English lost interest in the passage for a time and instead built the colonies that became the United States. But by the late 1700s, explorers were again searching the Arctic for the Northwest Passage. James COOK, George VANCOUVER, and other British navigators looked for the western end of the passage as they explored the Pacific coast of North America. Spanish explorers also probed this coast, without success.

By about 1800, geographers realized that there is no easy way to sail through or around North America. They knew that if the passage existed, it would certainly be dangerous, narrow, and clogged with ice. Merchants carrying cargo would not be able to use it. But in the early 1800s, Britain launched a new effort to find the passage, mainly to satisfy scientific curiosity and national pride. William Edward PARRY made much progress, but John FRANKLIN's expedition was never heard from again. During the long search for Franklin and his crew, explorers such as Francis Leopold McCLINTOCK and Robert John Le Mesurier McCLURE filled in the map of the Canadian Arctic. McClure also found the long-sought Northwest Passage, but he had to abandon his ship without sailing through it. This feat was at last completed by Roald AMUNDSEN of Norway in a small boat, on a voyage that lasted from 1903 to 1906.

The Northeast Passage

To sail from Europe to Asia was a cherished goal for many nations. In the 1500s, Portugal controlled the southern route around Africa. The western route across the Atlantic turned out to be blocked by

Northeast Passage water route connecting the Atlantic Ocean and Pacific Ocean along the Arctic coastline of Europe and Asia

the Americas, so some people looked to the northeast. They hoped to find a **Northeast Passage**—a sea route to Asia through the Arctic Ocean north of Europe and Russia. By the end of the 1500s, England's Sebastian CABOT and Richard CHANCELLOR and the Netherlands' Willem BARENTS had sailed north of Norway and reached ports in northern Russia. In the mid-1700s, Vitus BERING led a massive nine-year expedition to map Russia's Arctic coastline. Most people still believed that the Northeast Passage was too cold and dangerous for safe shipping. Nils Adolf Erik NORDENSKIÖLD proved them wrong in 1879 by becoming the first explorer to sail through the entire Northeast Passage. He had to spend the winter in a harbor along the way, but 53 years later, an icebreaking ship called the *Sibiryakov* crossed the passage in a single season. Since that time, the Northeast Passage has been used regularly to ship cargo between western Russia and Siberia.

The Arctic

boat-sledge boat mounted on sled runners to allow travel on both ice and water

The explorers who searched for the Northwest and Northeast Passages sometimes tried to sail as far north as possible. They were always forced to turn back where the Arctic Ocean had frozen to ice. William Parry tried to travel north over the ice, using **boat-sledges,** but he had little success. Some geographers and explorers believed that the ice was only a ring, beyond which the polar sea was open and free of ice. Elisha Kent KANE, Charles Francis HALL, and George Washington DE LONG were among the Americans who tried to cross the ice. Austro-Hungarians Julius von PAYER and Karl Weyprecht discovered land north of Russia that they named Franz Josef Land. Fridtjof NANSEN of Norway followed the drift of the polar ice, and Sweden's Salomon August ANDRÉE tried to reach the North Pole in a balloon.

By the time people realized that ice covered the entire polar region, Arctic exploration had become a race to reach the North Pole. Americans Frederick Albert COOK and Robert Edwin PEARY both claimed to have been first. The public accepted Peary as the victor, but today some researchers believe that both men's claims were false. There is no doubt that Walter William HERBERT crossed the pole by dogsled in 1969, and both the Russian icebreaker *Arktika* and the American submarine *Nautilus* reached it by sea. But by that time, people had long been exploring the Arctic by air. As early as the 1920s, Roald Amundsen, Richard Evelyn BYRD, Lincoln

THE EXPLORATION OF THE POLAR REGIONS

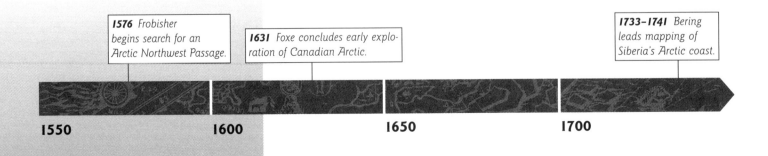

1576 *Frobisher begins search for an Arctic Northwest Passage.*

1631 *Foxe concludes early exploration of Canadian Arctic.*

1733–1741 *Bering leads mapping of Siberia's Arctic coast.*

1550   1600   1650   1700

In the polar regions, many explorers relied on sleds that were pulled by dogs and steered by a driver.

dirigible large aircraft filled with a lighter-than-air gas that keeps it aloft; similar to a blimp but with a rigid frame

ELLSWORTH, and Umberto NOBILE crossed over the pole in airplanes or **dirigibles.** An American Air Force plane landed at the pole in 1952, making Joseph Fletcher the first person known to have set foot there.

Antarctica

During the 1700s, mariners such as James COOK sailed far enough south to encounter the ice around Antarctica, but they could not see the continent itself. By 1800, ships hunting whales and seals were visiting seas and islands in the far south, and some of these crews may have seen the mainland. In 1820 Fabian von BELLING-SHAUSEN of Russia made the first confirmed sightings of the Antarctic coast. Jules-Sébastien-César DUMONT D'URVILLE, Charles WILKES, and James ROSS also sailed to Antarctica in the next few decades.

Like the North Pole, the South Pole became a magnet for explorers and nations seeking glory. Frederick Cook and Ernest SHACKLE-TON tried and failed to reach the pole. Roald Amundsen succeeded in 1911, beating Robert Falcon SCOTT by a matter of days. In the

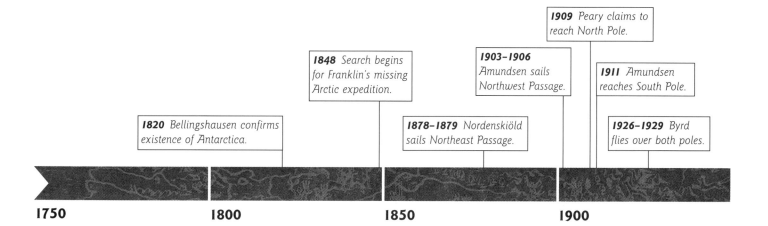

1909 *Peary claims to reach North Pole.*

1848 *Search begins for Franklin's missing Arctic expedition.*

1903–1906 *Amundsen sails Northwest Passage.*

1911 *Amundsen reaches South Pole.*

1820 *Bellingshausen confirms existence of Antarctica.*

1878–1879 *Nordenskiöld sails Northeast Passage.*

1926–1929 *Byrd flies over both poles.*

1750   1800   1850   1900

years that followed, George Hubert WILKINS, Lincoln Ellsworth, and Richard Byrd competed to reach the pole and to explore the continent by air. Fifteen nations have established bases in Antarctica, partly to support scientific research and partly to stake a claim to land and natural resources. The international Antarctic Treaty, signed in 1959, prohibits both commercial and military activities on the continent.

Space

Scientists have studied the solar system and outer space for many centuries by looking at the night sky. But the physical exploration of space began in the mid-1900s, when people first began using **rockets** to leave the earth. Rockets were developed mainly by military scientists, and the specially trained pilots who go into space are often officers in their nations' armed forces. The early exploration of space was in some ways a military competition between the United States and the **Soviet Union.** It was also a great scientific effort.

In 1957 the Soviets launched *Sputnik 1,* the first **satellite** to **orbit** the earth. Space scientists in both nations then raced feverishly toward the next goal: to send a human being into space. They trained elite groups of **astronauts** and **cosmonauts** to fly the next generation of spacecraft.

Orbiting the Earth

In 1961 cosmonaut Yuri GAGARIN began the Soviet Union's Vostok program in a **capsule** named *Swallow.* He was the first person to travel into space. Gagarin orbited the earth once and then piloted the *Swallow* back to the Soviet Union. A month later, American astronaut Alan SHEPARD rode a Mercury capsule called *Freedom 7* into space, and John GLENN made three orbits of the earth the following year in *Friendship 7.*

It was a period of intense rivalry between the United States and the Soviet Union. Both nations made rapid advances in space technology. For a time, the Soviets led the way, and they made history

rocket vehicle propelled by exploding fuel

Soviet Union nation that existed from 1922 to 1991, made up of Russia and 14 other republics in eastern Europe and northern Asia

satellite object launched into space to circle a planet or moon

orbit stable, circular route; one trip around; to revolve around

astronaut American term for a person who travels into space; literally, "traveler to the stars"

cosmonaut Russian term for a person who travels into space; literally, "traveler to the universe"

capsule small early spacecraft designed to carry a person around the earth

THE EXPLORATION OF SPACE

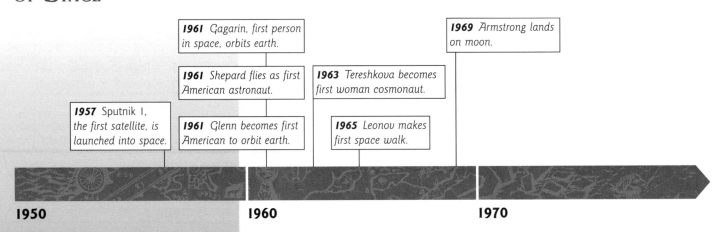

1961 *Gagarin, first person in space, orbits earth.*

1969 *Armstrong lands on moon.*

1961 *Shepard flies as first American astronaut.*

1963 *Tereshkova becomes first woman cosmonaut.*

1957 Sputnik I, the first satellite, is launched into space.

1961 *Glenn becomes first American to orbit earth.*

1965 *Leonov makes first space walk.*

1950   1960   1970

In a new era of discovery, people have left the earth and begun the exploration of space.

space station spacecraft that circles the earth for months or years with a human crew

NASA National Aeronautics and Space Administration, the U.S. space agency

space shuttle reusable spacecraft designed to transport both people and cargo between the earth and space

again when Valentina TERESHKOVA became the first woman in space, aboard Vostok 6, the *Sea Gull.* The Soviets launched the first two spacecraft to link together in space, as well as the first spacecraft to carry more than one person. Cosmonaut Aleksei LEONOV was the first person to "walk" in space, floating at the end of a cable outside the Voskhod 2 capsule *Diamond.*

Soon, however, American astronauts were setting new records for time spent in space. They were also the first to link two spacecraft flying in orbit around the earth. Such maneuvers were part of the American effort to reach a new goal, set by President John F. Kennedy: to land on the moon.

Missions to the Moon

For many years, Soviet and American space scientists launched small spacecraft without crews to photograph and study the moon. These probes prepared the way for the Soviet Soyuz and American Apollo programs. The United States won this stage of the "space race." In 1968 the crew of Apollo 8 made ten orbits of the moon. A year later, Apollo 11 landed Neil ARMSTRONG and Edwin "Buzz" Aldrin, Jr., on the moon's surface.

The United States sent six more missions to the moon, partly to demonstrate the nation's superiority in space and partly to conduct scientific research. The high cost of the missions and a decline in public interest ended the Apollo program in 1972. But some scientists predict that people will return to the moon at a later stage of space exploration—perhaps to establish bases, mines, or colonies.

Stations and Shuttles

While Americans explored the moon, Soviets experimented with **space stations,** on which cosmonauts could live and work for long periods. In 1971 the Soviet Union launched its first space station, *Salyut 1,* and cosmonauts began setting new records for time spent in space. Five more Salyut stations reached orbit, as did an American station, *Skylab.*

Meanwhile, **NASA** developed a series of **space shuttles** that took crews into orbit around the earth. Dozens of astronauts—including Sally RIDE, the first American woman to travel in space—conducted

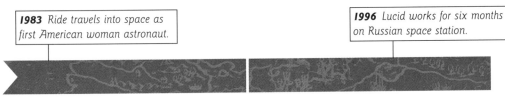

1983 *Ride travels into space as first American woman astronaut.*

1996 *Lucid works for six months on Russian space station.*

1980   **1990**

scientific experiments in the shuttles. The shuttles were also useful for retrieving old satellites and placing new ones in orbit. The program suffered a major setback when the shuttle *Challenger* exploded during a launch in 1986, but flights resumed at the end of the decade.

In 1986 the Soviet Union launched a large space station named *Mir,* which means "peace." As competition between the United States and the Soviet Union eased, *Mir* was visited by astronauts from several nations. Shannon LUCID, an American astronaut, spent six months aboard the station. In the 1990s, after the Soviet Union disbanded, the governments of Russia, the United States, and other countries began considering more international projects. Their ideas included a new space station and a landing on Mars. At the end of the decade, these nations practiced using space shuttles to assemble a space station in orbit around the earth.

European nations—as well as China, Japan, India, and others—continued to become more active in space in the 1980s. They launched satellites that joined the hundreds now orbiting the earth. These devices perform a wide range of services, from broadcasting television to predicting the weather.

The first human-made objects to leave our solar system were probes such as *Pioneer 10* and *Voyager 1.* But most space exploration is still carried out by scientists on the earth. They receive information from probes and satellites. For example, in 1997 the U.S. Mars Pathfinder project sent a remote-controlled robotic vehicle to the surface of Mars. Instruments such as telescopes—both on the earth and in orbit—are also used to study the planets and stars of the universe.

Biographical Profiles

Acuña, Cristóbal de

Spanish
b 1597?; Burgos, Spain
d 1676; Lima, Peru
***Produced earliest published account
of Amazon River***

Jesuit member of the Society of Jesus, a
Roman Catholic order founded by Ignatius of
Loyola in 1534

Treaty of Tordesillas agreement between
Spain and Portugal dividing the rights to
discovered lands along a north-south line

league unit of distance, usually used at sea,
roughly equal to 3.5 miles

In the first published description of South
America's Amazon region, Father Cristóbal
de Acuña described more than 150 Indian
nations.

In 1639 Father Cristóbal de Acuña left his post as head of a
Jesuit college in Spain to make an extraordinary journey. Acuña
was part of an expedition that sailed from Peru to Pará (now Belém),
Brazil, along the mighty Amazon River. During the trip, the Jesuit
priest wrote about everything he saw. His journal became the first
published description of South America's Amazon region.

From Priest to Explorer

Acuña was born in Burgos, a city in northern Spain. The exact date
of his birth is unknown, as are the details of his life before and after
his Amazon adventure. Acuña arrived in Peru in the 1620s, and he
was named the head of the college at Cuenca, then part of Peru.

At the time, Spain and Portugal were competing to control South
America, particularly the regions near the Amazon River. In 1638 a
Portuguese captain, Pedro de TEIXEIRA, sailed up the Amazon River
from Pará, Brazil, to the Spanish town of Quito (in modern-day
Ecuador). His journey alarmed Spanish officials, who worried that
the Portuguese would try to take control of Peru. The Spanish realized that a better knowledge of the Amazon would help them to
protect their territory and to support their claim to the Amazon as
stated in the **Treaty of Tordesillas.**

The Spanish decided that Teixeira could not be allowed to return
to Portuguese territory unless he took a Spaniard with him. The
governor of Quito, Don Juan Vásquez de Acuña, volunteered to
make the trip. His brother, Father Cristóbal de Acuña, was chosen
instead. Acuña's instructions were to "describe, with clearness, the
distance in **leagues,** the provinces, tribes of Indians, rivers, and
districts. . . ."

The Teixeira expedition left Quito on February 16, 1639, heading
down the Napo River toward the Amazon. Acuña noted the many
small rivers that fed into the Amazon from the upper Amazon Valley. These rivers would allow colonists to ship goods from the Spanish territories of Peru and New Granada (now Colombia) directly to
the Atlantic Ocean. The Teixeira expedition traveled down the
Marañón River (the upper Amazon). Acuña was particularly impressed by the Agua Indians, whom he described as the "most intel-
ligent and best governed of any tribe on the river."

The Wonders of the Amazon

When Acuña finally saw the Amazon itself, he wrote that it was
"the largest and most celebrated river in the world." Acuña's writings reflected the excitement he felt in seeing what seemed like a
paradise. He wrote that "the river is full of fish, the forests with
game, the air of birds, the trees are covered with fruit. . . ."

Acuña recommended that the Spanish develop the resources
along the river. He imagined a day when Spanish plantations would
grow tobacco and sugar cane, and shipyards would build with Amazon lumber. Medicines could be produced by learning from the Indians' knowledge of herbs. Acuña also found the climate pleasing,
neither too hot nor too cold.

Nearly everything the Jesuit priest saw impressed him, from the
land to the people who lived on it. He carefully documented more

than 150 Indian nations, describing their customs, languages, trading practices, and wars with one another.

Acuña took an interest in the Indians' turtle roundups. Captured turtles were kept in wooden holding tanks until the Indians needed them for food. Acuña reported that "turtle eggs were almost as good as hen's eggs," though harder to digest. He was also fascinated by an unusual method of fishing. The Indians beat the water with poisonous vines, causing the stunned fish to float to the surface.

Acuña was upset only by the Portuguese, who made raids along the river to kidnap Indians as slaves. This practice made the Indians fearful of all Europeans. The tribes either fled inland as Acuña's expedition passed or treated the Europeans with false kindness. Once, when the Portuguese soldiers wanted to capture Indians, Acuña protested strongly to Teixeira. The captain agreed to call off the raid and continue down the river.

Science and Legends

In his journal, Acuña wrote scientific reports about the creatures he saw. These included the manatee and what is now called the electric eel. In Acuña's words, the manatee "has hair all over its body, not very long, like soft bristles, and the animal moves in the water with short fins. . . ." The eel, Acuña wrote, "has the peculiarity that, when [it is] alive, whoever touches it trembles all over his body. . . ." These notes were the first recorded descriptions of the animals to reach Europe.

As they proceeded down the river, the explorers met the Tupinambá Indians, who had migrated 3,500 miles to escape the Portuguese invasion of Brazil. Acuña described these Indians as "noble-hearted" and welcoming. The Tupinambá told him the legends of the Amazons, a civilization of women warriors. They also repeated legends he had heard from other tribes, about lands filled with giants, pygmies, and men whose feet were turned backward. Acuña never judged the stories he heard; he simply wrote them down, believing that "time will discover the truth."

After the Journey

The expedition reached Pará on December 16, 1639. Acuña immediately wrote to the king of Spain, recommending that the king act quickly to take control of "Amazonia." The priest also urged the king to stop the Indian wars and to support a plan to convert the Indians to Christianity. Acuña eventually traveled to Spain to present his report in person.

Acuña's account of his journey, *New Discovery of the Great River of the Amazons,* was published in 1641. By that time, however, Spain had lost its claim to the Amazon. Captain Teixeira had succeeded in extending Portuguese control over the region. A disappointed Acuña returned to his religious duties in Peru. Though his efforts had not helped Spain, he was the first to provide a detailed account of the Amazon region and the vast potential of its natural resources.

Suggested Reading Cristóbal de Acuña, *Expeditions into the Valley of the Amazons,* edited by Clements R. Markham (Hakluyt Society, 1859).

Akeley, Delia Denning

American
b December 5, 1875; Beaver Dam, Wisconsin
d May 22, 1970; Daytona Beach, Florida
*Explored Africa, collecting plants and
animals for museums*

specimen sample of a plant, animal, or
mineral, usually collected for scientific study
or display

Delia Denning Akeley pursued a successful
career as a scientific explorer of Africa.

Africanus, Leo. *See Leo Africanus.*

Delia Denning Akeley studied the wildlife and peoples of Africa. Working mostly in the tropical lands along the equator, she collected **specimens** of the plants and animals she found. Akeley's work helped educate Americans, who were eager to learn about a distant, exotic continent.

African Adventures

We know very little about Delia Denning's life before she met the man who became her husband, Carl F. Akeley. He was a sculptor at the Milwaukee Art Museum. Working as his assistant, Delia helped him create realistic animal exhibits for museums. Akeley took a job at the Field Museum in Chicago, and shortly after, he and Delia were married.

At the Field Museum, Carl Akeley became famous for the lifelike animals in his exhibits. In 1905 he traveled to Kenya, in East Africa, to collect specimens for a new exhibit. Delia joined him on the journey.

The Akeleys spent 18 months in East Africa, searching for birds and animals to bring to America. Delia fell in love with Africa, and her strong passion for the continent deepened throughout her life.

In 1909 the Akeleys returned to Africa to collect elephants for the American Museum of Natural History in New York City. During the trip, Carl was often sick or injured, but Delia carried on with their work. In addition to searching for specimens, Delia also studied families of baboons, noting their similarities to humans.

On Her Own

Carl and Delia divorced in 1923, and in 1924 Carl married Mary Lee Jobe AKELEY. He died two years later. Delia did not generally receive credit for the contributions she had made to his early work. In the meantime, however, she had become a respected explorer herself. The Brooklyn Museum of Arts and Sciences sent her to East Africa to collect specimens for an exhibit.

Delia Akeley spent 10 weeks traveling on the Tana River and then crossed the desert of Somalia. From Kenya, she sent her completed collection to the United States. After finishing this work, she made a difficult journey into the Ituri Forest of the Belgian Congo (now the Democratic Republic of Congo). There she lived with and studied a local tribe, the Pygmies, who were known for their short stature. When she returned to the United States, Akeley wrote and lectured about her many African adventures.

Suggested Reading Delia Akeley, *J. T., Jr.: The Biography of an African Monkey* (Macmillan, 1928) and *Jungle Portraits* (Macmillan, 1930); Elizabeth Flagg Olds, *Women of the Four Winds* (Houghton Mifflin, 1985); Mignon Rittenhouse, *Seven Women Explorers* (Lippincott, 1964).

Akeley, Mary Lee Jobe

American
b January 28, 1878; Tappan, Ohio
d July 19, 1966; Stonington, Connecticut
Explored Africa and Canada

specimen sample of a plant, animal, or mineral, usually collected for scientific study or display

On her trips through the Canadian Rocky Mountains, Mary Lee Jobe Akeley won fame as a mountain climber, and a peak is named for her.

Mary Lee Jobe Akeley is best known for bringing public attention to the natural wonders of Africa. First with her husband and then on her own, she explored central and eastern Africa, photographing the beauty of the region's scenery and wildlife.

After studying in both Ohio and Pennsylvania, Mary Lee Jobe taught at Hunter College in New York City. In 1909 she took a break from teaching to make an expedition to British Columbia, Canada. That monthlong trip stirred her interest in exploration. She returned many times to the Canadian northwest to study the region's tribes and vegetation. In 1924 she married the naturalist Carl F. Akeley and turned her attention to his primary interest, Africa.

Bringing Africa to America

Carl Akeley wanted to create an exhibit called the Great African Hall at the American Museum of Natural History in New York City. In 1926 he led a trip to the Belgian Congo (now the Democratic Republic of Congo) to collect plant and animal **specimens** for the exhibit. He also intended to study the region's gorillas.

On the trip, Carl died of a fever, but Mary Lee completed the study of the gorillas and collected additional specimens for the museum. She also mapped areas of East Africa that had not yet been explored, and she studied the languages and cultures of local tribes.

The next year, Mary Lee Akeley came to New York with her specimens and helped assemble the African Hall exhibit. She returned to Africa in 1935 to gather more materials for the exhibit. Akeley's groundbreaking work led people to call her the woman who "brought the jungle to Central Park West." (The American Museum of Natural History is located on Central Park West in New York City.)

Preserving the Beauty of Africa

In the years between her first two trips to Africa, Akeley reported her work to King Albert of Belgium, who awarded her the Cross of the Knight. She also helped the Belgians expand a national park in the Congo.

Akeley became one of the leading voices in the growing effort to preserve Africa's natural beauty. Her numerous books and photos persuaded others to protect the continent's unique cultures and wildlife.

Suggested Reading Mary Lee Jobe Akeley, *Carl Akeley's Africa* (Dodd, Mead and Company, 1929) and *The Wilderness Lives Again* (Dodd, Mead and Company, 1940); Crowther Dawn-Starr, *Mary L. Jobe Akeley* (School of Art, Arizona State University, 1989).

Albuquerque, Afonso de

Portuguese
b 1453; Alhandra, near Lisbon, Portugal
d December 15, 1515; at sea off Goa, India
Strengthened Portuguese power in East Asia

courtier attendant at a royal court

corsair fast pirate ship

Afonso de Albuquerque was a charming **courtier,** a ruthless warrior, and a successful naval commander. While serving Portugal in India in the early 1500s, Albuquerque worked to strengthen his country's weak hold on these distant lands. He tried to create naval bases in the region to preserve the empire and to control the valuable spice trade.

Early Military Career

Albuquerque was born in 1453 in Alhandra, near Lisbon. He came from a wealthy military family with close ties to the royal family of Portugal. As a young soldier, Albuquerque fought in North Africa against Portugal's Muslim enemies. After 10 years in Africa, he returned to the court of Manuel I, king of Portugal.

At the time, Portugal was influential in the spice trade, thanks to its early expeditions to Asia. Vasco da GAMA had reached India in 1499, an achievement that led to a series of Portuguese trading posts along India's southwestern coast. The Asian spice trade was extremely profitable. Many Indian rulers, however, were hostile to the Europeans. To protect Portugal's interests in India, King Manuel sent a naval squadron there in 1503, led by Albuquerque.

Albuquerque's mission was to secure trade routes around the southern tip of Africa and into the Indian Ocean. A clever diplomat, he used words, not guns, to achieve his first victory. Albuquerque persuaded the ruler of Cochin, in southwest India, to let the Portuguese build a fortress there. It was Portugal's first military base in Asia.

Years of Battle

In 1506 Albuquerque led a naval expedition against the Muslims who lived near the Persian Gulf. He wanted to close off their way to India. The next year, the Portuguese captured the city of Hormuz, which overlooks the entrance to the Persian Gulf. After the battle, Albuquerque showed his savage side, ordering his men to cut off the noses and ears of the female prisoners. The male prisoners lost their noses and right hands.

In 1509 Albuquerque was named governor-general of Portugal's Indian lands. Seeking a better harbor for his ships, he invaded the port city of Goa. Backed by 23 ships as well as by Indian **corsairs,** the Portuguese waged a bitter struggle with Goa's Muslim forces. When Albuquerque's troops finally took the city, they slaughtered the defenders.

Using Goa as a base, Albuquerque continued to expand Portuguese power in Asia. He captured the city of Malacca, on the Malay Peninsula. Control of the nearby waterways gave Portugal a secure sea route to China.

Despite Albuquerque's successes, however, Portugal was unable to maintain its empire. The nation's forces were spread too thin to defend their territory against the Muslims and other European powers. During yet another military expedition in 1515, Albuquerque fell ill and died on board a ship near Goa.

Afonso de Albuquerque was a brilliant but cruel admiral who made the most of his limited resources.

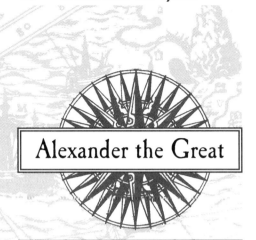

Alexander the Great

Greek
b 356 B.C.; Pella, Macedonia
d June 13, 323 B.C.; Babylon
***Explored and conquered Middle East
and central Asia***

As a young man, Alexander claimed to be a relative of Achilles, one of ancient Greece's greatest heroes.

Suggested Reading Afonso de Albuquerque, *The Commentaries of the Great Alfonso Dalboquerque, Second Viceroy of India,* translated by Walter de Gray Birch (B. Franklin, 1970); Elaine Sanceau, *Indies Adventure: The Amazing Career of Afonso de Albuquerque, Captain-General and Governor of India (1509-1515)* (Blackie, 1936).

Alexander the Great, king of Macedonia, was one of the most successful generals in history. By the time he was 30 years old, he had created a huge empire in Asia, Europe, and Africa. He led his army to regions that no European had ever fully explored.

More than just a skilled military leader, Alexander was also a learned man who appreciated science and the arts. As a young man, he had been tutored by Aristotle, the great thinker and scientist of ancient Greece. Exploration became one of Alexander's main goals as he led his armies through foreign lands. Although he could be cruel in war, he had the wisdom to treat his enemies well when they came under his rule. He built cities in the lands he conquered and spread Greek culture in Asia. His empire could not survive without him, however, and it collapsed after he died suddenly at the age of 33.

A Prince Becomes King

Alexander was born in 356 B.C. at Pella, north of Greece. He was the son of King Philip II of Macedonia and Queen Olympias. While Alexander was still a child, his parents divorced, and he and his mother fled the court. Alexander was later reunited with his father and fought by his side. Philip and Alexander defeated the Greeks and then led them against their common enemy, the Persians.

When Philip was assassinated in 336 B.C., Alexander acted quickly to take power. He executed the people he thought were responsible for his father's death—and anyone else who challenged his authority. At the age of 21, Alexander was secure as king, and he decided to carry out his father's plan to destroy the Persian Empire.

In the spring of 334 B.C., Alexander set out with an army of 35,000 soldiers. Along the Aegean coast (in what is now Turkey), he captured Greek cities that had been occupied by the Persians. Proceeding east, he defeated an army led by the Persian king Darius III at the Battle of Issus. Darius, however, managed to escape.

Conquering the Persians

Alexander next turned to Tyre (in modern-day Lebanon), Persia's main port on the Mediterranean Sea. After fierce fighting, the Greeks took Tyre in 332 B.C., and Alexander ordered that the city's women and children be sold as slaves. With this victory, Alexander was the master of the eastern Mediterranean. Later that year, Alexander reached Egypt. He was crowned pharaoh and founded the city of Alexandria.

Alexander returned north in pursuit of Darius. Greek and Persian forces clashed near the city of Nineveh (in present-day Iraq), and the Persians suffered their worst defeat of the war. Once again, Darius escaped, but he was later assassinated by one of his own generals. Alexander had reached the heart of the Persian Empire. He marched triumphantly to the great city of Persepolis and then occupied the Persian capital of Ecbatana (present-day Hamadan, Iran). After these victories, Alexander ruled all of Persia and commanded an army of more than 200,000.

East to India

For two years, Alexander remained in central Asia. Based in Tehran, his armies roamed eastward through the lands now known as Afghanistan, Turkmenistan, and Uzbekistan. Next, Alexander set his sights on India. He led his troops across the Hindu Kush mountain range, and in the summer of 327 B.C., they reached the northern part of the Indus River.

Alexander and his army marched across the plains of Punjab, the edge of the world known to Europeans at that time. Even the Persians had not crossed this region. After defeating a local army, Alexander heard about another great river to the east (most likely the Ganges River). He was determined to push deeper into India. He hoped to find the great sea that ancient Europeans believed surrounded the lands of the earth. Having already crossed the known world, Alexander's weary troops refused to go any further.

Alexander ordered a general named NEARCHUS to build a fleet to sail down the Indus River. He believed that the Indus was the source of the Nile River and would lead his army back to Egypt.

Like others in his time, Alexander did not know that east of India was the vast kingdom of China.

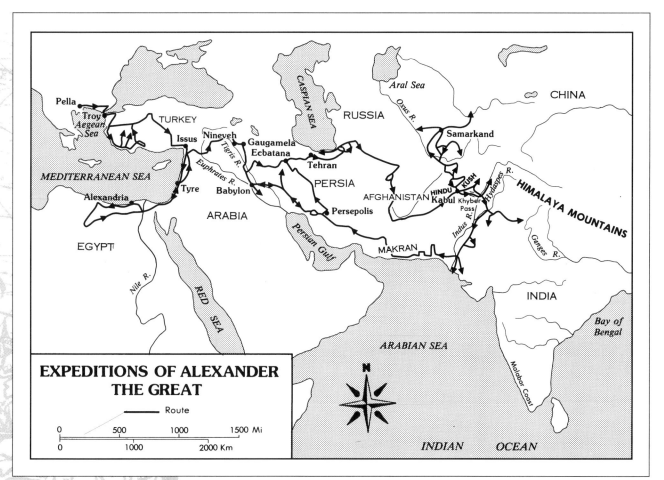

EXPEDITIONS OF ALEXANDER THE GREAT

—— Route

0   500   1000   1500 Mi
0   1000   2000 Km

The local people, however, told Alexander that the Indus led south to a great sea—the Indian Ocean. He decided to explore this sea, still convinced that it would take him back to Egypt.

A Disastrous Return Trip

Alexander loaded part of his army onto his new fleet of ships. He and the rest of his troops marched along the riverbank, battling local warriors as they went. For nine months, the army trudged on, covering 1,000 miles to the mouth of the Indus River on the Arabian Sea.

Alexander then divided his soldiers into three groups. The sick and wounded were ordered to march back to Persia. Nearchus and the fleet were to sail west along the coast, exploring the Arabian Sea and the Persian Gulf. Alexander's army was to march along the shore, providing the fleet with supplies.

In the fall of 325 B.C., the fleet set sail, but Alexander's plan soon went horribly wrong. During its 130-day voyage, Nearchus's fleet met Alexander's army only once. Food and water were scarce along the barren coast. Many of the men on the ships died before the fleet reached the mouth of the Euphrates River in Persia.

Meanwhile, the rough terrain along the shore forced Alexander to march inland. This trek was also a disaster. Crossing the Makran desert in the region now called Pakistan, the troops found little food or water. Many died from hunger or thirst. Eventually the soldiers found a **caravan** route that led back to Persepolis and on to what is now Iran.

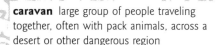

caravan large group of people traveling together, often with pack animals, across a desert or other dangerous region

The End of an Empire

Since the start of its expedition, Alexander's army had marched more than 25,000 miles. But Alexander's days of exploration and conquest were over. He spent his last two years trying to strengthen his control over his new lands. He hoped to combine the best of the Greek and Persian cultures by having his Greek officers marry Persian wives. Alexander himself married a daughter of King Darius.

Alexander, however, was showing signs of mental strain. He claimed he was a son of the gods and had divine powers. In fact, he was all too human. He fell ill after a long bout of drinking and died of a fever on June 13, 323 B.C.

Without his leadership, the empire quickly collapsed into several smaller parts ruled by his quarreling relatives and generals. Still, Alexander's achievements truly earned him the nickname "the Great." His travels and military conquests united the known world, planting the seeds for increased trade and the sharing of culture and knowledge among distant lands.

Suggested Reading Robin L. Fox, *The Search for Alexander* (Little, Brown, 1980); Harold Lamb, *Alexander of Macedon: The Journey to World's End* (Doubleday, 1946); Aubrey de Selincourt, *The Campaigns of Alexander* (Penguin, 1976).

al-Idrisi. See *Idrisi, al-*.

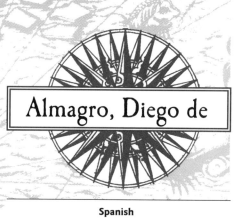

Almagro, Diego de

Spanish
b 1474?; Almagro, Spain
d July, 1538; near Cuzco, Peru
Explored Chile by land

conquistador Spanish or Portuguese explorer and military leader in the Americas

adelantado Spanish leader of a military expedition to America during the 1500s who also served as governor and judge

league unit of distance, usually used at sea, roughly equal to 3.5 miles

Diego de Almagro was described in his time as "a man of short stature, with ugly features, but of great courage and endurance."

Diego de Almagro, an explorer and **conquistador,** took part in one of the greatest adventures in the history of exploration. It was also one of the most brutal attacks on a native population. With Francisco PIZARRO, Almagro discovered and conquered the great Inca civilization of what is now Peru. Hoping to discover a vast fortune in gold, Almagro then led the first European expedition to explore the area that is now Chile by land.

Diego de Almagro was probably born about 1474 in the town of Almagro, in the Estremadura region of Spain. Until he was 40, he wandered across Spain, looking for adventure, and he once murdered a man in a brawl. In 1514 Almagro traveled to the Americas and arrived in what is now Colombia.

In Search of the Inca

After a decade in South America, Almagro teamed up with Francisco Pizarro. The two men pooled resources with a wealthy priest to invest in farming, mining, and the slave trade. The men then planned an expedition to find the Inca Empire, which was called Birú. The Inca were rumored to possess incredible wealth.

Almagro and Pizarro set out in 1525. During the first of two unsuccessful trips, Almagro lost an eye and several fingers in a battle with Indians. At the end of 1530, Pizarro tricked Almagro and made another trip, this time alone. He had won permission from the Spanish government to lead the Peruvian conquest and keep most of the Inca fortunes he found for himself. Almagro was angry, but he was apparently satisfied after Pizarro promised to share his future riches.

Almagro gathered recruits and supplies and met Pizarro at Cajamarca, Peru, in 1533. The combined forces of Almagro, Pizarro, and Hernando de SOTO marched 750 miles from Cajamarca to Cuzco, the Inca capital. The Spanish captured the city, and Pizarro named Almagro governor of Cuzco.

Exploration of Chile

In 1534 the king of Spain named Almagro **adelantado** of New Toledo, a province that extended some 200 **leagues** south from Pizarro's territory of New Castile. The two leaders quarreled over whose lands included the Inca capital. Pizarro avoided a war by encouraging Almagro to explore New Toledo along the Pacific Ocean.

Almagro left Cuzco on July 3, 1535. His forces included 750 Spaniards and 12,000 Indians, and he hoped to find a rich civilization like that of the Inca. Following the route used by the Incas, the expedition passed Lake Titicaca (on the border of modern Peru and Bolivia). Almagro then tried to march during the winter—a costly mistake. He lost many soldiers, Indians, and horses before he finally stopped in the Salta Valley.

When the journey was resumed, the expedition made a difficult trek across the Andes and then turned south into the plain of northern Chile. Almagro and his forces eventually reached the site of Santiago, today the capital of Chile.

During the long march, Almagro's forces committed many gruesome acts of violence against the Indians they met and captured.

Father Cristóbal de Molina, a priest who kept notes on the journey, described some of these brutal scenes. He wrote that the Indian prisoners walked in long lines, chained together at the neck. When a prisoner died, his head was cut off so that his body could be removed without undoing the chains.

Failure and Death

After months of exploration, Almagro and his forces had not found great treasures. Weary and disappointed, the expedition headed back to Cuzco. The explorers took a coastal route north, and they became the first Europeans to cross the 600-mile-long Atacama Desert in northern Chile.

When Almagro returned to Cuzco, he found the city under attack by Manco, an Inca leader. Almagro defeated Manco and claimed the city for himself. This action led to war between Almagro and his old partner, Pizarro, who was supported by his three half brothers. Almagro won an early battle but was eventually defeated and captured. After an unjust trial, held only for show, he was beheaded in July 1538. His son later took revenge by murdering Francisco Pizarro.

Diego de Almagro won wealth, power, and fame for his part in the conquest of Peru. His place among explorers, however, was guaranteed by his remarkable expedition through Chile.

Suggested Reading Gerald Green, *The Sword and the Sun: A Story of the Spanish Civil Wars in Peru* (Scribner, 1953).

---

al-Mas'udi. See *Mas'udi, al-*.

al-Nasibi, ibn Hawqal. See *Ibn Hawqal*.

Alvarado, Pedro de

Spanish
b 1485?; Badajoz, Spain
d June 29, 1541; Jalisco, Mexico
Explored Guatemala, El Salvador, Mexico, and Ecuador

---

conquistador Spanish or Portuguese explorer and military leader in the Americas

Beginning with his first expedition to Mexico in 1518, Pedro de Alvarado always sought unknown regions to explore. He first served under the command of others, then became a **conquistador** himself. He led a successful mission to Guatemala and El Salvador. Later Alvarado entered the province of Quito (present-day Ecuador) to look for Inca riches, only to find that Francisco PIZARRO had already arrived there.

Alvarado was born in about 1485 in Badajoz, in the Spanish province of Estremadura. We know little about his life before 1510, when he landed in the West Indies with his four brothers. For the next eight years, Alvarado helped run a plantation in Santo Domingo (now the capital of the Dominican Republic). He was then named commander of a ship sent to the Yucatán peninsula of Mexico. During the journey, Alvarado earned a reputation as a brave though sometimes cruel man.

Pedro de Alvarado survived bitter cold while exploring the Andes, but many of his soldiers froze to death in the heavy mountain snow.

plateau high, flat area of land

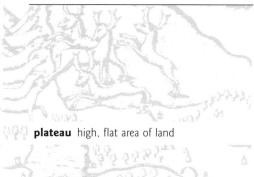

Trouble with the Aztecs

Alvarado next joined Hernán CORTÉS to push farther into Mexico. Cortés and his forces discovered and conquered the Aztecs, who had ruled the most powerful empire in Mexico. During this time, Alvarado became Cortés's second-in-command. When Cortés had to leave the Aztec capital of Tenochtitlán, he left Alvarado in charge.

Alvarado tried to intervene in the Aztec religious ceremonies, hoping to stop the practice of human sacrifice. The Aztecs' resistance resulted in the death of 200 of their nobles. When Cortés returned to the city, he and his forces had to retreat to avoid war with the Aztecs. By 1523, however, Cortés had regained Tenochtitlán as well as the rest of Mexico. Alvarado received permission to explore and conquer Central America.

Fighting Through Unknown Territory

During his expedition to Central America, Alvarado proved to be a strong leader. He won the loyalty of his men and the respect of the Indians he conquered. Details of this trip come primarily from two letters that Alvarado sent to Cortés.

Alvarado and his forces traveled south along the western coast of Mexico, reaching the city of Tehuantepac with little trouble. From there on, Alvarado constantly battled Indians as he headed east into Guatemala. The Indians' resistance, however, was greatly weakened by an epidemic of smallpox, a disease that had come with the Europeans to the Americas.

The expedition crossed "two rivers with very steep, rocky banks" and climbed a mountain pass. The pass led Alvarado to the great interior **plateau** of Guatemala. He called the scenery "magnificent," and he counted 16 volcanoes along the Pacific Ocean. Alvarado moved into an abandoned Indian city, where his forces later fought off an Indian attack. When he resumed his march, Alvarado took advantage of a war between two major Indian tribes. He won the friendship of one tribe, the Cakchiquel, by aiding them in their battle against the Quiché.

By autumn, Alvarado had reached the city of Tecpán and defeated the Atitlán Indians. He had also begun to build the first capital of Guatemala at the site of modern-day Guatemala City. Alvarado then continued into what is now El Salvador, going as far south as Cuzcaclan (near the present capital, San Salvador). Alvarado was eventually given full authority in Guatemala and El Salvador.

Jungles and Mountains

In 1533 Alvarado turned his attention to South America and the province of Quito. He hoped to find great wealth there, as Pizarro had done. Alvarado sailed to the coast and led his expedition into the rain forest. The heavy humidity of these interior lands rusted the men's weapons and armor. When the party reached the mountains of the Andes, they suffered greatly in the icy conditions. They also had trouble breathing because of ash from an erupting volcano.

When he finally reached Quito, Alvarado found that the land had already been claimed by Pizarro and his partner, Diego de ALMAGRO.

To avoid a war between the competing conquistadors, Almagro bought Alvarado's remaining army and supplies.

After returning to Guatemala, Alvarado planned a trip to the Spice Islands, in the East Indies, in 1540. Instead, the Spanish governor of Mexico persuaded him to lead an expedition to search for the legendary Mexican cities of Cíbola. Alvarado never accomplished either goal. He was killed on June 29, 1541, when a rearing horse fell on him.

Suggested Reading John E. Kelly, *Pedro de Alvarado, Conquistador* (Kennikat Press, 1971).

Alvares, Francisco

Portuguese
b 1465?; Portugal?
d 1541 or 1542; Rome, Italy
Explored Ethiopia

Francisco Alvares was a Roman Catholic priest. In 1515 he served as chaplain on an expedition to Abyssinia (now known as Ethiopia). Alvares wrote about his journey to this East African nation near the Red Sea. European readers were fascinated by their first look at Abyssinia's customs, society, and people.

The Search for a Mysterious King
Alvares was a member of a Portuguese expedition in search of Prester John, a great Christian king. Prester John later turned out to be a myth, but many Europeans believed that his kingdom existed somewhere in Africa or Asia. Alvares and his companions also hoped to establish official ties between Portugal and Abyssinia.

The expedition's commander died during the voyage from Portugal to East Africa, which took five years. In 1520, however, the party arrived at the court of Lebna Dengel, the emperor of Abyssinia.

Alvares, of course, did not discover Prester John or his fabled kingdom, but he did find a fellow Portuguese, Pêro da COVILHÃ. Once an explorer himself, Covilhã had been missing for almost 30 years. He had been captured by the Abyssinians, who forbade him to leave. During his captivity, he had learned a great deal about Abyssinia, and he helped Alvares to understand this foreign land.

Record of a Lost Empire
Alvares also made his own careful observations of the country and its people. When he returned to Portugal in 1527, he wrote a detailed description of Abyssinia. He called his work *True Information on the Countries of Prester John of the Indies.* The book was translated into several languages and read all across Europe. Alvares became famous. The book was also historically valuable. Not long after Alvares left Abyssinia, the country was destroyed by Muslim invaders. His book was the only detailed record of the Abyssinian Empire. Five years after he returned to Portugal, Alvares traveled to Italy. He delivered letters from the Abyssinian emperor to Pope Clement VII, the leader of the Roman Catholic Church. Alvares remained in Italy until his death.

Suggested Reading Francisco Alvares, *The Prester John of the Indies: A True Relation of the Lands of the Prester John, Being the Narrative of the Portuguese Embassy to Ethiopia in 1520,* translated by Lord Stanley of Alderley (Hakluyt Society, 1961).

Alvarez de Pineda, Alonso

Spanish?
b 1400s?; ?
d 1520; Pánuco River, Mexico
***Explored Gulf of Mexico and was first
European to see Mississippi River***

Alvarez de Pineda's map brought Europe its first knowledge of North America's mightiest river, the Mississippi.

In 1519 Alonso Alvarez de Pineda commanded a Spanish ship along the coast of the Gulf of Mexico, exploring from the southern tip of Florida to Veracruz, Mexico. During his expedition, Alvarez de Pineda proved that Florida was not an island, as most people believed at the time. He also became the first European explorer to see the mouth of the Mississippi River.

Nothing is known of Alvarez de Pineda's life before his historic journey. Historians have tried to trace his background through Spanish records, but they cannot find any mention of him. He was probably not actually Spanish. In any case, by 1519 Alvarez de Pineda had reached the Americas, where he met Francisco de Garay, the Spanish governor of Jamaica. Garay was in financial trouble and desperately needed money. He hoped that if he discovered new lands, he would find great riches. Garay received permission to send four ships to explore the mainland of North America. He hired Alvarez de Pineda to lead the expedition.

The Gulf of Mexico

Garay's four ships sailed from Jamaica with a combined crew of approximately 270. Their mission was to explore the area between Florida, which had been discovered by Juan PONCE DE LEÓN, and eastern Mexico, where Hernán CORTÉS was already active. Alvarez de Pineda and his crew were looking for a strait connecting the Gulf of Mexico with the South Sea. The South Sea, later known as the Pacific Ocean, had been discovered by Vasco Nuñez de BALBOA.

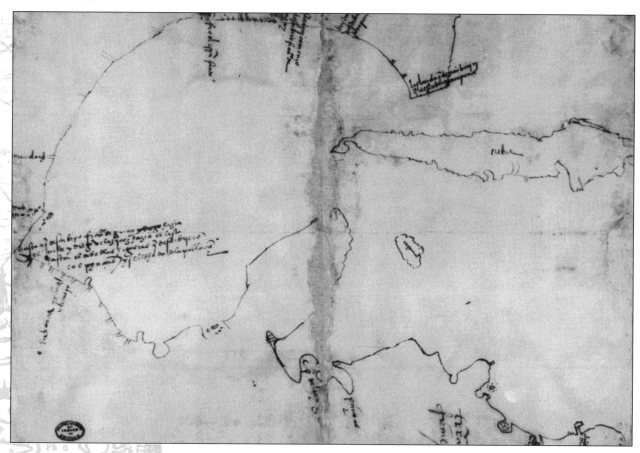

The explorers sailed through the Yucatán Channel between Mexico and Cuba and headed north until they sighted Florida. Ponce de León believed that Florida was an island, so the explorers looked for a waterway between Florida and the mainland. When they failed to find a channel, they knew that Florida was not an island after all.

Alvarez de Pineda then wanted to sail up Florida's east coast, but the wind and ocean currents forced him to change his plans. From Florida's west coast, he began to follow the Gulf of Mexico coastline toward Mexico. On the way, the expedition saw the waters of the Mississippi River pouring into the gulf. That day, June 2, 1519, was the feast day of the Holy Spirit, a Catholic holiday. Alvarez de Pineda named the river Rio del Espiritu Santo—the river of the Holy Spirit.

Conflict with Cortés

As Alvarez de Pineda sailed along the coast of the Gulf of Mexico, he observed "a very good land"—peaceful and fertile. The trees produced a variety of fruits, and he was sure that the rivers contained gold. He noted that the Indians wore gold jewelry "in their nostrils, on their ear lobes, and on other parts of their body."

Eventually the expedition came to Villa Rica de Vera Cruz (modern-day Veracruz). There, Hernán Cortés was preparing to launch an attack against the great Aztec Empire. Alvarez de Pineda sent four men ashore to inform Cortés that he planned to found a settlement nearby. Cortés was not happy about the arrival of another Spanish explorer in this region, which he wanted to claim for himself. However, he was too busy with his military planning to pay much attention to this nuisance. He seized the four messengers, but he let Alvarez de Pineda's ships sail north, to the mouth of the Pánuco River.

The ships traveled about 20 miles up the river, observing 40 villages of the friendly Huastec Indians. After about 40 days on the river, the expedition returned to Jamaica.

Mexico Becomes Deadly

Alvarez de Pineda gave Governor Garay the map he had made during the voyage. The map showed a fairly accurate outline of the Gulf of Mexico, and it was sent to Spain with the rest of the expedition's records. Even before Spanish officials granted their permission, Garay planned to settle the Mexican land that Alvarez de Pineda had explored. In fact, some historians believe that Alvarez de Pineda did not return to Jamaica with the original expedition. Instead, he may have stayed near the Pánuco River to start a settlement.

If Alvarez de Pineda did not stay in Mexico, then he certainly went back to the Pánuco region from Jamaica. Either way, this adventure was less successful than his first. The Huastec Indians, who had been friendly during the first visit, turned against the Spanish. Early in 1520, they killed all of the Spaniards' horses and all but 60 of the several hundred settlers. Alvarez de Pineda died in the fighting.

Suggested Reading Clotilde Garcia, *Captain Alonso Alvarez de Pineda and the Exploration of the Texas Coast and the Gulf of Mexico* (San Felipe, 1982).

Amundsen, Roald Engelbregt Gravning

Norwegian
b July 16, 1872; Borge, near Oslo, Norway
d June 1928; near Spitsbergen, Norway
*Sailed Northwest Passage; reached South Pole;
explored polar regions by sea, land, and air*

Northwest Passage water route connecting
the Atlantic Ocean and Pacific Ocean through
the Arctic islands of northern Canada

Northeast Passage water route connecting
the Atlantic Ocean and Pacific Ocean along
the Arctic coastline of Europe and Asia

plateau high, flat area of land

Sometimes called the last Viking, Roald
Amundsen was 54 years old when his
airplane crashed in the Arctic.

In 1903 Roald Engelbregt Gravning
Amundsen launched his exploring career
with a stunning success. He sailed through
the **Northwest Passage,** a feat other explorers had failed to accomplish for hundreds of years. During the trip, Amundsen spent three
sleepless weeks navigating through shallow, icy waters that threatened to wreck his tiny ship at any moment. The historic journey
was only the first of his many spectacular explorations in the
world's polar regions.

Amundsen later became the first to reach the South Pole. He also
sailed through the **Northeast Passage** and pioneered the use of aircraft to explore the Arctic Ocean. Sometimes called the last Viking,
Amundsen had trouble getting along in respectable society. But
throughout his life he showed skill, cunning, and bravery that few
explorers ever matched.

An Early Inspiration

Amundsen came from a middle-class Norwegian family. Although
his father and uncles made their living in the shipping business,
Roald Amundsen grew up in the city of Oslo. The only chance the
boy had to explore nature came when his family spent holidays
on a farm.

When he was 15, Amundsen read the works of John FRANKLIN, a
British explorer. These writings, Amundsen later said, "shaped the
whole course of my life." Franklin wrote vividly of his first Arctic
expedition and the great suffering he had endured.
Amundsen was particularly impressed by this account,
and he later wrote: "A strange ambition burned within me
to endure those same sufferings."

Amundsen's mother, however, had other plans. After
her husband died, Mrs. Amundsen wanted her son to become a doctor. He tried to obey her wishes but never did
well in medical school. His passion was to become an explorer. Amundsen stayed in school until he was 21, when
his mother died. He then decided to explore the Arctic.

A Brush with Death

Before tackling the Arctic, Amundsen took on an exploration closer to home. Along with his brother, he set out
to cross the Norwegian **plateau** in the dead of winter. If
Amundsen wanted to suffer as his hero Franklin had, he
was off to a good start. Amundsen did not prepare as carefully for this trip as he would for his future expeditions.
The two young men set out with only a small amount of
food and two sleeping bags. Without a tent, they were
soon freezing and starving.

One night Amundsen burrowed into the snow to sleep.
When the weather changed, the surrounding snow turned
into "a ghastly coffin of ice." It took his brother three
hours to chip Roald free. By the end of their ordeal, the
brothers were horribly thin and sickly, their skin a shade
of greenish yellow.

mate assistant to the commander of a ship

scurvy disease caused by a lack of vitamin C and once a major cause of death among sailors; symptoms include internal bleeding, loosened teeth, and extreme fatigue

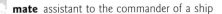

In case he did not return from the South Pole, Amundsen left a letter there for Robert Scott to take to Norway. The letter was found on Scott's frozen body.

Explorer in Training

Amundsen called his first experience a training exercise. It also marked his break from the civilized Norwegian society to which his family had belonged. Amundsen continued his training by working as a common sailor on a ship that often sailed the Arctic waters. He sailed for three summers and then qualified as a **mate.** In 1897 he was named first mate of the Belgian Antarctic Expedition. The trip was nearly a disaster, but Amundsen made it a triumph of survival.

The Belgian ship was not prepared for winter and became caught in an ice field near Graham Land, south of the tip of Chile. The situation worsened when the commanding officers were unable to provide fresh meat for the crew. As a result, the officers and many crew members developed **scurvy,** and Amundsen took command of the ship. He and the ship's physician, Dr. Frederick COOK, saved the expedition. They nursed everyone back to health, then maneuvered the ship out of the ice the following spring.

Adventure or Science?

When he returned to Norway, Amundsen received his captain's license and began preparing for his journey through the Northwest Passage. He thoroughly studied the British attempts of the past. His reading of

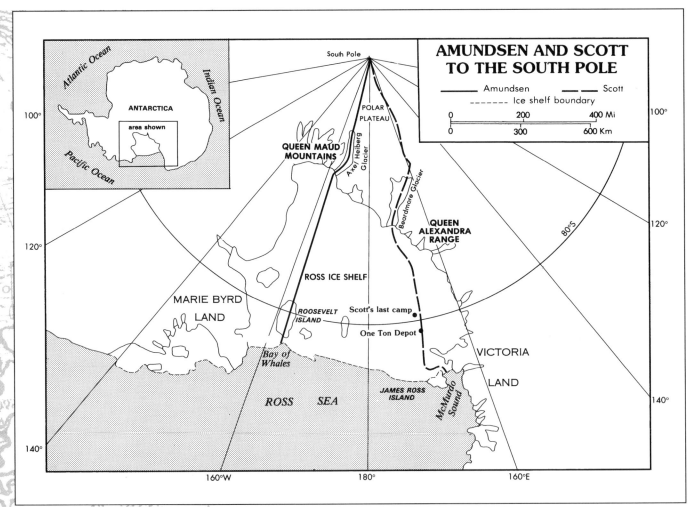

Francis Leopold McCLINTOCK's book convinced him that John Franklin's route offered the best chance of success. At the same time, Amundsen had in mind several improvements over Franklin's methods.

Rather than follow the main ice pack west of Canada's King William Island, Amundsen would sail east of the island. The waters there were more frequently free of ice. Amundsen also decided to use a new invention, the diesel engine, to power his small yacht, the *Gjoa.* Luckily the Arctic was enjoying some unusually warm weather at the time. He took his plan to Fridtjof NANSEN, a famous polar explorer. Nansen approved the plan and gave his encouragement.

To some, Amundsen's planned journey did not seem like a serious expedition. The lands through which he would be traveling had already been explored, and no one thought that the passage would ever be useful for shipping. Amundsen's critics charged that his voyage was a only a stunt to win public attention. Like the American polar explorer Robert PEARY, Amundsen was an adventurer who made his living by speaking and writing about his exploits. To raise money for this trip, he had to convince scientific organizations that his expedition would produce useful research.

Amundsen had no interest in science, but for the sake of his plan, he studied relentlessly and became an expert on magnetism. He promised to provide new information about the North Magnetic Pole, the place pointed to by magnetic compasses in the Northern Hemisphere. It had been 70 years since an earlier explorer, Sir

Amundsen wrote that on his yacht, the *Gjoa,* he and his crew felt like "seven as light-hearted pirates as ever flew the black flag. . . ."

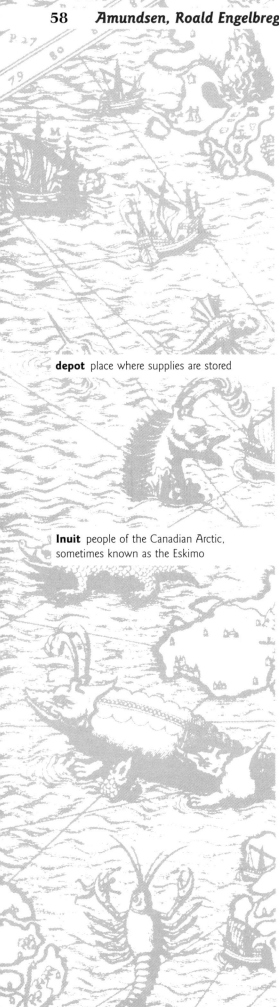

depot place where supplies are stored

Inuit people of the Canadian Arctic, sometimes known as the Eskimo

James Clark Ross, had studied the magnetic pole. During the winter and spring of 1903, Amundsen found educational societies and wealthy individuals who would fund his journey.

Still, many of Norway's scientists sensed that Amundsen was not sincere about his scientific interest. Funding for the trip soon dried up, and his debts mounted. Rather than go bankrupt and lose his yacht, Amundsen set sail in secret, one step ahead of his creditors.

Three Years' Voyage

It was midnight, June 16, 1903, when the *Gjoa* and its seven crew members sneaked out of Oslo. Amundsen was an untraditional captain. He did not believe in strict discipline and acted more like a president than a dictator. "Good work," Amundsen said, "can be done without the fear of the law."

Though the *Gjoa* was heavily loaded, the ship made good progress. By mid-August, the explorers were off the coast of northern Greenland, where they met fellow explorer Knud RASMUSSEN and the Danish Literary Greenland Expedition. Amundsen's party picked up supplies from a **depot** set up earlier and went on their way.

By August 22, they had arrived in the Canadian Arctic, at a camp once used by Amundsen's hero, John Franklin. From there, the party sailed to the point in Franklin Strait beyond which no one had sailed since Franklin's own journey. They pressed on, hoping that the waterway would remain clear of ice.

In early September, the *Gjoa* ran aground and was nearly wrecked. Finally the ship returned to the water, and the party reached its winter harbor on the south coast of King William Island. Amundsen spent two winters there, making observations and trading with the local **Inuit** people. In August 1905, he set sail again. In the shallow waters of Simpson Strait, Amundsen endured his three-week sleepless ordeal. But on August 27, a ship that had come east from the Bering Strait sailed into sight. Amundsen knew that he had made it through the Northwest Passage.

Unfortunately, the ice closed in too fast for the *Gjoa* to reach the Pacific Ocean that year. After another winter in the Arctic, the expedition arrived in San Francisco in October 1906. While still traveling along the Arctic coast, Amundsen had managed to come ashore and hike to a telegraph station on the Yukon River. He had sent word of his success, and a celebration was already organized when the *Gjoa* sailed into San Francisco Bay. When Amundsen finally returned to Norway, no one minded that he had left without paying his debts. Instead, he received a hero's welcome.

Plans and New Plans

With his new fame, Amundsen had no trouble raising money for his next adventure. He wanted to be the first person to reach the North Pole, and he planned to drift with the polar ice pack, as Fridtjof Nansen had done. But while Amundsen made his preparations, Robert Peary made his own attempt at the pole. On April 6, 1909, Peary announced that he had reached his goal.

Amundsen immediately decided to focus instead on the South Pole, which had also never been reached. But Amundsen had a

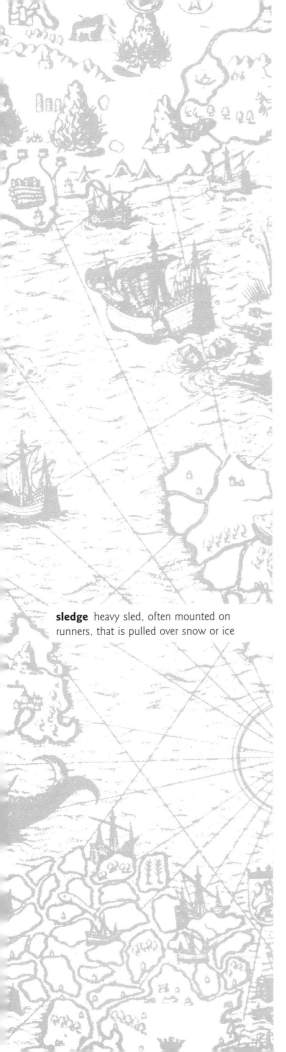

sledge heavy sled, often mounted on runners, that is pulled over snow or ice

competitor for that destination, too. Robert Falcon Scott, a British explorer, was already planning a trip to the southern continent. Amundsen feared that Scott would speed up his plans if he knew that the Norwegian was heading south. So instead of announcing his new plan, Amundsen lied. He claimed he was still going to the Arctic.

In the meantime, Amundsen built a house to serve as his base on the coast of Antarctica. He also bought 100 Greenland sled dogs. On August 9, 1910, Amundsen and his crew left Oslo on the *Fram,* the ship once used by Nansen. Their destination was Alaska—or so everyone thought. At Madeira, an island off the coast of Spain, Amundsen announced his real plan, both to the world and to his enthusiastic crew. Scott, upset that he had been deceived, hurried his own preparations. The race to the South Pole was on.

Amundsen had developed a brilliant but risky plan for his expedition. He had studied recent charts of the ice shelf that extended over the Ross Sea. By comparing these to earlier charts, Amundsen had guessed that part of the ice shelf was on top of land. Most other explorers assumed that the ice floated on water. By setting up his base on the ice over land in the Bay of Whales, he was 69 miles closer to the pole than Scott, who camped on James Ross Island. Luckily, Amundsen's conclusion about the ice shelf was correct. If he had been wrong, his camp could have dropped off the floating ice into the sea at any moment.

Amundsen's plan had another possible flaw. No one had ever explored the area he wanted to cross. He could not map out an exact route, and he might have run into a wall of mountains that he could not cross. Again, by good luck, Amundsen's risks paid off.

Harsh Realities

On October 19, 1911, Amundsen set off from his base with four **sledges,** four human companions, and 13 dogs. He had only limited experience in sledging, but Helmer Hanssen, who led the team, was an expert. They followed Amundsen's time schedule closely, though they faced dangers along the way. On the ice shelf, they were threatened by steep inclines and huge, bottomless cracks in the ice. But the team reached the Polar Plateau in early December, and the rest of the journey went smoothly.

To make his plan work, Amundsen had to follow an unpleasant but necessary strategy. Fewer sled dogs were needed to pull the sledges as the food was eaten. All the dogs, however, still would have to be fed with the remaining food. Amundsen had calculated that he could travel farther without the unneeded dogs. He was bothered by the idea of using the dogs for weeks and then killing them, but he stuck to this plan. It was practical but cruel, and it made him even less popular with some people.

The dogs were shot at the party's camp at the base of the plateau, a spot they named the Butcher Shop. The explorers, near starvation, were forced to join the remaining dogs in eating the dead animals. "But on this first evening," Amundsen later wrote, "we put a restraint on ourselves; we thought we could not fall upon our four-footed friends and devour them before they had time to grow cold. . . ."

Amundsen, a loyal subject of Norway's King Haakon VII, planted the Norwegian flag at the South Pole.

On December 6, the party reached its highest point on the plateau (11,024 feet), going on to arrive at the pole itself on December 14. All five men assisted in planting the Norwegian flag. Amundsen reported: "Five weather-beaten, frostbitten fists . . . grasped the waving flag in the air and planted it as the first at the geographic South Pole." The team then headed back to their base camp, reaching it on January 11, 1912. The expedition had covered 1,860 miles in 99 days.

Wartime Activities

Amundsen returned to Norway secretly. He wanted to write his book about the successful expedition quickly and then move on to his next adventure. He was once again bankrupt, but he found a wealthy Norwegian who was willing to support him. Amundsen returned to an old plan, to drift along with the polar ice pack in the Arctic. World War I, however, delayed this expedition.

Amundsen decided that the war could be an opportunity to earn money. He bought Norwegian ships and sold them at a profit to countries allied against Germany. With this money, he had the ship *Maud* built especially for his drift on the ice. Amundsen left in July 1918, planning to sail the Northeast Passage before heading into the pack ice. The crossing was successful, but before he could begin the polar drift, his ship was locked in ice for two years near the Bering Strait. During that time, Amundsen was injured in a fall and mauled by a bear. He decided to call off the expedition.

More Trouble than Money

During those two years, Amundsen's financial problems returned. He spent more than he had, always hopeful that he would find more money. The Norwegian government gave him some aid, but it was not enough to keep him out of debt. Still, even as he struggled with money, Amundsen discovered an exciting new way to undertake polar exploration—by airplane.

While waiting in Seattle to begin his intended polar drift, he bought a Junker—a German plane—and stored it on the *Maud.* Amundsen hoped to fly it from Point Barrow, Alaska, to Spitsbergen, Norway, across the Arctic Ocean. The *Maud* finally set sail in the summer of 1922, but Amundsen was not on it. He had decided to take his airplane to Point Barrow on a merchant ship. It was a lucky move, since the *Maud* was soon taken away by Amundsen's creditors. Meanwhile, Amundsen was finally ready to fly the Junker, but he damaged it in a trial flight.

At this point, Amundsen was deeply in debt. Even his brother gave up helping him. The great explorer tried to earn money by speaking across America, but this lecture tour did not bring in enough money. In his own words, he was "nearer to black despair than ever before in the 54 years of my life." Then an unexpected telephone call restored his hope.

While Amundsen was sitting in a hotel room, wondering how he was going to pay his bill, he received a call from an American, Lincoln ELLSWORTH. A college dropout and the son of a millionaire, Ellsworth was desperately searching for something to do with his life. He said that he would give Amundsen the necessary funds. In exchange,

Ellsworth wanted to share the command of a flight to the North Pole. Delighted and relieved, Amundsen agreed. "The gloom of the past year rolled away," Amundsen wrote, "and even the horrors of my business experience faded into forgetfulness in the activities of preparation."

Amundsen the Aviator

Amundsen and Ellsworth left for the North Pole in 1925, using two planes. In one sense, the journey was a failure because they never reached their destination. But the drama of the trip captivated the world. The two planes went down into the ice near the pole, and the explorers worked heroically to get the one working plane back into the air. The craft was overloaded, but the men managed to return safely. Amundsen was once again hailed as the brave and resourceful explorer of old.

A year later, Amundsen took part in another astounding flight. On the Italian **dirigible** *Norge,* he flew across the Arctic from Norway to Alaska. The dirigible floated over the polar ocean, dangerously weighed down by glittering blankets of ice. The trip was a marvel of technology, and Amundsen was once again at the center of the world's attention.

Unfortunately, Amundsen's later actions spoiled the glory of these achievements. In his autobiography, he attacked Umberto No-BILE, the Italian who had designed and piloted the *Norge.* He also criticized other explorers, including many of his partners and even his brother. When he could have appeared as a grand hero of exploration, he came across as a bitter old man.

Amundsen's image was restored on one last voyage. In 1928 Nobile tried to repeat his flight across the Arctic. He wanted to clear his name after the charges Amundsen had made against him. During the flight, however, Nobile's dirigible crashed. When he heard of the accident, Amundsen immediately put aside his conflicts with Nobile and boarded a plane to join in the search. Nobile was eventually rescued, but Amundsen did not return. His plane had gone down, and the Norwegian explorer sank unseen into the Arctic Ocean.

Suggested Reading Roald Amundsen, *My Life as an Explorer* (Doubleday, Doran and Company, 1928); Gerald Bowman, *Men of Antarctica* (Fleet, 1958); Roland Huntford, *Scott and Amundsen* (Atheneum, 1984); Theodore K. Mason, *Two Against the Ice: Amundsen and Ellsworth* (Dodd, Mead and Company, 1982); J. Gordon Naeth, *To the Ends of the Earth: The Explorations of Roald Amundsen* (Harper and Row, 1962); L.H. Neatby, *Conquest of the Last Frontier* (Ohio University Press, 1966); Bellamy Partridge, *Amundsen* (Robert Hale, 1933); Charles Turley, *Roald Amundsen Explorer* (Methuen, 1935).

dirigible large aircraft filled with a lighter-than-air gas that keeps it aloft; similar to a blimp but with a rigid frame

Andrée, Salomon August

Swedish
b October 18, 1854; Grenna, Sweden
d 1897?; White Island, Norway
Attempted balloon flight to North Pole

In July of 1897, Salomon August Andrée set out from Spitsbergen Island in his balloon, the *Ornen,* seeking to reach the North Pole. It was the last time he would be seen alive. His fate and the story of his trip would remain unknown for more than 30 years.

A Love of Science and Ballooning

Andrée was born in 1854, one of seven children of a pharmacist. He showed an early interest in science, and in 1869 he entered the Royal Institute of Technology in Stockholm. He graduated four

Salomon August Andrée named his balloon *Ornen,* which means Eagle.

sledge heavy sled, often mounted on runners, that is pulled over snow or ice

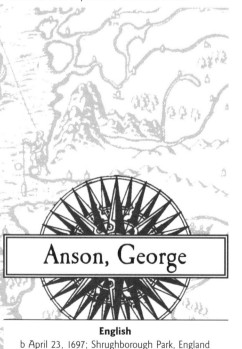

Anson, George

English
b April 23, 1697; Shrughborough Park, England
d June 6, 1762; Moor Park, England
Sailed around world, reformed British navy

years later and remained in Stockholm for two more years, working as a draftsman and designer. He went on to become chief engineer in the Swedish patent office.

Andrée became interested in balloons when he read a book called *Laws of the Wind.* In 1876 he traveled to Philadelphia to visit the exhibition celebrating the hundredth anniversary of the United States. There he met with an experienced balloon pilot who taught him the basics of ballooning. In 1894 Andrée received a grant to buy a balloon, the *Svea,* from which he conducted many scientific experiments.

The next year, Andrée announced his plan to travel by balloon to the North Pole. At that time, no one had ever reached the pole. Andrée began by making careful studies of the geography and winds of the Arctic. He designed special equipment that would allow him to steer his new balloon. He also gathered money to support the expedition. One of his sponsors was Alfred Nobel, the man who established the Nobel Prizes.

Forced Down

On July 11, 1897, Andrée and two companions took off from Spitsbergen aboard his new balloon. Problems at the launch caused some important equipment to be left behind. What happened next remained a mystery until August 6, 1930, when the remains and the records of the expedition were found on White Island, near Spitsbergen.

The records showed that the flight had lasted for 325 miles and three days. Then an unexpected lack of wind forced the balloon, weighted down by frost, to land on the ice. The men tried to return home by **sledge,** but heavy equipment, polar bears, and cold weather made the trip difficult. By early October, they had traveled 200 miles, but no one knows how much longer they might have survived. The bodies of Andrée and one companion were found in their tent. They had probably been poisoned by carbon monoxide gas that leaked from their kerosene stove. The journals, photos, and equipment they left behind told a moving story of a courageous and difficult journey.

Suggested Reading Edward Adams-Ray, translator, *Andrée's Story: The Complete Record of His Polar Flight, 1897,* revised edition (Viking, 1960); George Palmer Putnam, *Andrée: The Record of a Tragic Adventure* (Brewer and Warren, 1939); Per Olof Sundman *The Flight of the Eagle,* translated by Mary Sandbach (Pantheon, 1970).

George Anson was born into a distinguished family in Staffordshire in 1697 and went to sea with the navy when he was 15. He rose through the ranks and became a captain. From 1724 to 1739, Anson commanded three different ships, protecting Britain's territories in the Americas from Spanish attacks. Most of this military action took place along the southeast coast of North America. From 1740 to 1744, Anson led a British fleet on a voyage around the globe. When he returned home, he worked to turn the British navy into an efficient, professional force.

Setting Out to Circle the Globe

On September 18, 1740, Anson left Britain with six ships for the first part of a four-year trip around the world. His first task was to sail to the west coast of South America and attack Spanish settlements. Before reaching his goal, Anson lost half his fleet to shipwrecks, and many of his sailors died of **scurvy,** but Anson sailed on. He eventually captured the Spanish town of Paita on the coast of Peru and destroyed many Spanish ships in the region.

By that time, Anson's remaining ships had suffered damage. He put all his men on the most seaworthy of his vessels and sailed west to Tinian, an island in the western Pacific. They rested briefly there, then sailed farther west, reaching Macao, on the southern coast of China, in November 1742. The following summer, Anson captured a Spanish **galleon** sailing between the Philippines and the Americas. The ship carried a fortune in gold bars and coins. Back at Macao, Anson sold 32 wagonloads of this Spanish treasure to the Chinese and then headed home. When he reached Britain in 1744, Anson was a rich man for life.

Building a Better Navy

The determination Anson showed on his difficult global voyage appeared again during his next mission. At the time, the British navy was badly run and poorly organized. In 1745 Anson was named a rear admiral and began to reform the service.

Under his command, the navy dockyards were improved, and fleets were inspected regularly. To reduce theft and bribery, Anson checked the navy's finances carefully. He established new rules for awarding promotions and enforcing discipline. These reforms were partly why, for example, the wealthy civilian Alexander DALRYMPLE was denied the command of an expedition to the Pacific Ocean in 1768. Captain James COOK was the skilled naval officer who was chosen instead.

After making his reforms, Anson went back to active duty. In 1747 he commanded a British fleet against the French. He won a key victory, was promoted to vice admiral, and was given the title of baron. He continued working for the navy, and in 1755 he established the British marine corps.

When Anson died at Moor Park in 1762, he was Britain's highest-ranking admiral. His four-year trip around the world had stirred his country's interest in the Pacific, and he had turned the British navy into perhaps the best fleet in the world.

Suggested Reading Patrick O'Brian, *The Golden Ocean* (Norton, 1984); Richard Walter, *Anson's Voyage Round the World* (Charles E. Lauriat, 1928).

In 1748 Baron George Anson published a book describing his four-year global voyage. The work became a best-seller and was later translated into French.

scurvy disease caused by a lack of vitamin C and once a major cause of death among sailors; symptoms include internal bleeding, loosened teeth, and extreme fatigue

galleon large sailing ship used for war and trade

Anza, Juan Bautista de

Spanish
b 1735? Fronteras, Mexico
d December 19, 1788; Arizpe, Mexico
Established Sonora-California Trail

Colonel Juan Bautista de Anza has been called the last **conquistador.** He was born in **New Spain** and dedicated himself to defending its northern frontiers. He also blazed new trails to connect the widespread Spanish territories in North America. These trails included important land routes from Sonora (in what is now the state of Arizona) to upper California and from Sonora to Santa Fe (in what is now the state of New Mexico). In 1775 Anza led an expedition

conquistador Spanish or Portuguese explorer and military leader in the Americas

New Spain region of Spanish colonial empire that included the areas now occupied by Mexico, Florida, Texas, New Mexico, Arizona, California, and various Caribbean islands

presidio Spanish settlement in the Americas that was defended by soldiers

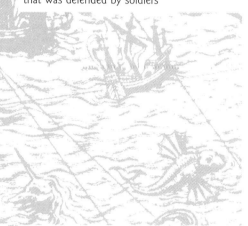

viceroy governor of a Spanish colony in the Americas

mission settlement founded by priests in a land where they hoped to convert people to Christianity

that established the first European settlement in the area of San Francisco Bay.

Young Soldier

Juan Bautista de Anza was born at the **presidio** of Fronteras, in the Sonora province in New Spain. Historians are unsure whether he was born in 1735 or 1736, and little is known of his early life. In 1752 he enlisted as a volunteer in Fronteras's armed forces, and by 1760 he had reached the rank of captain. That same year, he was named commander of the presidio of Tubac (near the present-day city of Douglas, Arizona). During the next 10 years, he led many successful campaigns against the Apache Indians.

The Sonora-California Trail

By 1770 the Spanish settlements in upper California were in trouble. The settlers had difficulty getting the supplies they needed by sea, and Russians in Alaska were pushing south toward California. Anza responded to these threats by suggesting a plan that his father had proposed 30 years earlier. Anza volunteered to open a land route from Sonora to upper California, using his own money to fund the expedition. Both the king of Spain and the **viceroy** of New Spain approved the plan.

Anza set out in January 1774 with 34 men, including Father Francisco GARCES. They headed north along the Gila River and followed it to the point where it flowed into the Colorado River. There Anza befriended the Yuma Indians, who controlled the lower Colorado River area. In his report on the journey, Anza emphasized the importance of friendly relations with the Yuma.

The expedition crossed the Colorado River, but Anza's party got lost in the desert west of the river and had to return to Yuma territory. They set out again, this time circling around the desert to the southwest and traveling through the Cocopah Mountains. Heading northwest, they reached the **mission** of San Gabriel. Anza left some soldiers at San Gabriel as reinforcements and then traveled north to the Monterey mission, which he also reinforced. Satisfied that the missions were safe, Anza then returned to Sonora, where he was promoted to lieutenant colonel. He was also chosen to lead a group of colonists to upper California and to find a site for a new presidio at San Francisco Bay.

Expedition to San Francisco

The new expedition left Tubac on October 23, 1775, with 240 colonists, 165 pack animals, 340 horses, and 300 cattle. Anza followed much the same route that he had taken on his previous expedition. This time, however, he marched across the desert instead of traveling around it. He divided the colonists into three groups that traveled a day apart. This way, the watering holes in the desert would have time to fill up again before the next group arrived. Rain, snow, and freezing temperatures made the winter journey difficult, and many of the animals died. At one point, Anza wrote, a storm was followed "with an earthquake which lasted four minutes." Despite the hardships, only one colonist died on the trip, and three healthy infants were born along the way.

Anza led the colonists to Monterey and then pushed on to explore the San Francisco Bay area. He discovered the Guadalupe River and found a good location for a presidio on a cliff at the mouth of San Francisco Bay. This expedition proved that Anza was an excellent leader. His outstanding performance earned him a promotion to colonel and an appointment as governor of New Mexico in 1777.

Anza's Governorship and His Legacy

Anza proved to be as capable a governor as he was an explorer. He brought peace to the northern frontier of New Mexico by defeating and befriending the Comanche, who then joined him against the Apache. He also continued to lead journeys of exploration, establishing the Sonora–Santa Fe Trail in 1780. The following year, he was unfairly blamed for an uprising by the Yuma and briefly lost his post as governor. In 1786 he requested a transfer to a more healthful climate, and two years later, he was named commander of the presidio at Tubac. However, he died in Arizpe, Mexico, on December 19, 1788, less than two months after being appointed to his new position.

Colonel Juan Bautista de Anza devoted himself to defending the northern frontier of Spain's empire in the Americas.

Anza was one of the best commanders and governors in New Spain. He established important routes connecting the heart of New Spain with remote outposts in California. He also kept detailed notes on the landscape, water supply, natural resources, and Indian tribes of the areas he explored. This information was valuable to later efforts at exploration and colonization. In the early 1900s, a legend grew that Anza was the founder of the city of San Francisco. In fact, the site of the city was chosen after Anza's expedition, although it was within the area that Anza had explored. Descendants of some of the settlers he led in 1775 still live in San Francisco today.

Suggested Reading Herbert E. Bolton, *Anza's California Expeditions*, 5 volumes (Russell and Russell, 1966), and *Outpost of Empire: The Story of the Founding of San Francisco* (Alfred A. Knopf, 1931); Frederick J. Teggart, editor, *The Anza Expedition of 1775-1776: Diary of Pedro Font* (University of California Press, 1913).

Armstrong, Neil Alden

American
b August 5, 1930; Wapakoneta, Ohio
living
First person on moon

Neil Alden Armstrong did something that no other explorer had ever done and none can ever repeat—he was the first person from the earth to set foot on another world. Millions of people watched on television in 1969 as Armstrong walked across the dusty, dark gray surface of the moon. The mission, named Apollo 11, was more than a personal achievement. Like all space flights, it was a triumph of technology and teamwork. For Americans, it was also a welcome victory in the "space race" with the **Soviet Union.** The whole world looked to Neil Armstrong as a symbol of what humanity could accomplish.

Soviet Union nation that existed from 1922 to 1991, made up of Russia and 14 other republics in eastern Europe and northern Asia

aeronautics the science of flight

NASA National Aeronautics and Space Administration, the U.S. space agency

supersonic faster than the speed of sound, which is about 740 miles per hour

rocket vehicle propelled by exploding fuel

astronaut American term for a person who travels into space; literally, "traveler to the stars"

capsule small early spacecraft designed to carry a person around the earth

orbit stable, circular route; one trip around; to revolve around

Dreams of Flying

As a boy living in small towns in Ohio, Armstrong built model airplanes and read about **aeronautics.** Sometimes he used a neighbor's telescope to look at the moon and stars in the night sky. His passion for airplanes led him to take flying lessons as a teenager, and he earned a pilot's license before he graduated from high school. He entered Purdue University in Indiana to study aeronautical engineering, but two years later, the United States became involved in the Korean War. Armstrong received flight training in Florida and then went to Korea as a fighter pilot. He flew 78 combat missions, winning three medals for what he called "bridge breaking, train stopping, tank shooting and that sort of thing." When his military service was completed, Armstrong returned to Purdue and finished his studies.

Into Space

Now an experienced flyer and an aeronautics engineer, Armstrong found a job as a research pilot for the National Advisory Committee for Aeronautics (NACA). The job took him to Edwards Air Force base in California, where he continued to work after NACA was replaced by **NASA** in 1958. As a test pilot, Armstrong flew more than 1,100 hours in new and experimental jets, trying to find out how high and how fast people and machines could travel. He flew **supersonic** fighter planes, and between 1960 and 1962, he flew six missions in a **rocket**-powered plane called the X-15. This plane was built to go to the highest parts of the earth's atmosphere—the very edge of space. Flying the X-15, Armstrong reached heights of 40 miles and speeds of 4,000 miles per hour.

By now, NASA had begun training **astronauts** to fly in small **capsules** that were launched into space by rockets. In early 1962, John GLENN became the first American to **orbit** the earth, kindling Armstrong's enthusiasm. Later that year, Armstrong was chosen by NASA to be one of the second group of astronauts. He was the first astronaut who was not a military officer.

Armstrong's first space flight was the Gemini 8 mission in 1966. He and copilot David Scott performed the first successful docking in space when their capsule met another spacecraft and joined with it. Despite problems that forced Armstrong to end the mission ahead of schedule, the docking was important to the progress of the American space program.

To the Moon

Armstrong's second space flight was his greatest contribution to exploration and one of mankind's greatest achievements. The United States had begun the Apollo program to reach the moon, and previous Apollo flights had taken astronauts near the moon and around it. Apollo 11 was intended to land astronauts on the moon's surface. NASA chose Armstrong to command the mission. Edwin "Buzz" Aldrin, Jr., and Michael Collins would accompany him.

On July 16, 1969, a Saturn 5 rocket blasted off from Cape Kennedy, Florida. It carried the command spacecraft, called the *Columbia,* and the landing craft, the *Eagle.* Three days later, the craft entered into orbit around the moon. While Collins stayed in the *Columbia,* Armstrong and Aldrin piloted the *Eagle* to a flat plain on the moon called the Sea of Tranquility. Six hours later, after adjusting his **space suit,** Armstrong opened the outer door and slowly climbed down a ladder to the powdery ground. Looking at his footprints on the moon's surface, he declared: "That's one small step for a man, one giant leap for mankind."

Armstrong and Aldrin spent two and a half hours walking on the moon. They set scientific instruments in place to record information about the moon's environment. They also gathered samples of soil and rocks and planted the American flag. A plaque they left behind reads: "Here men from the planet Earth first set foot upon the Moon, July 1969 A.D. We came in peace for all mankind." The next day they lifted off to dock with the *Columbia.* The three astronauts in the capsule splashed down in the Pacific Ocean on July 24. A navy ship picked them up and took them home.

Although Apollo 11 brought Armstrong worldwide fame, he did not enjoy the publicity. He preferred to work quietly at NASA's headquarters in Washington, D.C. He left the agency in 1971 for a career in education and business. In 1986 he served on the committee that investigated the explosion of the space shuttle *Challenger.*

space suit protective gear that allows a person who wears it to survive in space

From left to right: Neil Armstrong, Edwin Aldrin, Jr., and Michael Collins, the crew of the United States's Apollo 11 mission to the moon.

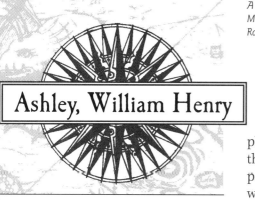

Ashley, William Henry

American
b 1778?; Powhatan, Virginia
d March 26, 1838; Cooper County, Missouri
Explored Green River

William Ashley founded the first annual rendezvous, a meeting of traders and trappers in the Rocky Mountains.

Suggested Reading Carmen Bredeson, *Neil Armstrong: A Space Biography* (Enslow, 1998); Andrew Chaikin, *A Man on the Moon: The Voyages of the Apollo Astronauts* (Viking, 1994); Michael D. Cole, *Apollo 11: First Moon Landing* (Enslow, 1995); Alan Shepard and Deke Slayton, *Moon Shot: The Inside Story of America's Race to the Moon* (Turner, 1994).

Although William Henry Ashley made only one journey of exploration in his life, he played a major role in opening the American West. His fur-trapping company employed many men who explored the Rocky Mountains in their search for beaver skins. During their travels, these men discovered new river routes and mountain passes that enabled settlers to cross the Rocky Mountains and push westward to the Pacific Ocean.

The Rocky Mountain Fur Company

Ashley was born in Virginia around 1778, but he migrated west to Missouri in 1805. He soon became a businessman in St. Louis, dealing in firearms and real estate. In fact, his involvement with exploration came more from his desire to make money than from the love of adventure. Ashley realized that there were great profits to be made from fur trapping in the Rocky Mountains, which were largely unexplored. In 1822 he and his partner Andrew Henry founded the Rocky Mountain Fur Company. They advertised for "enterprising young men" to go into the wilderness and make their fortunes by trapping beaver. Some of the men who joined Ashley's company would later be among the most important American explorers, such as Jedediah SMITH.

In 1823 Ashley led a party of men west along the Missouri River route established 20 years earlier by Meriwether LEWIS and William CLARK. They hoped to follow this route all the way to the Rockies.

Unfortunately, the group was attacked by Arikara Indians while traveling up the Missouri River, near the present-day border between North Dakota and South Dakota. Twelve of Ashley's men were killed, and the others were forced to turn back. One thousand armed men set out to subdue the Arikara, but the Indians defeated these men, too. With his first route blocked by the Arikara, Ashley had to rethink his plans. Since he was heavily in debt, he did not want to miss the entire trapping season and the profits that might be made. He decided to send his men to the Rockies by land instead of by river.

Two parties set out, one led by Jed Smith and the other by Andrew Henry. A year later, four men from Smith's group limped into St. Louis with both good news and bad news. The good news was that Smith had discovered rich fur-trapping territory around a river they called Seedskeedee, a name that means Prairie Hen (later named the Green River). The bad news was that Smith and his men were desperately in need of supplies.

A Businessman Becomes an Explorer

Ashley himself led the expedition to resupply his men, leaving Fort Atkinson, Missouri, in early November 1824 with 25 men, 50 pack horses, and several wagons. He followed the Platte River west before heading out across the open prairies and into the mountains. Despite the harsh winter weather, the party found excellent trapping in the Medicine Bow Mountains, in what is now southern Wyoming. After crossing the mountains, Ashley led his party south and west until they reached the Green River on April 15, 1825. Having resupplied Smith, he split his men into four groups and sent them out in different directions to trap beaver. The groups were instructed to meet 50 miles down the Green River on or before July 10.

Ashley led one group south on the Green River, hoping to find a river that would lead farther west. Traveling in buffalo-skin boats, the party explored the rough and often dangerous river. As the boats passed through deep, dark canyons, Ashley noticed the fear and gloom on his men's faces. They had heard tales of a giant whirlpool that would suck them all down to the center of the earth. Although they did come across several large whirlpools, none was as terrible as they had feared. Ashley, who could not swim, once nearly fell out of his boat. Still, the party pressed on until May 16, when they met two fur trappers who were traveling north from Taos, in the area now called New Mexico. These trappers told Ashley that there were no beaver farther south, so Ashley and his men turned back. Their journey on the Green River lasted 31 days and took them as far as what is now the state of Utah.

The Trappers' Rendezvous

Ashley's four groups met as planned. Their skillful trapping was a great success for Ashley, who had collected enough furs to pay off his debts and become a wealthy man. This gathering of trappers, called a rendezvous (the French word for meeting), started an annual tradition. The mountain men normally worked alone in the woods, but every year they came together at the rendezvous for a few weeks of trading, drinking, gambling, and storytelling.

Ashley went back to St. Louis, but he returned the next year for the rendezvous, which took place in Cache Valley, near the Great Salt Lake. There he sold his trapping business to Jed Smith and Smith's two partners. Ashley returned East to pursue a career in politics and was elected to the U.S. House of Representatives in 1831.

Ashley contributed in many ways to the exploration and settlement of the West. He personally explored the Green River, and the men he sent into the wilderness to trap furs found the South Pass through the Rockies. This pass, in present-day Wyoming, became a major route for settlers traveling to the west coast. Ashley's men also discovered and explored the Great Salt Lake. As a politician, Ashley used his enthusiasm for the riches of the West to encourage large groups of people to settle in that region.

Suggested Reading Harrison C. Dale, *The Ashley-Smith Explorations and the Discovery of a Central Route to the Pacific, 1822-1829* (Arthur H. Clark, 1941); Dale L. Morgan, *The West of William Ashley* (Old West, 1964).

---

ash-Sharif al Idrisi. See *Idrisi, al.*

Audubon, John James

French
b April 26, 1785; Cayes, Haiti
d January 27, 1851; New York, New York
Studied and drew birds of North America

Creole person of European ancestry born in Spanish colonies in the Americas; or, person descended from French settlers of what is now the southern United States

John James Audubon was not the usual kind of explorer. He did not blaze trails into the wilderness or discover new continents. But he added as much to the world's knowledge of North American wildlife as did any of the explorers whose trails he followed. Audubon's observations and drawings of birds in the wild provided a stunning record of the birds of North America in their natural environments.

Audubon's Early Life

Audubon was born on a plantation in what is now Haiti. He was the son of a French merchant and his **Creole** mistress. Before Audubon was a year old, his mother died, and his father took him and his half sister to live in France. His father's wife adopted both children as her own. By the age of 15, Audubon had become interested in drawing and in natural history, and he began a series of drawings of French birds. This passion would become his life's work.

In 1803 Audubon left France to avoid that country's political troubles. He moved to an estate that his father had bought in Pennsylvania and began his study of American birds. Audubon loved to draw his subjects, but he was also curious about their habits, which he studied closely. In one experiment, he tied silver threads around the legs of some young birds and noted that two returned to the same place the following year.

The Birth of an Idea

Audubon married in 1808 and spent most of the next 12 years in Kentucky, trying to support his family. He tried his hand at several businesses while continuing to draw birds. In 1820, while working

taxidermist scientist who preserves the bodies of animals by stuffing them for display

species type of plant or animal

specimen sample of a plant, animal, or mineral, usually collected for scientific study or display

John James Audubon's drawings of North American birds are among the most accurate and beautiful ever produced.

as a **taxidermist** at the Western Museum in Cincinnati, Ohio, he had the idea that would change his life. He decided to publish a series of life-size drawings of every North American **species** of bird. That year he took his first step toward that goal by making a birding trip by flatboat down the Ohio and Mississippi Rivers to New Orleans.

Audubon could not find an American publisher who was interested in his project. In 1826 he traveled to England and Scotland, where his work was more highly regarded. A printer in Scotland agreed to publish full-size reproductions of the drawings. Audubon and the printer found buyers who paid in advance to receive each new drawing as it was published. For the next 12 years, Audubon divided his time between business trips in England and Scotland and birding trips in North America.

Birds of America

In 1832 Audubon made two birding trips to Florida. The first was a difficult journey on the St. Johns River. He collected very few birds, but there were so many insects in the air that they put out his candle as he tried to write in his journal. His second try, a trip south along Florida's east coast, was more successful. Although he discovered only two new species, he collected over 1,000 **specimens** and made many drawings.

The following summer, Audubon organized an expedition to the coast of Labrador, in Canada. He hoped to discover new species and to study the feathers and breeding habits of the birds that spent the summer there. But Audubon saw few new species and found Labrador unbearable. He complained in his journal of the cold and the mosquitoes, and he later wrote about "the wonderful dreariness of the country."

In the spring of 1837, he traveled to the Republic of Texas, which had recently been created, and met its president, Sam Houston. Audubon failed to identify any new species of birds, but he learned much about the habits of birds west of the Mississippi River. Despite the difficulties of his travels, his project was completed the next year. In all, 435 color drawings were published as part of his series, *Birds of America.*

Audubon immediately began work on a series about four-legged animals, which was to be called *Quadrupeds of North America.* In March 1843, he set out to collect specimens for his new project. He also hoped to identify new species of birds for a new edition of *Birds of America.* He planned an eight-month journey and traveled to the regions of the upper Missouri and Yellowstone Rivers, but he never reached his goal, the Rocky Mountains. Audubon spent the rest of his life on his estate on the Hudson River. He died there in 1851.

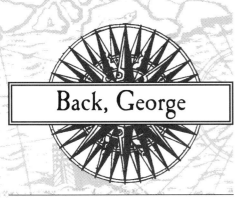

Back, George

English
b November 2, 1796; Stockport, England
d June 23, 1878; London, England
Explored central Canadian Arctic

Admiral Sir George Back was famous not only for his work as an explorer but also for his illustrations of the Arctic region.

Admiralty governing body of Britain's Royal Navy until 1964

Baffin, William

English
b 1584?; England?
d January 23, 1622; Qeshm, Iran
Explored Greenland and attempted Northwest Passage

Suggested Reading John J. Audubon, *Delineations of American Scenery and Character* (reprint, Ayer, 1970); Alice Ford, editor, *Audubon, By Himself* (Doubleday, 1969).

Admiral Sir George Back was called "in bravery, intelligence, and love of adventure . . . the very model of an English sailor." During his explorations of the Canadian Arctic, Back covered more than 10,000 miles on foot and by canoe. He not only led his own expeditions but also made significant contributions to the efforts and survival of others.

Before becoming an explorer, Back fought in naval battles against the French. While jailed in France as a prisoner of war, he studied mathematics and drawing. He continued to study art in Naples, Italy, after he was released. His first experience in exploration came in 1819, when he sailed with Sir John FRANKLIN's first Arctic expedition. Several of Franklin's starving men died, but more would have been lost without George Back's help.

Old Man of the Arctic

An attempt to save yet another expedition from disaster resulted in Back's most important discovery. When the British explorer John Ross disappeared in the Arctic, Back planned a voyage to find him. Ross turned up unexpectedly, but Back decided to go to the Arctic anyway, in 1833, to locate the mouth of Canada's Great Fish River, which was later renamed the Back River in his honor. He traveled the length of the river from the Great Slave Lake to the Arctic Ocean. When he returned to England, he published his account of the journey, together with his own illustrations.

In 1836 he accepted a new mission: to chart parts of the northern coast of Canada. The expedition ended in failure when his ship, the H.M.S. *Terror*, was trapped by ice in Hudson Bay. But Back won great admiration for his cool command during the crisis. When he returned to England in 1837, he was awarded the Royal Geographical Society's highest honors, and in 1839 he was knighted. He also served on the British **Admiralty's** Arctic Council. In late old age, he unveiled a monument in honor of John Franklin in Westminster Abbey, the church where many of Britain's great men and women are buried.

Suggested Reading George Back, *Arctic Artist: The Journal and Paintings of George Back, Midshipman with Franklin, 1819-1822*, edited by C. Stuart Houston, commentary by I. S. MacLaren (McGill-Queen's University Press, 1994) and *Narrative of the Arctic Land Expedition to the North of the Great Fish River, and Along the Shores of the Arctic Ocean, in the Years 1833, 1834, and 1835*, (reprint, M. G. Hurtig, 1970).

William Baffin was a brilliant navigator of the Arctic Ocean. In 1615 and 1616, he served as pilot for two expeditions that explored and charted the bay between northern Greenland and the largest Canadian island. Both the bay and the island now bear his name. Baffin also had an amazing natural talent for observation and measurement. His skills were so keen that he was able to make measurements nearly as accurate as those made by precision instruments hundreds of years later.

Inuit people of the Canadian Arctic, sometimes known as the Eskimo

longitude distance east or west of an imaginary line on the earth's surface; in 1884 most nations agreed to draw the line through Greenwich, England

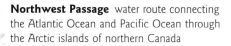

Northwest Passage water route connecting the Atlantic Ocean and Pacific Ocean through the Arctic islands of northern Canada

mate assistant to the commander of a ship

Baffin's Early Voyages

Nothing is known about Baffin's early life. He does not appear in any records before 1612, when he sailed to Greenland with Captain James Hall. Baffin served as pilot of Hall's ship. The mission ended tragically when Hall was killed by the local **Inuit** people. Hall had taken part in an earlier expedition with a Danish party that had treated the Inuit badly, and the Inuit had not forgotten.

While in Greenland, Baffin was the first navigator to try to determine **longitude** at sea by observing the position of the moon. Unfortunately, his results were not precise enough to be useful. After writing an account of that voyage, Baffin joined the English Muscovy Company as a pilot on several successful whaling expeditions to Spitsbergen, an island north of Norway. His experiences there sharpened his skills as an Arctic navigator.

Ice in the Arctic

In 1615 Baffin piloted Henry HUDSON's old ship, the *Discovery,* now under the command of Robert BYLOT. The expedition was sponsored by the **Northwest Passage** Company, which hoped to find a direct route to Asia by sailing north of Canada. Baffin sailed to the waters northwest of Hudson Strait, where his readings of the tides indicated that there was no passage to the north. Baffin's measurements were so accurate that 200 years later, they impressed the Arctic explorer William PARRY, who was using much better instruments. It was Parry who named Baffin Bay and Baffin Island.

The next year, again with Bylot, Baffin piloted the *Discovery* up Baffin Bay to Smith Sound. Although the voyage was a highly successful exploration, it was a failure for the Northwest Passage Company. The waters of Smith Sound were blocked by ice, and Baffin was forced to turn back. When he returned to England, Baffin wrote a detailed account of his voyage. He reported that there was no passage through the bay. This was not strictly correct, and Matthew Perry found a way out of the bay in 1821. However, this route was so badly blocked with ice that it was not only unprofitable but also extremely dangerous. In the end, Baffin saved the merchants much time and money by convincing them that it was best to focus their efforts elsewhere.

Despite his careful observations, many geographers doubted Baffin's story because of errors made by his publisher, Samuel PURCHAS. Purchas was rather careless with the text of Baffin's report, and he left out the detailed map that Baffin had drawn. In 1635 Luke FOXE published a map that included the bay described in Baffin's report, but later maps left the area blank. It was not until Captain John Ross rediscovered the bay in 1818 that Baffin received full credit.

Travels in the Middle East

Baffin wanted to try to find the Northwest Passage's western end in the Pacific Ocean. In 1617 he sailed from England to India as **mate** aboard the ship *Anne Royal,* which was owned by the British East India Company. The ship was sent to establish trade in the Red Sea. Baffin charted the waters there and in the Persian Gulf. He returned to England in 1619, having apparently given up on the Arctic.

The next year, Baffin signed on with the *London,* one of four ships sailing to the Middle East. At the entrance to the Persian Gulf, the fleet fought a combined force of two Portuguese ships and two Dutch ships. The captain of the *London* was killed in the battle, but the fleet sailed on, helping the ruler of Persia (now Iran) to drive out the Portuguese.

Baffin lost his life on this mission, but it seems fitting that he was taking measurements when he died. He had gone ashore near the castle of Qeshm to measure the height and distance of the castle walls so that the British could aim their guns more accurately. During a skirmish outside the walls, Baffin was killed. The British took the castle without the help of his measurements.

Baffin's Contributions to Navigation

Baffin's observations and notes proved invaluable to many later explorers and discoverers. His readings of **latitude** were always nearly perfect. He made brilliant attempts to determine longitude before the invention of the **chronometer.** Baffin also measured the earth's magnetic field in various places around the world. The first magnetic chart, published in 1701, would not have been possible without his efforts. Although Baffin's fame was delayed, his place in history is now secure.

Suggested Reading Clements R. Markham, *Voyages of William Baffin* (Hakluyt Society, 1881).

latitude distance north or south of the equator

chronometer clock designed to keep precise time in the rough conditions of sea travel

Baker, Samuel White

English
b June 8, 1821; London, England
d September 30, 1893; Devonshire, England
Explored Nile River and Lake Albert

Samuel White Baker went to Africa to search for the source of the Nile River. He is best known, however, for his attempts to create British colonies in Africa and to stop the slave trade in the Sudan. He and his second wife, Florence Baker, also explored the White Nile River and discovered Lake Albert.

Early Life and Travels

Baker was born into a wealthy English family. He was educated in Germany and developed a love of travel, hunting, and adventure. In his early 20s, he married a minister's daughter and managed his father's plantations on the island of Mauritius in the Indian Ocean. He later started his own successful agricultural business on the island of Ceylon (present-day Sri Lanka). After about 10 years overseas, Baker returned to England with his wife, Henrietta, who died of **typhus** shortly after.

Baker spent the next few years traveling in Asia Minor, the Crimea, and the Balkans. In 1860 Baker married a young Hungarian woman, Florence Ninian von Sass. Florence shared Baker's love of adventure, and the newlyweds decided to organize an expedition to search for the source of the Nile River.

Explorations and Emergencies

The Bakers arrived in Cairo, Egypt, in 1861. They had plenty of time and money for their journey because they were wealthy, independent travelers rather than military officers or hired adventurers.

typhus disease that causes high fever, dizziness, and rashes; often transmitted by body lice

tributary stream or river that flows into a larger stream or river

Samuel Baker was motivated by his love of adventure and his hatred of the African slave trade.

They spent their first year in Africa exploring the Nile and its **tributaries** at an easy pace. They traveled south on the Nile to Berber, in the Sudan, learning Arabic along the way. Then, when they reached Khartoum, the situation changed. The office of the Royal Geographical Society in Khartoum asked the Bakers to lead an expedition to locate two missing explorers, John Hanning SPEKE and James Augustus Grant. The two explorers, who had been sponsored by the society, had disappeared during the previous year while searching for the source of the Nile. The Bakers agreed to help find Speke and Grant, and they spent the next six months organizing the rescue expedition.

In December 1862, the Bakers began the 1,000-mile trip to Gondokoro. They arrived in six weeks, and the missing explorers showed up unharmed just two weeks later. Though they were relieved that the two men were safe, the Bakers were disappointed to learn that Speke and Grant had located the Nile's source. The two men suggested that the Bakers study a portion of the Nile that remained unexplored, as well as a lake that was rumored to be linked to the river. Speke and Grant gave the Bakers a map of their route, and the couple headed south.

The Bakers had to join a slave trader's caravan to travel safely through the kingdom of Bunyoro (in what is now Uganda). The ruler of Bunyoro and his people were not happy to have Europeans on their land. Even so, one year after leaving Gondokoro, the couple reached the eastern shore of the lake they had sought. The local tribes called the lake Luta N'zige, but Baker renamed it Lake Albert in honor of the husband of England's Queen Victoria. The Bakers also found Murchison Falls (now called Kabalega Falls), which they named for the president of the Royal Geographical Society. The society awarded Samuel Baker its gold medal for his accomplishments, and he was knighted by the queen in 1866. That year, Baker published a book entitled *The Albert N'yanza, Great Basin of the Nile, and Explorations of the Nile Sources.* Two years later, he released a second book, *Exploration of the Nile Tributaries.*

Fighting the Slave Trade

In 1869 Baker and his wife were in Egypt for the opening of the Suez Canal. Ismail, the ruler of Egypt, asked Baker to make a four-year expedition to claim for Egypt the lands that lay south along the White Nile toward Lake Victoria. It was a dangerous job, but Baker was eager for adventure, and he wanted to help Ismail wipe out the slave trade in the region. He was given command of a force of 1,200 men.

It took Baker a year to struggle through the Nile's swamps to Gondokoro. During the years since his previous journeys, the area had become poorer, the slave traders more powerful, and the local tribes more hostile. Baker was able to gain the confidence of some tribes by offering Egypt's protection. He established several military stations in 1871, but he also aroused the anger of many local chiefs and slave traders. More and more, Baker depended on military force to put down local uprisings, and he angered many tribes by taking their supplies for his soldiers.

One of Baker's toughest opponents was the ruler of the Bunyoro kingdom. During the Bakers' expedition of 1863, this ruler had forced Baker to surrender most of his possessions to buy passage through the Bunyoro kingdom. Now Baker and his troops were forced to fight the Bunyoro people. Baker captured the region for Ismail's empire, but Egypt's control over it was never secure.

Baker was unsuccessful in shutting down the slave traders, who had become the rulers of many areas. After Baker returned to Britain in 1873, Egyptian officials often simply took over the local slave trade from those who had run it before.

Although this expedition was a failure, Baker is credited with the first serious attempt to combat slavery in the Sudan. In addition, his extensive travels made him one of Britain's leading experts on the Nile River and central Africa.

Suggested Reading Richard Hall, *Lovers on the Nile: The Incredible African Journeys of Sam and Florence Baker* (Random House, 1980); Dorothy Middleton, *Baker of the Nile* (Falcon Press, 1949).

Balboa, Vasco Nuñez de

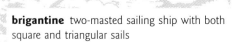

Spanish
b 1475; Jerez de los Caballeros, Spain
d January 21, 1519; Acla, Panama
Discovered Pacific Ocean

brigantine two-masted sailing ship with both square and triangular sails

Vasco Nuñez de Balboa founded the Spanish town of Darién (now in Colombia) and explored the areas nearby. In 1513 he left Darién without permission from Spanish authorities. Using information given him by local Indians, Balboa led an expedition to find the "Great Waters." He became the first European to see the Pacific Ocean from North America.

Caribbean Troubles

Balboa was born in 1475 into a family of poor nobles in the province of Badajoz, Spain. We know very little about his youth. In 1501 he sailed for Hispaniola, the island where Haiti and the Dominican Republic are located today.

On Hispaniola, Balboa settled down as a planter, but he was not suited for that life and soon ran up very large debts. To escape the men to whom he owed money, he hid himself and his dog Leoncico in a huge jug. They were smuggled onto a ship carrying supplies for the Spanish colony at San Sebastián on the Gulf of Urabá. On the way, the ship met a **brigantine** commanded by Francisco PIZARRO. Pizarro had come from San Sebastián and said that all the members of the colony, except his crew, had died from disease and Indian attacks. Pizarro and the commander of the supply ship, Martín Fernández de Enciso, sailed together to the shore and found San Sebastián in ashes.

Rise to Power

By then, Balboa had been accepted as a member of Enciso's crew. He told Enciso about an Indian village on the mainland (in what is now Panama) that he had seen on his way to Hispaniola. The Spaniards went to the village, where they seized control of the Indians and their rich supplies of food, cotton, and treasures. The Spaniards set up a headquarters, and Balboa officially founded the

Vasco Nuñez de Balboa crossed land that cost many later explorers their health and strength—and even their lives.

pirogue canoe usually made from a hollow tree trunk

plateau high, flat area of land

town of Santa María la Antigua del Darién. He quickly set about building his power.

Balboa convinced the Spanish colonists that Enciso, a weak leader, had no authority in Darién. Enciso was forced to return to Spain to ask for help from King Ferdinand. Diego de Nicuesa arrived as the king's new governor, but Balboa pressured the colonists to reject him. The colonists picked Balboa and a man named Zamudio to rule as mayors. Balboa then got rid of Zamudio, too, by sending him to Spain to defend Balboa against the accusations made by Enciso.

Balboa ruled wisely for two years and had a talent for making friends with the local Indians. On the other hand, he conquered and looted the villages of any Indians who were hostile. He collected a fortune in gold and jewels. Many Indians told Balboa stories about "Great Waters" beyond the mountains. He was convinced that a large sea existed, so he wrote to King Ferdinand, asking for 1,000 men for an expedition of discovery. Before Balboa got his answer, he learned that the king was going to order him back to Spain. Realizing that he had to act quickly, Balboa started the expedition on his own.

The Far Side of America

Bolboa's party left Darién on September 1, 1513, in one brigantine and ten **pirogues,** with 190 Spaniards, 800 Indians, and several dogs, including Leoncico. They dropped anchor near the colony of Acla. The spot was at the narrowest part of Panama—a lucky choice. Balboa made an alliance with the local Indian chief, Careta, who presented the Spaniard with his daughter as a bride. Leaving with about half of his men, Balboa started south. Carrying heavy weapons and armor in the hot and humid climate, the Spanish found the going extremely tough. Few parts of the world were as hard to pass through, but after three days, they reached a deserted Indian village. Balboa needed new guides for the rest of the trip, so he found the Indians who had left that village and befriended them. Their chief was so impressed that he gave Balboa guides to take him to a mountain ridge. From there, the chief said, the "Great Waters" could be seen.

Travel was no easier when they continued, and it took the group four days to cover about 30 miles. They met a tribe of hostile Indians and defeated them in a bloody battle. The Spanish tortured many of the captured Indians and looted their village, collecting much treasure. Finally the Spanish party reached a small **plateau** near the top of a high mountain. On September 27, 1513, Balboa climbed alone to the summit and gazed past the rocks and greenery. He became the first European to see the vast Pacific Ocean from North America. When the rest of his party joined him, they sang the Te Deum, a Christian hymn, and built a cross.

Balboa sent out three separate groups to find the best way to the shore. They decided on a path and went together to the ocean's edge. Balboa waded into the water carrying his sword in one hand and the banner of Spain's royal family in the other. He claimed the

The Spanish flag, as it appeared in Balboa's time, combined the symbols of the provinces of Castile and León.

ocean, its islands, and all the lands around it as the property of Spain. He named the ocean the Mar del Sur, which means South Sea in Spanish.

Glory and Conflict

For the return trip, Balboa chose a different route, but it was as difficult as the first. The explorers nearly died of hunger because they were carrying so much treasure instead of food. They won even more treasure when they surprised and captured a powerful chief called Tubanama and held him for ransom. (His name may be the source of the name of the country of Panama.) Balboa then caught a feverish illness and had to be carried into town when his party reached Darién, about four and a half months after they had left.

While Balboa had been away, King Ferdinand had made Pedro Arias de Ávila, known as Pedrarias, the new mayor of Darién. Pedrarias asked Balboa if it was true that Leoncico was getting the same share of the booty as a soldier. Balboa said that it was true, because the soldiers had agreed that the dog was worth several fighting men.

Pedrarias was not a strong leader, and he was always jealous of Balboa's popularity. At a rare time when there was less tension between them, Balboa began a bold new adventure. He built ships on the shore of the Pacific Ocean, intending to explore the unknown coastline. Hundreds of Indian slaves died while carrying the parts of the ships over the mountains and through the jungles. Balboa managed to have two ships built. He set sail and soon encountered the Pearl Islands off the coast. However, poor winds forced him to return to the mainland.

Trouble Catches Up with Balboa

Meanwhile, Pedrarias had become certain that Balboa was plotting to set up a separate government on the west coast of Panama. Pedrarias sent a message to Balboa, asking him to come to Darién. He said he wanted to hold discussions, but he actually planned to arrest Balboa. Soon Pedrarias worried that Balboa might not show up, so he ordered Pizarro to take an armed force to the west coast. Balboa met Pizarro, who had once been his lieutenant, halfway across Panama. He went with Pizarro without fighting. When they reached Darién, Pedrarias had Balboa put on trial and convicted of treason. Although the colonists supported their popular hero, he was sentenced to die. Balboa was beheaded in Acla on January 21, 1519, not far from the town he had founded and made famous in the world of his time.

Vasco Nuñez de Balboa was always loyal to Spain, but he was also a brash and independent explorer. He often ignored his leaders, set his own goals, and organized his own plans. The area he explored was fairly small, but it included some of the most forbidding terrain in the world. His discovery of the Pacific Ocean stands out in history as a tremendous feat.

Suggested Reading Charles L. G. Anderson, *Life and Letters of Vasco Nuñez de Balboa* (Fleming H. Revell Company, 1941); Kathleen Romoli, *Balboa of Darién: Discoverer of the Pacific* (Doubleday, 1953).

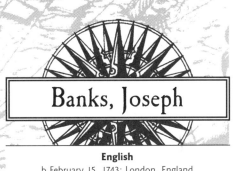

Banks, Joseph

English
b February 15, 1743; London, England
d June 19, 1820; London, England
Sailed as naturalist with James Cook

circumnavigation journey around the world

specimen sample of a plant, animal, or mineral, usually collected for scientific study or display

botany the scientific study of plants

Joseph Banks's descriptions of the culture of Tahiti sparked Europe's scientific interest in the Pacific.

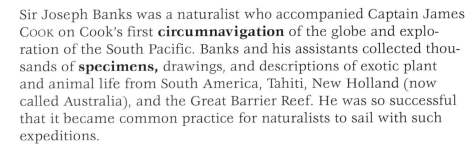

Sir Joseph Banks was a naturalist who accompanied Captain James COOK on Cook's first **circumnavigation** of the globe and exploration of the South Pacific. Banks and his assistants collected thousands of **specimens,** drawings, and descriptions of exotic plant and animal life from South America, Tahiti, New Holland (now called Australia), and the Great Barrier Reef. He was so successful that it became common practice for naturalists to sail with such expeditions.

Young Man with a Bright Future

Banks was born in 1743, the son of a wealthy doctor. He was educated at Harrow, Eton, and Oxford—the finest schools in Britain. As a student, he showed a keen interest in **botany** and the natural sciences. When he was 15, he took part in a voyage to Newfoundland to collect specimens and nearly died of a fever. The collection of plants he gathered is now on display in the British Museum.

Banks was 18 when his father died. The young man inherited an annual income and was able to live comfortably while pursuing his interest in the natural sciences. Seven years later, he persuaded the British government to allow him to join James Cook's expedition to the Pacific Ocean. Cook's mission was to observe the planet Venus as it passed between the earth and the sun.

Banks contributed a substantial amount of money to hire a team of assistants and artists. Such a well-equipped group of scientists had never before sailed with an expedition. They brought with them an entire library of books about natural history. One man who knew Banks reported that the team had "all sorts of machines for catching and preserving insects, all types of nets, trawls, drags, and hooks for coral fishing, they even have a curious contrivance of a telescope by which, put into the water, you can see the bottom at great depth."

Island Adventures

Cook's ship, the *Endeavour,* left Britain in August 1768, headed for the Pacific Ocean by way of South America. Banks and his team spent the days at sea dragging nets through the water and cataloging their finds. In December the ship reached the large island known as Tierra del Fuego, at the southern tip of South America. The scientists went ashore to study plants in the mountains, where two of Banks's servants froze to death.

The next stop was Tahiti, a tropical island with a more pleasant climate than Tierra del Fuego. Banks learned to speak the islanders' language and served as an interpreter for the Tahitians and the British. Presenting gifts, he went to great lengths to win the trust of the islanders. He even removed his clothes and darkened his skin with charcoal and water in order to fit in better. With or without this disguise, the Tahitians seemed to accept him. He was allowed to visit burial grounds that no European had ever seen before.

Banks was a sharp observer of Tahitian culture, and his journal provided a fascinating picture of their way of life. He recorded every detail of daily living, describing how the islanders made

dysentery disease that causes severe diarrhea

fishhooks from bones and wove nets from jungle vines. He also provided the first descriptions of surfing ever to reach Europe. Not content just to observe, he allowed himself to be tattooed. The tradition of sailors being tattooed may have begun in this way. Like so many Europeans who visited Tahiti, Banks also noted the charms of Tahitian women, including one named Queen Obarea.

The voyage continued to New Zealand, Australia, and the Great Barrier Reef, where Banks added to his growing collection of specimens. The Australian Aborigines were not as friendly as the Tahitians. Skirmishes with the people of New Guinea, along with an outbreak of **dysentery,** cut short his activities there. Even so, Banks made several discoveries. He was the first European to describe a kangaroo, and he found a spot near what is now Sydney, Australia, that was so rich in plant life that he called it Botany Bay. He later recommended Botany Bay as the site for a new British prison colony.

Life as a Famous Scientist

The trip was a huge success for Banks, who collected more than 1,000 plants, 500 fish, 500 birds, and countless insects, shells, corals, and rocks. He also acquired many small objects, cloths, and carvings made by the peoples of the Pacific. In fact, upon his return to Britain in 1771, the public considered Banks, rather than Cook, to be the hero of the voyage. Banks found himself very popular in the circles of London's high society, and he was honored when even King George III asked to meet with him.

One year later, Banks planned to accompany Cook on a second voyage, this time with an even larger team, including several musicians. But Cook's ship could not sail with the extra cabins and cargo, so the captain asked Banks to make do with fewer assistants. Banks angrily refused and instead made a private journey to conduct research in Iceland and the Hebrides, islands in the Atlantic Ocean northwest of Scotland.

Despite this disagreement, the captain and the naturalist remained friends. When Cook returned to Britain from his next voyage, he brought with him a young Tahitian man named Omai. Banks took the visitor in, dressed him in the finest clothes, and introduced him to London society. He even took him on hunting trips to Yorkshire. Omai soon returned to the Pacific with Cook, who continued to bring Banks new specimens.

In 1777 Banks was named president of the Royal Society, an organization of British scientists, and he held this post for the next 42 years. When Cook died, Banks persuaded the society to produce a medal to commemorate the captain's achievements. He also promoted many new expeditions and explorers, such as William BLIGH, Mungo PARK, and Matthew FLINDERS. He served as royal adviser for London's Kew Gardens and played a key role in establishing botanical gardens in Jamaica, St. Vincent, and Ceylon (now known as Sri Lanka). After his death, a statue in his honor was placed in London's Natural History Museum.

Suggested Reading J. C. Beaglehole, *The Endeavour Journal of Joseph Banks,* 2 volumes (Angus and Robertson, 1962); Harold B. Carter, *Sir Joseph Banks, 1743–1820* (Omnigraphics, 1987).

Barbosa, Duarte

Portuguese
b 1480?; Portugal
d June 6, 1521; Cebu, Philippines
*Explored Indian Ocean;
sailed with Magellan in service of Spain*

Duarte Barbosa was related to the wife of Ferdinand MAGELLAN and became one of Magellan's most loyal supporters on the first journey around the world. Barbosa was already an experienced seaman when he played a major role in Magellan's historic expedition.

In Love with the Sea

Barbosa was born in Portugal in the late 1400s, but he may have grown up in Spain. Historians believe that he was the son or nephew of Diogo Barbosa, an official in the Spanish government. Duarte was lured to the sea, as were many young Portuguese men at that exciting time. He traveled widely, sailing to the Cape of Good Hope, the east coast of Africa, and Arabia. He helped make important trade deals at Aden and Hormuz, on the Persian Gulf. He proceeded from there to western India and as far east as Sumatra, in present-day Indonesia. India was probably where Barbosa first met Magellan, who was traveling there with a Portuguese official.

Duarte returned to Lisbon, Portugal, around 1516 and published a book about his adventures, *The Book of Duarte Barbosa.* He was eager to continue his explorations but received little support from Portugal's King Manuel I. Disappointed, Barbosa headed to the city of Pôrto, where many discontented sailors gathered. There he met Magellan and interested him in sailing around South America to the Spice Islands (now called the Moluccas). The two men left Pôrto in October 1517 and traveled to Spain. They stayed in the household of Diogo Barbosa, and Magellan married Diogo's daughter, Beatriz. Spain's King Charles I gave Magellan his support for the ocean voyage.

Leadership on a Difficult Journey

Tensions were high from the start between the Spanish and Portuguese crew members of Magellan's expedition. On April 2, 1520, the fleet was off the southern coast of South America when 30 sailors seized one of the ships. Barbosa handpicked a group of reliable crewmen, and they easily recaptured the ship of rebels. For his loyalty, Barbosa was rewarded by Magellan with command of the *Victoria,* which would be the only ship to complete the voyage.

Barbosa proved to be a natural leader. He set an example by showing the physical and mental strength to endure the hardships of the journey. The explorers sailed in uncharted waters for months without seeing land. When the food ran out, the men were forced to eat rats and leather. They reached Asia in the spring of 1521, but Magellan was killed in the Philippines soon afterward. Barbosa and his countryman Juan Serrano were chosen as the new leaders of the expedition.

Barbosa did not survive much longer than Magellan. The ruler of the island of Cebu in the Philippines invited Barbosa and 26 crewmen to a banquet on shore. Serrano was opposed to the idea, but Barbosa persuaded him to go along. At the banquet, all the sailors except Serrano and one other were ambushed and killed. Serrano was stripped naked and bound in chains—his shipmates had to abandon him to die on the island. Although Barbosa never made it back to Europe, the *Victoria* did complete the journey, thanks in part to his leadership and courage.

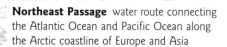

Dutch

b 1550?; Terschelling Island, Netherlands
d June 20, 1597; Barents Sea
*Explored Northeast Passage and
discovered Spitsbergen Island*

Northeast Passage water route connecting the Atlantic Ocean and Pacific Ocean along the Arctic coastline of Europe and Asia

Suggested Reading Duarte Barbosa, *The Book of Duarte Barbosa*, 2 volumes, translated by M. L. Dames (Hakluyt Society, 1921).

At a time when many explorers sailed to East Asia around the southern tip of Africa, Willem Barents searched for a route through the Arctic. Between 1594 and 1597, Barents made three voyages to locate a **Northeast Passage** that would make trade with China easier. Although he never found a passage free of ice, he did discover Spitsbergen Island, the largest of a group of islands that are now part of Norway.

Two Early Failures

On Barents's first expedition in 1594, two of his ships, piloted by other captains, made significant progress in the Northeast Passage. The *Swan* and the *Mercury* sailed through the Pet Strait, which lies between the northern coast of Russia and the island of Novaya Zemlya. The strait was named after the English explorer Arthur Pet, whose sailing directions Barents had translated. The ships reached the Kara Sea and then turned back, for their captains were sure that they had discovered the passage to China. In fact, they were many hundreds of miles away. Barents himself tried to sail north of Novaya Zemlya but was stopped by ice.

A second expedition was organized the next year by Dutch leaders who were confident that Barents could reach China. Seven ships in four Dutch ports were loaded with goods to be traded in the East. This expedition was a failure. The ships found the Pet Strait clogged by ice, and they returned home. Both of Barents's voyages had been funded with public money, and the Dutch government now voted to waste no more money exploring this route.

Over 200 years later, the Swedish explorer Nils Adolf Erik NOR-DENSKIÖLD studied Barents's voyages. Nordenskiöld believed that if Barents had persevered, he could have passed the ice and reached the Russian settlements on the Obi and Yenisei Rivers. In this way, Barents could have established trade between Europe and central Asia. But the lure of trade with China must have been much stronger for both Barents and his sponsors.

The Discovery of Spitsbergen

Barents refused to give up on the route to China. Both he and his scientific adviser, the Reverend Peter Plancius, believed that ice was a problem only near the shore. They hoped that ships sailing far north of Novaya Zemlya would find open waters. Barents persuaded the merchants of Amsterdam to finance another voyage, and he set out again in 1596.

Barents piloted a vessel commanded by Jacob van Heemskerck. A second ship was commanded by Jan Cornelius Rijp. On June 9 both ships discovered Bear Island, and 10 days later, they found Spitsbergen Island, which they thought was Greenland. The two captains then disagreed about the best course to take, and the ships separated. Rijp sailed a short distance farther north and then returned home. Barents headed for Novaya Zemlya, but on August 26

The islands discovered by Willem Barents were later a rich source of profits for Dutch and English hunters of whales, seals, and walrus.

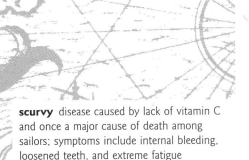

scurvy disease caused by lack of vitamin C and once a major cause of death among sailors; symptoms include internal bleeding, loosened teeth, and extreme fatigue

the ship was trapped in ice near the island. The crew was forced to abandon the ship and spend the winter on the ice.

Survival in the Arctic

Barents and his men knew of only one crew that had wintered in the Arctic before then. Those English sailors, led by Hugh Willoughby 40 years earlier, had all frozen to death. The Dutch knew that their chances of survival were not good. With driftwood and some of the ship's timbers, they built a cabin with a fireplace. The area's many foxes were a good supply of food. Polar bears were the biggest problem, but the men overcame even this danger. They also made careful astronomical and geographical observations.

Of the 17 men on the ice, 15 survived the winter. (The other two probably died of **scurvy.**) But when summer came, the ship remained stuck in the ice. The men had no choice but to use the ship's two small boats. Before leaving the cabin, Captain Heemskerck wrote out two copies of an account of the voyage—one copy for each boat. Barents wrote his own account, which he placed in the cabin's chimney. It was found 274 years later, just where Barents had left it.

The two small boats set out in June 1597. Barents never reached home—on the seventh day of the journey, he died of scurvy. After 80 days of rowing and sailing over 1,600 miles, the boats reached a Dutch trading settlement on the coast of Russia. There they met Captain Rijp, who took them home. All of Europe marveled at their story.

Suggested Reading Rayner Unwin, *A Winter Away from Home: William Barents and the North-east Passage* (Seafarer Books, 1995); Gerrit de Veer, *The Three Voyages of William Barents to the Arctic Regions (1594, 1595, and 1596)*, edited by Charles T. Beke (B. Franklin, 1964).

Barrow, John

English
b June 19, 1764; Ulverston, England
d November 23, 1848; London, England
Founded Royal Geographical Society

Admiralty governing body of Britain's Royal Navy until 1964

Northwest Passage water route connecting the Atlantic Ocean and Pacific Ocean through the Arctic islands of northern Canada

John Barrow founded the Royal Geographical Society, which sponsored the work of hundreds of explorers.

As a young man, John Barrow showed himself to be a hard worker with a sense of adventure. When he grew up, these qualities led him to support Arctic exploration and to found England's Royal Geographical Society.

England, China, and Africa

Barrow had an active and difficult youth. In his early teens, he worked in an iron factory in Liverpool, England. At the age of 15, he became a crewman on a whaling ship in the Arctic Ocean. This sailing experience marked the beginning of his interest in Arctic exploration. He was also the first person to make a balloon flight in England. Barrow later worked as a tutor to the son of Sir George Leonard Staunton. Sir George was the chief assistant of a British nobleman named Lord Macartney. This connection would launch Barrow's brilliant career in the service of his country.

Lord Macartney was named Britain's ambassador to China, and Barrow was invited to join him as a scientific adviser. Barrow's observations and writings helped shape Europe's understanding of China's culture and history. Macartney was then appointed governor of Cape Colony in South Africa. He again invited Barrow to join him as an adviser, and Barrow accepted. In 1803 Barrow returned to Britain and became permanent secretary of the **Admiralty.** He held this post for almost 40 years.

The Arctic and the World

When the Napoleonic Wars ended in 1815, large numbers of skilled British naval officers were released from duty. Barrow used his influence with the Admiralty to employ many of these sailors in the search for a **Northwest Passage.** In the early 1800s, European ships sailing to Asia had to make a long and dangerous journey around either South America or Africa. Barrow hoped to find a shorter sea route to Asia across the Arctic Ocean. The passage was not found until years after Barrow's death. However, the expeditions he sent out made many important geographic discoveries. Explorers of the Canadian Arctic named Barrow Strait and Cape Barrow after the secretary who supported their work.

In 1830 Barrow made perhaps his most important contribution to exploration. Together with six others, he founded the Royal Geographical Society. The society soon became the world's leading independent sponsor of exploration. It backed many of history's most important explorers, including David LIVINGSTONE and John Hanning SPEKE.

Suggested Reading John Barrow, *The Mutiny of the Bounty* (Oxford University Press, 1975); Christopher Lloyd, *Mr. Barrow of the Admiralty: A Life of Sir John Barrow, 1764-1848* (Collins, 1970).

Barth, Heinrich

German
b February 16, 1821; Hamburg, Germany
d November 25, 1865; Berlin, Germany
Explored North Africa and central Africa

Heinrich Barth covered 10,000 miles during his six-year exploration of the African interior.

Heinrich Barth is now considered one of the leading explorers and scholars of Africa, although his work was not fully appreciated during his lifetime. He traveled in the Sahara and the Sudan regions for nearly six years through territory that was largely unknown to Europeans. His knowledge of history, geography, and archaeology enabled him to make important observations about these lands and the people who lived there.

Young Loner

Barth was the son of a wealthy merchant. As a child, he became obsessed with the desire to impress his mother by becoming more successful than his father. The young Barth applied himself to his schoolwork, ignoring all social activities. He spent his time reading books on science, geography, and languages. As a student at the University of Berlin, he excelled in archaeology, history, and geography, but he did not develop any social skills.

Concerned about his son's lack of personal contact, Barth's father sent him on a lengthy tour of London, Paris, and the Mediterranean region. He hoped that new people and places would bring his son out of his shell. The trip did nothing to cure Barth's inability to relate to others, but it did spark his interest in Africa. After visiting the North African coast, he became fascinated with the idea of exploring the vast lands to the south. Instead, he returned to Germany after three years to take a teaching position at the University of Berlin.

Barth's social difficulties continued to be a problem. He was so unpopular with his students and fellow instructors that the archaeology course he taught was canceled. Barth suffered another blow when the woman he had been seeing suddenly ended their relationship. Those disappointments were soon forgotten. The batch of mail that brought his sweetheart's letter also included an invitation to join an expedition to the African interior. The 28-year-old Barth accepted immediately, and two months later, he was back in North Africa as a member of the English Mixed Scientific and Commercial Expedition.

Explorations in Libya

The leader of the expedition was a British former missionary, James Richardson, who was an accomplished explorer. He planned to gather information about the Sahara while making trade arrangements for British merchants. In March 1850, the party left the Libyan city of Tripoli and traveled south toward the city of Kano in what is now Nigeria.

Barth made his first major discovery about 500 miles south of Tripoli, near the desert town of Murzuch. He found the ruins of an ancient Roman settlement along a dry river valley. Farther south, he found rock paintings made by peoples who had lived there from the Stone Age to about A.D. 100. The paintings showed how the once fertile land had gradually become a desert. The earliest paintings showed tropical animals, such as elephants and ostriches. Later images featured cattle and horses, which thrive on grassy plains. The most recent paintings were of the desert's best-known animal, the camel.

sultan ruler of a Muslim nation

malaria disease that is spread by mosquitoes in tropical areas

sheikh Arab chief

Barth's social skills were still not as good as his scientific skills. He and Richardson quickly grew to dislike each other. But Barth had the support of a German geologist on the expedition, Adolf Overweg. The two Germans began riding and camping apart from their leader. Several times they left the party to explore on their own, but one such trip nearly cost Barth his life. While climbing the supposedly haunted Mount Idinen, Barth and Overweg became separated. Barth was trapped on the hot, barren mountain. At one point, he became so thirsty that he sucked blood from his own veins. He almost died before he was rescued.

The journey was also made difficult by the Tuareg people of the Sahara. The explorers faced the constant threat of attack as they made their way to the city of Ghat. After a few months, though, they made a truce with the Tuareg and were allowed safe passage. Barth then struck out on his own to visit Agadès, where he was an honored guest at the crowning of the new **sultan.** He spent several weeks investigating the ancient town and befriending its citizens, who called him *Abd-el-Kerim,* which means "servant of God." In October, Barth rejoined his companions at the oasis of Tintellust in the Aïr Mountains. Three months later, they parted company to pursue three separate paths to Lake Chad. They agreed to meet in the city of Kuka (now Kukawa, Nigeria), near the lake's western shore.

The Loner Becomes a Diplomat

Within three weeks, Barth traveled 375 miles south, reaching the city of Kano in February 1851. Although his supplies were running low, he wisely offered expensive gifts to the chief officials of the province. They rewarded him with their full hospitality during his monthlong stay. In addition to studying the society and geography of the area, Barth paved the way for profitable trade agreements between Kano and Europe. While on his way to meet Richardson and Overweg at Kuka, he learned that Richardson had died of **malaria.**

Barth was becoming much more skilled at dealing with people, and he received a warm welcome from Sultan Omar of Bornu. The sultan gave him access to the entire territory and provided guides to help him explore Lake Chad. But Barth left that task to Overweg and traveled south to Yola, where he discovered parts of the Benue River. He then went east to explore the Shari River.

Barth was now almost out of money, so he wrote to his sponsors in London to ask for more. The funds arrived with instructions to head west to Timbuktu (in present-day Mali). While the explorers prepared for this journey, Overweg died of malaria.

The Dangerous Journey to Timbuktu

Barth left Bornu and headed west across the plains to Sokoto (in present-day Nigeria). Without the sultan's protection, Barth and his six-man party had to beware of the area's tribesmen and bandits. He kept his men constantly on guard and posed as a holy man delivering religious books to the **sheikh** of Timbuktu. His disguise was so convincing that some local people believed that he was the Messiah.

Timbuktu proved to be a disappointment. Europeans had thought that it was a rich and beautiful city, but Barth discovered

For a map of Barth's travels, see the article about Gustav NACHTIGAL in Volume 2.

that it was a dull, poor place. The city's residents disliked foreigners and accused him of being a spy. Barth later said that he was safe in Timbuktu only because people feared his Colt six-shooter pistol, a recent invention. When he was permitted to leave Timbuktu in May 1854, Barth returned to Kuka, where he was welcomed by the tribes he had befriended earlier.

In Kuka he learned that his sponsors in Europe feared that he was dead and had sent an explorer named Eduard Vogel to discover his fate. Barth met Vogel in the Bundi jungle and brought him to Kuka. In August 1855, Barth returned to Tripoli and then to Europe, exhausted after nearly six years in Africa.

Return to Europe

When Barth arrived in London, he was honored with the Patron's Medal of the Royal Geographical Society. He again withdrew from the company of others and spent the next three years writing a full account of his experiences. The five-volume work met with a mixed reception from its readers, who considered it believable but dull. Years later the book was more fully appreciated for its wealth of useful facts, keen insights, and detailed maps and drawings.

Barth returned to Germany and was welcomed back to the University of Berlin as a professor of geography. He remained disappointed that the public did not acclaim his work, but he did not live long enough to see that opinion change. Two years after coming home, he died at the age of 44 from a stomach ailment that had begun in Africa.

Suggested Reading Brian Gardner, *The Quest for Timbuctoo* (Harcourt, Brace and World 1968); Robert I. Rotberg, *Africa and its Explorers* (Harvard University Press, 1970).

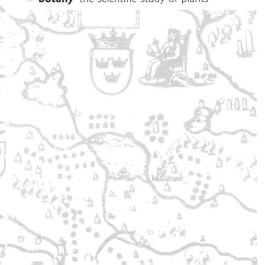

Bartram, John

American
b March 23, 1699; near Darby, Pennsylvania
d September 22, 1777; Kingsessing, Pennsylvania
Studied plants of eastern North America

botanist scientist who studies plants
botany the scientific study of plants

John Bartram has been called the first American **botanist.** His passion for collecting and studying plants led him throughout eastern North America. His studies took him as far north as Lake Ontario and as far south as Florida.

Bartram became interested in plants while growing up on a farm in colonial Pennsylvania. He later traveled to Philadelphia to buy books about plants, and he taught himself **botany.** At the age of 29, he bought property on the Schuylkill River near Philadelphia. He planted gardens and conducted experiments in creating new types of plants. George Washington and Benjamin Franklin often came to Bartram's gardens to relax and talk.

Travels in the American Wilderness

Bartram made the first of many trips to study America's plant life in 1738. He began in Williamsburg, Virginia, and then traveled up the James River and across the Blue Ridge Mountains, covering more than 1,000 miles in five weeks. In 1751 he published his journals from a trip to Lake Ontario. Over the next decade, he visited the Catskill Mountains, North Carolina, South Carolina, and the frontier fort that became the city of Pittsburgh.

Soon afterward, a British friend managed to have Bartram named botanist to King George III, a position with a comfortable salary.

Bartram was grateful and relieved, since he had always traveled at his own expense. In 1765 he traveled as royal botanist to Charleston, South Carolina, where he joined his son William. Together father and son explored the Carolina wilderness for two months and then found a trail to Georgia. They continued south to Florida, where they charted the St. Johns River. Enduring swamps and mosquitoes, they studied Florida's natural world—trees, flowers, fruits, birds, fish, and minerals.

Although this effort was Bartram's last major expedition, he had a great influence on the exploration of America. He suggested the importance of studying the American West to Benjamin Franklin. Franklin took the idea to Thomas Jefferson, who sent Meriwether LEWIS and William CLARK on their famous journey from 1803 to 1806. Jefferson's instructions to Lewis and Clark were very similar to John Bartram's original proposal.

Suggested Reading Edmund Berkeley, *The Life and Travels of John Bartram* (University Presses of Florida, 1990); Helen Gere Cruickshank, editor, *John and William Bartram's America* (Devin-Adair, 1957); Thomas Slaughter, *The Natures of John and William Bartram* (Alfred A. Knopf, 1996).

Bastidas, Rodrigo de

Spanish
b 1460?; Triana, Spain
d 1526; Caribbean Sea
Explored coasts of Colombia and Panama

Spanish Main area of the Spanish Empire including the Caribbean coasts of Central America and South America

Rodrigo de Bastidas made his fortune as a merchant and sailor before he became an explorer. He was motivated to begin his new career by the profits other Spaniards had made in the Americas. He explored most of the coastline of present-day Colombia, and he became the first European to reach Central America.

Shipwrecked by Worms

Bastidas was about 40 years old when the Spanish crown gave him permission to discover new lands in South America. He was not, however, allowed to enter areas that had been discovered by Christopher COLUMBUS or were controlled by Portugal. Teaming up with the great mapmaker Juan de LA COSA, Bastidas sailed in February 1501, following Columbus's route across the Atlantic Ocean.

Bastidas found an island rich in vegetation and called it Isla Verde, which means "Green Island" in Spanish. This island is either present-day Barbados or Grenada. He reached the coast of South America in what is now Colombia and traded with the Sinu (or Zenu) Indians. He then sailed north along the coast to Panama. It was the first expedition to reach Central America, but he could not take time to explore. He was forced to turn back because worms were slowly eating the wood of his ships. The collapsing vessels were wrecked on the southwest coast of Hispaniola (the island now occupied by Haiti and the Dominican Republic). Bastidas and La Cosa walked to the island's capital carrying a treasure of gold and pearls. For their trouble, they were arrested for trading in an area that was off-limits to them. After their release, they returned to Spain in 1504.

A Troubled Colony

Twenty years later, Bastidas was granted a license to found a colony on the **Spanish Main.** He recruited 500 settlers on Hispaniola and took them to the coast of Colombia, where he founded the city of Santa Marta. Unlike most Spanish explorers, Bastidas protected the local Indians from slavery. He encouraged the colonists to do their own manual labor, but they rebelled against him. The settlement also suffered an epidemic of **dysentery.** Under such difficult conditions, Bastidas had to seek help in Hispaniola. He too had come down with dysentery, and he died aboard ship 12 days after leaving Santa Marta.

Suggested Reading Washington Irving, *Voyages and Discoveries of the Companions of Columbus* (reprint, Twayne, 1986).

Bates, Henry Walter

English
b February 8, 1825; Leicester, England
d February 16, 1892; London, England
Explored upper Amazon River valley

species type of plant or animal

zoology the scientific study of animals

specimen sample of a plant, animal, or mineral, usually collected for scientific study or display

Henry Walter Bates was an expert on insects. He journeyed to the Amazon River valley in Brazil in 1848 and explored the region for 11 years. He studied the lives of its people and discovered thousands of insect **species** that had been unknown to European scientists. In Britain he was greatly honored for his work.

Bates had little formal education. His father, a manufacturer, pushed him into business by getting him a job at a company that made stockings. Bates worked long hours during the day, but he found time to attend school at night. He read as much as he could and became interested in **zoology.** He began to roam the countryside, collecting **specimens** of animal life. At 18, he published a paper about beetles in a new scientific magazine.

The next year, his life was changed when he met Alfred Russel WALLACE, a schoolteacher. The two friends shared a love for zoology and collected specimens together outside of town. Then Wallace suggested that they study a more exciting region: the Amazon River valley in South America. Bates jumped at the chance to make zoology more than just a hobby.

Into the Jungle

In May 1848, the two young scientists arrived in the Brazilian town of Pará (now called Belém), where the Amazon River meets the Atlantic Ocean. Journeying inland, they explored the Tocantins River and the Black River (Río Negro). Then they separated to cover a wider area. Bates worked near Pará for more than a year. He collected specimens of many animals, including anteaters and bats. He then headed upriver for Óbidos, a town on the Amazon River. He studied insects and spider monkeys for several months and then reunited with Wallace.

The two friends soon split up again. For the next seven years, Bates explored the upper Amazon region. Most of this time was spent near two smaller rivers, the Solimões and the Tapajós. He gathered 14,500 specimens, of which 8,000 types had been unknown. He discovered more than 500 species of butterflies alone. While studying insects, he noticed that some species try to escape their enemies by imitating the shape or color of a different species. Bates's research proved to be very valuable to later scientists who studied insects.

An Honored Return Home

Bates had hoped to follow the Amazon as far west as the Andes, but his years in the jungle had damaged his health. He had no choice but to return to Britain. His work met with great praise from his fellow

A famous naturalist, Henry Walter Bates was also a skilled student of human cultures and languages.

dysentery disease that causes severe diarrhea

scientists, and he took an important position with the Royal Geographical Society. He wrote a very popular book about his travels and also won a high honor from Brazil, a country that rarely praised foreign scientists. His home in England is now a museum where thousands of his specimens are still on display. However, a desire for fame was not what drove him. Though he had suffered through illness, loneliness, hunger, and hard work, he wrote that the "pleasure of finding another new species . . . supports one against everything."

Suggested Reading Henry Walter Bates, *The Naturalist on the River Amazon*, abridged edition (University of California Press, 1962); Monica Lee, *300 Year Journey: Leicester Naturalist Henry Walter Bates, F.R.S. and His Family, 1665–1985* (Penguin, 1989).

Battuta, Ibn. See *Ibn Battuta*.

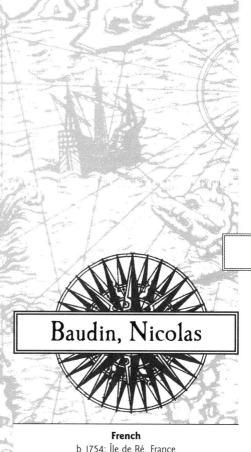

Baudin, Nicolas

French
b 1754; Île de Ré, France
d September 16, 1803; Port Louis, Mauritius
Explored coastline of Australia

---

specimen sample of a plant, animal, or mineral, usually collected for scientific study or display

species type of plant or animal

scurvy disease caused by a lack of vitamin C and once a major cause of death among sailors; symptoms include internal bleeding, loosened teeth, and extreme fatigue

The French scientist Nicolas Baudin led an expedition along the coast of New Holland (now Australia). He was a tough commander who pushed his crew members beyond their limits. Many of the scientists and sailors under Baudin's command deserted the mission. Others died along the way—including Baudin himself. Still, the Frenchmen managed to collect more than 10,000 plant and animal **specimens** and to discover 2,500 **species** that had been unknown to science.

Science and Sickness

After an early career in the French navy, Baudin sailed on an Austrian ship for 12 years, exploring parts of Asia and South America. He gathered many samples of the plant and animal life that he found. His career took a new turn in 1800, when Napoleon, the emperor of France, ordered him to explore New Holland. The east coast of that continent had already been claimed by the British. If Baudin found that the western part of New Holland was separated from the eastern part by water, he could claim the west for France.

Baudin set sail with two ships. It was five months before they stopped at an island port in the Indian Ocean. Forty crewmen, officers, and scientists went ashore and refused to return to the ships. Some were physically ill. Others were simply tired of Baudin's harsh command. The rest of the team reached New Holland three months later. The two ships were soon separated in a storm, and each charted sections of the coastline before they met again at Timor, an island to the north. Again many crew members went ashore, most of them suffering from **scurvy.**

A Suffering Crew

The ships set sail again, this time for the island of Van Diemen's Land (now called Tasmania). With little fresh food or water, crew members were dying every day. But Baudin would not give up. He pushed his men onward, reaching the Tasmanian rain forest in early 1802. Half the crew became too ill to sail the ships. When the

sloop small ship with one mast and triangular sails

expedition struggled into the port of Sydney, a **sloop** had to be sent to bring the sick men to shore.

After a short rest, the expedition headed south again to explore more of the coast of New Holland. The British settlers watched suspiciously. In June 1803, Baudin sent one ship back to France and took the other to Timor. He wanted to continue exploring, but now his own ill health held him back. The next month, he began the return trip to France, but he never got there. The surviving crew members arrived home more than three years after their disastrous expedition had left.

Suggested Reading Frank Horner, *The French Reconnaissance: Baudin in Australia, 1801–1803* (Melbourne University Press, 1987); N. J. B. Plomley, *The Baudin Expedition and the Tasmanian Aborigines* (Blubber Head, 1983).

Bautista de Anza, Juan. *See Anza, Juan Bautista de.*

Belalcázar, Sebastinán, de. *See Benalcázar, Sebastián de.*

Bell, Gertrude Margaret Lowthian

English
b July 14, 1868; Washington, England
d July 12, 1926; Baghdad, Iraq
Traveled in Middle East

Gertrude Bell was a scholar of the culture and history of the Middle East, and she took great risks to travel and study in that region. She was highly respected for her knowledge of the Arab world. Her understanding enabled her not only to translate medieval Persian poetry but also to serve Great Britain as a diplomat and adviser.

Exploring the Mysteries of Persia

Bell showed her talent early, earning a university degree in natural history in less time than it took most students. In 1892, at the age of 23, she made her first trip to Persia (modern-day Iran). She wrote in a letter to a friend that it was "the place I have always longed to see."

Bell was introduced to Persia by her uncle, a British diplomat in the city of Tehran. She was thrilled by the beauty of the land and its language. She quickly learned to read Persian and began to translate Persian poetry into English. She won high praise for her translations of poems by Divan of Hafiz, a Persian poet of the 1300s.

In 1897 Bell went on a six-month trip around the world. She then returned to her studies of the Middle East. She visited Jerusalem and the desert region east of the Dead Sea. Seeing the ruins of a grand Persian palace was, she wrote, "a thing one will never forget as long as one lives." She then traveled through the flat Syrian Desert, enduring a slow and exhausting caravan journey to see ruins from the time of the ancient Roman Empire.

Bell returned to Europe and spent several summers climbing mountains in France. But she found herself traveling to the Middle East again and again between 1900 and 1914. She was often the first European woman to see the places she visited. Although Arab women

Gertrude Bell risked her life to study ancient ruins and modern kingdoms in the deserts of the Middle East.

often lived separately from the men, the desert leaders treated Bell with the courtesy and respect they showed to male visitors. They helped her to find sites that would teach her more about the history of the Middle East. Her quest took her all the way to Constantinople (now Istanbul), a Turkish city with a long and rich history.

Dangers of the Desert

Bell again proved her daring and courage during her last desert expedition. In 1913 she traveled to Damascus in the Turkish Ottoman Empire, where she bought 20 camels and hired three camel drivers and two servants. In great secrecy, she set out for Hail, a city in the Arabian desert. She feared that the government would try to stop her from traveling through the harsh desert areas that were controlled by bandits. In fact, a Turkish official did try to bar her way soon after she began her journey. He let her continue only after she signed a letter saying that he was not to blame for anything that might happen to her.

As expected, Bell's caravan ran into trouble with a desert ruler. Bell offered him gifts, but the bandit suggested to her servants and drivers that they murder her and take her belongings. Luckily, they stayed loyal and refused to hurt her. At last the caravan was allowed to travel on, but matters only got worse when they reached their destination. The prince of Hail was away fighting a war. His grandmother suspected that Bell was an enemy spy, so she had her arrested. When one of the prince's advisers set them free, Bell spent a day taking photographs of the city before traveling north to Baghdad. She arrived in May 1914, a few months before World War I broke out.

Service to Britain

When Britain entered the war, Bell was sent to Egypt to gather information for Britain's Arab allies. After the war ended, she settled in Baghdad to work for the British government and was later put in charge of the British collections of historical objects in Iraq. She worked to have a museum built to preserve and display these collections. Even after her death in 1926, her devotion to historical study was felt. In her will, she left money to create the British School of Archaeology in Iraq.

Suggested Reading Janet Wallach, *Desert Queen: The Extraordinary Life of Gertrude Bell, Adventurer, Adviser to Kings, Ally of Lawrence of Arabia* (Doubleday, 1996); H. V. F. Winstone, *Gertrude Bell* (Quartet Books, 1978).

Belleborne, Jean Nicolett de. See *Nicolett de Belleborne, Jean.*

Bellingshausen, Fabian Gottlieb von

Russian
b September 9, 1778; Saaremaa, Estonia
d January 13, 1852; Kronstadt, Russia
Discovered mainland of Antarctica

Fabian Gottlieb von Bellingshausen, an officer in the Russian navy, led the first major expedition to Antarctica. Bellingshausen observed and wrote descriptions of parts of the continent during this journey, but he did not formally claim it for Russia. In the years that followed, explorers from several other countries continued Bellingshausen's explorations of Antarctica.

When Fabian Gottlieb von Bellingshausen sailed around Antarctica, he found it hard to tell whether icebergs were actually snow-covered mountains.

frigate small, agile warship with three masts and square sails

czar title of Russian monarchs from the 1200s to 1917

Their territorial claims have left the status of the continent in question to this day.

Bellingshausen was born into a family of German nobles who lived on the coast of the Baltic Sea. He joined the Russian navy when he was only 10 years old and became an officer at 19. His first assignment as an officer was to serve under Adam Ivan von KRUSEN-STERN on a voyage around the world. Bellingshausen was next given command of a **frigate** in the Black Sea.

The New Continent

In 1819 **Czar** Alexander I chose Bellingshausen to lead an expedition to the southern polar seas. At that time, no one was sure whether a continent existed there. In the 1700s, James COOK and several whaling captains had reported seeing only islands and ice. The czar wanted to investigate this mysterious region and find harbors that could hold supplies for Russian ships. In the winter of 1819 to 1820, Bellingshausen investigated these islands and found that they were not connected to a mainland. As he sailed, he corrected errors in existing maps and added details.

He then headed farther south into uncharted territory, pushing into the icy seas that had stopped Cook. Sailing east around the pole, he sighted the mainland, exploring the coasts of what would later be called Queen Maud Land and Enderby Land. When the southern winter came, he sailed north to avoid being caught in the ice. The following spring, he hurried south again and continued to follow the coast, reaching what is now known as the Bellingshausen Sea. He loyally named two islands, Peter I Island and Alexander Island, after Russian czars.

The fleet returned to Russia on August 5, 1821, three years after setting sail. Many people were now convinced that an entire continent existed at the South Pole. The story of its exploration had only just begun. Bellingshausen himself never visited such remote seas again, but he served the Russian navy for many years and retired with the rank of admiral.

Suggested Reading Glynn Barratt, *Bellingshausen: A Visit to New Zealand* (Dunmore Press, 1979); Charles Neider, *Antarctica: Authentic Accounts of Life and Exploration in the World's Highest, Driest, Windiest, Coldest and Most Remote Continent* (Random House, 1972).

Benalcázar, Sebastián de

Spanish
b 1495?; Belalcázar, Spain
d April 1551; Cartagena, Colombia
Explored parts of Ecuador, Peru, and Colombia

conquistador Spanish or Portuguese explorer and military leader in the Americas

encomendero Spanish colonist who received a grant of land in the Americas and had control over the Indians who lived there

Sebastián de Benalcázar was a Spanish **conquistador** whose life was ruled by greed and ambition. He fought the Indians of South America—and sometimes even his own countrymen—to gain wealth and power. As a soldier, he helped conquer Peru and Ecuador. As an explorer and colonial official, he founded several cities that still stand in Ecuador and Colombia.

Sebastián de Benalcázar's real name was Sebastián Moyano, but he was known by the name of Belalcázar, his hometown in southern Spain. He was born into a poor family and never learned to read. As a young man, he began his quest for fame and fortune in the West Indies. Within a few years, he had become an **encomendero** in what is now Panama and was involved in heavy fighting. The Spanish waged war against Indian tribes for control of regions that are

El Dorado mythical ruler, city, or area of South America believed to possess much gold

adelantado Spanish leader of a military expedition to America during the 1500s who also served as governor and judge

now Nicaragua and Honduras. When the Spanish were victorious after three years of battle, they founded the city of Léon. Benalcázar helped to found the city and served as its first mayor.

Fortunes Rising

Five years later, Benalcázar went to Peru to help Francisco PIZARRO and Diego de ALMAGRO conquer the Inca Empire. Benalcázar was the captain of the Spanish horsemen and received a share of the enormous riches won by the conquistadors. He was also named the commander of San Miguel de Piura, a city in northern Peru. As a result, he was no longer a part of the Spanish military force that continued to move through Peru.

But he was not out of the fighting for long. When the Inca general Rumiñavi attacked the city of Quito, Pizarro asked Benalcázar to crush the uprising. Benalcázar left Piura and headed north over a wide, empty plain. He convinced local enemies of the Inca, the Cañari Indians, to join him. The Inca surprised the war party on a slippery mountain road, but Benalcázar's troops won this first battle. As the Spanish and Cañari marched through the Andes toward Quito, the Inca attacked again and again.

Benalcázar arrived at Quito to find that the Inca had deserted the city and burned it to the ground. Taking control of the ruined city, he fought off one last Inca attack and then rebuilt the city for the Spanish. He cruelly tortured his Inca prisoners to find out where they had hidden their treasures of gold and silver.

The Land of the Golden Man

Benalcázar pushed on into southern Ecuador and founded two cities, Riobamba and Guayaquil. He then turned his attention to rumors of a golden man whose country was full of great riches. This legendary land became known to the Spanish as **El Dorado.** It may have been Benalcázar who first used this name. Excited by the stories of wealth, he led several expeditions in search of El Dorado. In his travels, he explored much of what is now Colombia. He crossed rugged lands and followed the Cauca River valley north to the lands of the Popayán Indians, whom he conquered. He founded two cities in the region, Popayán and Cali. He then crossed a mountain range and discovered the source of a major river, the Magdalena. As he made his way along this river, the Pijáo Indians attacked with poison darts, killing 20 men. One Spanish soldier said that this march was filled with "bad mountains, bad roads, and bad Indians."

When Benalcázar finally came to a land of wealth, he was upset to find out that Gonzalo JIMÉNEZ DE QUESADA had already claimed the area. This area, which had belonged to the Chibcha Indians and was rich in emeralds, was also claimed by Nikolaus FEDERMANN. The three rivals returned to Spain and asked the king to resolve the conflict. The king named Benalcázar captain general and **adelantado** of a large part of eastern Colombia. Benalcázar returned to South America and fought for the king in the Peruvian Civil Wars, which lasted for five years. During the fighting he killed another Spaniard, Jorge Robeldo, who had tried to take control of some of Benalcázar's lands. Robeldo's widow took revenge by having Benalcázar arrested for murder. He was ordered to travel to the coast of Colombia, where he was to board a ship for Spain. But he died on the way to the coast, still on the continent he had explored and looted for over 30 years.

Suggested Reading James Lockhart, *The Men of Cajamarca, a Social and Biographical Study of the Conquerers of Peru* (University of Texas Press, 1972).

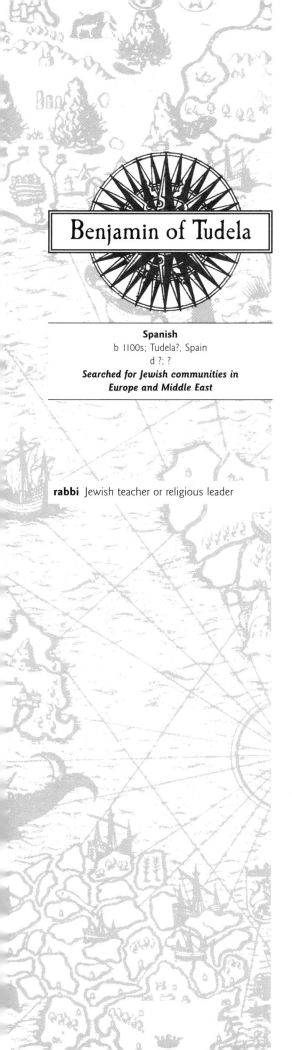

Benjamin of Tudela

Spanish
b 1100s; Tudela?, Spain
d ?; ?
Searched for Jewish communities in Europe and Middle East

rabbi Jewish teacher or religious leader

Benjamin of Tudela spent years traveling to Jewish communities in Europe, North Africa, and the Middle East. Upon his return to his home in Spain, he wrote a book about what he had seen and heard. It was first published in printed form as *The Itinerary of Benjamin of Tudela* in 1543. Like other medieval writers, Benjamin did not always distinguish between legends and facts. He may have stretched the truth for the sake of a colorful tale, or he may have been mistaken. Even so, historians consider his account to be one of the most complete and accurate travel narratives of the Middle Ages. Modern scholars value its record of the life and customs of medieval Jews in many parts of the world.

Traveling with a Mission

Other than a few hints contained in his writings, the details of Benjamin's life are a mystery. He was born sometime in the 1100s and lived in the town of Tudela near the city of Saragossa in northern Spain. People knew him as Benjamin ben Jonah or **Rabbi** Benjamin. But scholars who have studied his book think that he was most likely a merchant, not a rabbi. He may have been called Rabbi Benjamin simply out of respect for his learning.

Benjamin's travels were inspired by the situation of the Jews who lived in Europe during the Middle Ages. In many nations, Jews suffered verbal and physical attacks by Christians. Spain's large Jewish population lived in relative comfort, but some Spanish Jews feared that one day the Christians would force them to leave. Benjamin wanted to give Spanish Jews useful information about places where they could live if they had to leave their country.

The Beginning of a Long Journey

Benjamin left Saragossa around 1160. He traveled to the port of Barcelona and then to southern France, where he boarded a ship for the Italian city of Genoa. His account of the trip lists every town and city in which he stopped. It is a practical guide, in which he noted how many days' travel separated each place from the next. Benjamin also recorded how many Jews lived in each community, and sometimes named their leading citizens. He described the circumstances in which the Jews lived, what kinds of work they did, and whether they were on good terms with Christian rulers and citizens. He also discussed many political and economic matters, such as the democratic government of Genoa and the bustling docks at Montpellier, France.

Constantinople and the Holy Land

From Italy, Benjamin traveled to Greece, which was then part of the great empire of the Byzantine Christians. The empire's capital

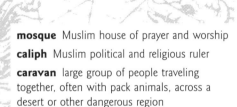

mosque Muslim house of prayer and worship

caliph Muslim political and religious ruler

caravan large group of people traveling together, often with pack animals, across a desert or other dangerous region

Fearing that Spanish Jews might be forced to leave Spain, Benjamin of Tudela traveled widely to learn about life in other Jewish communities.

was Constantinople, where Jews had to live in a separate section of the city. "They are exposed to be beaten in the streets," he wrote, "and must submit to all sorts of bad treatment." Despite the Jews' oppression, he was impressed with the city's magnificence and wealth. He wrote that people came to Constantinople "from all parts of the world for purposes of trade."

Benjamin then traveled south through the region of greatest interest to the Jews—Palestine, the ancient Holy Land of the Bible. At the time of his visit, Jerusalem was in the hands of European Christian knights who had captured it from Muslims. Benjamin described the Christians' activities, the city's temples and shrines, and other points of interest. For example, he claimed to have seen the pillar of salt into which Lot's wife was transformed, as told in the Bible. Benjamin wrote that "although the sheep continually lick it, the pillar grows again, and retains its original state." He also mentioned an early tourist attraction in the city of Hebron, where visitors paid to see fake tombs of biblical heroes. For an extra fee, Benjamin explained, Jews could see the real tombs.

The Distant Lands of Islam

From Jerusalem, Benjamin traveled to Damascus, in Syria, where he admired the lush gardens and the splendid **mosque.** Moving on, he went east into the region called Mesopotamia (present-day Iraq), where he found large and prosperous communities of Jews. They lived peacefully under the rule of the **caliph** of Baghdad. The leader of Mesopotamia's Jews was treated with respect by the Muslims. Benjamin painted a favorable picture of Jewish life in Mesopotamia. Some scholars think that he exaggerated, especially in his high estimate of the number of Jews living there. Still, it is known that a large Jewish community had long existed in Mesopotamia and was on good terms with the Muslim people at the time of Benjamin's visit.

Benjamin also described the ruins of Babylon, one of the great cities of ancient Mesopotamia. It is impossible to tell whether Benjamin really saw the ruins or merely heard about them from other travelers. Similarly, he discussed the eastern lands of Persia, now known as Iran, as well as Samarkand and other cities in central Asia. He even mentioned such distant lands as China, India, and Tibet. He did not claim to have visited these places, and it is very unlikely that he did so. Like other medieval writers, Benjamin probably expanded on his own firsthand observations by including common knowledge and travelers' tales in his writings.

He was on more familiar ground when he visited North Africa and described the cities and **caravan** routes of Egypt and the Sahara. He wrote that Alexandria in Egypt was home to about 3,000 Jews and was "an excellent market to all nations," filled with Christian, Muslim, and Asian traders. From Egypt he sailed to the island of Sicily and then returned home by way of Italy, Germany, and France. He reached Tudela around 1173, after completing an impressive tour of the parts of the world known to medieval Europeans. Jewish scholars learned of Benjamin's journey and admired his book. After his writings were translated from Hebrew into Latin in 1575, other Europeans also became aware of his achievement.

Suggested Reading Sandra Benjamin, *The World of Benjamin of Tudela* (Fairleigh Dickinson University Press, 1995); Manuel Komroff, editor, *Contemporaries of Marco Polo* (Dorset Press, 1989); Yosef Levanon, *The Jewish Travellers in the Twelfth Century* (University Press of America, 1980).

Bennett, Floyd

American
b October 25, 1890; Warrensburg, New York
d April 25, 1928; Québec, Canada
Piloted Richard Byrd's plane over North Pole

Floyd Bennett's heroism as a pilot and explorer won him the Congressional Medal of Honor for his role in the first flight over the North Pole.

Floyd Bennett was an expert pilot and mechanic. He flew for Richard Byrd from 1925 until his early death at the age of 37. The two men were the first to fly over the North Pole.

Bennett worked as a car mechanic before joining the navy in 1917. There he learned how to fly and fix airplanes. Byrd, a navy pilot, spotted Bennett's talent and recruited him to be his copilot. They both flew in the Arctic region with Donald B. MacMillan in 1925. The next year, Bennett and Byrd set out to make the first flight over the North Pole. They took off from Spitsbergen, an island north of Norway. They had a scare when an engine began to leak oil, but when the oil level dropped below the hole, the leak stopped. The successful journey lasted 15½ hours and covered 1,360 miles. The U.S. Congress awarded Bennett the Medal of Honor.

Byrd and Bennett then aimed to be the first pilots to carry passengers across the Atlantic Ocean. In a test flight, the front of the plane was too heavy, and they made a crash landing. Everyone survived, but Bennett was seriously injured. He did not recover in time to make the ocean crossing in 1927. One year later, Byrd made Bennett his second-in-command for a flight to the South Pole. Before they were ready to leave the United States, Bennett flew off to rescue two German pilots who had crashed into a river in Canada. He made the rescue in the wet cold of early spring. Still weak from his own crash, he caught pneumonia and died. Byrd later flew over the South Pole in a plane named *Floyd Bennett*. He tied an American flag to a stone from Bennett's grave and dropped it from the plane into the snow below.

Suggested Reading Cora L. Bennett, *Floyd Bennett* (W. F. Payson, 1932); Basil Clarke, *Polar Flight* (Ian Allen, 1964).

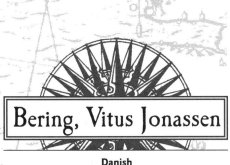

Bering, Vitus Jonassen

Danish
b August 12, 1681; Horsens, Denmark
d December 6, 1741; Bering Island, Russia
***Commanded first European crossing
from Siberia to Alaska***

Vitus Jonassen Bering was a Danish naval officer who led two difficult Russian expeditions to the coast of Alaska. He was sent to find out whether North America and Russia were connected by land or divided by water. Bering showed himself to be a strong leader, a capable organizer, and a skilled navigator. He led hundreds of men across Siberia, which is more than three times as wide as North America. His explorations helped the Russian fur trade expand along the Alaskan coastline. The strait between Siberia and Alaska had already been found in 1648 by a Russian pioneer named Semyon Ivanov DEZHNEV. But Dezhnev's report had gone unnoticed at the time. Bering repeated Dezhnev's discovery on a much larger and more challenging scale.

The Captain and the Czar

Little is known about Bering's life before he led these missions. After he returned from an ocean voyage to the East Indies in 1703, he was asked to join the Russian navy. He served with Russian fleets in battles on the Baltic, Black, and White Seas for 20 years. By 1723 he had achieved the rank of captain second class. When he applied to become a captain first class, he was turned down, so he retired from the navy. But within a year, Bering was asked to return as captain first class to lead a voyage of exploration.

Czar Peter the Great had written the mission's instructions before he died. The explorers were to start from the western city of St. Petersburg, march across Siberia, sail to the Kamchatka Peninsula, then cross Kamchatka to its east coast on the Pacific Ocean. There they would build ships to explore the area between Russia and North America. It would have been easier to sail ships from western Russia around Africa to the East Indies and then sail north past Japan. But Czar Peter had purposely chosen the exhausting overland route. Because it passed only through Russian territory, other

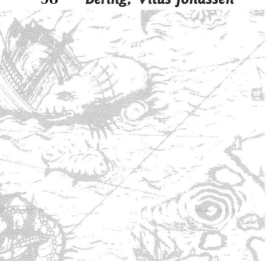

czar title of Russian monarchs from the 1200s to 1917

Bering's two voyages led to greater knowledge of the seas between Russia and Alaska.

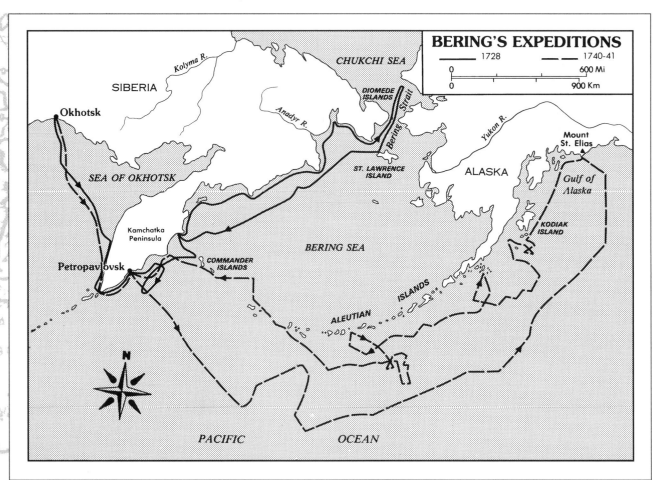

countries would have no idea that Russia intended to explore North America. Peter also wanted to impress his new subjects in Siberia, which had recently come under his empire's control. By sending a large and well-equipped expedition through Siberia, he could show the people that their distant ruler was quite powerful.

Hard Roads and Foggy Seas

Bering accepted the challenge and left St. Petersburg in 1725 with 100 men. He had two lieutenants, Martin Spanberg and Aleksei CHIRIKOV. As they crossed Siberia, they gathered hundreds of laborers. The growing party crossed mountain ranges and floated down rivers, sometimes fighting Siberian tribes along the way. They carried supplies and boats through a frozen land where the snow was deeper than the horses were high.

The **caravan** finally reached Okhotsk, on the Siberian coast, more than two years after setting out. There the men built a ship and moved their supplies across the Sea of Okhotsk to Kamchatka. They crossed Kamchatka and built another ship, the *St. Gabriel.* After 3½ years, the actual voyage of discovery could finally begin.

Through the Bering Strait

The *St. Gabriel* followed the shore northeast toward the distant corner of Asia. In the sea north of the Pacific Ocean, Bering landed on an island, which he named after Saint Lawrence. The island is now part of Alaska, and the sea is now known as the Bering Sea. The ship continued north, and after two days, it had passed out of sight of land. The czar's orders had been to travel along the coast. If the ship looped around Asia and back to the west, it would mean that water separated Asia from America. If the shore turned east, away from Russia, it would prove that the continents were connected by land.

Lieutenant Chirikov wanted to continue the search, even if it meant spending the entire winter in that barren region after the waters froze. But Bering felt that wintering so far north would be dangerous. He sailed on for a few more days and entered the narrow strait he had been looking for. Bering should have been able to see North America, but there was too much fog, and he returned to Kamchatka. Although he did not have solid proof, he was convinced that the strait existed. The Russian public was not so certain.

Another Chance at Discovery

When Bering returned to St. Petersburg two years later, his superiors scolded him for failing to complete his mission. Still, they admired his ability to organize and lead such a large and lengthy expedition. After all, Bering had had to cope with many details, such as providing food and clothing for all the men. He had ensured that the weary and homesick officers and workers got along well and performed their duties. He had also had to deal with the people in the hundreds of villages he passed.

Bering proposed a new mission to the eastern seas. He also wanted to explore the northern coast of Siberia. The Russian government set aside its doubts about Bering's first journey and named

Vitus Jonassen Bering was among the hundreds of western Europeans whom Czar Peter enlisted to help modernize Russia.

caravan large group of people traveling together, often with pack animals, across a desert or other dangerous region

This Russian flag would have flown over Bering's expeditions as they advanced eastward across northern Asia.

surveyor one who makes precise measurements of a location's geography

scurvy disease caused by a lack of vitamin C and once a major cause of death among sailors; symptoms include internal bleeding, loosened teeth, and extreme fatigue

him captain commander of the Great Northern Expedition. This huge project would take nine years to chart the hundreds of miles of Siberia's Arctic coastline. Bering commanded 13 ships and 3,000 men. He hired two landscape painters, five **surveyors,** and 30 scientists with hundreds of books and nine wagons full of instruments. Bering himself would study the easternmost section of the coast. Each time the expedition met with problems, the government sent him angry letters, and it took his men eight years just to reach Okhotsk. By the time he sailed for Alaska with two ships, he was exhausted and dispirited.

The two ships were separated in a summer storm. Bering's ship, the *St. Peter,* sailed southeast to the Gulf of Alaska, where Bering finally sighted the Alaskan mainland. Even this discovery, toward which Bering had worked for 15 years, did not lift his spirits. He was too busy worrying about the challenges ahead. The crew made several landings to explore the Alaskan coast, and the chief scientist wanted to stay there and do research all winter. Bering, however, insisted on returning to Kamchatka before the winter weather struck. Storms blew the ship to a group of islands now known as the Commander Islands.

The party was forced to winter in an unsafe harbor with no hope of receiving supplies. Bering was one of 30 men who died that winter from **scurvy** and cold weather. The following summer, the survivors built another boat from what was left of the *St. Peter* and made their way back to Kamchatka. The other ship, captained by Chirikov, was waiting for them there.

A Place in History

Historians still argue about Bering's importance as an explorer. After all, Dezhnev had already discovered the strait almost a hundred years earlier. But it was Bering's mission that brought back the news that Alaska was rich in furs of many kinds. Russian trappers headed for North America, and the Russian Empire slowly expanded down the North American coast. Today's maps also show that Bering's hard work has been remembered. The Bering Strait, the Bering Sea, and even Bering Island, where he died and was buried, still carry the name of this dedicated explorer.

Suggested Reading Raymond H. Fisher, *Bering's Voyages: Whither and Why* (University of Washington Press, 1977); F. A. Golder, *Russian Expansion on the Pacific, 1641-1850* (Peter Smith, 1960); Gerhard Friedrich Müller, *Bering's Voyages: The Reports from Russia,* translated by Carol Urness (University of Alaska Press, 1986); Georg Wilhelm Steller, *Journal of a Voyage with Bering, 1741-1742,* translated by Margritt A. Engel and O. W. Frost, edited by O. W. Frost (Stanford University Press, 1988).

Bethencourt, Jean de

French
b 1360?; Normandy, France
d 1422; Grainville, France
Explored Canary Islands for Spain

Jean de Bethencourt was a French nobleman who conquered the Canary Islands, which lie off the coast of Africa. He brought the islands under the rule of King Henry III of Spain. They later became a major port where ships stopped to pick up supplies for journeys to the Americas and beyond.

Bethencourt was raised to live in the luxurious style of French nobles. Then, at the court of King Charles VI of France, he heard exciting stories of exploration and adventure. These tales of glory gave him an idea: he would conquer the Canary Islands and teach the people there about his religion, Christianity.

Mysterious Islands

There are 14 small islands that make up the Canaries, located 700 miles south of Spain and 70 miles west of Morocco. In Bethencourt's time, Europeans knew little about them. Decades earlier, Portuguese and Italian sailors had been to the Canaries. Since then, however, only a handful of merchants and pirates paid any attention to these islands.

Bethencourt used his own money to pay for the expedition. On May 1, 1402, he sailed from France with two ships. During the voyage, he was threatened by crew members who were planning a mutiny. He squashed the rebellion and safely reached the Canary Island known as Lanzarote in a few weeks. The people who lived on the island wore clothes made from animal skins and woven grass. Bethencourt conquered these people and settled on Lanzarote. However, he felt that he needed more men to fight for control of the other islands. He traveled to Spain and sought help from the Spanish king, Henry III, who was a family friend.

A New Spanish Colony

Bethencourt soon returned as the royally appointed ruler of the Canary Islands, which he claimed for Spain. While he was gone, his second-in-command had conquered another island, Fuerteventura. With two islands under his control, Bethencourt hurried home to Normandy to gather colonists and take them to a third island, Hierro.

At the end of 1406, Bethencourt left the Canary Islands for good. He kept his royal title and his rights to the colony's profits, but he hired his nephew to live there and govern. Bethencourt returned to Normandy and wrote an account of his expeditions, but many historians doubt his truthfulness. He died in Normandy in 1422.

Suggested Reading Jean de Bethencourt, *The Canarian; or, Book of the Conquest and Conversion of the Canarians in the Year 1402: by Messire Jean de Béthencourt,* translated and edited by Richard Henry Major (B. Franklin, 1969).

In the early 1400s, Jean de Bethencourt explored the Canary Islands, which later became an important point of departure for voyages to the Americas.

Bilot, Robert. See *Bylot, Robert.*

Bingham, Hiram

American
b November 19, 1875; Honolulu, Hawaii
d June 6, 1956; Washington, D.C.
Discovered Machu Picchu and Vitcos in Peru

Hiram Bingham held many impressive positions in his lifetime. He was a professor of Latin American history and geography at Yale University. He was the governor of Connecticut and a United States senator. He was even the pastor of a small church in Hawaii. But he always listed "explorer" as his main occupation. He made several trips to South America, and in 1911 he discovered the ruins of two lost Inca cities, Machu Picchu and Vitcos.

Hiram Bingham discovered Machu Picchu. The ancient Inca city is built on terraces, which look like steps carved out of the mountainside.

El Dorado mythical ruler, city, or area of South America believed to possess much gold

Although he led a life of great adventure, Bingham had been raised to be a humble, religious man. His parents were missionaries who had moved to Honolulu just before he was born. One of his grandfathers had also been a missionary in the Pacific, and Hiram grew up in the shadow of his family's history. In 1894 he entered Yale University, where he was drawn toward a more worldly life. But when he graduated, he returned to Hawaii and served as pastor of the Palama Chapel in a poor neighborhood in Honolulu.

The Road to Adventure

Bingham's outlook on life changed when he fell in love with the young and wealthy Alfreda Mitchell, who was vacationing in Hawaii with her family. He wanted to marry her, but he knew that he would have to earn a better living. He left his job as a pastor and earned a master's degree in South American history from the University of California at Berkeley. After that, he and Alfreda were married. Bingham then studied at Harvard University and was later hired to teach at Princeton University, but he soon became bored with the life he led at these schools. Within a year, he was off on his first field trip. He traveled across Venezuela and Colombia, tracing the route of Simon Bolívar, who had freed much of South America from Spanish rule in the 1800s.

When Bingham returned, he was hired as a lecturer at Yale. The president of the United States, Theodore ROOSEVELT, then asked him to attend a scientific conference in Santiago, Chile. This trip gave Bingham a chance to explore the old Spanish trade route from Buenos Aires, Argentina, to Lima, Peru. He also visited the ruins of Choqquequirau. This ancient city had once been thought to be the last capital of the Inca Empire and maybe even **El Dorado,** the legendary city of gold. Bingham became interested in searching for Vitcos, the true last capital of the Inca.

To Find a Lost City

In 1911 Bingham set out on the most important trip of his career, the Yale Peruvian Expedition. One of his goals was to search for Inca ruins in the Urubamba Valley of the Andes in Peru. On July 24, Bingham discovered the ruins of Machu Picchu perched atop a high cliff between steep mountain peaks. The Inca city was almost impossible to reach. Bingham crawled on his hands and knees across a decaying bridge over a roaring river. He then climbed the mountainside leading to the ancient city. "I felt utterly alone," he wrote later. But when at last he saw the grand ruins up close, "breathless with excitement, I forgot my fatigue. . . ." Still, Bingham did not believe that this was Vitcos, the last capital of the Inca Empire. A local guide helped him continue his search. They arrived at a place called Nũsta Isppana. Seeing a landmark, a large white rock near the ruins of a temple, he felt certain that he had found Vitcos.

Return to a Life of Service

Back in the United States, some historians questioned whether Bingham had been the first to discover Machu Picchu in 1911. He had found the name "Lizarraga" and the date "1902" written in charcoal on a temple wall. It turned out that a man named Augustine Lizarraga had in fact been there and left this inscription but had never reported his find. Bingham is usually credited as the "scientific discoverer" of Machu Picchu. His careful records and notes added much to earlier knowledge about the Inca. His work also created new interest in scientific exploration of both South America and North America.

Bingham made two other expeditions to Peru with the support of Yale University and the National Geographic Society. He served in World War I and was elected governor of Connecticut in 1924. He resigned as governor soon after taking office, when he was appointed to fill an open seat in the United States Senate. He was a senator for eight years. Bingham had lived up to his early sense of duty. He added to human knowledge and led a life of service. At the same time, he was a man who loved to have adventures, dance at parties, and socialize with the rich and powerful.

Suggested Reading Alfred M. Bingham, *Portrait of an Explorer: Hiram Bingham, Discoverer of Machu Picchu* (Iowa State University Press, 1989); Hiram Bingham, *Lost City of the Incas* (reprint, Greenwood, 1981).

Bird, Isabella. See *Bishop, Isabella Bird.*

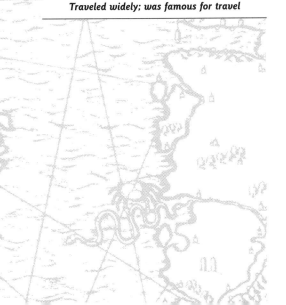

Bishop, Isabella Bird

English
b October 15, 1831; Yorkshire, England
d October 7, 1904; Edinburgh, Scotland
Traveled widely; was famous for travel

During the 1800s, a number of strong-willed, adventurous women traveled to remote parts of the world. Many of them later wrote popular books about their journeys. They proved that exploration was not only for men, and they expanded people's ideas about what women could do. One of the best-known and most widely traveled of these women was Isabella Bird, who became Isabella Bird Bishop when she married in 1881. Her journeys through North America and Asia and across the Pacific Ocean sometimes seemed like ordinary sightseeing—but at other times, they held all the mystery of true exploration.

Traveling for Her Health

Bird, a daughter of an English minister, grew up in a household that emphasized service to others. Her family shared the belief, commonly held in England and elsewhere in the 1800s, that a woman's place was in the home. Bird was often sick as a child. During her early 20s, she felt so weak, ill, and tired that she sometimes spent months in bed. A doctor recommended a sea voyage. Bird's father gave her some money and told her that she could go anywhere she wanted for as long as the money lasted. She boarded a ship and crossed the Atlantic Ocean to visit a cousin in Canada.

The experience of traveling on her own filled Bird with humor and energy. She toured part of North America by train and

caravan large group of people traveling together, often with pack animals, across a desert or other dangerous region

stagecoach, writing lively letters home to her beloved sister, Henrietta. When she returned home, her family encouraged her to make a book out of the letters. *The Englishwoman in America,* Bird's first book, appeared in 1856. In the years that followed, however, she again became weary and sick. Short trips to North America and the Mediterranean Sea failed to improve her health or her spirits. In 1872 a doctor suggested another long sea voyage, and Bird decided to visit Australia and New Zealand. At the age of 40, she stood on the edge of a new life.

Delights and Dangers of Travel

Bird was not impressed with Australia or New Zealand, so she set sail for San Francisco. When her ship stopped in Hawaii (then called the Sandwich Islands), she decided to stay. For six months, she rode over the islands on horseback, exploring volcanoes and delighting in her freedom. She experienced what she called "the height of enjoyment in traveling" when she camped under a tree with her saddle for a pillow. Bird had discovered the great love of her life, travel in wild places.

From Hawaii she went to San Francisco and toured the American West, determined to visit a remote valley in Colorado that she had heard about. Her adventures in Colorado included mountain climbs, blizzards, and a romance with "Mountain Jim" Nugent, a tattered but generous character whom Bird called a "Desperado." Bird eventually returned home after a two-year absence.

The books she wrote about her visits to Hawaii and the Rocky Mountains, *The Hawaiian Archipelago* and *A Lady's Life in the Rocky Mountains,* became immensely popular. By the time the second book appeared, she had already left on her next long trip, this time to Japan. There she immersed herself in the daily lives of people in remote rural districts seldom visited by tourists. She also passed through several Chinese cities before reaching the island of Singapore. She was offered a chance to board a ship bound for Malaysia, then a little-known land of rain forests in southeast Asia. "I was only allowed five minutes for decision," she wrote, "but I have no difficulty in making up my mind when an escape from civilization is possible." After returning from her Asian trip, Bird seemed to settle down, writing books and marrying Dr. John Bishop, who had proposed marriage on many occasions. During this time, her sister Henrietta died. Five years later, Isabella's husband also died.

Last Adventures

In 1888, with her loved ones gone, Isabella Bird Bishop left England for Tibet, a region that had long fascinated her. Starting in India, she made a horseback journey to Ladakh, a mountain kingdom in the Himalayas, and reached the fringes of Tibet. She then joined a British army officer who was riding through Persia (now Iran). They traveled together for several months before Bishop joined a **caravan** to the Black Sea.

Back in Europe, politicians sought her opinion on conditions in Persia and the Middle East, and she once again published her

The daring and determined Isabella Bird Bishop gained worldwide fame through the books she wrote about her travels.

adventures. By now many people had realized that Bishop was more than a tireless traveler and a good writer. She was also a careful observer, whose reports on the places she visited contained valuable geographic information. In 1892 Britain's Royal Geographical Society made Bishop its first woman member.

Bishop's last long trip began in 1894. After passing through Korea, she spent almost three years in China. Several times she came close to dying at the hands of mobs who were hostile to foreigners, and she began carrying a pistol. Despite these dangers, Bishop did not turn back. She continued the trip she had planned, advanced to the foothills of Tibet, and spent the rest of her time camping with Buddhist nomads whom she met there. Although she was by then close to 70, Bishop refused to give up the travel that had given meaning and purpose to her life. After a trip to Morocco in 1900, her health failed, and she remained at home until her death three years later.

Suggested Reading Pat Barr, *A Curious Life for a Lady: The Story of Isabella Bird, a Remarkable Victorian Traveller* (Doubleday, 1970); Cicely P. Havely, editor, *This Grand Beyond: Travels of Isabella Bird Bishop* (Century, 1984); Dorothy Middleton, *Victorian Lady Travellers* (Dutton, 1965); Rebecca Stefoff, *Women of the World: Women Travelers and Explorers* (Oxford University Press, 1992).

Blaxland, Gregory

English
b June 27, 1778; Newington, England
d January 1853; North Parramatta, Australia
Explored Australia's Blue Mountains

Gregory Blaxland was the first European to cross Australia's Blue Mountains, part of the Great Dividing Range that separates Australia's east coast from the rest of the continent. His journey opened the way for other important explorations of Australia.

He was born into a wealthy English family and had many important and influential friends. One of these friends was the naturalist Sir Joseph BANKS, who had explored Australia's Botany Bay in 1770 with Captain James Cook. At Banks's suggestion, Britain created a prison colony in Australia. In 1805 Blaxland became one of the first free men to move to Australia, hoping to start a farm there. The British government gave him 4,000 acres of land and 40 convicts to do the farmwork. The government also agreed to pay for the prisoners' food and clothing for the first 18 months.

The Search for Greener Grass

Blaxland settled at the foot of the Blue Mountains. In 1813 a lack of rain ruined his harvest. He and two other landowners, William Lawson and William Charles Wentworth, decided to look for more fertile land on the other side of the mountains. Previous explorers had tried and failed to cross the mountains by traveling in the valleys between peaks—but Blaxland and his group stayed atop the ridges, and they succeeded.

After about three weeks of hiking, the group reached a **tributary** of the Nepean River. On both sides of the river, later named the Lett River, rich grasslands stretched for miles. The men compared the area to the biblical land of Canaan. Blaxland said that it had enough grass to support all the colony's cattle for 30 years.

It turned out that they had not actually crossed the whole mountain range. The land they saw was only a valley known as the Bathurst Plains. Even so, their technique of staying on the ridges proved that the mountains could be crossed. Other colonists were convinced that the continent west of the mountains was worth exploring. Blaxland wrote an account of the trip in 1823 and spent the rest of his life as a farmer. He killed himself 30 years later in a fit of severe depression.

Suggested Reading Victor Hyde, *Gregory Blaxland* (Oxford University Press, 1958); Arthur W. Jose, *Builders and Pioneers of Australia* (Books for Libraries, 1970).

tributary stream or river that flows into a larger stream or river

Bligh, William

English
b September 9, 1754; Tyntan, England
d December 7, 1817; London, England
Charted northeast coast of Australia; explored southern Pacific Ocean

mutiny rebellion by a ship's crew against the officers

William Bligh was a skilled seaman who had an adventurous and troublesome career. He showed early promise as a navigator, and at 22 he served on the *Resolution* under Captain James Cook. He must have learned a great deal from Cook as they visited the southern Pacific Ocean, North America, and the Arctic Ocean. Bligh himself commanded British warships in several major battles. Late in his career, he served as a colonial governor in Australia. He is best known, however, as the captain of the *Bounty.* His crew staged a **mutiny,** setting him and 19 loyal crew members adrift in a small boat.

The Floating Greenhouse

At the age of 33, Bligh was a lieutenant in the British navy. He was given command of the *Bounty* on a mission to Tahiti, an island in the South Pacific Ocean. Sir Joseph Banks, a well-known scientist, had proposed that breadfruit trees be taken from Tahiti and replanted in the West Indies. The new breadfruit crops would feed the slaves on West Indian plantations. The *Bounty* was remodeled as a floating greenhouse to carry the young trees.

Bligh set sail from Britain in the winter of 1787 with a crew of 44 men. He was the only naval officer on board and had hired an old

The crew of the *Bounty* rebelled against William Bligh, setting him and 19 loyal men adrift in a small boat.

mate assistant to the commander of a ship

circumnavigation journey around the world

friend, Fletcher Christian, as a **mate.** The trip got off to a bad start. Crew members were frustrated by rough weather, cramped living quarters, and short supplies of bad food. They got no sympathy from Bligh, a strict and moody commander. He planned to sail west around the southern tip of South America. This was not the safest route to the South Pacific, especially in winter, but he wanted to make this trip a complete **circumnavigation.** The overworked crew was very unhappy with this plan, and Bligh finally agreed to sail east around the southern tip of Africa instead.

The Mutiny on the Bounty

The expedition reached Tahiti 10 months after leaving Britain and spent 5 months there. This period was longer than the usual visit, but they had to wait for the breadfruit seedlings to sprout. During these months, many of the crewmen formed relationships with Tahitian women and came to enjoy the island's simple life. They also grew even more tired of Bligh's strict discipline and bad temper.

When the *Bounty* left Tahiti for the Friendly Islands (present-day Tonga), Bligh was frustrated by the crew's sulky attitude. He punished the men who did not work hard enough to suit him by putting them in chains. He even accused Christian of stealing coconuts from him. Christian grew angry and started planning to escape to Tahiti. About three weeks after the *Bounty* had left the

chronometer clock designed to keep precise time in the rough conditions of sea travel

island, Christian led a mutiny. Bligh and the crewmen who stayed loyal to him were put aboard a 23-foot-long boat and set adrift with some food and a **chronometer.**

Luckily, Bligh was a skillful navigator. He brought the small boat safely across nearly 4,000 miles of ocean to Timor, an island that is now part of Indonesia. Bligh and his men were taken back to Britain, where he was not blamed for losing the *Bounty*. In fact, he was praised as a hero for having survived.

Meanwhile, Christian had taken the *Bounty* back to Tahiti, where another British ship soon arrived to capture the rebels. Christian escaped with 11 other mutineers and 12 Tahitian women to Pitcairn Island. They burned the *Bounty* when they arrived, so that passing ships would not see it and know where they were hiding. When an American whaling ship visited Pitcairn about 20 years later, only one mutineer was still alive. Five had been killed in quarrels over land and women, and the rest had died of natural causes. But their children survived, and by 1825 the Pitcairn settlement had become a colony of 65 people.

Back in Command

Bligh repeated his expedition to Tahiti in 1791. This time he did carry breadfruit trees to Jamaica. He also charted Australia's northern coast on the way. In later years, Bligh commanded ships in battle, winning honors for his service in the Napoleonic Wars. But he had not seen his last mutiny.

In 1805 he was named governor of New South Wales (now a province of Australia). When he arrived at the colony, he found that the soldiers there were more interested in moneymaking schemes than in their military duties. Bligh tried to whip these corrupt men into shape. After three years under Bligh's strict dicipline, the officers rebelled and put him in prison. He was held for two years, until he was recalled to Britain. The soldiers were put on trial and dismissed from the army. Despite his misfortune, Bligh continued his career in the navy and died with the rank of vice admiral.

Suggested Reading Gavin Kennedy, *Captain Bligh: The Man and his Mutinies* (Duckworth, 1989); Richard A. Mansir, *The Journal of Bounty's Launch* (Kittiwake, 1989); Sam McKinney, *Bligh: A True Account of the Mutiny Aboard His Majesty's Ship Bounty* (International Marine Publishing, 1989); Charles Nordhoff and James Norman Hall, *Mutiny on the Bounty* (Little, Brown, 1932).

Bodega y Quadra, Juan Francisco de la

Spanish
b 1743; Lima, Peru
d March 26, 1794; Mexico City, Mexico
Explored northwest coast of North America

Juan Francisco de la Bodega y Quadra was a Spanish naval officer who explored the Pacific coast of North America. Known as a gentleman who loved to entertain guests, he was also a friend to the Indians he met. In 1775 and 1779, he sailed north as far as Alaska, making Spain's northernmost claims of territory.

Overcoming Prejudice

In the late 1700s, Spain was working to strengthen its control of areas north of Mexico. San Blas, a city on the west coast of Mexico, was the base for Spanish exploration of North America's Pacific coast. In 1774 Bodega and five other young officers were sent to San

Creole person of European ancestry born in Spanish colonies in the Americas; or, person descended from French settlers of what is now the southern United States

schooner fast, easy-to-maneuver sailing ship with two or more masts and triangular sails

scurvy disease caused by a lack of vitamin C and once a major cause of death among sailors; symptoms include internal bleeding, loosened teeth, and extreme fatigue

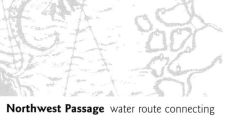

Northwest Passage water route connecting the Atlantic Ocean and Pacific Ocean through the Arctic islands of northern Canada

viceroy governor of a Spanish colony in the Americas

New Spain region of Spanish colonial empire that included the areas now occupied by Mexico, Florida, Texas, New Mexico, Arizona, California, and various Caribbean islands

Blas to lead sea voyages to the north. To his dismay, Bodega was passed over for command in favor of the younger Bruno de HEZETA. Bodega was probably discriminated against because he was a **Creole** born in Peru. Spanish authorities often looked down on Creoles and preferred people who were born in Spain, such as Hezeta. Despite this prejudice, Bodega volunteered to serve as second-in-command of another ship, the *Sonora,* a light, narrow **schooner.** The ship was intended only for short trips, and 10 of the 17 crew members had never before been to sea.

Hezeta's instructions were to sail far to the north, going ashore to claim land for Spain wherever he could do so safely. He was to avoid the settlements of other nations. He was also ordered to be friendly to the Indians and find out what goods they had to trade. Shortly after the Spaniards left San Blas, the captain of one ship began to show signs of insanity. He was replaced by the captain of the *Sonora,* who left his own ship to Bodega's command.

Parting Ways

The mission began to have more problems. When the ships anchored off the coast of what is now the state of Washington, a party went ashore to find fresh water. Several men were killed in a sudden attack by Indians. Also, some of Hezeta's crewmen were beginning to suffer from **scurvy.** Hezeta decided to turn back and return to San Blas. When the sun rose the next morning, the *Sonora* and Hezeta's ship had become separated. Most historians agree that Bodega lost Hezeta on purpose, thinking his commander too timid. Bodega and his pilot, Mourelle, felt that it was their duty to sail as far north as they could in their small, fragile craft.

Fresh water was in short supply, and food had to be divided carefully, but the crew agreed to continue. They sailed north along the coast for two more weeks and then landed on an island now known as Prince of Wales Island, near the southern tip of Alaska. Bodega explored every inlet and bay he could find, searching for the **Northwest Passage.**

The *Sonora* entered a calm bay of warmer water. Bodega thought that the water was warmed by the glowing volcanoes that could be seen from the ship at night. He claimed the bay for Spain and named it for Antonio Bucareli, the **viceroy** of **New Spain.** He headed north again, but he soon turned back because five men had scurvy. By the time the *Sonora* reached Monterey Bay in California a month later, every man on board had become ill. Bodega and his crew were nursed back to health by Spanish priests.

Sailing North Again

Four years later, Bodega served as second-in-command of a new expedition to the north. The Spanish had learned that the British captain James COOK would be arriving in the northwest Pacific Ocean. The Spanish ships were sent to warn Cook away from Spanish territory and also to find out how far the Russians had expanded into Alaska.

The Spaniards left San Blas in February 1779 and arrived in May at Bucareli Sound. They explored the area for a month and then sailed north. In Alaska the party went ashore near what is now Prince William Sound and claimed the land for Spain. It was the northernmost territory that Spain would ever claim in the Americas. Heavy rains, several cases of scurvy, and seven deaths forced the explorers to return to San Blas.

Bodega continued to serve Spain in North America. He commanded the Nootka settlement off the coast of what is now called Vancouver Island. He oversaw exploration of the nearby coast, continuing the search for the Northwest Passage. He was still in command in 1792 when Captain George VANCOUVER came to reclaim British land from Spain. Although Spain eventually lost its hold on the Alaskan and Canadian coastlines, Bodega's work long delayed that day. Throughout his career, he was a courageous explorer who faced many dangers to carry out orders.

Suggested Reading Warren L. Cook, *Flood Tide of Empire: Spain and the Pacific Northwest, 1543-1819* (Yale University Press, 1973).

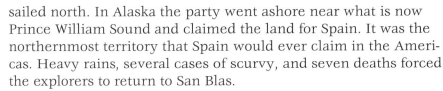

Bonneville, Benjamin Louis Eulalie de

American
b April 14,1796; Paris, France
d June 12, 1878; Fort Smith, Arkansas
Explored American West

Benjamin Bonneville claimed that he explored the West to seek his fortune in the fur trade, but he may have been a spy for the U.S. government.

Captain Benjamin Louis Eulalie de Bonneville traveled widely over the Rocky Mountains and beyond. He did not discover any new territory, but his research added greatly to the United States government's knowledge of the West. Although he claimed to be a fur trapper, many historians suggest that he was actually a spy. In any case, Bonneville was an important figure who helped open the Rockies and California to American settlers.

Businessman or Spy?

When he was a boy, his family moved from France to the United States. He graduated from the U.S. Military Academy at West Point at age 19. For the next several years, he served on the frontier at two army posts in what are now the states of Arkansas and Oklahoma. He also became interested in the fur trade. In 1830 he requested a leave of absence from the army, saying that he wanted to travel west and try his luck at trapping furs. He easily found wealthy people who loaned him money to help him start his new business.

Bonneville's true reasons for going west are one of the unsolved mysteries of American history. Perhaps he really did want to get rich in the fur trade. Some historians, however, claim that Bonneville was a spy for the U.S. government. Much of the territory he explored was also claimed by Great Britain. The army had granted him a leave of absence but had also given him detailed instructions as to what he was to do in that time.

Bonneville was ordered to explore the country as far as the Rocky Mountains and the territory beyond. He was to study the soil, mineral deposits, natural history, and climate of the lands he explored. He was also to observe the Indian tribes, noting opportunities for trade, the number of warriors in each tribe, and their methods of warfare. In sum, his mission was to gather any information that might help the United States expand westward.

Western Trails

On May 1, 1832, Bonneville led a caravan of wagons with 110 men out of Fort Osage, Missouri. They headed through the South Pass in the Rockies and arrived at the Green River. It was the first time that wagons had come so far west. Bonneville immediately built a fort as his headquarters. Other fur trappers called the fort "Bonneville's Folly." They knew that it was too far north to be useful for trapping in winter—or even late fall and early spring. However, the fort was in a good place for watching who came and went through the Rockies. The location of Bonneville's fort supports the theory that he was a spy.

During his first winter, Bonneville and his men set traps near the Snake and Salmon Rivers with little success. The next summer, he sent his field commander, Joseph Reddeford WALKER, with about 50 men to explore land west of the Great Salt Lake. It is not known whether Walker had orders to reach the west coast of California, but he did end up at the Pacific Ocean. The trail Walker blazed would later be the main route for settlers going to California.

Bonneville himself made two expeditions to the Columbia River, which runs through present-day Washington and Oregon. He may have been trying to find out more about the British settlements in that area. Both times the British at Fort Walla Walla forced him to turn back. He also sent a party into the northern Rockies to contact the Crow Indians. Just before leaving the West, he himself made a lengthy tour of Crow territory.

Surprise and Success

After three years in the Rockies, Bonneville returned to the East. He was surprised to find that he had been discharged from the army for staying in the West longer than his leave of absence allowed. He had sent a letter asking for more time, but the letter never made it to Washington. President Andrew Jackson personally made sure that Bonneville was readmitted to the army. Bonneville later served in the Mexican War and retired with the rank of brigadier general.

Although he failed to make any money from his fur trapping, Benjamin Bonneville's time in the West was well spent. His report to the government gave detailed information on each of the subjects he had been asked to investigate. It was thought to be one of the best intelligence reports ever written about the West.

Suggested Reading Washington Irving, *The Adventures of Captain Bonneville* (Twayne, 1977); Edith Haroldsen Lovell, *Benjamin Bonneville: Soldier of the American Frontier* (Horizon, 1992).

Boone, Daniel

American
b November 2, 1734; Pennsylvania
d September 26, 1820; Missouri
Explored Kentucky

Daniel Boone may be the most famous pioneer in the history of the American frontier. He was a skilled woodsman who was never happier than when he was alone in the wilderness. Yet he devoted himself to helping others settle lands west of the British colonies that would soon become the United States. His greatest achievement was to blaze the Wilderness Road to Kentucky through the Cumberland Gap, a pass in the Appalachian Mountains.

Daniel Boone defended early settlements in Kentucky from Indian attacks. He was captured by the Shawnee in 1778, but he managed to escape.

The Call of Bluegrass Country

Boone fought for the British during the French and Indian War, which lasted from 1754 to 1763. A fellow soldier named John Finley told him about a fertile bluegrass region west of the Appalachian Mountains. In the winter of 1767 to 1768, Boone tried and failed to reach bluegrass country from his home in Yadkin County, North Carolina. The next winter, Finley arrived in Yadkin County, and the two friends planned a spring expedition through the Cumberland Gap with four other men. This trip was a success. The travelers camped by a small creek near the edge of the bluegrass plain. By day they hunted and explored, and by night they read *Gulliver's Travels* by the British writer Jonathan Swift.

Unfortunately, one member of the party was killed by Indians. Boone refused to leave the plain, but the others returned to North Carolina before the end of the year. Boone's brother Squire came for several visits. During his time alone, Daniel explored the Kentucky and Licking River valleys. After two years, he packed up his furs and headed home. He was passing through the Cumberland Gap when a band of Cherokee Indians stole his supplies and every fur that he had collected during the last two years. It was neither the first nor the last time he would encounter conflict with Indians.

The Wilderness Road

In 1773 Boone attempted to lead seven families, including his own, through the Cumberland Gap into Kentucky. They were ambushed by Indians. Boone's son and five other members of the party were killed in the attack. Boone wanted to press on toward Kentucky, but the other survivors persuaded him to end the expedition and turn back.

Two years later, a man named Judge Henderson bought land from the Cherokee through an illegal treaty. He planned to sell the land to settlers. He hired Boone and 28 other men to mark a trail across Cherokee territory to the Cumberland Gap and into Kentucky. This trail was the famous Wilderness Road. On the south bank of the Kentucky River, Boone and his men built a few crude cabins. This settlement grew to become Boonesborough, the first white settlement in Kentucky.

Boone later found that Kentucky was getting too crowded for him, so he moved on. He settled first in what is now West Virginia and then in Spanish territory in what is now Missouri. He died there in 1820. Since then many myths and legends have grown up around his life. What is certain is that his love of the wilderness was unmatched. Without him, the first settlements in Kentucky would probably not have survived.

Suggested Reading John Bakeless, *Daniel Boone* (William Morrow, 1939); Lawrence Elliot, *The Long Hunter: A New Life of Daniel Boone* (Reader's Digest Press, 1976); Timothy Flint, *The Life and Adventures of Daniel Boone* (U. P. James, 1958).

Borchgrevink, Carstens Egeberg

Norwegian
b December 1, 1864; Oslo, Norway
d April 21, 1934; Oslo, Norway
Explored Antarctica

surveyor one who makes precise measurements of a location's geography

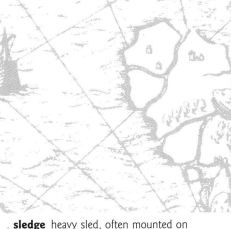

sledge heavy sled, often mounted on runners, that is pulled over snow or ice

Carstens Egeberg Borchgrevink was one of the first people to set foot on the mainland of Antarctica. He later led the first expedition to spend a winter on that frozen continent. His stay set the stage for a new period of Antarctic exploration. Teams of scientists and explorers learned to work there all year round.

In just four years, Borchgrevink went from being an unknown language teacher and **surveyor** in Australia to leading a major expedition. In 1894 he quit his job to follow his dream of going to Antarctica. He volunteered to serve on the *Antarctic,* a Norwegian whaling ship. A party landed on the shore of Antarctica, near Cape Adare in Victoria Land. They were the first people known to have set foot on the mainland. They were astonished to find plants in this frozen world. Borchgrevink was determined to return to the harbor with a team of scientists.

Penniless, he managed to raise money for a trip to London, where a conference on geography was to be held. Although he was neither famous nor experienced, he gave a passionate speech that caused a stir of excitement. He was soon sharing his plans with the leaders of the conference. But he did not realize that he had offended the president of the conference, who was also planning an Antarctic expedition. Unwilling to be upstaged, the president opposed Borchgrevink's plans. Luckily, a British newspaper saw a good story and offered to pay for Borchgrevink's voyage.

The Long Winter

In December 1898, the 34-year-old Norwegian set sail from an island south of Australia on the *Southern Cross.* The ship arrived off Cape Adare two months later. The team members built a house on the shore, and the ship left them to spend the winter in the most severe climate in the world. Borchgrevink's nine-person staff included experts on magnetism, weather, and natural science. Two men from Finland were in charge of a team of **sledge** dogs. Borchgrevink climbed to the highest point on the cape and studied the area in detail. After nearly a year, the *Southern Cross* returned. With new supplies, a sledge party was sent across the Ross Ice Shelf. The scientists gathered much useful information. Even more important, Borchgrevink had proved that it was physically possible to spend the winter in Antarctica. Within the next 10 years, explorers such as Robert Falcon SCOTT and Ernest SHACKLETON were doing just that.

Suggested Reading C. E. Borchgrevink, *First on the Antarctic Continent: Being an Account of the British Antarctic Expedition, 1898-1900* (C. Hurst and Company, 1992).

Bougainville, Louis-Antoine de

French
b November 12, 1729; Paris, France
d August 31, 1811; Paris, France
Sailed around world; explored Pacific Ocean

Louis-Antoine de Bougainville led the first French expedition to **circumnavigate** the globe. His voyage took place soon after the Seven Years' War with Britain. France was discouraged after losing its colonies in Canada and India to the British. Bougainville boosted French spirits by exploring, charting, and claiming islands in the South Pacific Ocean.

He was the son of a lawyer in Paris and studied law as a young man. His real interests, though, were mathematics and science. A

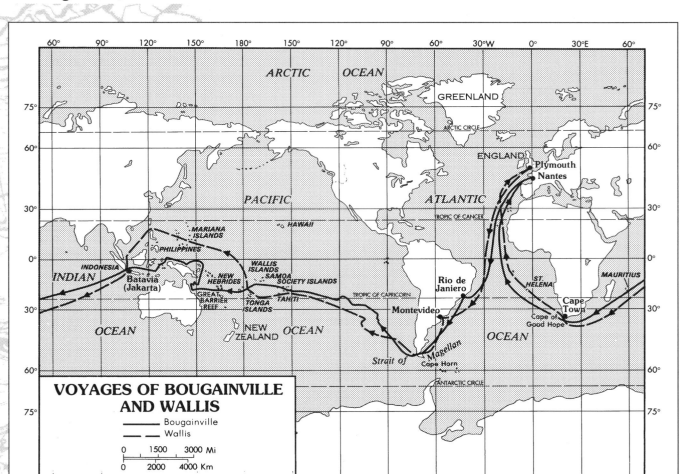

VOYAGES OF BOUGAINVILLE AND WALLIS

——— Bougainville
- - - Wallis

0   1500   3000 Mi
0   2000   4000 Km

France's Louis-Antoine de Bougainville and Britain's Samuel WALLIS both commanded voyages around the world in the 1760s.

circumnavigate to travel around

aide-de-camp assistant to a high-ranking military officer

botanist scientist who studies plants

scurvy disease caused by a lack of vitamin C and once a major cause of death among sailors; symptoms include internal bleeding, loosened teeth, and extreme fatigue

mathematical paper he wrote was well received, and he was elected to the British Royal Society. In 1756, during the Seven Years' War, Bougainville served in Canada as **aide-de-camp** to a general. When he returned to France, he searched for a new way to serve his country. He decided to explore the Pacific Ocean for new islands. As a first step, he started a French settlement in the Falkland Islands (also called the Malvinas), off the southeast coast of South America. The British and Spanish governments saw the colony as a threat and asked King Louis XV of France to abandon it. Louis backed down, and the Spanish refunded Bougainville the money he had spent to establish the colony.

Around the World

In 1766 King Louis sent Bougainville on a voyage through the Pacific Ocean and around the world. Bougainville had no formal training as a sea captain, but he had learned a great deal while crossing the Atlantic Ocean during the war. He hired skilled men to serve as second-in-command, pilot, and **botanist.** Two ships set sail from Nantes, France. They stopped in South America and formally gave up the colony in the Falklands. Then they sailed west around Cape Horn into the Pacific Ocean.

The crews endured foul weather and **scurvy** until they found a safe harbor on the island of Tahiti. Although Bougainville knew that he was not the first European to reach Tahiti, he claimed the island for France. He also took a guest on board, Ahu-toru, the son of a Tahitian chief. After 12 days on Tahiti, the French sailed on. Supplies ran so low that the sailors had to eat the rats that lived on board. With a sick and starving crew, Bougainville decided to avoid the dangerous Australian coast, passing up the chance to claim Australia for France. Meanwhile, it was discovered that the botanist's chief assistant was a woman named Jeanne Baret disguised as a man. Baret may have been the first woman to sail around the world.

Public Success

After charting the Solomon Islands and picking up supplies in the Dutch East Indies, the two ships arrived in France. In over two years, only nine men out of 200 had died, an impressively low number for that time. Ahu-toru, who had been eager to visit France, created a public sensation on his arrival. Bougainville himself became a popular hero, and his book, *Voyage Around the World,* was widely read.

In 1772 Bougainville became secretary to Louis XV and commanded the French fleet that helped the Americans during their revolution against the British. An island and a strait in the South Pacific bear his name, as does Bougainvillea, a South American plant that he introduced to Europe.

Suggested Reading David Hammond, *News from New Cythera: A Report of Bougainville's Voyage 1766-69* (Minnesota University Press, 1970); Maurice Thiery, *Bougainville: Soldier and Sailor* (Grayson and Grayson, 1932).

After long service to France, Louis-Antoine de Bougainville made scientific studies at his estate and was honored by Emperor Napoleon I.

Boyd, Louise Arner

American
b September 16, 1887; San Rafael, California
d September 14, 1972; San Francisco, California
Explored Greenland

For her Arctic rescue work, Louise Boyd was awarded Norway's Chevalier Cross of the Order of Saint Olav and France's Cross of the Legion of Honor.

Louise Arner Boyd was a highly respected leader of expeditions to the Arctic. A wealthy heiress, she used her money to break into a scientific world that was dominated by men. Boyd began as a tourist but became an expert on the geography and natural history of Greenland. She was also a skilled photographer and the first woman to fly over the North Pole.

The Lure of the Arctic

Boyd inherited her family's fortune in 1920. Four years later, without any special purpose in life, she took a summer cruise to the Arctic on a Norwegian tour boat. It was on this cruise that she first felt what she called the "Arctic lure." Her second trip was just as lighthearted as the first. She passed her time hunting polar bears and taking photographs.

Boyd soon had a chance to work with "real" explorers, as she called them. Back in the Arctic in 1928, she had intended to do more hunting, but an emergency changed her plans. The **dirigible** flown by the Italian Umberto NOBILE went down in the Arctic Ocean. During a rescue attempt, the famous Norwegian explorer Roald AMUNDSEN disappeared. Boyd joined the international search for Amundsen and his plane, working closely with members of his earlier expeditions for four months. Though Nobile was rescued, Amundsen was never found. By the time the searchers gave up, Boyd was determined to become an Arctic explorer herself.

dirigible large aircraft filled with a lighter-than-air gas that keeps it aloft; similar to a blimp but with a rigid frame

fjord narrow inlet where the sea meets the shore between steep cliffs

For Science and Country

In 1931 she made the first of four important scientific studies in the Greenland **fjord** named after Franz Josef, a former emperor of Austria. Her writings and photographs greatly impressed the American Geographical Society, which funded her work. During World War II, Greenland became an important area, and the U.S. War Department recruited Boyd as an adviser.

In 1955 Boyd became the first woman to fly over the North Pole. She was also the first woman elected to the council of the American Geographical Society in 1960. She succeeded brilliantly as a woman working in a world of men.

Suggested Reading Louise Boyd, *The Coast of Northeast Greenland, with Hydrographic Studies in the Greenland Sea* (American Geographical Society, 1948) and *The Fjord Region of East Greenland* (American Geographical Society, 1935).

Brandon. See *Brendan*.

Brazza, Pierre-Paul-François-Camille Savorgnan de

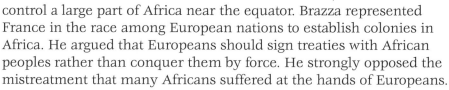

Italian-French
b January 25, 1852; Rome, Italy
d September 14, 1905; Dakar, Senegal
Explored central Africa

Pierre Savorgnan de Brazza spent most of his adult life in central Africa, working to protect the rights of Africans in the French colonies he had helped to create.

Thanks to the explorations of Count Pierre Savorgnan de Brazza, France came to control a large part of Africa near the equator. Brazza represented France in the race among European nations to establish colonies in Africa. He argued that Europeans should sign treaties with African peoples rather than conquer them by force. He strongly opposed the mistreatment that many Africans suffered at the hands of Europeans.

Competition in the Congo

An Italian noble by birth, Brazza studied at France's naval academy and served in the French navy. He later became a citizen of France. In 1874, while stationed in Gabon on the west coast of Africa, Brazza received permission to explore the Ogowe River. He discovered the Ogowe's source, and with the help of the friendly Bateke tribe, he almost reached the Congo River. Attacks by cannibals in the region forced him to turn back in 1878. Later that year, Brazza was outraged to learn that Henry Morton STANLEY had succeeded in traveling down the Congo. Brazza returned to France and asked the government to fund another trip. The French agreed when they realized that Belgium had hired Stanley to colonize the area.

Brazza returned to Gabon, traveled up the Ogowe, and stopped at the village of Mbe. During his monthlong stay, he convinced the Bateke ruler to sign a treaty that placed the Bateke kingdom under French control. The Bateke allowed Brazza to build a fort in Mbe, which later became known as Brazzaville, the capital of the Republic of the Congo.

The Dark Side of Colonial Rule

Thanks in part to Brazza's explorations, France created a large colonial empire in central Africa. Brazza remained there as a French governor. He stirred up controversy by exposing the way

Ancient Times
and
Middle Ages

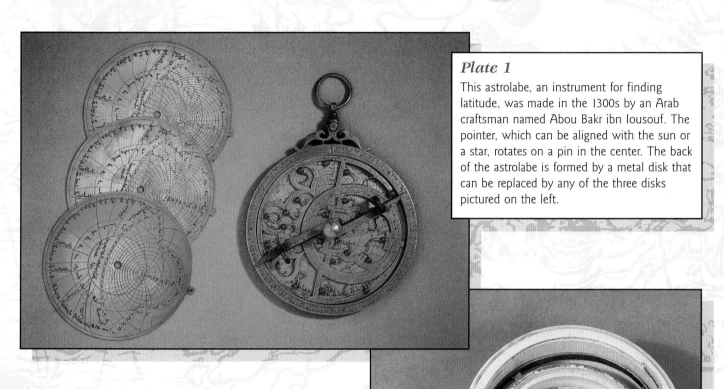

Plate 1
This astrolabe, an instrument for finding latitude, was made in the 1300s by an Arab craftsman named Abou Bakr ibn Iousouf. The pointer, which can be aligned with the sun or a star, rotates on a pin in the center. The back of the astrolabe is formed by a metal disk that can be replaced by any of the three disks pictured on the left.

Plate 2
Navigators have used compasses as the principal instruments for determining direction since the 1200s. The first compasses were probably just pieces of lodestone, a mineral that aligns itself with the earth's magnetic field. The mariner's compass consisted of a magnetized needle stuck through a piece of wood, cork, or straw. An ivory case houses this Italian mariner's compass dating from the 1500s.

Plate 3

Phoenicians were among the greatest mariners, explorers, and traders of the ancient world. This relief sculpture, dating from between 721 B.C. and 705 B.C., depicts ancient Phoenician sailors hauling cargoes of timber on galleys.

Plate 4

This mosaic from the early 500s, found in a cathedral in Ravenna, Italy, shows ancient Roman sailing vessels. The ships, with single masts and square sails, carried Roman merchants and soldiers throughout the Mediterranean Sea.

Plate 5

Arab merchants and sailors of the 700s and 800s used a type of ship called a dhow. These ships carried exotic items such as cloves, pepper, silks, and tea—goods that later attracted Europeans to the region.

Plate 6

A port city welcomes the fleet of the emperor Yang Di, who ruled China in the early 600s. In this Chinese painting, the ships, known as junks, display common features including tall sterns, ornate figureheads, and rectangular sails made of fiber mats.

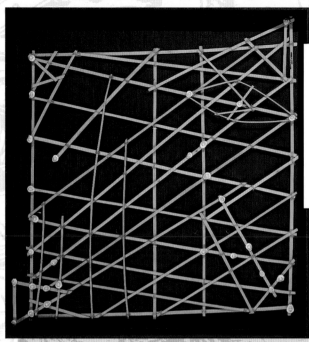

Plate 7

Long before the arrival of European explorers, people sailed across the vast expanses of the Pacific Ocean. Some charted its widely scattered island chains. Maps made by the people of the Marshall Islands had grids formed of straight sticks. Curved sticks represented wave swells, and small shells showed the locations of islands.

Plate 8

This map appears in an English book of Psalms from the early 1200s. Its "T-and-O" organization places Asia at the top, Europe at bottom left, and Africa at bottom right. Such maps often had a religious, symbolic purpose.

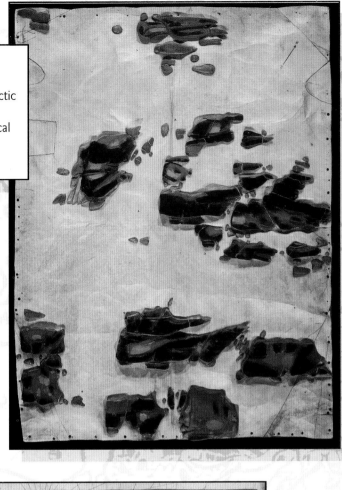

Plate 9

The Inuit people of northern Canada made three-dimensional maps of islands in the Arctic Ocean. They affixed pieces of fur or carved driftwood to sealskin. The Inuit's geographical knowledge was crucial to the survival and success of European explorers in the Arctic.

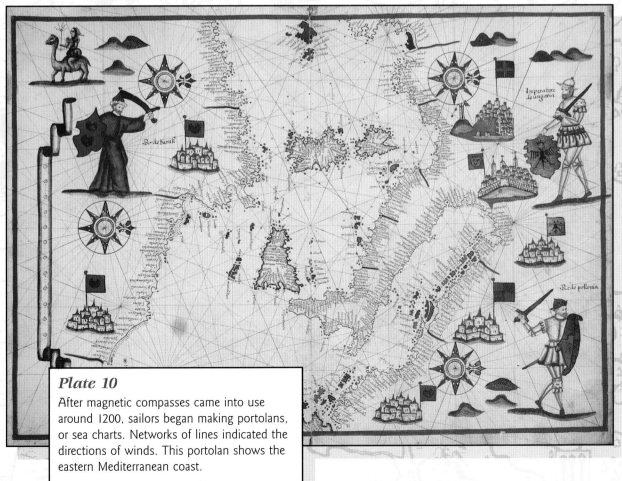

Plate 10

After magnetic compasses came into use around 1200, sailors began making portolans, or sea charts. Networks of lines indicated the directions of winds. This portolan shows the eastern Mediterranean coast.

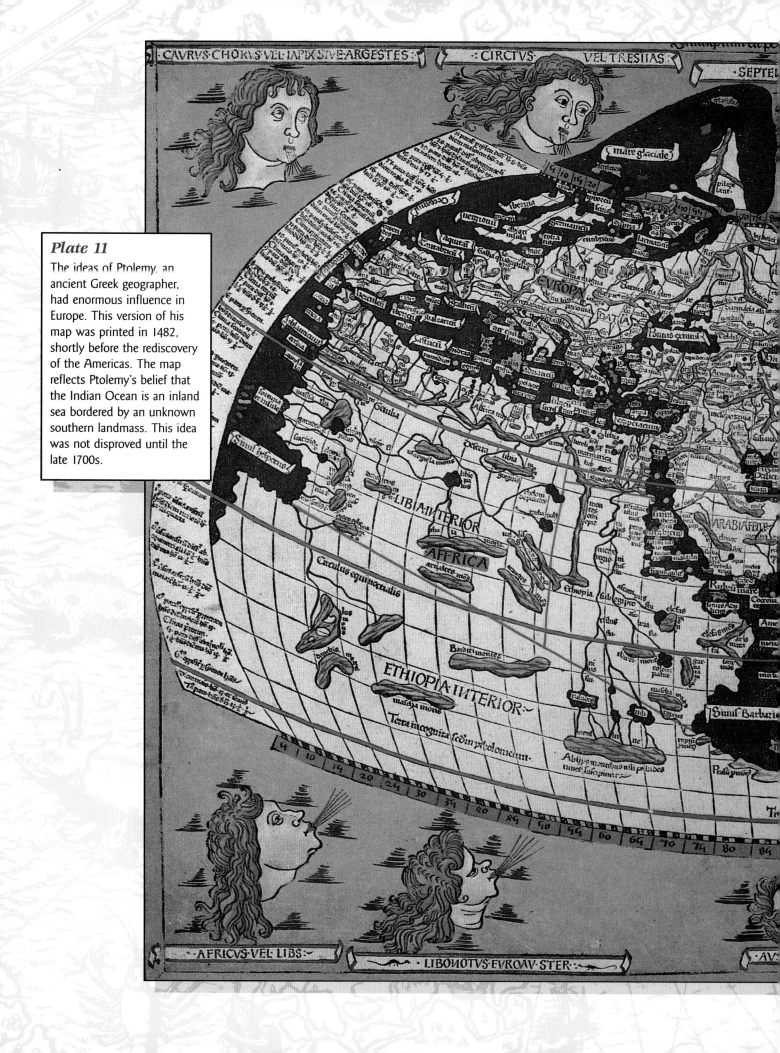

Plate 11

The ideas of Ptolemy, an ancient Greek geographer, had enormous influence in Europe. This version of his map was printed in 1482, shortly before the rediscovery of the Americas. The map reflects Ptolemy's belief that the Indian Ocean is an inland sea bordered by an unknown southern landmass. This idea was not disproved until the late 1700s.

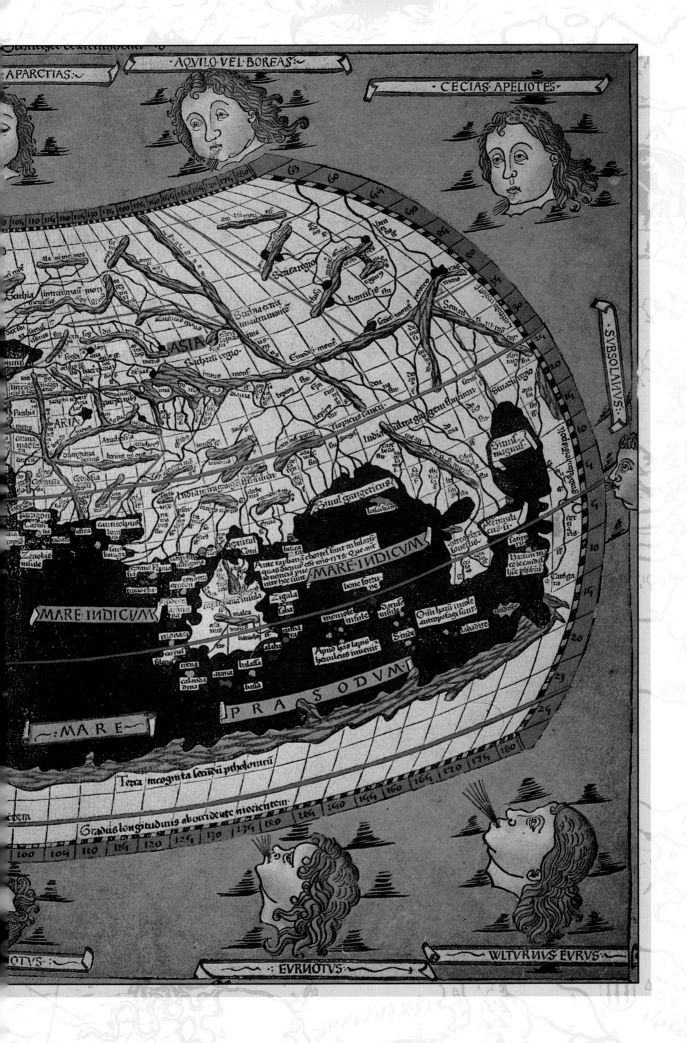

Plate 12

In the imaginations of medieval Europeans, the far reaches of the globe were populated by strange creatures, including humans with monstrous deformities. This image is a detail of a French illustration from about 1460.

Plate 13

The story of the Polo family's journey through Asia in the late 1200s was very popular in medieval Europe and inspired much exploration in the following centuries. This illustration of the Polo family decorated a manuscript produced in 1375.

Plate 14

According to legend, an Irish abbot named Brendan, who lived in the A.D. 500s, may have been the first European to reach North America. This colored woodcut shows Brendan and several other monks on a missionary voyage, with a sea monster lurking near their boat.

French soldiers and officials abused the rights of Africans. The French government began to work on reforms, but Brazza died before he could see these take effect.

Suggested Reading Jean Carbonnier, *Congo Explorer, Pierre Savorgnan de Brazza* (Scribner, 1960); Richard West, *Brazza of the Congo: European Exploration and Exploitation in French Equatorial Africa* (Victorian Book Club, 1973).

Brendan

Irish
b between 484 and 489?; Tralee, Ireland
d between 577 and 583?; ?
May have reached the Americas

This map illustrates part of the tale of Saint Brendan's voyage, in which the monks built an altar to God on the back of a whale.

Brendan, later called Saint Brendan, became a Christian monk in 512 and founded several monasteries. He himself headed the Clonfert monastery in Galway, Ireland. Centuries later, Brendan became associated in legend with at least one fantastic ocean voyage. Some historians believe that Brendan and several other monks, or other Irish explorers of his time, may have been the first Europeans to reach the Americas.

A book was written in the 800s called *Navigatio Sancti Brendani,* which means, in Latin, "The Voyage of Saint Brendan." According to this book, Brendan and 17 other monks made a sea journey in a 30-foot-long boat made of animal skins. They were searching for a mythical place called the Saints' Promised Land, which they believed was in the Atlantic Ocean.

On their journey, Brendan and his monks came to several islands, which may have been the Outer Hebrides and the Faeroes, north of Ireland. They crossed a spot where the sea resembled a "thick, curdled mass." This may be history's first description of seaweed in the Sargasso Sea. Eventually they reached large, flat islands in clear water, possibly the Bahamas. One monk was left behind

there as a missionary. They also found a "fragrant island of mountains" which may have been Jamaica. Brendan and his crew sailed north to a large continent and then returned to Ireland.

"St. Brendan's Isle" remained on many maps until as late as 1759, although mapmakers could not agree on its location. Known also as Brendan the Voyager, Brendan is considered the patron saint of sailors.

Suggested Reading Geoffrey Ashe, *Land to the West: St. Brendan's Voyage to America* (Collins, 1962); Timothy Severin, *The Brendan Voyage* (McGraw-Hill, 1978); George Simms, *Brendan the Voyager* (O'Brien, 1989).

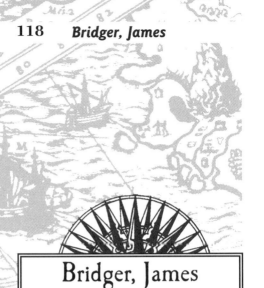

Bridger, James

American
b March 17, 1804; Richmond, Virginia
d July 17, 1881; Washington, Missouri
Explored American West

surveyor one who makes precise measurements of a location's geography

Many tales and legends surround the adventures of Jim Bridger, Mountain Man of the American West.

The exploration of the American West was carried out in part by a loosely knit group known as the Mountain Men. These rough and ready trailblazers pushed west of the Mississippi River in the early 1800s in search of beaver furs, which were in great demand. Jim Bridger was one of the first and best-known of the Mountain Men. He spent much time among Indians, and over the course of his life, he married three Indian women. He learned a great deal from the western tribes about local geography and wildlife, and he put this knowledge to use as a guide for many travelers. In so doing, he helped open the West to other Americans, who settled the lands he had explored.

An Orphan on the Frontier
Jim Bridger spent the first years of his life in Virginia, where his father was an innkeeper and **surveyor.** The frontier appealed to many Americans in the early 1800s, and in 1812 Bridger's father moved the family to a farm near St. Louis, Missouri. The move did not turn out well. Within a year, every member of the family except Jim was dead. Now an orphan, the nine-year-old boy went to work for a blacksmith in St. Louis.

When Jim was 18, he heard about an advertisement that called for "enterprising young men" to follow the Missouri River to its source and work there as fur trappers. The ad had been placed by the lieutenant governor of Missouri, General William Henry ASHLEY. Like other Americans, Ashley was eager to take part in the profitable trade that Canadian fur trappers had already established west of the Mississippi River. The United States had bought the region from France in 1803, and Meriwether LEWIS and William CLARK had explored it. Their glowing reports encouraged other adventurers to go west.

Adventures in the Rockies
Bridger signed on with Ashley's venture and was soon on his way up the Missouri River. The trip was an eventful one. Another trapper, Hugh Glass, was savagely attacked by a grizzly bear. According to some sources, Bridger was one of two men assigned to bury their companion. Bridger and the other man did not bury Glass but simply took his rifle. Luckily,

it turned out that Glass was not dead after all. Despite his horrible injuries, he managed to crawl many miles to a fort, where he regained his health.

Another story involving Bridger is set in the winter of 1824 to 1825, when he and another of Ashley's men reached the shore of the Great Salt Lake, in what is now Utah. Upon tasting the water and finding it salty, Bridger mistakenly thought that he had arrived at the Pacific Ocean. For years Bridger was credited with being the first person, other than Indians, to see the Great Salt Lake. Although historians now believe that others probably came across the lake before him, his name is still linked to its discovery.

"Old Gabe" the Mountain Man

Bridger's first trip into the West introduced him to a land and a way of life that he made his own. From then on, he spent much of his time exploring and guiding others through the territory now occupied by the states of Montana, Idaho, Utah, Wyoming, North Dakota, and South Dakota.

In the 20 years following the Ashley expedition, Bridger supported himself by trapping and trading furs. For a time, he and some partners owned a trading company. He attended many rendezvous, the rowdy annual gatherings of fur trappers that were part business meeting and part festival. His fellow Mountain Men called him "Old Gabe" and knew him as a skilled frontiersman and an inspired teller of tall tales. They scoffed at his wild stories about a strange land of multicolored fountains and odd-smelling springs. But Bridger's account proved to be accurate when other explorers followed his trail to what is now Yellowstone National Park.

Opening the Way to the West

By the early 1840s, few beaver were left to be trapped, and the demand for beaver hats in Europe had ended. But the number of people heading west for other reasons was increasing, and Bridger saw a new opportunity to make a living. He and a partner sold supplies and services to these travelers at a fort and trading post on the Green River in southwestern Wyoming. Fort Bridger became a landmark of the Oregon Trail and a gateway to the West. Travelers who passed through included the explorers John Charles FRÉMONT and Benjamin BONNEVILLE, as well as Brigham Young, leader of a new religious group known as the Mormons. After the Mormons settled near the Great Salt Lake, Bridger came into conflict with them and was forced to surrender his fort to them.

Bridger retired to a farm he had bought in Missouri. He seems to have missed the mountain life, and he soon returned to the West as a guide. One of his missions was to lead U.S. Army troops to the Salt Lake region, where they fought with the Mormons. The army took control of Fort Bridger and used it as a post until 1890. Bridger was also employed by mapmakers and surveyors and by army units that protected shipments of mail. He finally retired in 1868 and spent his final years on his farm, ill and blind.

During his time in the West, Bridger's knowledge and skills won him great fame. An official of the Montana Historical Society wrote in 1900,

"James Bridger was the Daniel BOONE of the Rocky Mountains . . . yet most of his life history is lost to us. We obtain glimpses of him here and there, but the many eventful scenes of his life are now forever lost."

Suggested Reading J. Cecil Alter, *Jim Bridger* (University of Oklahoma Press, 1962); Gene Caesar, *King of the Mountain Men: The Life of Jim Bridger* (Dutton, 1961); Clide Hollman, *Jim Bridger, King of Scouts* (Vantage, 1953); William Luce, *Jim Bridger, Man of the Mountains* (Chelsea Juniors, 1992); Dan Zadra, *Jim Bridger: The Mountain Man* (Creative Education, 1988).

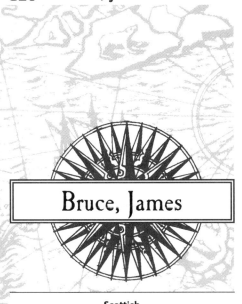

Bruce, James

Scottish
b December 14, 1730; Stirling, Scotland
d April 27, 1794; Stirling, Scotland
Explored Blue Nile River

tributary stream or river that flows into a larger stream or river

headwaters source of a river

James Bruce's tales of war in Abyssinia were so shocking that many people in Britain doubted his claim to have found the source of the Nile River.

From the first time he visited Africa, James Bruce had one goal as an explorer: to find the source of the Nile River. This river, the longest in the world, has two main **tributaries,** the White Nile and the Blue Nile. When Bruce reached the **headwaters** of the Blue Nile, he rejoiced in his success, but in fact the Nile River's source is at the head of the White Nile. Still, Bruce's exploration of the Blue Nile stands out as an impressive feat.

Tragedy Strikes Early

Bruce came from a wealthy Scottish family. As a young man, he studied both law and medicine, but a severe illness forced him to give up his studies. After he recovered, he married the daughter of a Scottish wine merchant and joined her family's business. His wife died just one year later, and the grieving Bruce left Scotland to cope with his loss.

He visited Spain and Portugal and studied a number of languages, including Arabic. In 1758, his father died. Bruce inherited a large sum of money and decided to continue traveling. First, however, he served in the British military. The British government then made him a diplomat in Algiers, a North African city on the Mediterranean Sea. Bruce's fascination with Africa deepened. Two years later, he traveled to Egypt to make plans for the journey he dreamed of, an expedition up the Blue Nile.

River, Desert, and War

Bruce left Cairo in 1768 with about 20 men. They sailed up the river to Aswan, then crossed the Eastern Desert to Abyssinia (modern-day Ethiopia), where Bruce believed that he would find the source of the Blue Nile. The expedition arrived at the Abyssinian capital of Gondar to find a country torn by civil war. The party's survival depended on the good will of the emperor of Abyssinia. By the end of 1770, Bruce reached Lake Tana, the source of the Blue Nile. He believed that he had succeeded where others had failed for centuries. He wrote: "I triumphed here, in my own mind, over kings and their armies." But he still faced a difficult return trip. He arrived in Cairo only after another year in Abyssinia and a 20-day trip across the desert of Sudan.

Doubts and Attacks at Home

When he returned to Britain, Bruce found that many people did not believe his written account of the journey. He was a colorful writer and displayed a high opinion of himself. Some critics charged that everything he had written was a lie.

Frustrated and disgusted, Bruce returned to his family's home in Scotland. He married again, but this marriage also ended in the death of his wife. Bruce spent his time compiling the writings and drawings from his trip. A five-volume work was published in 1790. The book became very popular, especially after later explorers confirmed much of what he wrote. Soon after, Bruce died of a fall down the front steps of his manor.

Suggested Reading James Macarthur Reid, *Traveller Extraordinary, the Life of James Bruce of Kinnaird* (Norton, 1968).

Brulé, Etienne

French
b 1592?; Champigny-sur-Marne?, France
d June 1632?; Huron lands near the Great Lakes
***Explored Great Lakes, Susquehanna River,
and Chesapeake Bay***

Etienne Brulé may have been the first European to explore four of the five Great Lakes.

Since Etienne Brulé produced no written record of his explorations, much of his life remains a mystery. It is known, however, that he lived among the Huron Indians for many years. He also traveled the length of the Susquehanna River, so that he was probably the first European to set foot in what is now Pennsylvania. According to the reports of other explorers, he may have also been the first European to see four of the five Great Lakes.

Brulé arrived in Québec, in French Canada, in 1608. Two years later, the French explorer and colonizer Samuel de CHAMPLAIN sent him to live among the Indians and learn their languages and customs. Brulé spent a year with the Algonquin in the Ottawa Valley and returned, Champlain wrote, "dressed like an Indian." It was only the beginning of Brulé's fascination with the Indian way of life.

Huron Country

Little is known about Brulé's travels between 1611 and 1615. He probably stayed with the Huron near Georgian Bay on the east side of Lake Huron. He is credited with being the first European to see that lake. In 1615 he served as Champlain's interpreter on a trip to Huron country. The French hoped to arrange fur trading with the Indians and to add new territory to the French Empire.

Champlain and his Huron allies prepared to attack the Iroquois near Oneida Lake. Meanwhile, Brulé went with a small party of Hurons to seek the support of the Andaste, a tribe in what is now the state of New York. The journey led around the west end of Lake Ontario, so it is likely that Brulé was the first European to see that lake as well.

Conflicts near the Great Lakes

When Brulé and the Andaste arrived at the Iroquois village that had been targeted for attack, Champlain was gone. He and the Huron had been defeated by the Iroquois and had left two days earlier. Brulé then returned to the Andaste village, near the source of the Susquehanna River. Always ready for adventure, he set out on his own to explore. He followed the Susquehanna south and eventually reached Chesapeake Bay. He explored the bay and some of its many islands. As he traveled back to Québec, he was captured by the Iroquois. The Indians tortured Brulé until a violent thunderstorm struck. Seeing the storm as an omen, the Iroquois allowed Brulé to leave.

In 1618 he met Champlain again and told him of his travels. Champlain urged him to continue exploring, so Brulé and another Frenchman named Grenolle explored the north shore of Lake Huron as far as Lake Superior. Some accounts say that several years later, Brulé was in the country of the Neutrals, a tribe of Indians who lived near Lake Erie. If Brulé really did visit the Neutrals, he was the first European to see Lake Erie.

In 1629 the British attacked the city of Québec. Brulé abandoned Champlain and joined the British, who may have lured him with money. After the French surrendered Québec, Brulé returned to Huron country. Sometime around 1632, for reasons that no one else ever learned, the Hurons killed and ate him. It was a strange end for a man who had admired the Huron culture and had adopted it so well.

Suggested Reading C. W. Butterfield, *History of Brulé's Discoveries and Explorations* (Helman-Taylor, 1898); James Herbert Cranston, *Etienne Brulé, Immortal Scoundrel* (Ryerson, 1949).

Bruni, Antoine Raymond Joseph de. See *Entrecasteaux, Antoine Raymond Joseph de Bruni d'.*

Burckhardt, Johann Ludwig

Swiss
b November 24, 1784; Lausanne, Switzerland
d October 15, 1817; Cairo, Egypt
Explored Arabian Peninsula and East Africa

Johann Ludwig Burckhardt was one of the first Europeans to combine the two careers of scholar and explorer. In the early 1800s, he made detailed studies of Muslim communities and cities in Arabia and traveled south along the Nile River. He learned about ancient cultures that were largely unknown—and even forbidden—to Europeans. Burckhardt was highly regarded by other explorers for the many facts he provided on obscure areas and customs of the Muslim world.

Burckhardt came from a wealthy Swiss family, but he spent much of his youth in Germany. He was an excellent student at German universities, where he studied science and languages. In 1806 he traveled to Britain, looking for work. Intrigued with the idea of visiting foreign lands, Burckhardt applied to the Association for Promoting the Discovery of the Interior Parts of Africa, known as the African Association. Its founder, Sir Joseph BANKS, hired Burckhardt to explore the Niger River and the city of Timbuktu in western Africa. Banks suggested that Burckhardt study the Arabic language before beginning his travels.

Studies Become an Obsession

Burckhardt's studies went far beyond what the African Association had expected. Determined to be an effective explorer, the dedicated young scholar spent more than four years in training. In Britain he

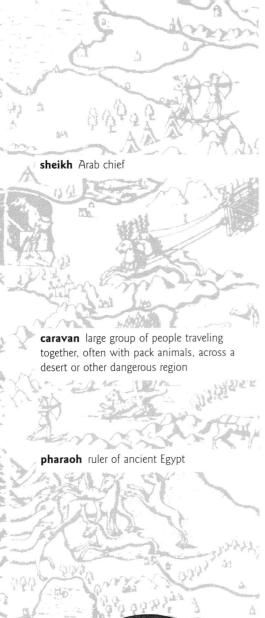

sheikh Arab chief

caravan large group of people traveling together, often with pack animals, across a desert or other dangerous region

pharaoh ruler of ancient Egypt

To travel in Muslim lands, the Swiss scholar Johann Ludwig Burckhardt disguised himself as Sheikh Ibrahim ibn Abdullah.

studied Arabic and researched Muslim culture. He walked barefoot, slept outdoors, and lived on a diet of vegetables and water. In early 1809, he traveled to Syria, where he continued to study the region's language and customs. He also created a disguise, pretending to be a **sheikh** named Ibrahim ibn Abdullah. Dressed in Arab clothing, he made three trial journeys in Syria before heading for Egypt in June 1812.

Burckhardt had planned to start from Cairo on his trip southwest to the Niger River and Timbuktu. Even before he reached Cairo, however, he changed his route. By now he was completely immersed in Muslim culture, and he wanted to learn more. He decided to visit Muslim cities that were closed to outsiders and became the first European since the Middle Ages to see Petra, a city in what is now Jordan. Arriving in Cairo later that year, he could not locate a **caravan** heading west and decided instead to follow the Nile River south.

Ancient Lands

Traveling by donkey, Burckhardt covered more than 1,000 miles and made one of his few actual discoveries. At the village of Abu Simbel in southern Egypt, he came upon the temples of Ramses II, a great **pharaoh.** The temples had been carved into the side of a cliff approximately 3,000 years before Burckhardt's visit. He was the first European traveler to see these impressive monuments since ancient times. Farther south, in the region of Nubia, Burckhardt found more temples and ruins. Taking detailed notes, he provided keen insights into the history and geography of this ancient region and its people. Although he admired the Nubians he met, he was also at risk among them. Their customs allowed robbers to take what they wanted from travelers—and kill those who refused to give up their valuables. Burckhardt had several narrow escapes.

The Swiss scholar developed an eye infection and had to stay in the area for several months to recover. In March 1814 he set out again, taking a caravan route south across the Nubian Desert and then continuing to follow the Nile River. He eventually turned east, reached the Red Sea, and sailed across it to Arabia.

Forbidden Cities

Arriving in the town of Jidda, Burckhardt wrote to the African Association to tell them of his detour. He planned to stay in Arabia until he could join the annual caravan from Cairo to the Niger River. He was anxious to explore the Muslim region known as the Hejaz. Its capital, Mecca, is the holiest city of Islam, and non-Muslims were forbidden to enter.

In his Egyptian disguise, Burckhardt visited Mecca and another holy city, Medina. His descriptions of those cities and their citizens were the most accurate yet written by a European. He returned to Cairo the following year to find that an epidemic of disease had broken out. He left quickly and headed east once again. This time he traveled to the Sinai Peninsula, where he studied manuscripts kept in a monastery at Mount Sinai.

dysentery disease that causes severe diarrhea

The Mission Uncompleted

In 1816 Burckhardt returned to Cairo to wait for the caravan to take him to Timbuktu. While he prepared for his journey, he came down with **dysentery** and died the following year. He was buried as Sheikh Ibrahim ibn Abdullah in a Muslim funeral. Although Burckhardt never made the expedition for which he had been hired, the African Association was impressed with the length and quality of his journals. He had written in great detail about the terrain, climate, people, and wildlife of the regions he had visited. Over the next few years, the association published his accounts. They were too scholarly to be popular with the general public, but they proved invaluable to later students of the Muslim world.

Suggested Reading Katherine Sim, *Desert Traveller: The Life of Jean Louis Burckhardt* (Victor Gollancz, 1969).

Burke, Robert O'Hara

Irish
b 1821; St. Clerans, Ireland
d June 28, 1861; Cooper's Creek, Australia
**Led Great Northern Exploration Expedition
across Australia**

Robert O'Hara Burke commanded perhaps the most tragic expedition in Australia's history. Burke had courage, but he was inexperienced and impatient. His first trip into Australia's barren interior was his last. However, he and William John WILLS did succeed in crossing the continent from south to north.

A Police Officer Enters History

Burke was born in Ireland and educated in Belgium. At the age of 20 he joined the army of Austria-Hungary, then one of Europe's most powerful nations. He achieved the rank of captain but then returned to Ireland and became a police officer. In 1853 he went to live in Tasmania, an island south of Australia, and soon moved to Melbourne, a city on the mainland. Burke served in Melbourne as a police sergeant and inspector.

In 1860 he was selected to lead an expedition across Australia from south to north. His sponsors wanted to build a telegraph line across the continent. Burke unfortunately lacked many of the qualities that explorers need. He was not a careful planner, and he had no real experience in the harsh Australian interior. But he did have the finest expedition money could buy. He left Melbourne with 18 men, 24 camels, 28 horses, and 21 tons of supplies. The camels were imported from India and were cared for by three handlers from Pakistan.

A stubborn and sometimes misguided man, Robert Burke (left) ignored the advice of the younger William Wills (right), a decision that led both to their deaths.

Early Troubles

At Menindee, some 400 miles north of Melbourne, Burke faced his first major problem. Tired of Burke's fiery temper, the group's second-in-command, camel master, and doctor all quit. Burke made William John Wills his new second-in-command. He then decided to leave most of his staff and supplies at Menindee and move quickly with just six men to Cooper's Creek, a river to the north. He instructed a guide, William Wright, to follow with the rest of the men and supplies.

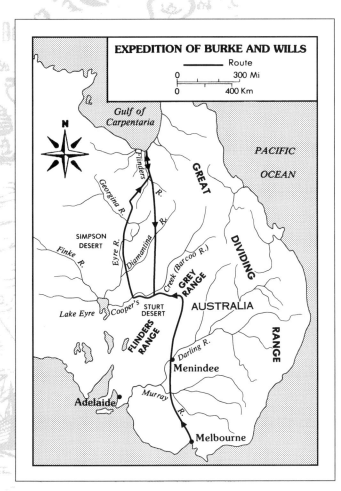

EXPEDITION OF BURKE AND WILLS

After crossing Australia, Burke and Wills became lost in the desert interior and never made it back to Melbourne.

---

depot place where supplies are stored

dysentery disease that causes severe diarrhea

When Burke reached Cooper's Creek, he set up a **depot.** He had planned to stay there until Wright arrived, but he became too impatient. Leaving William Brahe at the depot, Burke set out with Wills, John King, and Charles Gray. They took six camels, a horse, and supplies for 12 weeks. Brahe was told to wait three months for their return.

The Struggle North and South

The four explorers faced a brutal journey. They marched 12 hours a day for two months in searing heat. The temperature rose as high as 140 degrees Fahrenheit. They ate little along the way. Exhausted, the men finally reached the mouth of the Flinders River at the Gulf of Carpentaria. They never actually saw the Indian Ocean because wide marshes lay between them and the shore. But they were close enough to know that they had completed their mission. They began the return journey almost immediately.

The trek south was as wet as the trip north had been hot and dry. Burke, Wills, King, and Gray traveled slowly through heavy rains and lightning storms. Once they ran over a snake almost as thick as a log. They killed it and ate it. As they grew more desperate for food, the men had to eat their horse and two of their camels. When Gray came down with **dysentery,** the others thought that he was faking, but he died two weeks later.

The three remaining explorers spent a day burying their dead companion. That delay in their trip probably cost them their lives. When they arrived back at Cooper's Creek on April 21, the depot was deserted. William Brahe had left the camp earlier that day. He had headed back toward Menindee and had left some food and a note saying what route he was taking. Brahe was only about 14 miles away. Wills and King wanted to try to follow him, but Burke was sure that they could not catch up. Instead, Burke insisted on heading for Mount Hopeless, some 150 miles to the southwest, which was the nearest inhabited area.

The Last Journey

The three men headed southwest, but they soon lost their way and ended up wandering in circles. They were forced to eat nardoo, a type of grass seed, along with fish and rats. Each day the search for food became more difficult, and the men grew weaker. Burke and Wills died of starvation within two days of each other at the end of June 1861. King was found by a group of Aborigines, the people native to Australia. They cared for him until he was rescued by a search party. Back in Melbourne, the public was critical of Burke's foolish decisions. In later years, however, he and Wills were recognized for their bravery in reaching their goal. They had covered 1,500 miles and had established a land route across the continent.

Suggested Reading Tim Bonyhady, *Burke and Wills: From Melbourne to Myth* (David Ell, 1991); Max Colwell, *The Journey of Burke and Wills* (Hamlyn, 1971); Randal Flynn, *Burke and Wills, Crossing the Continent* (Macmillan Australia, 1991).

Burton, Richard Francis

English
b March 19, 1821; Torquay, England
d October 20, 1890; Trieste, Italy
*Explored Africa and Asia;
discovered Lake Tanganyika*

The explorer Richard Burton gained fame and notoriety for his translations of Eastern classics such as the *Arabian Nights* and the *Kama Sutra*.

Sir Richard Francis Burton was among the most notable and controversial explorers of the 1800s. He discovered Lake Tanganyika in central Africa and went on two expeditions to search for the source of the Nile River. He later traveled through much of western Africa and the Arabian Peninsula. A sharp observer and talented student of languages, Burton gathered an enormous amount of information about the lands and people he saw. He shared his knowledge in more than 50 books. These included volumes of poetry and translations of works from Arabia and India, as well as original accounts of his travels. Burton's works have often been criticized—both then and now—for their racist attitudes and shocking content. However, they are widely respected for their contributions to the study of Africa and Asia.

Interest in Foreign Lands

The son of a British army colonel, Burton traveled through Europe with his family as a boy. Even then he showed signs of being a rebel. He fought often in school and did poorly in his classes. At Oxford University, he developed what became a lifelong interest in foreign languages, but he was expelled for disobedience. He learned 6 languages before he was 18 years old, and he eventually mastered some 25 more.

Thrilled with travel and adventure, Burton joined the army of the British East India Company, which controlled much of India's trade and politics. During a seven-year stay, he researched the history and culture of Indian cities, also learning Arabic and 10 other languages. In 1849 he took an extended leave from the army to perfect his command of Arabic and prepare for his next adventure.

Holy Cities

Burton was fascinated by the famed Islamic cities of Mecca and Medina on the Arabian Peninsula. Christians were forbidden to enter these heavily guarded cities. Burton wore Arab clothing and darkened his skin with henna, a natural dye. In 1853 he spent several months in Mecca and Medina, posing as a doctor from Afghanistan. He wrote about his experiences in a book called *Personal Narrative of a Pilgrimage to Mecca and El Medina,* which is considered one of his best travel books. Burton's disguise also enabled him to be the first European to visit the holy city of Harar in Ethiopia.

Burton was in Ethiopia as part of an expedition with a fellow army officer named John Hanning SPEKE. The two men explored eastern Ethiopia and Somaliland (now known as Somalia) and searched for the source of the Nile River. They were both wounded in an

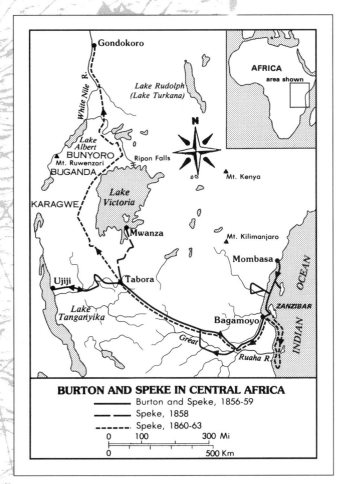

BURTON AND SPEKE IN CENTRAL AFRICA
———— Burton and Speke, 1856-59
— — — Speke, 1858
- - - - Speke, 1860-63

| 0 | 100 | | 300 Mi |
| 0 | | 500 Km | |

Richard Burton and John Speke had angry public disagreements over whether Speke had found the source of the Nile River.

tributary stream or river that flows into a larger stream or river

malaria disease that is spread by mosquitoes in tropical areas

attack by Somalis at Berbera in 1855, and they were forced to flee the country. After recovering from their injuries, they returned to Africa for a second journey. It would prove more successful than the first, but it would also lead to a bitter feud.

Searching for the Source of Nile

Burton won the support of Britain's Royal Geographical Society and was named the mission's leader. His assignment was to find the origin of the White Nile, the Nile River's largest **tributary.** He was also to locate an unexplored body of water called the Sea of Ujiji, which is now known as Lake Tanganyika. The party traveled west from the coastal region of Zanzibar to Kazeh (now Tabora, Tanzania). By the time the party reached the Sea of Ujiji in February 1858, Burton was suffering from **malaria,** and Speke was temporarily blinded by a tropical eye disease. They explored the lake only briefly before returning to Kazeh to regain their health.

Speke recovered more quickly than Burton and set out on his own to locate a larger body of water rumored to be northeast of the Sea of Ujiji. He found Lake Ukerewe in late July and renamed it in honor of Britain's Queen Victoria. Speke learned from local tribes and missionaries that a large river flowed from the lake's north side. He correctly assumed that he had discovered the source of the Nile, and he rushed back to Kazeh to share the good news with Burton. The fiercely competitive Burton doubted Speke's claim and ridiculed him for lacking proof. Speke returned to Britain first and claimed that he had indeed found the source of the Nile. He received funds from the Royal Geographical Society to continue exploring Lake Victoria on his own. As Speke's reputation grew, so did Burton's anger.

New Travels and Studies

Burton recovered from his malaria in 1860 while traveling across the United States. He studied the Mormon communities of Utah and wrote a book about them the following year. He then took an unimportant position as a British official in West Africa. He also became involved in another bitter controversy. In this case, however, Burton supported the explorer in question, Paul Belloni Du CHAILLU. This French-American traveler claimed to have observed gorillas in the highlands of West Africa. Burton believed that Du Chaillu was telling the truth and defended him at a public debate. Burton was also inspired to travel to the Gabon River region eight months later, and he too caught a brief glimpse of a gorilla. He also studied the area's Fang people, also know as Oahouins, who were known to practice cannibalism.

Burton's travels west and south led him through Nigeria, Cameroon, and Angola. He was assigned to visit Benin to try to reduce the slave trade there. He failed to persuade Benin's King

Gelele to stop the practice, but he did study the region and produce a two-volume account of what he learned. He wrote several other books about the lands and peoples of West Africa.

Burton's work for the British government next took him to continents other than Africa. He traveled extensively in Brazil, Syria, Palestine, Iceland, Italy, and the Balkans. He also made a return visit to India and tried unsuccessfully to find gold in Arabia and West Africa. This tireless traveler spent his last years as a diplomat in Italy, where he died at the age of 69.

In his writings, Burton often offended the readers of his day. He described the peoples he met in very unflattering ways, making fun of their appearance, habits, and religious beliefs. He also insulted other groups, such as Jews and the French. Few would deny, however, that Burton was an extraordinary man who achieved greatness as both an explorer and a writer.

Suggested Reading Thomas J. Assad, *Three Victorian Travelers* (Routledge and Kegan Paul, 1964); Fawn M. Brodie, *The Devil Drives; A Life of Sir Richard Burton* (W. W. Norton, 1967); Byron Farwell, *Burton* (Holt, Rinehart, and Winston, 1963); Edward Rice, *Captain Sir Richard Francis Burton* (Charles Scribner's Sons, 1990).

Button, Thomas

Welsh
b 1500s; St. Lythans, Wales
d April 1634; Worlton, Wales
Searched for Northwest Passage

Northwest Passage water route connecting the Atlantic Ocean and Pacific Ocean through the Arctic islands of northern Canada

mutiny rebellion by a ship's crew against the officers

In 1613, while sailing in northern Canada in search of the **Northwest Passage,** Admiral Sir Thomas Button discovered the west side of what is now Hudson Bay. The discovery was not an occasion for joy, since it meant that the bay was not part of the passage. Button had followed the route of Henry HUDSON, who had sailed those waters one year before. After a **mutiny** by his crew, Hudson had been set adrift on the bay in a small, open boat. The rebellious crew had returned to England, and now Button was back on the bay on Hudson's ship, the *Discovery,* sailed by Hudson's treacherous pilot, Robert BYLOT. Though Hudson, his son, and the loyal members of his crew may still have been alive, the Button expedition did not try to find them.

After reaching the west end of the bay, Button and his crew wintered at Port Nelson, where several sailors froze to death. Button kept the surviving men in order with strict discipline. When summer came, they explored 600 miles of the bay's coastline and then sailed home. The area would prove to be a rich source of furs for Britain. Button continued to succeed in the navy, reaching the rank of admiral. His later years were troubled by charges that he was involved in illegal financial dealings.

Suggested Reading George Thomas Clark, *Some Account of Sir Robert Mansel Kt, Vice Admiral of England, and Member of Parliament for the County of Glamorgan, and of Admiral Sir Thomas Button Kt, of Worlton, and of Cardiff in the County of Glamorgan* (Dowlais, 1883).

Bylot, Robert

English
b 1500s; England?
d 1600s; ?
Searched for Northwest Passage

Robert Bylot was a natural leader who won the respect of everyone who sailed with him. In 1611, however, he damaged his reputation forever by joining a **mutiny** against Henry HUDSON, captain of the *Discovery.* Bylot had certainly earned Hudson's respect. After Hudson fired the first **mate** during the voyage, he gave the position to Bylot. But when the mutiny occurred, Bylot chose not to support his captain, who was left to die in the freezing Canadian wilderness.

mutiny rebellion by a ship's crew against the officers

mate assistant to the commander of a ship

Northwest Passage water route connecting the Atlantic Ocean and Pacific Ocean through the Arctic islands of northern Canada

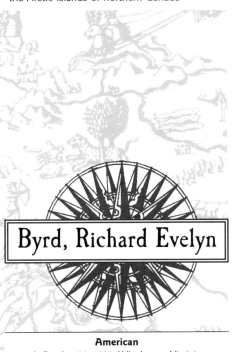

Byrd, Richard Evelyn

American
b October 25, 1888; Winchester, Virginia
d March 11, 1957; Boston, Massachusetts
Explored Arctic Ocean and Antarctica by plane; flew over North and South Poles

Inuit people of the Canadian Arctic, sometimes known as the Eskimo

sledge heavy sled, often mounted on runners, that is pulled over snow or ice

The rebel crew put Bylot in charge of the return trip to England. He proved his abilities by sailing the ship with only seven crewmen, who were ill. They were all arrested when they arrived in England. The usual penalty for mutiny was death by hanging, but Bylot persuaded the navy to let them live. In fact, he was soon back on the *Discovery,* sailing in search of the **Northwest Passage.**

Within a year after his trial, he piloted that ship for Sir Thomas BUTTON on an expedition to Hudson Bay. Bylot then sailed as the *Discovery*'s captain on two important voyages to the Canadian Arctic in 1615 and 1616. Although Bylot led those missions, his pilot, William BAFFIN, has received all the credit for discovering Baffin Bay and the south shore of Baffin Island. History does not record how Bylot spent the rest of his life. The circumstances of his death, like those of his birth, are a mystery.

Suggested Reading Christy Miller, *The Voyages of Captain Luke Foxe of Hull, and Captain Thomas James of Bristol, in Search of a Northwest Passage in 1631-32 with Narratives of the Earlier Northwest Voyages of Frobisher, David, Weymouth, Hall, Knight, Hudson, Button, Gibbons, Bylot, Hawkridge, and Others* (B. Franklin, 1963).

Admiral Richard Evelyn Byrd brought modern machines to the world's polar regions. Until Byrd's time, explorers in the Arctic and Antarctica used **Inuit** methods of travel, such as **sledges** pulled by dogs. Byrd relied on airplanes and snow tractors, which he equipped with cameras and radios. Although these machines could be very dangerous, they put the poles in easy reach. When the American explorer Robert PEARY conquered the North Pole in 1909, he risked his life for five hard weeks on a dog sledge. Seventeen years later, Byrd's round-trip to the pole from the Norwegian island of Spitsbergen took only 15½ hours. "To think," Byrd wrote in his log, "that men toiled for years over this ice, a few hard-won miles a day; and we travel luxuriously a hundred miles an hour. How motors have changed the burdens of man."

Career in the Navy

Byrd's adventures began at an early age. He came from an upperclass Virginia family, and his parents sent him on a trip around the world when he was just 12 years old. Two years later, he decided that someday he would reach the North Pole. After high school, he entered the U.S. Naval Academy, where he was a gifted athlete in football and gymnastics. However, he broke his foot twice in school. When he injured it again while serving on the battleship *Wyoming,* he had no choice but to retire from active duty in 1916.

Byrd had already decided that he wanted to fly planes on missions of exploration. The United States was close to entering World War I, however, and the navy needed instructors. Byrd trained sailors in Rhode Island and briefly held a command position. When the United States declared war on Germany in 1917, he took a desk job, but he was eager to see action. He persuaded the navy to train him as a pilot. Byrd quickly showed his skills and was made a flight instructor in Florida. There he helped invent a device for navigating a new flying boat called the NC-1. In the summer of 1917, he went

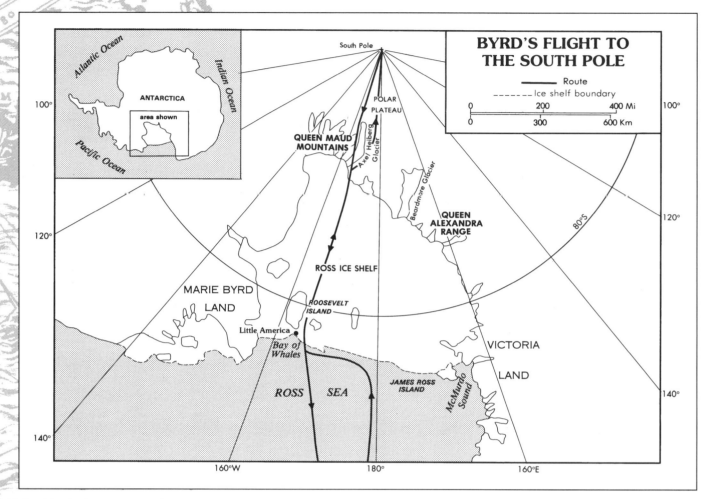

BYRD'S FLIGHT TO THE SOUTH POLE

——— Route
------ Ice shelf boundary

Richard Byrd's base camp, Little America, was built on the same site that Roald Amundsen used for his 1911 overland journey to the South Pole.

dirigible large aircraft filled with a lighter-than-air gas that keeps it aloft; similar to a blimp but with a rigid frame

to a base in Nova Scotia, Canada, to train pilots to fly the NC-1 across the Atlantic Ocean. The war ended before his work in Canada was finished. For the next five years, he worked for the navy in Washington, D.C. He helped persuade Congress to let the navy pursue the use of airplanes in combat.

Dreams Come True

Byrd began to realize his ambitions as an explorer in 1925, when he was put in charge of the airplanes on an expedition to Greenland led by Donald MACMILLAN. In those early days of flight, mechanical failures were not the only dangers. A plane could easily run out of fuel if the pilot made an error in navigation. That would mean a crash landing in the ice and water of the Arctic Ocean. But Byrd and MacMillan proved that planes could be useful tools for exploring the Arctic.

The next year, Byrd had a chance to achieve his boyhood goal of traveling to the North Pole. He and his copilot, Floyd BENNETT, set up camp on Spitsbergen Island, north of Norway. They had company—the famous Norwegian explorer Roald AMUNDSEN was there planning his own flight in an Italian **dirigible.** Byrd and Bennett reached the pole first, however, in their three-motor plane, the

Richard Byrd devoted his life to exploring the earth's polar regions. He was the first to fly over both the North Pole and the South Pole.

Josephine Ford. During the flight, oil began to leak from one of the engines. Bennett wanted to land to make repairs, but the risks of landing on the rough and unstable ice were too great. Luckily, the leak stopped when the oil level dropped below the hole in the tank. The relieved pilots circled the pole and returned safely to their base. Even Amundsen greeted them with embraces and praise. He said that "few more hazardous ventures have ever been undertaken in history."

Byrd's next feat was to cross the Atlantic Ocean in a plane large enough to carry passengers. On June 29, 1927, he flew from New York to Paris, France, with a cargo of 15,000 pounds. Just as he approached Europe, a faulty compass and bad weather forced him to bring the plane down in the ocean. Still, he had shown that airplanes could be used for trade and travel across the Atlantic. He and his crew received a hero's welcome in both Paris and New York.

The South Pole Is Next

Byrd turned his attention south. He prepared the largest and most expensive expedition ever to visit Antarctica. He raised close to one million dollars and bought four ships, four planes, and a variety of advanced cameras for photographs and motion pictures. Little America, his camp at the Bay of Whales on the Ross Ice Shelf, was more like a village, housing 42 workers and 94 dogs. Byrd began by making short trips with planes and sledges. He then turned to his main goal, a flight to the South Pole.

His plane was named *Floyd Bennett* after his former partner, who had died the year before. On November 28, 1929, Byrd took to the air with the Norwegian-American pilot Bernt Balchen at the controls. Their greatest fear was that the plane would not make it over a mountain range that lay between their base and the pole. But the two men dumped some of their cargo, and the plane cleared the icy mountains at a height of 10,500 feet. The flight was a success.

No Escape from Danger

The 1930s were tough times economically for Americans, and Byrd had trouble raising money for another trip to Antarctica. After deciding on less ambitious plans, he raised enough money for a two-year expedition. On this visit, he and his teams covered more ground than before and recorded a great deal of scientific information. The mission was a success, but Byrd almost died.

He was alone at a scientific station 125 miles from his base camp. A leaking stovepipe released carbon monoxide, a poisonous gas, into the station. His radio messages to the base camp were strange and confused, so his staff knew that something was seriously wrong. Because of bad weather, he could not be rescued for more than a month. Byrd later wrote about this experience in *Alone,* published in 1938. In this book, he doubted the value and wisdom of exploration. He realized that he had nearly killed himself to collect a "tiny heap of data" that might have no practical use. He was, he wrote, "a fool, lost on a fool's errand. . . ."

However, Byrd did not abandon his work in Antarctica. In 1939 he led the first Antarctic expedition to be sponsored by the U.S. government. Over the next few years, he led several more trips, one with 13 ships and 4,000 crew members. He made his last flight over the South Pole in 1956. A year later, he died in his sleep, and the world mourned the loss of the explorer it had admired for 30 years.

Suggested Reading Richard Evelyn Byrd, *Alone* (reprint, Island, 1984) and *Discovery: The Story of the Second Byrd Antarctic Expedition* (reprint, Gale, 1971); Edwin P. Hoyt, *The Last Explorer: The Adventures of Admiral Byrd* (John Day, 1968); Lisle A. Rose, *Assault on Eternity: Richard E. Byrd and the Exploration of Antarctica* (Naval Institute Press, 1980).

Byron, John

English
b November 8, 1723; Newstead Abbey, England
d April 10, 1786; London, England
*Explored southern Pacific Ocean
and Falkland Islands*

circumnavigation journey around the world

Northwest Passage water route connecting the Atlantic Ocean and Pacific Ocean through the Arctic islands of northern Canada

frigate small, agile warship with three masts and square sails

sloop small ship with one mast and triangular sails

John Byron led one of the first British voyages of discovery in the Pacific Ocean. He also set a long-standing record for the fastest **circumnavigation.** Byron joined the navy as a youth and at 17 served under George ANSON aboard the *Wager.* The ship was one of six on a mission to raid Spanish settlements on the west coast of South America. In 1741 the *Wager* was shipwrecked on the coast of Patagonia, the southernmost region of the South American mainland. Byron and his shipmates were captured by a local tribe of Patagonians and held for a year. The Patagonians then turned the sailors over to Spanish officials, who also imprisoned the Englishmen. Byron did not return home until four years after the shipwreck. Back in England, he published an account of his difficult time in Patagonia. But those experiences did not keep him from going back to sea. In 1758 he served bravely in naval battles against France and was promoted to the rank of commodore.

Competition at Sea

In the mid-1700s, both Britain and France took pride in the successes of their navies. They competed for control of distant lands and new sources of wealth. These territories were also important as ports for ships on long voyages. Byron was named commander of an expedition to find and claim new lands for England in the southern Atlantic Ocean, between the Cape of Good Hope in Africa and the Strait of Magellan in South America. The commodore was asked to look for a large and fertile land, known as Pepys Island, that was rumored to be somewhere in the southern Atlantic. He was also instructed to explore the area of the California coast that Sir Francis DRAKE had named New Albion in 1579. Farther north in the Pacific Ocean, he was to search for the western end of the **Northwest Passage.**

On June 21, 1764, Byron sailed with the *Dolphin,* one of the first **frigates** covered with copper, and the *Tamar,* a **sloop.** To keep the plans secret, the crews were told that the expedition was headed for

After sailing through some of the worst storms ever recorded at sea, Byron earned the nickname "Foul Weather Jack."

the Caribbean Sea. Only after the ships reached Brazil did Byron tell them their real orders. He promised to double their pay if they would carry out the mission. They agreed, and the ships continued down the South American coast, staying at Port Desire in Patagonia for two weeks before heading south.

On to the Pacific

Byron never found Pepys Island, but in early 1765 he reached the Falkland Islands and claimed them for England. He did not know that the explorer Louis-Antoine de BOUGAINVILLE had just established a French colony in those islands. Entering the Pacific Ocean shortly after, Byron tried to anchor at the Tuamotu Islands. When he could not find a suitable harbor, he named two of the islands the Disappointment Islands. He also named two islands for England's King George and one for himself, but the names would not be permanent.

From this point on, Byron ignored his instructions. He did not sail north to explore California or seek the Northwest Passage. Instead, he continued sailing west and reached Batavia (now Jakarta, Indonesia) in November 1765. He may have been worried about the condition of the copper on his experimental ship. He raced toward Cape Town, South Africa, and reached it in three months. Byron and his crew returned to England having set a record for the fastest circumnavigation—less than two years. But since Byron had not completed his assignment, the voyage was considered a failure.

Naval Duty

In 1769 Byron was named governor of Newfoundland, a British colony in what is now Canada. During the American Revolution, the navy called him back to active service. His fleet brought English troops to the war and tracked the movements of French ships off the American coast. In 1779 Byron took part in his last naval campaign, fighting the French at the Battle of Grenada in the Caribbean Sea. He then returned to England and retired with the rank of vice admiral. The family name was carried on by his grandson, the famous Romantic poet George Gordon Lord Byron.

Suggested Reading John Byron, *The Wreck of the* Wager (Book Club of California, 1940); Peter Shankland, *Byron of the* Wager (Coward, McCann and Geoghegan, 1975).

Cabeza de Vaca, Álvar Núñez

Spanish
b 1490?; Jerez, Spain
d 1556; Seville?, Spain
Explored American Southwest and northern Mexico

Bad luck and poor planning helped make Álvar Núñez Cabeza de Vaca an explorer, and his unexpected travels had lasting effects on the history of Spanish America. After a failed expedition left him stranded in Florida, he and three other men wandered for eight years in the lands between Florida and Mexico. They were the first Europeans to cross North America from the Gulf of Mexico to the Gulf of California. Cabeza de Vaca's travels proved that there was a massive continent north of **New Spain.** His reports inspired Francisco Vásquez de CORONADO, Hernando de SOTO, and others to explore a land about which Europeans knew almost nothing.

This engraving shows Cabeza de Vaca and his companions trading with Indians.

New Spain region of Spanish colonial empire that included the areas now occupied by Mexico, Florida, Texas, New Mexico, Arizona, California, and various Caribbean islands

barge flat-bottomed boat without sails

Early Struggles and Later Disasters

There are few details known of Cabeza de Vaca's early life. Both his mother and father came from distinguished military families, and he too joined the military as a young man. He took part in several battles in Italy and Spain before joining an expedition to Florida led by Pánfilo de NARVÁEZ.

Cabeza de Vaca served as treasurer of the mission, which sailed from Spain on June 27, 1527, with five ships and about 600 men. Problems began as soon as the ships landed at Santo Domingo on the island of Hispaniola in the Caribbean Sea. There, about 140 men deserted, thinking they would enjoy an easier life on the island.

Narváez recruited more soldiers in Cuba and then sailed to Vera Cruz, Mexico. He left Cabeza de Vaca in command of two ships and sent him to another island, Trinidad, for more supplies. Cabeza de Vaca was ashore with about 30 men when a hurricane struck the island. The storm wrecked both ships and drowned the 60 crew members left on board. A few days later, Narváez arrived and picked up the survivors. The reunited force then spent the winter at Spanish settlements along the Gulf of Mexico. Narváez purchased two more ships, and in the spring of 1528, he set sail with about 400 men. They sighted Florida on April 12. Two days later, they landed at Tampa Bay and took official possession of the land that Juan PONCE DE LEÓN had claimed for Spain 15 years before.

Deadly Decisions

The Spaniards' supply of food was already low, but Indians near Tampa Bay told the Spaniards that they would find food and gold farther north, in a city called Apalachen. Narváez then made a fatal error. He took about 300 men and set out for Apalachen on foot. He ordered his fleet to follow the coastline and meet him and his soldiers to the north.

Harassed by hostile Indians, Narváez, Cabeza de Vaca, and the other hungry Spaniards trudged north to Apalachen. They found corn but little else. They moved on, looking for food and waiting for the ships, which never appeared. The ships had spent nearly a year searching for Narváez's party and had sailed back to New Spain.

As they marched along the west coast of Florida, the Spanish soldiers died one by one from hunger, disease, and Indian arrows. Narváez decided to build **barges** and float across the Gulf of Mexico to the Spanish settlement at Pánuco. It was about 600 miles away, much farther than he realized. On September 22, the Spaniards slaughtered and ate the last of their horses. They then sailed west in five barges.

The Sole Survivors

The men sailed the barges close to the coast, but the poorly built boats were difficult to control and barely stayed afloat. Narváez ordered the crews to fend for themselves, and the barges slowly drifted apart. Later, Cabeza de Vaca learned from local Indians what had happened to three of the barges. The crewmen of one, weak from hunger and thirst, went ashore and were killed by Indians. Another barge was stranded on the water, and all aboard starved to death. The barge led by Narváez disappeared at sea and was never seen again.

In November 1528, the two remaining barges, one of which carried Cabeza de Vaca, were wrecked on what is now Galveston Island in Texas. There were now only 90 men left of the 300 who had begun the long march through Florida. The Indians who now greeted the Spaniards were friendly, but an unusually cold winter struck hard. Many Spaniards and Indians died from hunger, disease, and cold, and Cabeza de Vaca fell ill. When spring came, most of the Spanish survivors left the region, but he remained behind, too weak to travel.

Life Among the Indians

For the next five years, Cabeza de Vaca lived among the Indians. At first he was held captive. Later he wandered alone, trading with various tribes along Galveston Bay and elsewhere in the Texas region. In the winter of 1534 to 1535, he met two Spanish soldiers and their Arab slave—the only other survivors of his expedition. The four men decided to make another attempt to reach Spanish territory by heading inland to the west. They began their trek in 1535 at a point near modern-day San Antonio. Accompanied by Indian guides, they crossed into the region that is now New Mexico and possibly Arizona. They then headed south through the Mexican province of Sonora, toward the Gulf of California.

A Happy Return and a Bitter End

In July 1536, Cabeza de Vaca and his companions reached Mexico City, where they were hailed as heroes. They submitted a report of their adventures before Cabeza de Vaca left for Spain the following year. Five years later, he published *The Shipwrecks,* a more personal story of his years in the wilderness.

Back in Spain, Cabeza de Vaca turned down an invitation from Hernando de Soto to join a new expedition to Florida. But he had not completely lost his taste for adventure. In 1540 he went to Asunción (in present-day Paraguay) to govern Spanish settlements in the area. To get there, he had to make a difficult four-month journey by land from Brazil. On the way, he probably became the first European to see Iguaçu Falls, on the border between Argentina and Brazil.

Unfortunately, Cabeza de Vaca's time in Paraguay did not turn out well. In 1542 he led an unsuccessful search for gold. When he returned to Asunción, he was arrested—for reasons that are unclear—and was taken back to Spain to stand trial. The case dragged on for six years. He was found guilty and was banished to Africa,

> For a map of the route taken by Cabeza de Vaca, see the profile of Hernando de Soto in Volume 3.

but the king of Spain overturned the sentence and allowed Cabeza de Vaca to remain in Spain with a small income.

Suggested Reading Morris Bishop, *The Odyssey of Cabeza de Vaca* (Century, 1933); Álvar Núñez Cabeza de Vaca, *Adventures in the Unknown Interiors of America,* edited and translated by Cyclone Covey (University of New Mexico Press, 1966); Lissa Jones Johnston, *Crossing a Continent: The Incredible Journey of Cabeza de Vaca* (Eakin Press, 1997).

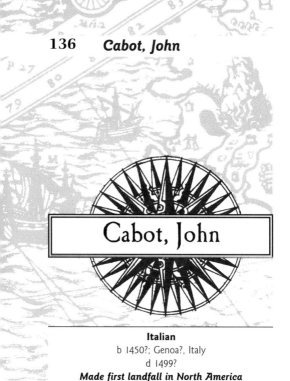

Cabot, John

Italian
b 1450?; Genoa?, Italy
d 1499?
*Made first landfall in North America
after Leif Erikson*

John Cabot was an Italian who believed that he could find a quick route to the spices of eastern Asia by sailing west across the northern Atlantic Ocean. He was unable to interest the rulers of Spain and Portugal in his idea, so he approached King Henry VII of England, who encouraged and supported his plan. In 1497 Cabot led the first European expedition to land in North America since the Norseman Leif ERIKSON's expedition 500 years before. Cabot's voyage would prove to be as important for England as Christopher Columbus's had been for Spain.

Italy and the Spice Trade

Like most details about his life, the date and place of John Cabot's birth are unknown. Letters about Cabot mention that he came from Genoa, a city-state in what is now Italy. However, official records in Genoa do not include a "Caboto" family living there at that time. Other records indicate that he became a citizen of Venice, another Italian city-state, in 1476.

These Italian port cities thrived on the spice trade, and Cabot became interested in the money that could be made. In the days before refrigerators, spices were not simply a luxury—they were a necessity to hide the unpleasant taste of spoiling meat. Demand for spices was high in Europe. Italian merchants grew rich by buying spices from Arab traders and then selling them at a higher price in western and northern Europe. To avoid paying the high prices of the Italian and Arab middlemen, the buyers wished for a way to get the spices directly from Asia.

Cabot thought that he knew of such a way. He claimed that as a young man, he had traveled east to Mecca (in modern-day Saudi Arabia) to buy spices from Arab traders. According to Cabot, when he asked the Arabs where the spices came from, they told him they did not know. They said that the spices were brought from the east by traders in **caravans,** and that these traders had bought the spices from other traders who came from even more distant lands. It was apparent to Cabot that the spices came from lands very far to the east of Europe. Believing that the earth was round, he reasoned that he could reach the spices' source by sailing west across the Atlantic Ocean.

It is not known whether Cabot developed this idea on his own, or whether he was inspired by the similar voyage made by Christopher Columbus in 1492. There is evidence that Cabot was in Valencia, Spain, when Columbus returned from that journey. If so, Cabot may have witnessed Columbus's triumphant arrival. In any case, Cabot improved upon Columbus's idea. He suggested that since the circumference of the globe is smaller at a northern **latitude** than at

caravan large group of people traveling together, often with pack animals, across a desert or other dangerous region

latitude distance north or south of the equator

John Cabot (with flag), pictured here with his son Sebastian, may have been the first European to land in North America since the time of the Vikings.

the equator, ships sailing in the north would have a shorter trip around the world. Thus, Cabot could make the trip more quickly than Columbus. At the time, of course, neither man realized that Columbus had not reached Asia at all—he had found an unknown continent.

Cabot for the English

Cabot took his idea to the royal courts of both Spain and Portugal, but neither wanted to fund his voyage. He then moved his family to England to see if he could interest King Henry VII in the plan. Since England was at the very end of the route of the spice trade, the English paid the highest price for spices. Cabot believed that they would be very interested in a shorter, cheaper route to Asia.

Cabot chose to settle in the port of Bristol on the west coast of England. It was a good choice, because the merchants of Bristol were already looking for new ways to obtain spices. About 40 years earlier, a Bristol merchant named Robert Stormy had tried to bypass the Italians by sending two ships to Arab lands on the Mediterranean Sea. One of the ships was wrecked. The other was destroyed by Italian cargo shippers, who did not appreciate Stormy's attempts to deny them their usual profits.

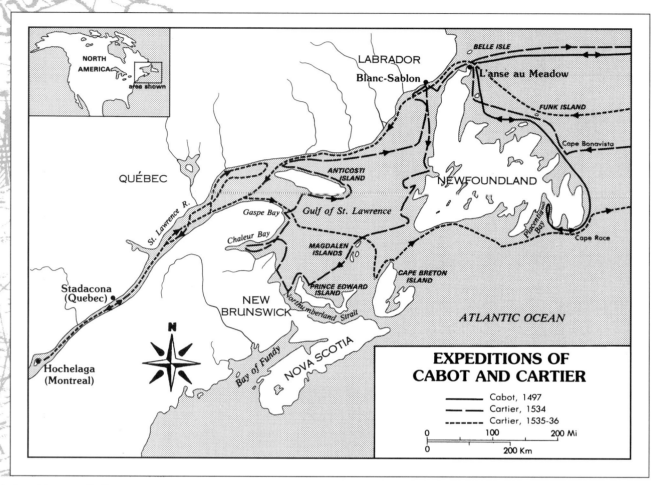

John Cabot and Jacques Cartier were among the earliest explorers of the St. Lawrence River region.

The Bristol merchants were also interested in Cabot's proposed voyage to the western Atlantic because they were looking for new fishing waters. They had been trying for years to locate a legendary island, which they called Hy-Brasil. They believed that this island lay west of Ireland and was surrounded by waters rich in fish. No one had yet located such an island, but some sailors claimed to have reached a large landmass before 1494. This land may even have been North America itself. With so much at stake, the merchants of Bristol offered Cabot not only their interest but also their financial support.

Preparing for Discovery

Cabot still needed the approval of the king. He presented his plan to Henry, who reacted with great enthusiasm. England's rival, Spain, was already profiting from newly discovered lands to the west, and Henry was eager for England to do so as well. On March 5, 1496, he granted permission to Cabot and Cabot's three sons to sail under the flag of England. He wrote a letter that granted the family of explorers permission to find new lands "in whatsoever part of the world they may be, which before this time were unknown to Christians." Cabot was also allowed to bring any spices or other products back to England and sell them. In return, the king was to receive one-fifth of the profits.

quadrant navigational instrument used since the Middle Ages to determine distance north or south of the equator

Cabot's instructions allowed him five ships, but he was able to find only one. It was called the *Matthew* and was about the same size as the *Niña,* the smallest of Columbus's three ships. He hired about 20 sailors, and it is likely that his son Sebastian CABOT was also on board. On May 20, 1497, the ship sailed west from Bristol to Dursey Head, on the west coast of Ireland. John Cabot then used a method of navigation called latitude sailing. He sailed the Atlantic at a single chosen latitude and maintained his course by finding the North Star at night. He also used a compass and **quadrant** to help him find the correct latitude if he was blown off course. Thirty-three days after leaving Dursey Head, the *Matthew* reached the coast of North America. Although Cabot had traveled a much shorter distance than Columbus had, it took about the same amount of time because the winds in the north were less favorable.

Landfall in North America

No one is sure exactly where Cabot landed, since neither he nor any member of his crew kept a journal during the voyage. Because of Cabot's practice of latitude sailing, many historians locate his landfall at present-day Griquet Harbor. This bay, on the northern tip of what is now called Newfoundland, lies on the same latitude as Dursey Head, Ireland. This theory is supported by Cabot's report of a large island, which could be Belle Isle, about 15 miles to the north of his landfall. If so, it would mean that Cabot landed within five miles of where Leif ERIKSON had landed nearly 500 years before. Other historians have placed Cabot's landfall father south, perhaps at Cape Breton Island.

The exact spot remains a mystery, but the time when land was sighted was 5 A.M. on June 24, according to an inscription on a map made by Sebastian. For some reason, this was the only landing made by John Cabot and his crew. The captain apparently feared that any people who lived there might be hostile. Though the Europeans did not see anyone else, they did see signs of life: snares, fishing nets, and a red stick with holes at both ends that was probably used for weaving the nets. Cabot forbade his men to go farther from the ship than the distance a crossbow could be shot. At least one historian has suggested that the explorers might also have been discouraged by the swarms of mosquitoes that plague Newfoundland during the summer. Whatever the reason, Cabot chose to spend the rest of the voyage observing the coast from the relative safety of his ship.

The extent of Cabot's exploration is also unknown. Historians who think that he landed in Griquet Harbor believe that he sailed south along Newfoundland's east coast before heading back to England. Those who believe that he landed farther south assume that he sailed north before turning homeward. Wherever he was, Cabot noted that fish were so plentiful that the crew could let down weighted buckets and draw them up full of cod. On the shore they saw tall trees that would make excellent masts, as well as tended fields of plants that may have been blueberry bushes. At one point, they also saw two figures chasing each other in the woods, but they could not tell whether the figures were animals or humans.

khan title of an Asian ruler

Northwest Passage water route connecting the Atlantic Ocean and Pacific Ocean through the Arctic islands of northern Canada

Return to Bristol, Return to America

Heading home, Cabot sailed east for 15 days and found himself off the coast of Brittany, France. He then turned north and arrived back in Bristol on August 6. After he had made his own map and globe to show his route and discoveries, he went to London to inform the king. Cabot was convinced that he had reached the northern shores of Asia—"the land of the Great **Khan.**" Though he had not returned with spices or jewels, he told Henry about the rich fishing he had found and falsely claimed that the new land produced exotic wood and silk.

King Henry named the discovery New Isle, but by 1502 he was calling it "the newe founde lande", the name that it bears today. Henry was excited by the reports, but his rewards to Cabot were modest. Cabot received a prize from the royal treasury and a small yearly income to be paid by the city of Bristol. But what Cabot lacked in riches was made up for in fame. A letter written at the time says that Cabot "is called the Great Admiral and vast honour is paid to him and he goes dressed in silk, and these English run after him like mad."

With this new status, Cabot was able to plan a second trip. He intended to sail farther to the southwest to look for Cipangu, which is now known as Japan. According to Marco Polo, the great Italian traveler of the 1200s, all the spices and jewels of the world came from Cipangu. King Henry granted Cabot permission to sail with six English ships and to enlist any English sailor willing to make the trip. The king paid for one ship, and the merchants of Bristol provided four more. The fleet set sail from Bristol early in May 1498.

The fate of Cabot's second voyage is still a mystery. One book written in the 1500s claims that the expedition sailed up the west coast of Greenland before it was stopped by huge icebergs. That account goes on to say that Cabot sailed south along the coasts of what are now called Baffin Island, Newfoundland, Nova Scotia, and New England, and as far south as Chesapeake Bay, before returning to England empty-handed. Other historians believe that this source confuses Cabot's second voyage with one made much later by his son Sebastian, who was searching for a **Northwest Passage.** These historians believe that one of John Cabot's ships was forced to return to England for reasons that are not clear, and that the other four were never heard from again.

Cabot's Place in History

Only one fact is known for certain about Cabot after he departed on his second voyage. Records show that his reward money was last collected from the Bristol city government on the holiday of Michaelmas, September 29, 1498. It is not clear whether the money was collected by Cabot himself or by his wife. After that, John Cabot does not appear in history. His son Sebastian may be one reason why. Although Sebastian became an accomplished explorer himself, he also took credit for much of his father's work. Not until the 1800s did historians realize that John Cabot, not Sebastian, was the man who led England's first voyage of exploration across the Atlantic.

Opinions of John Cabot written by those who lived in his time say that he was an excellent navigator and a skilled maker of maps and globes. He also seems to have been a careful explorer who would not needlessly risk the lives of his crew. Although he believed to the end that he had found a sea route to Asia, he had in fact discovered something equally valuable. His idea of crossing the Atlantic at a more northernly latitude than Columbus brought many benefits to England. In the short run, it gave the English food and profits from fertile new fishing waters. In the long run, it opened the English exploration of North America, the continent they would eventually claim and colonize.

Suggested Reading C. Raymond Beazley, *John and Sebastian Cabot; the Discovery of North America* (B. Franklin, 1964); Brian Cuthbertson, *John Cabot and the Voyage of the* Matthew (Formac, 1997); Henry Kurtz, *John and Sebastian Cabot* (Franklin Watts, 1973); James A. Williamson, *The Cabot Voyages and Bristol Discovery Under Henry VII* (Hakluyt Society, 1962).

Cabot, Sebastian

Italian
b 1476?; Venice, Italy
d 1557; London, England
Explored waterways in South America and Canada

Northwest Passage water route connecting the Atlantic Ocean and Pacific Ocean through the Arctic islands of northern Canada

Northeast Passage water route connecting the Atlantic Ocean and Pacific Ocean along the Arctic coastline of Europe and Asia

cartography the science of mapmaking

cosmography the scientific study of the structure of the universe

Sebastian Cabot, one of the most accomplished mapmakers of his time, was the first explorer to search for a **Northwest Passage** to Asia. On an expedition sponsored by England, he explored the coast of Labrador and reached Hudson Bay. He later organized three missions to seek a **Northeast Passage** to Asia. One of these missions led to trade between England and Russia. Cabot's most famous journey, however, was one he made to South America. Sponsored by Spain, he explored the Río de la Plata, the Paraná River, and part of the Paraguay River.

A Family of Explorers

Sebastian Cabot was a son of the famed navigator and explorer, John CABOT. Although he probably learned navigation, **cartography,** and **cosmography** from his father, the two men had little else in common. John was friendly and good-natured. Sebastian, on the other hand, was vain and self-centered and had a habit of exaggerating his own importance. He even claimed credit for some of his father's accomplishments.

In the 1490s, the Cabot family moved to Bristol, England. Sebastian probably accompanied his father in 1497 on a voyage to North America sponsored by King Henry VII of England. On this expedition, the Cabots sailed along the east coast of what is now Canada. It was the first journey across the North Atlantic since Leif ERIKSON had landed on those same shores 500 years before.

Historians disagree about how many voyages Sebastian himself led, as well as about the extent of his explorations. Several authors list as his first voyage an expedition across the North Atlantic from 1508 to 1509, which was sponsored by Henry VII. The goal was to find a direct route to Asia by sailing north of Canada. Cabot sailed northward along the coasts of Newfoundland and Labrador and reached Hudson Bay. At the entrance to the bay, he mistakenly believed that he had found the Northwest Passage, and he did not press forward. He may have sailed as far north as Foxe Channel, between present-day Baffin Island and the Northwest Territories.

Sebastian Cabot was famous both as an explorer and as a mapmaker, but he spent much of his time chasing legends.

cartographer mapmaker
Council of the Indies governing body of Spain's colonial empire from 1524 to 1834

tributary stream or river that flows into a larger stream or river

There, dangerous chunks of floating ice would have caused Cabot to abandon the journey and head back to England.

Sailing for Spain

For three years after his return, Cabot served as royal **cartographer** for the new English king, Henry VIII. In 1512 Cabot accompanied English troops who were sent to help the Spanish king, Ferdinand of Aragon, in his war against the French. Since Henry VIII was not really interested in exploration, Cabot offered his services to King Ferdinand. Ferdinand hired Cabot as Spain's royal cartographer. Within a few years, Cabot was awarded the rank of pilot major and became a member of the **Council of the Indies.**

In 1526 Charles I, the new king of Spain, asked Cabot to sail to eastern Asia in search of trade and riches. Cabot had a theory that there was a shorter route to Asia than the one taken by Ferdinand MAGELLAN just five years earlier. To that end, he was instructed to map the coast of South America in detail. On April 3, 1526, he sailed west from the Spanish port of Sanlúcar de Barrameda with four ships and about 200 men. On September 29, he reached a harbor that today is the site of the Brazilian city Recife.

From Indians living on the Brazilian coast, Cabot heard the first of several reports of the "White King." This king supposedly dressed like Europeans and ruled a wealthy realm that included a mountain of silver. Continuing south along the coast, Cabot found an island he named Ilha de Santa Catarina, in honor of his wife. Farther south, he picked up two castaways from an earlier, ill-fated expedition. These men repeated the tale of the White King, claiming that his kingdom was located north of the region now called Paraguay. Cabot, attracted by the tales of great wealth, changed his plans in order to search for the legendary king. When several of his officers objected, he simply abandoned them on the coast.

The Search for the White King

On February 21, 1527, Cabot entered the mouth of a large river that led into the interior of Argentina. He named it the Río de la Plata (Silver River) after the pieces of silver he obtained from local Indians. The silver had come from the Inca civilization in Peru, but Cabot thought its source was much closer. He built a fort on the Río Carcarañá, a **tributary** of the Río de la Plata. Then he left in search of the silver. He sailed up another tributary, the Paraná River, going about 50 miles past the point where it meets the Paraguay River. At the end of March, he began exploring the Paraguay River, but he was forced to turn back because food was running low and Indians had begun to attack.

Cabot returned to the fort he had built. Soon he heard another local legend, this one about the "Enchanted City of the Caesars."

According to the legend, the city was part of a wealthy, advanced, and peaceful civilization, perhaps in the Andes of Peru. After failing to find the city, Cabot met another explorer, Diego Garcia, and the two men decided to combine forces to look for the White King. Attacks by Indians once again forced Cabot to retreat to the fort, but he found that it had been destroyed, and the troops there had been killed. With nothing but seal meat left to eat, Cabot decided to return to Spain in November 1529. He reached Spain the following year without any of the Asian treasure that the Spanish had expected. He was stripped of his rank and banished to Africa for two years for disobeying his orders.

New Honors in Later Years

Eventually Cabot's rank as pilot major was restored, and in 1547 he returned to England at the invitation of King Edward VI. He became a founder of the Company of Merchant Adventurers (also known as the Muscovy Company), which had the right to claim lands north of the British Isles. In the 1550s, Cabot organized three expeditions that searched for a Northeast Passage to Asia by sailing north of Russia. Although none of the explorers found such a passage, one ship, piloted by Richard CHANCELLOR, entered the White Sea north of Russia in 1553. Chancellor and his crew traveled south by land to Moscow, where he negotiated a trade agreement between England and Russia.

Cabot never found a northern sea route to Asia, but his maps and voyages greatly influenced the next generation of European explorers. His map of the world was a landmark in the history of cartography, and his voyages to Canada and South America paved the way for future expeditions. Many explorers, inspired by Cabot's stories about the White King and the Enchanted City of the Caesars, risked everything to find the sources of these legends.

Suggested Reading Raymond Beazley, *John and Sebastian Cabot* (Burt Franklin, 1964); Henry Kurtz, *John and Sebastian Cabot* (Franklin Watts, 1973); John Williamson, *The Cabot Voyages and Bristol Discovery Under Henry VII* (Hakluyt Society, 1962).

Caboto, Giovanni. See *Cabot, John.*

Caboto, Sebastiano. See *Cabot, Sebastian.*

Cabral, Pedro Álvares

Portuguese
b 1467?; Belmonte, Portugal
d 1520; Santarém, Portugal
Discovered Brazil

As the leader of the first successful trade mission to India, Pedro Álvares Cabral was the first person to sign treaties for direct trade between Europe and the East Indies. He is best known, however, as the man who discovered Brazil. Historians are still unsure whether the discovery was intentional or accidental. They are not even certain whether Cabral should receive credit for finding Brazil. But Brazilians today celebrate him as the discoverer of their country.

Pedro Álvares Cabral discovered Brazil while on an expedition to establish trading posts in India.

trade winds winds that blow from east to west in the tropics

Noble Service to the Crown

Cabral was born in about 1467 on an estate in Belmonte, Portugal, to a wealthy noble family that had influence at the Portuguese royal court. As a boy, Cabral served as a page to King John II. Other details of his life as a young man are unknown, except that he grew up to serve on the council of Portugal's King Manuel I and was made a knight of the Order of Christ.

In 1499 Cabral was named chief captain of a fleet sent to establish trading posts on the west coast of southern India, known as the Malabar Coast. The expedition sailed from the Tagus River in Lisbon, Portugal, on March 9, 1500, with 13 ships and 1,000 men. The commander of one of Cabral's ships was Bartolomeu DIAS, who had reached the Cape of Good Hope at the southern tip of Africa 12 years before.

The Discovery of Brazil

On his earlier voyage, Dias had had no choice but to follow the unknown west coast of Africa. This time Cabral decided to take the route first charted by Vasco da GAMA a year earlier. Cabral first sailed to the Canary Islands and then continued southwest past the Cape Verde Islands off the coast of Africa. He turned south on March 22 but soon switched to a southwesterly course to take advantage of the strong **trade winds.** When he reached the southern latitude of the Cape of Good Hope, he tried to turn east, but winds and currents continued to push him farther west. On April 22, near Easter, the crew sighted Mount Pascal in Brazil. Cabral claimed the land for Portugal and named it Terra da Vera Cruz, which means "land of the true cross" in Portuguese. In later years, the land came to be known as Terra do Brazil, named for the brazilwood that traders valued for its red dye. The name Brazil was the one that stuck.

Cabral spent little time in this new land, exploring about 50 miles of the coast in 12 days. He landed on an island just north of the site of the present-day city of Rio de Janeiro. Cabral planted a cross on the island, and the crew celebrated mass. They also met Indians, whom Cabral described in a letter to King Manuel as friendly and peaceful. In the same letter, he described the Indians' houses and their custom of wearing feathers as decorations.

No official log of the journey exists, but some details are provided by Cabral's letters to the king and by the eyewitness account of one of the crew, Pêro Vaz. At one point, Cabral asked the crew to vote on whether to send a ship back to Portugal with news of the discovery and whether the ship should take some Indians along. Such a democratic approach was quite unusual at the time. Most captains exercised complete authority over their missions and their men. Cabral's crew voted to send the ship to Portugal but without the Indians.

Trade Mission to the Indies

On May 2, Cabral resumed his journey to the Cape of Good Hope, but three weeks later, a storm at sea sank four of the ships and scattered the rest. The remaining ships regrouped off the east coast of Africa and reached Calicut on the Malabar Coast in September.

Cabral set up a trading post, but the Muslims of Calicut did not want the Portuguese there. A party of Muslims attacked the post, killing about 50 Europeans. Cabral retaliated by burning Arab ships and firing his own ships' cannons at the city. He finally left Calicut, sailing south along the coast to Cochin and Cannanore, where he received a warmer welcome. He established trading posts in these towns and signed trade treaties on behalf of Portugal.

Cabral returned to Lisbon in 1501, carrying pearls, diamonds, porcelain, and valuable spices such as pepper, ginger, cinnamon, and cloves. The trip had cost many lives, including that of Dias, who had gone down with his ship during the storm off the Cape of Good Hope. Cabral was welcomed home by King Manuel, but the two men seem to have had a disagreement later. Vasco da Gama was chosen over Cabral to lead the next Portuguese voyage to the Indies. Cabral left the royal court at this time and never returned. He settled on his estate near Santarém, married, and had six children.

Questions About the Discovery

Some historians believe that Cabral's discovery of Brazil was not an accident. Under the **Treaty of Tordesillas,** Portugal was given the right to claim lands lying east of a line drawn through the Atlantic Ocean on maps. King Manuel may have given Cabral secret orders to sail as far west as possible without crossing that line, to see if Portugal could claim any new lands.

Another difficult question is whether Cabral was actually the first European to discover Brazil. At least three other explorers—Amerigo VESPUCCI, Vicente Yáñez PINZÓN, and Diego de Lepe—landed on the Brazilian coast before Cabral. These explorers, however, were mainly interested in the Caribbean islands. When they reached the north coast of Brazil, they were not surprised to have found land south of those islands. Cabral was the first to discover Brazilian land where it was not expected to be. Today monuments in both Lisbon and Rio de Janeiro honor him as the discoverer of Brazil.

Suggested Reading William Brooks Greenlee, *The Voyage of Pedro Álvares Cabral to Brazil and India, from Contemporary Documents and Narratives* (Hakluyt Society, 1938).

Treaty of Tordesillas agreement between Spain and Portugal dividing the rights to discovered lands along a north-south line

Cabrillo, Juan Rodriguez

Portuguese
b 1498?; ?
d January 3, 1543; San Miguel Island, California
Explored California and Central America

During a lifetime filled with adventure, Juan Rodriguez Cabrillo was a soldier, sailor, shipbuilder, miner, explorer, and author. His travels took him to many parts of the Americas. In 1518 he served under Pánfilo de Narváez during the exploration and conquest of Cuba. In the years that followed, he helped Hernán Cortés to conquer the Aztec capital of Tenochtitlán (present-day Mexico City). With Tenochtitlán secure, he joined Pedro de Alvarado in the region that is now Honduras, Guatemala, and El Salvador. Today Cabrillo is known in the United States as the first European explorer of the coast of California.

Seeking Adventure and Wealth

Nothing is known about Cabrillo's parents or the date and place of his birth. The first recorded information about him shows that he

encomendero Spanish colonist who received a grant of land in the Americas and had control over the Indians who lived there

brigantine two-masted sailing ship with both square and triangular sails

received military training in Cuba from 1510 to 1511. He was reported to be in his early 20s when he left for Mexico in 1520, so he was probably born around 1498. It is unlikely that he came from a noble family, but as an adult, he earned the privileges of an **encomendero** in both Cuba and Guatemala. Most historians have believed that Cabrillo was a Portuguese who had entered the service of Spain, but recently some scholars have claimed that he was actually Spanish.

Cabrillo proved to be an outstanding soldier and seaman during Narváez's conquest of Cuba in 1518. Two years later, he went to Mexico with Narváez on a mission to control the ambitious activities of Cortés. A battle ensued, and Cortés defeated Narváez. Like many of the remaining men in Narváez's army, Cabrillo then changed sides, and Cortés put him in charge of building 13 **brigantines** for the final assault on Tenochtitlán. During the battle, Cabrillo was wounded, but the Spanish were victorious. He recovered in time to join Francisco de Orozco on an expedition in late 1521. Orozco founded the Mexican city of Oaxaca.

Beginning in 1523, Cabrillo spent several years under the command of Pedro de Alvarado, exploring and conquering large parts of Central America. Cabrillo became a citizen of the colonial province of Guatemala. He lived with his Indian wife and their children, and he became wealthy from gold mines that he had discovered. In 1532 he sailed to Spain to marry the sister of a friend and then returned to Guatemala the following year. Upon his arrival, he received a commission to build a fleet for an expedition to the Spice Islands (also called the Moluccas) that Alvarado was planning.

The Exploration of California

In 1542 Cabrillo was chosen to lead a journey along the Pacific coast to the northern limits of Spanish territory. He was instructed to find and claim new lands. One of the vessels built for Alvarado, the *San Salvador,* served as Cabrillo's flagship. He sailed on June 27, and by July 2, he had reached the Baja California peninsula. He is the first European known to have made contact with the Indians of that area.

Cabrillo explored every inlet and bay along the coast. One of these he named San Diego Bay after the smallest of his ships. Today it is the site of the city of San Diego. He sailed as far north as the Russian River but then turned back to find a safe port in which to spend the winter. While spending the winter on San Miguel Island, one of several large islands off the coast, his party was attacked by Indians. His leg was broken in the fighting, and the injury led to his death soon after. In the spring, Cabrillo's chosen successor, Bartolomé Ferrera, led the Spanish force as far north as Oregon before returning to Mexico.

Cabrillo's account of this expedition was not published until the 1800s. However, it is the oldest written record of human activity on the west coast of the United States. Today Cabrillo is remembered as the discoverer and explorer of the California coast, and his name can be found on schools, monuments, and roads throughout the state.

Suggested Reading Harry Kelsey, *Juan Rodriguez Cabrillo* (Huntington Library, 1986); Nancy Lemke, *Cabrillo: First European Explorer of the California Coast* (EZ Nature, 1991); Francis J. Weber, *Explorer of California: Juan Rodriguez Cabrillo* (Opuscula, 1992).

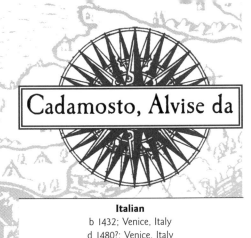

Cadamosto, Alvise da

Italian
b 1432; Venice, Italy
d 1480?; Venice, Italy
Explored west coast of Africa

galley ship with oars and sails, used in ancient and medieval times

caravel small ship with three masts and both square and triangular sails

Alvise da Cadamosto was one of the first Europeans to explore the seas south of Spain and Portugal. He made two journeys of discovery along the west coast of Africa, sailing as far south as what is now Gambia. He may also have discovered the Cape Verde Islands.

In the Service of Henry the Navigator

As a young man, Cadamosto decided to become a sailor. In 1454 he left Venice, Italy, on a **galley** bound for Flanders, a region that is now part of France and Belgium. When winds delayed the ship off Portugal's Cape St. Vincent, he met the famous prince of Portugal, Henry the Navigator. Prince Henry, who sponsored many voyages of discovery, persuaded Cadamosto to lead a Portuguese trading fleet to the west coast of Africa.

The prince provided Cadamosto with a **caravel** in return for half of the profits of the voyage. Cadamosto set sail on March 22, 1455. Within a week, his ship reached the island of Madeira, off the northwest coast of Africa. From Madeira, Cadamosto continued south past the Canary Islands. He then headed to an island known as Arguin Island. For a third of the trip to Arguin Island, the ship sailed out of sight of land—a daring feat at the time. Eventually Cadamosto reached the mouth of the Senegal River (in modern-day Senegal). He and his crew spent about a month in the area. At a local marketplace, Cadamosto saw many unfamiliar plants and foods, as well as such animals as lions, panthers, and elephants. The Africans were fascinated by Cadamosto. They rubbed his hands to see if the light color of his skin would come off.

After leaving the Senegal River region, Cadamosto searched for riches farther south. He was joined by two other ships, one belonging to Prince Henry and another commanded by an Italian named Uso di Mare. They discovered a river about 60 miles south of Cape Verde, Senegal, but hostile Africans prevented them from exploring it. When they reached the Gambia River (in what is now Gambia), they traveled upstream. They were soon followed by canoes filled with Africans who carried shields and wore white clothes and feathered headdresses. The Europeans attempted to show that they were on a peaceful mission, but fighting broke out. Although the Europeans had superior weapons, they tried to frighten the Africans away rather than harm them.

A Second Voyage to Africa

Cadamosto returned to Portugal around 1456. Four years later, he and Uso di Mare went to Africa again. As they were sailing along the African coast, their ships were blown out to sea by a storm. Three days later, they spotted two large islands that may have been the Cape Verde Islands. Returning to the Gambia River, they followed it inland for 10 miles and met a group of Mandingo people. The Mandingo king, Batti, welcomed the Europeans kindly. Cadamosto and di Mare traded with the Mandingo for slaves, gold, exotic animals, nuts, cotton, and ivory. After two weeks, the Europeans continued south, traveling about 150 miles to explore the mouths of five smaller rivers before returning to Portugal.

Cadamosto's colorful account of his travels was published in Venice in 1507.

Suggested Reading G. R. Crone, *The Voyages of Cadamosto and Other Documents on Western Africa in the Second Half of the Fifteenth Century* (Hakluyt Society, 1937).

Caillié, René-Auguste

French
b November 19, 1799; Mauzé, France
d May 17, 1838; Mauzé, France
Explored Africa

René-Auguste Caillié was the first European to return alive from Timbuktu.

caravan large group of people traveling together, often with pack animals, across a desert or other dangerous region

scurvy disease caused by a lack of vitamin C and once a major cause of death among sailors; symptoms include internal bleeding, loosened teeth, and extreme fatigue

René-Auguste Caillié was the first explorer to travel to the African city of Timbuktu (in present-day Mali) and live to tell about it. He traveled through many miles of desert, often while severely ill. After he left the city, hostile Africans made his return trip every bit as difficult. Caillié's account of his trip was widely doubted and criticized in Europe, but other explorers confirmed his reports after his death.

Chasing a Childhood Dream

As a child, Caillié was left on his own after his mother died and his father was sent to prison. He dropped out of school to learn to be a shoemaker, but his greatest interest was Africa. He read a great deal about the continent and was especially fascinated by tales of a fabulous city called Timbuktu.

At age 16, Caillé left his village and found a job as a cabin boy aboard a ship bound for Africa. He arrived at Cape Verde, the westernmost point in Africa, in July 1816. He deserted his ship to join an expedition traveling up the Senegal River. He soon became seriously ill, however, and he returned to France, where he remained for three years. His second trip was also cut short by illness, but the attempt would not be his last.

In 1824 Caillié returned to Senegal, but this time he decided to prepare more thoroughly for his journey inland. For eight months, he lived among the area's Arab tribes, studying their languages and customs. He sought money from the French government to fund his travels, but his request was denied. Luckily, a British colonial official gave him a job to help him raise the needed money. In 1827 Caillié set out with a small Arab **caravan.** He posed as an Egyptian Arab who wanted to pass through Timbuktu on the way back to Egypt.

Difficulties and Disappointments

Caillié's skin was fairly dark, and he was fluent in the local language, so he had little trouble with his disguise. Still, the journey was very difficult, and he suffered tremendous physical hardships. He fell ill with **scurvy** and fever and was forced to interrupt his trip for several days. He finally reached Timbuktu in April 1828.

What he saw in Timbuktu was a great disappointment. Some Arab histories, as well as the famous book *Arabian Nights,* had portrayed Timbuktu as a lively, wealthy, and exotic city. Caillié found a city of "badly built houses of clay" and streets that were "monotonous and melancholy like the desert."

To add to his disappointment, he was not, after all, the first European to see Timbuktu. He found out that the Scottish explorer Alexander Gordon LAING had visited the city two years earlier. Laing had been killed before he was able to return to Europe to tell of his travels. Despite the fact that the journey had lost much of its glamor and glory, Caillié took detailed notes on the city and its residents during his two-week visit.

Triumph and Heartbreak

From Timbuktu, Caillié began the 1,200-mile trek across the western Sahara to Morocco. He traveled through the desert with a caravan that included 600 camels. At first he was able to ride a camel, but his fellow travelers gradually became hostile toward him. They began to treat him like a slave, forcing him to walk and even beating him. Caillié left the caravan to travel on his own. He made a dangerous journey through Moroccan territory that was forbidden to Christians. After three months, he arrived in the Moroccan city of Fès. The French colonial official there did not believe that this dark, ragged stranger was French, and he refused to help Caillié. Continuing north, Caillié reached Tangier, where a sympathetic official arranged for his passage home.

Caillié received a hero's welcome in France. He was made a knight of the Legion of Honor. The Paris Geographical Society gave him a large reward for being the first traveler to return from Timbuktu. He published an account of his journey, but many readers refused to believe that Timbuktu was not a magnificent city. Some pointed to Caillié's humble background and lack of scientific training. They claimed that he had invented his entire story. Heartbroken, Caillié returned to his childhood village, where he died of **tuberculosis** in 1838. Ten years later, the German explorer Heinrich BARTH confirmed Caillié's reports and praised him as "one of the most reliable explorers of Africa."

Suggested Reading Gailbraith Welch, *The Unveiling of Timbuktoo: The Astounding Adventures of Caillié* (Carroll and Graf, 1991).

Cam, Diego. See *Cão, Diogo.*

Cameron, Verney Lovett

English
b July 1, 1844; Radipole, England
d March 27, 1894; near Leighton Buzzard, England
Explored central Africa

Verney Lovett Cameron was the first European to travel across central Africa from coast to coast. He explored Lake Tanganyika and located the outlet where the lake water flows into a **tributary** of the Congo River. He also led an expedition to locate the missing explorer David LIVINGSTONE. Cameron became known for his strong opposition to the African slave trade and for his efforts to develop trade and transportation in Africa.

The Search for David Livingstone

Cameron, the son of a clergyman, left his village at age 13 to join the British navy. He took part in Britain's military campaign in Abyssinia (present-day Ethiopia) in 1868. He also joined patrols on Zanzibar, an island off the coast of Tanzania, that were organized to find and arrest slave traders. After spending so much time in eastern Africa, he became interested in exploring the continent's

tuberculosis infection of the lungs

tributary stream or river that flows into a larger stream or river

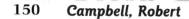

malaria disease that is spread by mosquitoes in tropical areas

interior. When he was 28, Britain's Royal Geographical Society offered him a chance to lead a search for Livingstone.

Members of the expedition met at Bagamoyo on the east coast of Tanzania in February 1873 and departed for the interior the next month. By the time they reached Tabora (in central Tanzania), one man had died of **malaria,** and the rest were seriously ill. On October 20, while still in Tabora, Cameron received a letter announcing Livingstone's death. A few days later, Livingstone's servants arrived with the explorer's body, which was returned to England. Some members of Cameron's expedition, believing their mission complete, left with Livingstone's servants. Cameron, though, was determined to continue exploring with the help of Livingstone's papers and equipment.

Across Africa

Cameron traveled to the southern end of Lake Tanganyika, where he identified the Lukuga River as the lake's outlet. He tried to reach the Congo River by sailing north on the Lualaba River, but he failed and was uncertain what to do next. He then met one of Livingstone's former guides, an Arab slave trader named Tippoo Tib. Learning of Cameron's difficulties, Tippoo Tib suggested that Cameron travel west to what is now Angola, on Africa's west coast. Cameron agreed and left the town of Nyangwe (in modern-day Democratic Republic of Congo) in August 1874. He crossed the Congo River basin and arrived at the coastal village of Catumbela, in Angola, on November 7, 1875. He was the first European to travel all the way across tropical Africa.

Upon his return to England a few months later, Cameron was awarded the Founder's Medal of the Royal Geographical Society. In 1877 he published an account of his journey, entitled *Across Africa.* For the rest of his life, he was an active spokesman for British involvement in Africa. He took part in several efforts to develop trade on the continent, and he proposed building a railway across Africa from north to south. He also spoke publicly against the slave trade. In 1883 he returned to Africa with Richard Francis Bur-ton. The two men wrote a book about their adventures, *To the Gold Coast for Gold.*

Suggested Reading Verney Lovett Cameron, *Across Africa* (Negro Universities Press, 1969); Robert W. Foran, *African Odyssey: The Life of Verney Lovett Cameron* (Hutchinson, 1937).

Verney Lovett Cameron was the first European to cross tropical Africa from coast to coast.

Campbell, Robert

Scottish
b February 21, 1808; Glenlyon, Scotland
d May 9, 1894; Manitoba, Canada
Explored sources of Yukon River

Fur trader Robert Campbell was one of the first explorers of the Yukon region of Canada. From 1834 to 1852, he investigated the far northwest of North America. He is particularly known for his accomplishments on the Yukon River, which flows from Canada through Alaska to the Bering Sea.

Early Explorations of the Northwest

In 1830 Campbell joined the Hudson's Bay Company, a British company involved in trade in Canada. Four years later, he was assigned to the Mackenzie River region in northwestern Canada. He was instructed to explore the area and to build a network of trading posts there. In 1837 he traveled up the Stikine River (in what is now British Columbia), and a year later, he built a post on Dease Lake. In his journal, he described how he and his companions were forced to endure "a winter of constant danger...and of much suffering from starvation." They were so short of food, he wrote, that "our last meal before abandoning Dease Lake on 8th May, 1839, consisted of the lacing of our snow-shoes."

The following year, Campbell and seven others explored the northern branch of the Liard River. They also discovered a body of water Campbell called a "beautiful lake." He named it Frances Lake after the wife of Sir George Simpson, an official of the Hudson's Bay Company. Leaving their canoe and continuing on foot, the explorers eventually came to a stream that flowed to the west. Campbell named the stream Pelly after the company's governor. Campbell would later discover that the Pelly River was one of the main branches of the Yukon River. He would also learn that the Yukon River system can be navigated for over 1,500 miles to its mouth in the Bering Sea.

Expanding Trade in the Northwest

Campbell and his men built a trading post at Frances Lake and then set off on a journey down the Pelly River by canoe in June 1843. Eventually they came to a place where the upper Yukon River joins the Pelly to form the main flow of the Yukon River. A group of Wood Indians there warned the explorers that many fierce Indians lived farther down the Yukon. Campbell's companions were alarmed by this information, and rather than risk their lives, they forced him to call off the trip and turn back.

In 1850 Campbell followed the Yukon to the place where it meets one of its large northern **tributaries,** the Porcupine River. He traveled up the Porcupine River and crossed the Richardson Mountains to the Mackenzie River, which empties into the Arctic Ocean. Following the Mackenzie River inland, he reached Fort Simpson, a major trading post west of Great Slave Lake. Campbell's discovery of the routes between the Mackenzie, the Porcupine, and the Yukon Rivers was valuable information that provided a great boost to trade in the region. He left the Yukon territory in 1852 and traveled south and east to Montréal. He made that entire journey of over 3,000 miles on snowshoes.

Robert Campbell braved the cold and isolation of the far northwest of North America mainly to expand the business activities of the Hudson's Bay Company. As an explorer, he also greatly expanded knowledge of one of the most remote regions of the earth. He demonstrated his remarkable courage, skill, and endurance in that harsh terrain for 18 years.

Suggested Reading Clifford Wilson, *Campbell of the Yukon* (Macmillan of Canada, 1970).

tributary stream or river that flows into a larger stream or river

Candish, Thomas. See *Cavendish, Thomas.*

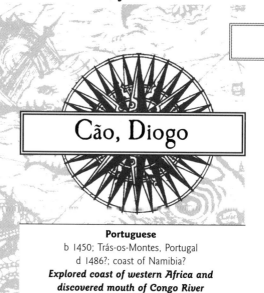

Cão, Diogo

Portuguese
b 1450; Trás-os-Montes, Portugal
d 1486?; coast of Namibia?
Explored coast of western Africa and discovered mouth of Congo River

cartographer mapmaker

Cano, Juan Sebastián del. *See Elcano, Juan Sebastián de.*

Diogo Cão was one of the most capable navigators of his day. He discovered the lower course of Africa's Congo River and gave it and the surrounding region the name Zaire. He was chosen by King John II of Portugal to sail down the Atlantic coast of Africa. King John hoped that Cão would find the southern tip of Africa, sail around it, and reach the trade markets of Asia. Cão's first expedition covered some 800 miles of mostly unexplored coastline and took him to the mouth of the Congo River and beyond. A second journey, from which he apparently never returned, covered nearly twice this distance. Even so, he never found the southern tip of Africa and could not complete his mission.

The Discovery of the Congo River

Cão was born into a Portuguese military family. He joined the Portuguese navy as a youth, eventually becoming a captain and proving his skill in combat off the west coast of Africa. In his early 30s, his reputation as a brave and talented navigator brought him to the attention of the king of Portugal, John II.

King John gave Cão the opportunity to explore Africa's western coastline. The king supplied him with limestone pillars to use as markers for claiming new territory. The pillars, known as *padrãos,* were five feet tall and featured a cross at the top. Each *padrão* was inscribed with the names of the king and the expedition's commander.

Cão left Portugal in June, 1482, sailing down the coast of Africa by way of the Canary Islands and the Gulf of Guinea. He made his way along the rugged coastline against dangerous currents, traveling 280 miles past the southernmost point previously explored. Late in the year, he reached the mouth of the Congo River and left a *padrão* on the river's southern bank.

Cão spent a month near the river, known to the native Bakongo people as the Nzadi, meaning "great water." Because Cão misunderstood the Bakongo name for the river, the Portuguese royal **cartographers** would later list the river and the surrounding area, as Zaire or Kongo.

The friendly Bakongo told Cão that far upriver was the royal city of the Mani Kongo, Lord of the Kongo. Cão hoped that the Mani Kongo might prove to be Prester John, a legendary Christian king whom the Portuguese had long hoped to find. Before leaving the area, Cão sent four of his African slaves on a mission to the city of the Mani Kongo, bearing gifts for the ruler.

The rest of the expedition continued 500 miles farther south along the coast, reaching Cape St. Mary (in present-day Angola), where Cão erected another *padrão.* When he returned to the Congo River for his slaves, he found no trace of them nor any explanation for their disappearance. Certain that his men were being held captive, Cão kidnapped four of the Bakongo and sent word to the Mani Kongo that the captives would be held until Cão's men were freed. He then sailed for Portugal, promising to return to the Congo region.

The Disappearance of Diogo Cão

Cão arrived in Portugal in April 1484 and was knighted for his accomplishments. King John treated the Bakongo captives as honored guests, since he believed that they would help him find Prester John. Confident that Cão had almost found the route around Africa, the king agreed to finance a second journey.

Cão left Portugal on his second voyage in late 1485. First he went to the Congo River to exchange his Bakongo hostages for the slaves he had left behind. He sailed about 100 miles up the river but was forced to turn back when he reached dangerous rapids. He returned to the coast and continued south, still searching for a route to Asia. He reached Cape Negro (now in Angola) and Cape Cross (now in Namibia), placing *padrãos* at both sites. Here his story abruptly ends. There is no further record of Cão's journey, and his disappearance remains a mystery to this day.

Historians have speculated that Cão may have been shipwrecked on Cape Cross or lost at sea on his way back to Portugal. His slaves, however, arrived safely in Lisbon. Some scholars suggest that Cão returned to Portugal but was executed by King John for twice failing to find the route around Africa.

Suggested Reading Eric Axelson, *Congo to Cape; Early Portuguese Explorers* (Barnes and Noble, 1973); Ernest Ravenstein, *The Voyages of Diogo Cão and Bartholomeu Dias, 1482–1488* (State Library, 1986).

Carpini, Giovanni de Plano

Italian
b 1180?; Umbria, near Perugia, Italy
d August 1, 1252; Italy?
***Traveled across Europe and Asia
to Mongol Empire***

Giovanni de Plano Carpini, a member of the Franciscan order of monks, made a historic journey across Asia when he was 65 years old. He was sent by Pope Innocent IV as an ambassador to the powerful Mongols (also called Tartars), whose warriors had invaded eastern Europe. During his mission to the Mongol court, Carpini traveled over 15,000 miles, finding routes to the previously unknown lands of eastern Asia. His description of Asia and the Mongols is considered one of the best provided by a Christian writer of the Middle Ages.

In the Service of the Church

Carpini was a follower of Saint Francis of Assisi, the founder of the Franciscan order. As a monk, Carpini became a leading teacher in northern Europe and one of the pope's most trusted representatives. He made lengthy trips to both Spain and Scandinavia on behalf of the Franciscan order. When Pope Innocent IV decided to send an ambassador to the Mongols in 1245, he chose Carpini.

The pope had two reasons to communicate with the Mongols. The first was the Mongol invasion of eastern Europe in 1241. The pope hoped to discover why the Mongols had attacked. The second reason was the fall of Jerusalem to the Saracens, a Muslim tribe from the Arabian desert. The pope hoped to enlist the Mongols' aid in driving the Saracens from Jerusalem and the surrounding area.

khan title of an Asian ruler

European leaders knew little about the Mongols. Stories about a Christian kingdom in Asia, ruled by the legendary Prester John, had fascinated Europeans for many years. Some people suggested that the Mongols were descendants of Prester John's followers. But, Europeans asked, if the Mongols were somehow connected with Prester John, why were they invading Christian Europe? To find out, Pope Innocent wrote a letter to the Mongol ruler, known as the Great **Khan.** Carpini was instructed to deliver this letter and bring back a reply.

Journey into the Unknown

Since the Great Khan's location was unknown, Innocent decided to increase his chances of success by sending two separate groups. Carpini led one party. The other was led by Laurentius of Portugal, who did not succeed in reaching the khan.

Carpini set out from Lyon, France, on Easter Day, 1245. He and the other members of the mission traveled to Prague (in the present-day Czech Republic), where they were told to continue east into Poland. There they would meet a Russian prince who would escort them to meet Batu, the Mongol conqueror of eastern Europe. This general was camped near the Volga River in Russia. After weeks of winter travel, they arrived at the city of Kiev (now in Ukraine), which had been almost totally destroyed by the Mongols. Some Mongols in Kiev offered to take Carpini's group on horseback to Batu's camp. According to Carpini, they rode as fast as the horses could run, changing horses three or four times a day. Even so, they did not reach Batu's camp until the day before the next Easter, nearly a year after they had left France.

The Heart of the Mongol Empire

Batu ordered Carpini's group to continue east to Mongolia, where they could meet with the khan, whose name was Guyug. Accompanied by two Mongol escorts, they traveled into the heart of Mongol territory. Heading north of the Caspian and Aral Seas, they rode through a bitterly cold June snowstorm. They arrived at Guyug's palace on July 22, just in time to see Mongol leaders elect him as their ruler.

Over 4,000 foreign ambassadors were present for the election. Carpini was one of only a handful of Europeans. After Guyug had been officially named khan, Carpini was given an opportunity to present the pope's message. Guyug gave Carpini a letter in response and instructed him to begin his trip back to Europe.

Carpini's Return

Carpini's group left immediately and traveled right through the winter. Carpini later wrote: "We often had to lie in snow in the wilderness. . . . When we awoke in the morning, we often found ourselves completely covered with snow that the wind had blown over us." They arrived at Batu's camp on May 9, 1247. When Carpini asked if Batu had any message of his own for the pope, Batu said that he had nothing to add to Guyug's reply. Carpini sensed some tension between Batu and the new emperor. This observation would be welcome news to the Europeans, who hoped that the Mongols would be too busy fighting among themselves to continue their attacks against Europe.

Carpini reached France in November and made a full report to the pope. Guyug's letter was not encouraging. The khan claimed that eastern Europe had been conquered by the Mongols because the people there "did not comply with the commandments of God and [the] Khan, but rather, in their infamy, deliberately murdered Our ambassadors." His message to the Europeans was: "Today you shall say from the depths of your heart: we wish to be Your subjects and give You some of our power." Of course, the leaders of Europe would not choose to submit to the khan, but they continued to fear the powerful Mongol armies.

Although Carpini's expedition did not achieve friendly relations between the Europeans and the Mongols, he brought back much valuable information. In his book, *History of the Mongols,* Carpini described the climate and geography of the Mongol lands as well as the Mongols' religion, history, customs, leaders, and armies. Carpini's journey also opened a route to the east that was soon followed by others. One such traveler was another Franciscan monk, WILLIAM OF RUBRUCK, who unraveled the story of Prester John and the Asian Christians.

Suggested Reading Christopher Dawson, *Mission to Asia* (reprint, Toronto University Press, 1980); Manuel Komroff, *Contemporaries of Marco Polo* (reprint, Dorset, 1989); Sherwood Merriam, *The Road to Cathay* (Macmillan, 1928).

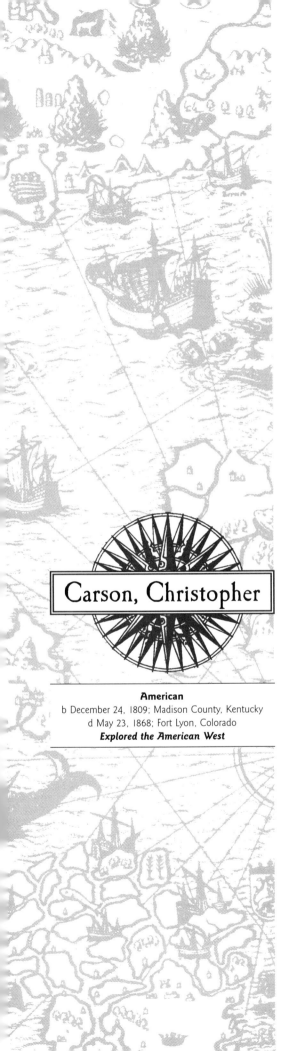

Carson, Christopher

American
b December 24, 1809; Madison County, Kentucky
d May 23, 1868; Fort Lyon, Colorado
Explored the American West

Christopher Carson, better known as Kit, was one of those Americans known as the Mountain Men. From the 1820s to the 1840s, they roamed the West, trapping beaver and selling furs. Along the way, the Mountain Men came to know more about the mountains, rivers, and plains of the West than any geographer. They were also popular heroes, famous for their astonishing adventures and colorful personalities. Perhaps none was better known or more admired than Kit Carson.

To the Mountains

Carson's father had fought in the American Revolution, and after the war, he headed west to Kentucky. Christopher was born in 1809, and the family moved to Missouri a year later. Carson's childhood on the frontier was not an easy one. The community he lived in was always in danger of attack by Indians. He received no schooling and did not know how to read or write. When he was nine years old, his father died, and his mother found him work with a saddle-maker in a nearby town. Carson did not stay with this man for long. Years later he recalled: "The business did not suit me and, having heard so many tales of life in the Mountains of the West, I concluded to leave him."

For a young man like Carson, the mysterious western lands held the promise of freedom and adventure. Only 20 years had passed since Meriwether LEWIS and William CLARK had returned from their

Many tales and legends were told about Christopher "Kit" Carson, but his real life as a Mountain Man was more than enough to secure his fame.

famous expedition to the Pacific Northwest. Large portions of the West were still unexplored and unmapped, but already some people were seeking their fortunes there. In 1826 Carson joined a group of traders bound for Santa Fe, which was then in Mexican territory.

After spending some time in Taos, north of Santa Fe, Carson joined a party of trappers led by Ewing Young, one of the first Mountain Men. They made a hard journey through mountains and deserts to California, trapping beaver in every river along the way. Carson then headed northwest and spent about 10 years in the Rocky Mountains, hunting beaver and buffalo. Sometimes the group in which he traveled included another Mountain Man, James BRIDGER. By the early 1840s, however, beaver were becoming scarce, and trappers found it hard to make a living. When Carson's Indian wife died in 1842, he took their daughter to Missouri to be raised. During this trip, a chance meeting changed his life and led to his fame throughout the nation.

Carson and Frémont

On a steamboat, Carson met John Charles FRÉMONT, a U.S. Army officer who was leading the exploration and mapping of the Oregon Trail through the Rocky Mountains. Frémont discovered that Carson knew the territory well, and he eventually hired him as a guide for two expeditions through the Rockies, Oregon, Utah, and California. In 1845 the government published Frémont's report, which became a huge public success. Americans had developed a great interest in the West. Thousands of people were moving to the frontier on the Oregon Trail. Also, a growing number of Americans felt that U.S. territory should include western regions that belonged to Mexico. People eagerly bought and read Frémont's report, which included glowing descriptions of the man Frémont called "My good and reliable friend, Kit Carson." The tough but soft-spoken Mountain Man became a hero.

In 1845 Carson made a third journey with Frémont. They crossed the Great Basin of Nevada and the Sierra Nevada mountain range on their way to California. There they became involved in a war between the United States and Mexico. Among other activities, Carson guided American soldiers over the Sierra Nevada. The war ended with the United States in control of California and the Southwest.

Military Career

In 1847 Frémont sent Carson to Washington, D.C., with reports of the events in California. President James K. Polk was impressed with Carson and made him a lieutenant in the Mounted Riflemen, an army unit. About a year later, members of Congress who opposed Frémont's activities in the West had Carson's appointment canceled. But there was nothing they could do about his fame.

Carson returned to Taos—by then part of the United States as a result of the war—and spent the next few years farming, fighting

Indians, and driving sheep to market. In the mid-1850s, increasing numbers of Indians were coming under U.S. control. The federal government put Carson in charge of relations between whites and Indians in his area. His job was to maintain order, supervise trade, and see that the Indians received the benefits that the government had promised them. Carson tried to represent the Indians fairly and often came into conflict with the territory's governor.

The governor did not agree with some of Carson's suggestions for improving conditions for the Indians. On one occasion, he went so far as have Carson arrested.

In 1861, when the Civil War broke out, Carson resigned his post to serve with the Union army. He fought in the West against the Apache, Navajo, and Comanche Indians, who were allied with the Confederacy. After the war, the army sent Carson to Colorado, but he left the service in 1867 because of ill health. He was appointed superintendent of Indian affairs for Colorado, but he died before taking up the job.

The Real Kit Carson

Kit Carson became a legend in his own lifetime. Once Frémont's reports had made him known to the public, other people began telling and publishing colorful stories about him. Some of these were exaggerations of events that had really happened, and some were completely false. Carson even became the hero of several works of fiction, such as the novel *Kit Carson, Prince of the Gold Hunters*, published in 1849. More recently, scholars have worked to replace the myths with a more accurate picture of the honest, loyal, and courageous Mountain Man who helped open the American West.

Suggested Reading Harvey L. Carter, *"Dear Old Kit": The Historical Christopher Carson* (Oklahoma University Press, 1968); Thelma S. Carter and Harvey L. Carter, *Kit Carson: A Pattern for Heroes* (Nebraska University Press, 1984); R. C. Gordon-McCutchan, editor, *Kit Carson: Indian Fighter or Indian Killer?* (Colorado University Press, 1996); Edward L. Sabin, *Kit Carson Days*, 2 volumes (reprint, Nebraska University Press, 1995).

Carteret, Philip

English
b January 22, 1733; Jersey Island, England
d July 21, 1796; Southampton, England
Discovered Pitcairn Island; sailed around world

frigate small, agile warship with three masts and square sails

sloop small ship with one mast and triangular sails

Philip Carteret was an English naval officer and explorer who survived a difficult 31-month sea voyage around the world. During his long journey, he made several discoveries in the Pacific Ocean, pointing the way for later explorers. At the time, however, he did not gain the recognition he deserved. His achievements were overshadowed by those of other famed English explorers, such as Samuel WALLIS and James COOK.

The Dolphin Voyages

Carteret was born into a distinguished family on the island of Jersey in the English Channel. He joined the navy as a teenager and served bravely during the Seven Years' War against France. One of the officers under whom he served was a commander named John BYRON. When Byron was planning an expedition on the **frigate** *Dolphin* in 1764, he asked Carteret to join him. Carteret agreed to serve as first lieutenant on the **sloop** *Tamar*, which was to sail alongside the *Dolphin*. The expedition lasted two years and traveled to the

Though his ship was barely seaworthy and his crew was desperately ill, Philip Carteret led a voyage around the world in the 1760s.

Falkland Islands, near the southern tip of South America. The two ships also sailed to several islands in the southern Pacific Ocean. By the end of the voyage, Carteret had been promoted to first lieutenant on the *Dolphin.*

When the *Dolphin* went to sea again, it was under a new commander, Samuel Wallis. The purpose of this voyage was to search for *Terra Australis Incognita,* an undiscovered southern continent believed to lie somewhere in the Pacific Ocean. Carteret was to command the *Swallow,* an old ship in poor condition. He was disappointed with the *Swallow,* but he was told that it would be replaced in the Falkland Islands. Carteret set sail with Wallis from Plymouth, England, late in the summer of 1766.

When they arrived in the Falklands, Carteret found that no new ship was waiting for him. He wanted to turn back, but Wallis would not allow it. To make sure that Carteret did not try to return to England, Wallis forced him to lead the way through the dangerous Strait of Magellan. This strait would take them across the southern tip of South America and into the Pacific Ocean.

In bad weather and high seas, the passage through the strait took four months. Just before the ships reached the Pacific Ocean, a strong wind pushed Wallis's *Dolphin* far ahead of the *Swallow,* and the two ships were separated. Carteret was now free of Wallis and could choose his own route. Although his ship was in terrible condition and many of his crew members were suffering from **scurvy,** Carteret continued to sail west.

Surviving on the High Seas

The *Swallow*'s voyage lasted for the next two years. In the southern Pacific Ocean, Carteret discovered Pitcairn Island, which later served as a hiding place for rebel sailors on the *Bounty,* a ship commanded by William BLIGH. Carteret also sailed to Santa Cruz and the Solomon Islands, which no European had seen since the 1500s. He did not realize that these islands had already been discovered by Alvaro de MENDAÑA DE NEHRA and Pedro Fernandez de QUIRÓS.

Sailing west from the Solomon Islands, Carteret reached New Britain, off the east coast of New Guinea. He discovered that New Britain was part of a group of three islands, not two as previously thought. He claimed New Britain and named the other two islands New Ireland and New Hanover. He also discovered and named the St. George Channel, which lay between New Britain and New Ireland. He named the strait between New Ireland and New Hanover after Byron and a harbor on New Ireland after himself. Further north and west, he reached another island group, which had been explored earlier by the Dutch navigator Abel TASMAN. Carteret named this group the Admiralty Islands.

More than a year after leaving England, Carteret reached an island in Indonesia. He hoped that he could finally repair his damaged ship, but Dutch officials there refused to help him. Carteret continued west, reaching what is now Jakarta, Indonesia, a year later. He spent four months there while the *Swallow* was repaired at last.

On his return journey to Britain, Carteret met a mysterious French navigator, who gave him news of the *Dolphin* but would say nothing about himself. He was Louis-Antoine de BOUGAINVILLE, another explorer sailing around the world. After this strange meeting, Carteret sailed on. He reached Britain in March 1769, after 31 months at sea. Half his crew had died during the voyage.

Ten years later, Carteret was again given command of a ship, the *Endymion.* He held this post for three years. Afterwards he remained a navy officer, but he never again went to sea.

Suggested Reading Helen Wallis, editor, *Carteret's Voyage Around the World,* (Hakluyt Society, 1965).

Cartier, Jacques

French
b 1491; St.-Malo, France
d September 1, 1557; St.-Malo, France
Explored Gulf of St. Lawrence and
St. Lawrence River

Jacques Cartier was an expert navigator who led three French expeditions to North America. In 1534 he sailed into the Gulf of St. Lawrence but did not find the St. Lawrence River. On the second voyage, a year later, he discovered the river and explored it as far as the site of present-day Montréal. In 1541 Cartier returned to the region to search for a mythical kingdom of great wealth and to start a French colony. Although he accomplished neither of these goals, Cartier was honored in his home country. His careful explorations were the first steps toward the empire France would build in North America.

On his three ocean crossings from France to North America, Jacques Cartier never lost a single ship or crew member to an accident at sea.

Treaty of Tordesillas agreement between Spain and Portugal dividing rights to discovered lands along a north-south line

Northwest Passage water route connecting the Atlantic Ocean and Pacific Ocean through the Arctic islands of northern Canada

A Search for Historical Evidence

Little is known of Jacques Cartier's life before he made his voyage to North America in 1534. Some historians believe that he took part in Giovanni da VERRAZANO's voyages to the Americas in the 1520s. In his writings, Cartier mentioned the food and native people of Brazil, one of the places explored by Verrazano. Records show that Cartier was away from France during Verrazano's expeditions. But other scholars point out that Cartier never wrote about those voyages or about the sections of the North American coast that Verrazano also explored.

Whether or not Cartier visited North America with Verrazano, he did become known as a skillful sailor. The abbot of the monastery at Mont-Saint-Michel, France, brought Cartier to the attention of the French king Francis I. At the time, Francis was looking for someone to lead a French expedition to North America. The abbot told the king that Cartier had traveled to both Brazil and Newfoundland (in present-day Canada).

Eyes on North America

King Francis hoped to find riches in the Americas like the gold and silver which Spain and Portugal had been mining for the last 30 years. However, a church decree of 1494, called the **Treaty of Tordesillas,** had given Spain and Portugal the right to claim newly discovered lands. The treaty excluded other nations. In 1533 King Francis persuaded Pope Clement VII to change the decree so that it would apply only to lands that were already known. Under the revised decree, any other lands could be claimed by the country that found them. Francis had won the opportunity for his country to join Spain and Portugal as a colonial power.

The king asked Cartier to lead the first French voyage to North America. In April 1534, Cartier sailed from St.-Malo in Brittany, France, with two ships and 61 men. His goals were to find new sources of precious metals and to discover a **Northwest Passage** to eastern Asia. Thanks to fair weather, the trip across the Atlantic Ocean was easy, taking only 20 days. The two ships reached land at what is now Cape Bonavista, Newfoundland. The island of Newfoundland was already being visited by French fishermen who needed to resupply or repair their vessels.

The Bleak and Rocky Coast

Even though it was early May, there was still much ice floating in the water. Cartier's ships sailed southeast to a warmer harbor before heading north again to what is now Funk Island. The French paused there to hunt sea birds called great auks for food. Soon the ships entered the Strait of Belle Isle between Newfoundland and the mainland coast of Labrador. This strait was the way into the bay later known as the Gulf of St. Lawrence.

As Cartier sailed along the rocky coast of Labrador, he was disappointed by what he saw. Although he landed in many places, he wrote that he found "nothing but moss and stunted shrubs." He described the few Indians he met as "untamed." Cartier soon grew weary of the bleak coast and headed south along the west coast of Newfoundland. When he reached the island's southern end, he guessed that there was a channel between Newfoundland and Nova Scotia, which was known to lie to the south. For some reason, he did not try to find this channel. Instead, he turned west and crossed over to what are now called the Magdalen Islands. Cartier did not name these islands—he thought that they were part of the mainland.

On June 29, Cartier's ships left the islands and sailed west all night. The crew sighted what is now called Prince Edward Island in the morning. Cartier mistakenly thought that this island, too, was part of the mainland. He took the ships across the entrance to the Northumberland Strait and sailed into Miramichi Bay, on the coast of modern-day New Brunswick. He then headed farther north and discovered another waterway, which he named Chaleur Bay. At last Cartier had found something to delight him, for he thought this bay lovelier than any other place he had seen during the voyage. He praised the warm air and water, the plentiful fish, and the rich soil. Chaleur Bay was long and narrow and seemed to stretch on without end. Cartier hoped that he had discovered a passage to China.

New Friends in North America

On the north shore of Chaleur Bay, Cartier had his first meeting with the Micmac Indians. They surrounded his ships in their canoes. Cartier wrote that the Indians made "signs of joy" to indicate friendship. Still, Cartier did not trust them, so his men shot small guns over the Indians' heads. The Micmac paid no attention to Cartier's threats. They returned the next day and offered fur pelts for sale. The French and Indians traded peacefully. Cartier sailed on, but he soon reached the end of the bay and knew that he would not find a Northwest Passage there.

The expedition sailed back out of the bay and then north to the tip of the Gaspé Peninsula. There the French met about 200 Huron Indians, who had come from what is now called Québec to fish along the coast. Cartier did not realize that the Indians were a fishing party, and he wrote that they were the "poorest people that can be in the world," because they carried so little with them.

The French raised a 30-foot-high cross at Gaspé Harbor. On the cross they wrote, "Long live the King of France." The Indians' chief, Donnaconna, could not understand the French language, but he could tell that these strangers were claiming the land. Donnaconna quickly made it clear to the French that the territory belonged to his people. The French were apparently able to reassure Donnaconna as to their peaceful intentions. The chief agreed to send his two sons, Domagaya and Taignoagny, to France to learn to speak French. Cartier promised to return the next year with Donnaconna's sons, who would then be able to serve as interpreters.

tributary stream or river that flows into a larger stream or river

Cartier set sail from Gaspé Harbor and explored nearby Anticosti Island. With summer nearly over, Cartier and his crew decided to return to France. They reached St.-Malo with both ships in good condition. Not one member of the crew had been lost. Although Cartier had failed to find gold, jewels, or a route to Asia, he was given a hero's welcome in France. He had added to European knowledge of North America, and he had made valuable allies among the Huron Indians.

The St. Lawrence River

Cartier had been back in France for less than two months when the king hired him to lead another expedition. This time Cartier was given three ships and 110 men. They set sail in the late spring of 1535. Bad weather and strong winds caused the ocean crossing to take more than twice as long as it had the first time. The ships finally landed at Funk Island in early July. Cartier then headed directly to the Strait of Belle Isle to search for a water route into the interior of the continent. He named a harbor after St. Lawrence on August 10, the feast day of that saint. In later years, that name would also be applied to the Gulf of St. Lawrence and the St. Lawrence River.

With Donnaconna's two sons as guides, Cartier easily found the mouth of the St. Lawrence River. Domagaya and Taignoagny told Cartier that this river was the route to "Canada," meaning the area that is now the province of Québec. They told him that the waters came from so far away that no one had ever seen their source. Cartier decided that this river must be the passage to Asia that he was seeking. Soon after entering the St. Lawrence River, the explorers saw a deep and rapid river joining the flow from the west. The Huron guides told them that this **tributary** was the way to Saguenay, a kingdom of great riches. The search for Saguenay later became the main purpose of Cartier's final voyage.

Demons and Deceptions

In September the ships reached the village of Stadacona, where the city of Québec is located today. Donnaconna was there to greet them. Donnaconna's sons had promised to lead Cartier all the way to the village of Hochelaga, the site of modern-day Montréal. Then, however, the guides began to stall. Cartier later learned that Hochelaga's chief claimed to rule Donnaconna's people. Donnaconna wanted to keep his French allies to himself.

Cartier decided to go to Hochelaga, even without the two guides, so Donnaconna tried to scare the French into staying at Stadacona. He had three Indians dress up as devils. They blackened their faces and wore long horns and dog skins. They warned the French that snow and ice upriver would cause the death of the entire crew if they tried to go to Hochelaga. The French only laughed at this trick. Donnaconna laughed along, pretending that he had meant the incident as a joke. Unsure of the chief's intentions, Cartier proceeded with his plans.

Cartier left part of his crew behind with Donnaconna's tribe and sailed up the river aboard one of his ships. He arrived at Hochelaga

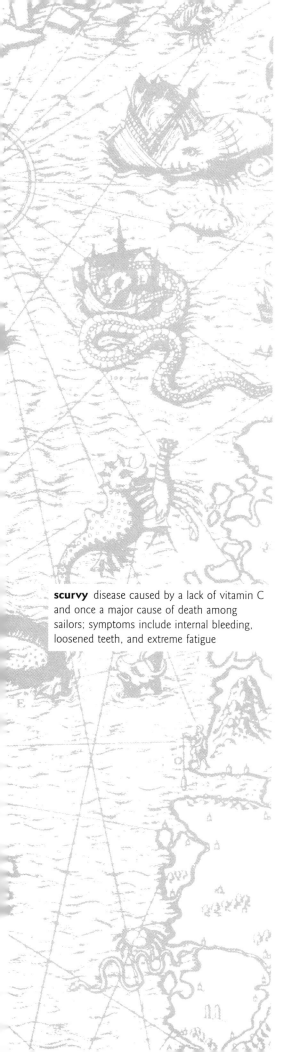

scurvy disease caused by a lack of vitamin C and once a major cause of death among sailors; symptoms include internal bleeding, loosened teeth, and extreme fatigue

about two weeks later. One thousand Huron Indians came to the riverbank to greet the explorers. They offered gifts and threw corn bread to the sailors. The Huron brought sick members of the tribe to Cartier, believing that he could heal with the touch of his hands. A grand ceremony was staged in the village's main plaza to welcome the visitors.

Some of the Frenchmen climbed a peak that Cartier named Mont Réal, which means "Royal Mountain" in French. From the top, they could see rapids on the river, just beyond Hochelaga. These rapids made it impossible to travel farther up the St. Lawrence River without canoes, which the French did not have. Cartier was very disappointed that he could not continue up the river, for he believed that it would have led him to Asia. He was forced to return to Stadacona. Before leaving Hochelaga, he asked the Indians about the legendary land of Saguenay. They told him that the stories he had heard earlier were true. They described the land's precious metals and said that its people had a reputation as skilled warriors.

Long Winter Nights

Unable to search for Saguenay, Cartier headed back east to the mouth of what is now called the St. Charles River. Near Stadacona, at a port that he named Ste.-Croix, he rejoined the sailors he had left behind. Those men had built a fort, and Cartier's entire party spent the winter there. Cartier used the time to write about the customs of local Indians. His notes contain the first written mention of tobacco in northern North America.

The winter was extremely cold. From mid-November to mid-April, the French ships were frozen in ice at the mouth of the St. Charles River. Many of the sailors suffered from **scurvy.** The disease caused their legs to swell up, their gums to turn black, and their teeth to fall out. Cartier wrote, "Out of the 110 men that we were, not 10 were well enough to help the others, a thing pitiful to see." Some of the crew were saved by a cure that they had learned from Domagaya. He had taught them to prepare a kind of tea from the bark and needles of the white cedar tree. Everyone who took this medicine recovered. At the end of the winter, 85 men were still alive.

Dreams of Saguenay

The relationship between the French and the Indians had become tense. Even so, many of the long winter nights were spent around fires, listening to Donnaconna tell stories. His elaborate and detailed accounts of the land of Saguenay were more amazing than any the French had yet heard. He gave glowing descriptions of Saguenay's gold and jewels. He claimed that the land's people included white men and one-legged monsters. Cartier did not realize that this kind of storytelling was a tradition among the Huron. Eager to please and entertain their guests, they said whatever they thought the French wanted to hear. The Huron saw the Frenchmen's eyes light up at the mention of gold, so they made sure to talk about gold as often as possible.

Donnaconna soon regretted having told these tales. Cartier decided that King Francis should hear the stories of Saguenay directly from the chief. Just before leaving for France, he kidnapped Donnaconna, Domagaya, Taignoagny, and several other important members of the tribe. The Huron people raised a great cry for the return of their captured chief. Cartier promised to bring Donnaconna back within a year with gifts from the French king.

The ships set sail in May 1536. During the voyage, Cartier made progress in his exploration of the Gulf of St. Lawrence. He had seen the Magdalen Islands two years earlier but had thought that they were part of the mainland. Now, sailing past them again, he realized that they were islands. He also became the first French explorer to sail between Newfoundland and Nova Scotia.

When the ships reached France, Cartier presented Donnaconna to the royal court. The Huron chief became very popular, once again spinning his tales about the kingdom of Saguenay. Donnaconna noticed that King Francis was interested in spices and exotic fruits as well as gold. Soon the stories were full of cloves, nutmeg, pepper, oranges, and pomegranates. King Francis decided to send Cartier back to North America to find Saguenay.

Journey of Disappointments

Cartier's departure was held up for five years. France was at war with Spain, and all of its money was spent on the French army and navy. The king could not afford to sponsor Cartier at that time. Once the war was over, Cartier spent three years preparing five ships. Intending to establish the first French colony in North America, he took hundreds of people on board to settle there.

By January 1541, Cartier was ready to set sail. Suddenly, the king placed Jean-François de la Rocque de Roberval in command in place of Cartier. All the settlers and crewmen, including Cartier, had to swear an oath of loyalty to Roberval. Cartier would still be the chief navigator, but he was no longer in charge. There is no record of his feeling about being replaced.

Cartier and the five ships left St.-Malo in May. Roberval would follow as soon as his own ships were ready. Three months later, Cartier's party arrived in Stadacona. A Huron named Agona had taken Donnaconna's place as chief of the tribe. Agona was relieved to hear that his rival Donnaconna had died in France. Cartier had a feeling that the Huron were not as friendly as they seemed. To prevent a conflict, he lied and said that the others were happy in France and did not want to return. In fact, except for one girl, all of the kidnapped Indians had died.

It was probably this same feeling of distrust that caused Cartier to abandon his old fort at Ste.-Croix. The French built a new fort several miles farther from Stadacona. They called it Charlesbourg-Royal, and the colonists planted a garden there. In the surrounding area, they began to collect what they thought were diamonds and gold. Actually, they had only found quartz and iron pyrite, which is also known as "fool's gold."

Meanwhile, Cartier and some of his men began the search for Saguenay. They traveled west toward Hochelaga, passing through

For a map of Cartier's routes, see the profile of John CABOT in this volume.

the territory of Achelacy, a chief whom Cartier had met on the previous expedition. Cartier left two French youths with Achelacy to learn the tribe's language. This example was later followed by other French explorers, such as Samuel de CHAMPLAIN, who sent Etienne BRULÉ and other young men to live among the Indians.

Just before reaching Hochelaga, Cartier's party reached a waterfall. The explorers left their boats and followed an Indian trail along the shore. The path led them to a village called Tutonaguy, where the French were treated kindly. Four Indians joined Cartier to help him reach Saguenay. These guides took the French to another village and drew a map with sticks to show the way to Saguenay. However, they also told Cartier that another series of waterfalls blocked the way. At this news, Cartier had to turn back again.

The Colony in Ruins

When Cartier got back to Charlesbourg-Royal, he found that he had been right to mistrust the Huron. The Indians had become violent, probably because they realized that the French visitors intended to stay. There are no records to show what actually happened during the long winter of 1541 to 1542. According to hearsay later gathered from French sailors, the Indians attacked the settlement more than once. They killed about 35 people during the winter. Scurvy broke out, but it was quickly cured with the medicine made from the white cedar tree. The settlers were depressed and miserable, and to make matters worse, no one knew why Roberval had not yet arrived.

In early summer, the French ships headed back to France with all of the colonists aboard. The settlers brought back barrels of what they thought were gold, silver, and jewels. On the way, the ships anchored in the harbor of St. John's in Newfoundland. There they found Roberval with three ships. Roberval ordered Cartier to turn around and go back to Stadacona. Cartier may have thought that his crew and the colonists would rebel against this plan. He may also have been eager to show his cargo to the king. Whatever his reasons, Cartier and his ships slipped away in the night and returned to St.-Malo.

Cartier was not punished for disobeying Roberval's order. Instead, the king rewarded him by giving him two of the ships. Cartier lived out the rest of his life in St.-Malo and at his nearby manor, Limoïlou. He died at the age of 66.

The riches that Cartier brought back turned out to be worthless rocks. No one ever found the land of Saguenay—it had existed only in the Indians' stories and in the Frenchmen's greedy imaginations. But Cartier is rightly remembered for his skill and leadership. His three missions were among the most important voyages of discovery ever made. The St. Lawrence River region became the heart of the French empire in North America.

Suggested Reading Henry S. Burrage, editor, *Early English and French Voyages Chiefly from Hakluyt, 1534-1608* (Barnes and Noble, 1934); Josef Berger, *Discoverers of the New World* (American Heritage Publishing Company, 1960); Harold Lamb, *New Found World* (Doubleday, 1955); Samuel Eliot Morison, *The European Discovery of America* (Oxford University Press, 1971); David B. Quinn, *North America from Earliest Discovery to First Settlements* (Harper and Row, 1977).

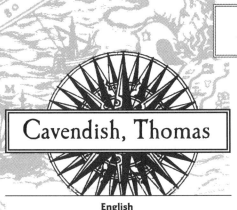

Cavendish, Thomas

English
b 1560; England
d October 1592; southern Atlantic Ocean
Sailed around world;
discovered Port Desire, Argentina

Thomas Cavendish commanded the third sea voyage around the world—and captured dozens of Spanish treasure ships along the way.

circumnavigate to travel around

courtier attendant at a royal court

buccaneer pirate, especially one who attacked Spanish colonies and ships in the 1600s

topsail second-lowest sail on the mast of a ship

Cavelier, René Robert de La Salle. *See La Salle, René Robert Cavelier de.*

Sir Thomas Cavendish was an English navigator who led the third expedition to **circumnavigate** the globe. His journey around the world followed those of Ferdinand MAGELLAN and Sir Francis DRAKE. Cavendish also spent time in South America, where he explored Patagonia and discovered Port Desire (in what is now Argentina).

High Hopes for Success

Cavendish attended Cambridge University in England but left without earning a degree. He was a **courtier** and a member of the English Parliament. During this time, he enjoyed an expensive lifestyle and almost ran out of money. He decided to seek his fortune at sea.

In 1585 he joined the British admiral Sir Richard Grenville on a voyage to the colony of Virginia in North America. When he returned to England, Cavendish began to plan his own ocean adventure. He wanted to make a full journey around the world, similar to that completed by Sir Francis Drake in 1580. In July 1586, Cavendish set sail from Plymouth, England, with 123 men in three ships. The ships were named the *Desire,* the *Content,* and the *Gallant.* They sailed south along the west coast of Africa to Sierra Leone, then crossed the Atlantic Ocean to Cape Frio, Brazil. Cavendish continued south and explored Patagonia (now part of southern Argentina). On the coast of Argentina, he made his major discovery—Port Desire, which he named for his ship. In later years, ships preparing to sail through the Strait of Magellan would often stop at Port Desire for supplies and repairs.

Pirates of the Pacific Ocean

Cavendish and his crew continued south and then sailed west through the Strait of Magellan into the Pacific Ocean. They made their way up the west coasts of South America, Central America, and Mexico. Like Sir Francis Drake, Cavendish and his men were **buccaneers**—they raided settlements and other ships.

Cavendish and his men captured some 19 vessels as they crossed the Pacific Ocean. Their route took them to many islands, including the Philippines and Java (in modern-day Indonesia). They then crossed the Indian Ocean and rounded the Cape of Good Hope at the southern tip of Africa. They reached England in September 1588 after two years and 50 days at sea.

Although Cavendish returned with only one ship, the *Desire,* he brought home the riches he had set out to find. When his ship reached England, the crew was wearing silk, and the **topsail** was said to be of gold cloth. Three years later, however, Cavendish again found himself in financial trouble. He decided to repeat his earlier journey. He gathered five ships and set sail, but he never made it back to England. He died at sea in 1592, somewhere in the southern Atlantic Ocean.

Suggested Reading Thomas Cavendish, *The Last Voyage of Thomas Cavendish, 1591–1592: The Autograph Manuscript of his Own Account of the Voyage, Written Shortly Before his Death,* edited by David Beers Quinn (Chicago University Press, 1975); Philip Edwards, editor, *Last Voyages—Cavendish, Hudson, Raleigh: The Original Narratives* (Oxford University Press, 1988).

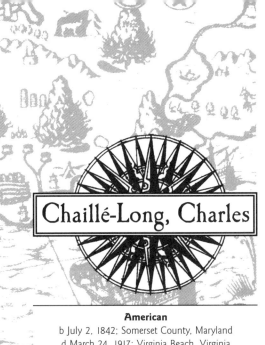

American
b July 2, 1842; Somerset County, Maryland
d March 24, 1917; Virginia Beach, Virginia
Explored Nile River region of Africa

In the late 1800s, Egypt and central Africa attracted explorers from all over the world. Charles Chaillé-Long, an American soldier, was one of these adventurers. He worked in Africa for the Egyptian government as a diplomat, officer, and geographer. During his journeys, he discovered a lake that is now in Uganda. He also gathered information about the White Nile River and other rivers of the region.

Into Central Africa

Chaillé-Long was born in Maryland. In 1861 he left school to fight in the Civil War, serving as a captain in the Union army. After the war, Chaillé-Long traveled to Egypt in hopes of finding more excitement. In 1869 he was appointed a lieutenant colonel in the Egyptian army. Within five years, he became chief of staff to General Charles "China" Gordon.

Gordon sent Chaillé-Long to explore the lands south of the Sudan in central Africa. Chaillé-Long was instructed to study the region's geography and to gather any information about the land and its people that might help Egypt gain control of the area. In Buganda (now Uganda), Chaillé-Long discussed a treaty with the local ruler, King Mutesa. They met in Rubaga, the capital city of Buganda. Chaillé-Long later reported that Rubaga was a large settlement that covered the hills for several miles around. He described the luxurious housing that was offered to visitors. He also noted that King Mutesa had an army of 150,000 warriors and a fleet of war canoes on Lake Victoria.

The Geographer Adds to the Maps

Chaillé-Long examined the geography of the lake regions of East Africa. He charted the course of the upper part of the Nile River, known as the White Nile River. He followed the White Nile from its source to Karuma Falls in central Uganda. This work added to the earlier discoveries of John Hanning SPEKE. While in Uganda, Chaillé-Long discovered Lake Ibrahim (now known as Lake Kyoga). In 1875 he traveled to the region between the Nile and Congo Rivers. Here, too, he added to knowledge that had been obtained by earlier explorers. After his journey into the continental interior, he worked at a new career as an official of the United States government in Egypt and Korea.

In later life, Chaillé-Long gained a reputation for boasting about his accomplishments. In his writings, he described his discoveries in grander terms than they really deserved. He wrote about his work as an explorer and diplomat in his autobiography, *My Life in Four Continents.*

Charles Chaillé-Long explored the Nile River region and was known for his boastful nature.

Suggested Reading Charles Chaillé-Long, *My Life in Four Continents* (Hutchinson and Company, 1912); Pierre Crabitès, *Americans in the Egyptian Army* (Routledge, 1938).

French
b 1567?; Brouage, France
d December 25, 1635; Québec, Canada
Explored and colonized eastern Canada

Chaillu, Paul Belloni Du. *See Du Chaillu, Paul Belloni.*

Samuel de Champlain was an adventurer, a mapmaker, and a leader of colonists. He devoted the last 30 years of his life to building France's North American empire. He founded the first permanent French colony on the continent and explored the Atlantic coast as far south as Cape Cod, Massachusetts. He journeyed inland as far west as Lake Huron and was the first European to reach the lake that bears his name, Lake Champlain (in present-day New York).

The son of a French sea captain, Champlain was born around 1567 on the coast of the Bay of Biscay. He fought for France's King Henry IV in religious wars between Protestants and Roman Catholics during the late 1500s. In 1599 Champlain spent two years in the West Indies as part of a Spanish expedition. During this time, he suggested that a canal connecting the Atlantic and the Pacific Oceans be built across Panama. His idea was ahead of his time— the canal was built about 300 years later.

The Geographer's Adventure

When Champlain returned to France, he wrote and illustrated a book about his experiences. King Henry was so impressed by the book that he made Champlain the royal geographer. Champlain, however, was bored by the easy life at the French court. He persuaded Henry to let him go to North America. At that time, France could not afford to send colonists to settle in the Americas. King Henry knew, though, that France needed to compete with Portugal, Spain, and England, which were already creating empires around the world. He offered a deal to French businessmen, giving them the right to trap and trade furs in North America if they used some of their profits to build and support French colonies.

In 1603 Champlain traveled to North America as the geographer for a party of fur traders. He and a few others sailed up the St. Lawrence River to the Indian village of Tadoussac. From there they continued 60 miles up the Saguenay River and also surveyed the St.-Maurice River. They traveled as far as the site of the modern-day city of Montréal. There the Indians spoke of a lake to the west that was so large that they were afraid to sail on it. Champlain thought that this might be the Pacific Ocean. He headed west, hoping to discover a sea route to China, but his travel on the St. Lawrence was blocked just west of Montréal by the dangerous Lachine Rapids. Frustrated, Champlain realized that the way to navigate North America's rivers was to use lightweight canoes like those of the Indians. Explorers who encountered rapids or falls could simply carry their canoes along the riverbanks until they passed the dangerous waters. This solution became the key to future French exploration in North America.

While traveling these rivers, Champlain formed an **alliance** with the Algonquin Indians against their enemies, the Iroquois Indians.

alliance formal agreement of friendship or common defense

The friendship of the Algonquin was helpful to Champlain at the time, but the Iroquois became bitter enemies of France. They later allied themselves with the British and helped cause the downfall of the French empire in Canada.

"The Narrowing of the Waters"

Champlain returned to France to report his findings and was back in North America less than a year later, now with a different fur company. He scouted the east coast as far south as Cape Cod in search of a good location for a settlement. He finally chose the east coast of the Bay of Fundy in the area the French called Acadie (Acadia, now Nova Scotia). After two years, however, the king took away the fur company's trading rights. Champlain's new colony had depended on the fur traders' profits, so Champlain and the other colonists were forced to return to France.

In 1608 the fur company regained its trading rights for a year, and Champlain again crossed the Atlantic. This time he started a colony on the St. Lawrence River at a place the Indians called Kebec, which means "the narrowing of the waters." Champlain named the settlement Québec. He hoped to use it as a base for more exploration. Just as he was about to leave for the west, a group of Algonquin and Huron Indians came to Québec to ask for his help in an attack on the Iroquois. He traveled south with them toward the homeland of the Mohawk Iroquois. On the way, they came upon the lake that now bears Champlain's name.

When the war party finally faced the Iroquois, Champlain's allies gathered around him. As they marched towards the Iroquois, the Algonquin suddenly stepped aside to reveal Champlain, a light-skinned stranger in gleaming steel armor and helmet. The sight surely amazed the Iroquois, who were even more shocked when Champlain raised his small musket and fired four shots. He killed two chiefs and wounded another. The Iroquois scattered in dismay while the Algonquin and Huron celebrated their powerful new ally.

Champlain returned to **New France** from Iroquois country in 1610. He built a trading post at what is now Montréal. By this time, many different fur companies were competing to trade with the Indians. Champlain spent most of his time building friendly relations between the French and the Indians. Yet he made sure that the work of exploration was continued by others even when he could not do it himself. He also sent selected young men, including Etienne BRULÉ, to live with the Indians in order to learn their customs and languages and explore their lands.

Samuel de Champlain never gave up on his dream of building a strong French colony in North America.

New France French colony that included the St. Lawrence River valley, the Great Lakes region, and until 1713, Acadia (now called Nova Scotia)

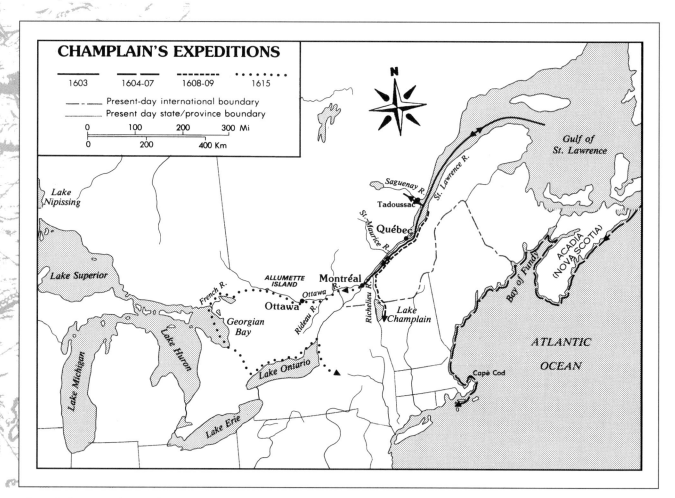

CHAMPLAIN'S EXPEDITIONS

———	————	- - - - -	• • • • •
1603	1604-07	1608-09	1615

— · — Present-day international boundary
——— Present day state/province boundary

For his work exploring, mapping, and settling French America, Champlain was called the "Father of New France."

coureur de bois French or French-Indian fur trapper

The Wrong River

In 1613 a **coureur de bois** named Vignau told Champlain that the source of the Ottawa River was a lake that emptied into a northern sea. Vignau, who had lived with the Algonquin, claimed that he had visited this sea and that it could be reached by a journey of 17 days from Montréal. Champlain was again hopeful that he might find a water route to Asia, so he decided to travel up the Ottawa River himself. The trip was difficult—the men sometimes had to tie their canoes to their wrists and pull them over the rapids. Champlain nearly drowned doing this, and all the explorers suffered from swarms of mosquitoes. They also had to struggle around an enormous waterfall at the mouth of the Rideau River, near what is now Ottawa. Champlain wrote that the waterfall "forms an archway nearly four hundred yards in width. The Indians, for the fun of it, pass underneath this without getting wet, except for the spray made by the falling water."

The party arrived at Allumette Island in the Ottawa River, where the Algonquin told Champlain that Vignau's story was false. Vignau was probably talking about Hudson Bay, far to the north. But the Algonquin held back this information because they did not want the French to know too much about the territory. Champlain was furious with Vignau, and the explorers returned to Montréal just three weeks after setting out.

Champlain carried the flag of the French monarchy. The emblem on the flag is called a *fleur-de-lis.*

Years of Conflict

Champlain made his last great journey into the North American wilderness in 1615. He got as far west as Georgian Bay on the eastern shore of Lake Huron, where he saw the villages and beautiful lands of his Huron allies. The route that Champlain took to get there became the fur traders' road west for many decades.

At Georgian Bay, Champlain and the Huron prepared for another attack against the Iroquois. Etienne Brulé went as interpreter with a small group of Huron to gather more Indian allies. Champlain and the main Huron war party made their way south around the eastern end of Lake Ontario to the home of the Onondaga Iroquois. The Huron launched a wild and disordered attack and were badly defeated. Even French firearms could not save the day, and Champlain was wounded in the battle. He and his allies were forced to retreat before Brulé and the additional warriors even arrived. Champlain had to spend the winter with the Huron near Lake Ontario. He used the time to visit tribes and explore areas he had not seen before, returning to Montréal in the spring.

In 1616 Champlain sailed back to France, where the king gave him official authority in Québec. Champlain spent the rest of his life trying to make his colony stable and prosperous. In 1629 Québec was captured by the English, and Champlain was taken to England as a prisoner. When the city was given back to France by a treaty in 1633, Champlain returned to Québec, where he lived a short while longer and then died in his late 60s.

Suggested Reading Morris Bishop, *Champlain* (Macdonald, 1949); Samuel Eliot Morison, *Samuel de Champlain: Father of New France* (Little, Brown, 1972); Francis Parkman, *Pioneers of France in the New World* (Little, Brown, 1897).

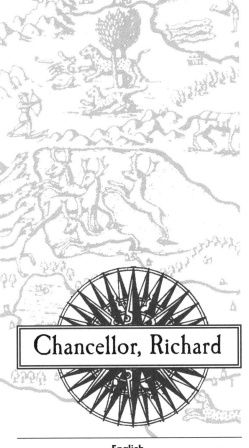

Chancellor, Richard

English
b 1500s?; England?
d November 10, 1556; Aberdour Bay, Scotland
Opened trade with Russia on White Sea

Northeast Passage water route connecting the Atlantic Ocean and Pacific Ocean along the Arctic coastline of Europe and Asia

The facts of Richard Chancellor's birth and background are unknown, but it is clear that he was a skilled navigator. In 1553 he was assigned to pilot a small English fleet eastward to China by sailing through the seas north of Europe. It was one of the first attempts to find what became known as the **Northeast Passage.** Although he did not find such a route, he made a great success out of a voyage that was in other ways a terrible disaster. Piloting the expedition's only ship that survived the Arctic seas, Chancellor discovered the northern sea route to Russia. His mission opened the first political and commercial relations between Russia and England.

The Muscovy Company

The idea of searching for a Northeast Passage to eastern Asia came from John Dudley, the English duke of Northumberland. Dudley had been lord admiral under England's King Henry VIII. During the reign of Henry's successor, the young and sickly Edward VI, Dudley was a major force on the ruling council that held power. He gathered some 200 traders to form the new Company of Merchant Adventurers. The company had a royal charter that made it the only company allowed to sail along northern trade routes. The merchants hoped to find the same kind of wealth that the Spanish and

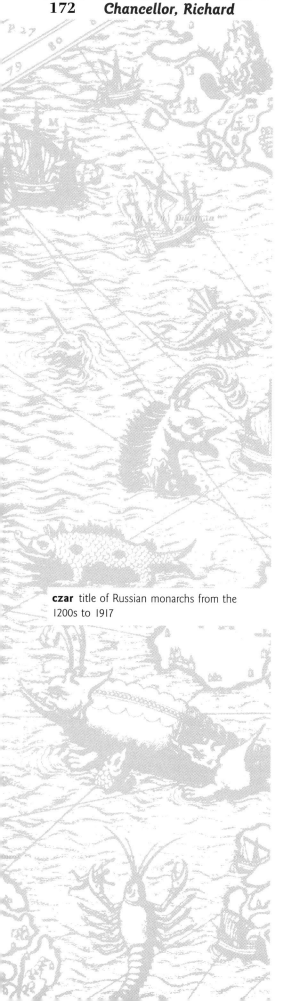

Portuguese had gained through their voyages of discovery to the south. The explorer Sebastian CABOT was appointed governor of the company. His first duty was to organize an expedition to China, which Europeans then called Cathay.

Cabot named Sir Hugh Willoughby commander of the voyage and fitted out three ships: the *Bona Esperanza,* captained by Willoughby; the *Edward Bonaventure,* captained by Chancellor; and the *Bona Confidentia.* Willoughby was a curious choice, since he had no experience as a navigator. He was a soldier who had been knighted for his role in a campaign against the Scots in 1544, but more recently he had fallen out of favor with the royal court. After he was removed from his command of a castle on the Scottish border, Willoughby's friends persuaded him to try his luck as a navigator. Cabot must have believed that as long as Willoughby kept the crews in order, Chancellor would take care of the sailing.

Separated at Sea

The expedition left England on May 10, 1553. In July the ships were separated by a storm off the coast of Finnmark (now the northern part of Norway). Chancellor took his ship to the meeting place that had been agreed on in case of such a separation. When Willoughby and the other two ships failed to arrive after seven days, Chancellor sailed on into the White Sea, north of Russia. At the mouth of Russia's Northern Dvina River, he met Russian fishermen. According to an account written in the late 1500s, the Russians were "amazed with the strange greatnesse of his shippe" and began to flee in terror. Chancellor caught up with them and "looked pleasantly upon them, comforting them by signs and gestures." The reassured fishermen soon supplied Chancellor and his crew with food and information.

Trade with Ivan's Russia

When the Russian **czar** Ivan IV (also known as Ivan the Terrible) received word of the visitors, he invited them to his capital, Moscow. Ivan welcomed the chance to open a new trade route with England. At the time, the only way for Russia to trade with western Europe was through the German merchants of central Europe. A sea route to the north would allow Russia and western European countries to trade with each other directly. Ivan gave Chancellor letters for King Edward VI, offering free and open trade between their two nations.

When Chancellor returned to England, he found that Edward had died two months after the expedition had set sail. John Dudley had been executed for opposing the new queen, Mary. The Company of Merchant Adventurers was reorganized as the Muscovy Company, and Queen Mary granted it a new charter.

The company's first agents in northern Russia learned the fate of the Willoughby expedition. Willoughby had sailed his two remaining ships in a wild series of zigzags and landed on Novaya Zemlya, a large island off the north coast of Russia. A leak in one ship forced him to sail back toward England, but the ships were trapped in the Arctic ice on the northern coast of Scandinavia. The men had

plenty of food, but they were unprepared for the cold. Russian fishermen had found their frozen bodies and turned them over to the agents of the Muscovy Company, who had shipped them back to England.

Chancellor's Second Voyage

In October 1555, Chancellor returned to Russia with the ships *Edward Bonaventure* and *Philip and Mary* to establish English markets there. After completing that task, he sailed for home with the first Russian ambassador to England on board. Off the coast of Scotland, his good luck ran out. A storm dashed the *Edward Bonaventure* against the shore, breaking the ship apart. Chancellor was killed, but the ambassador was one of a few survivors. He was rescued by some Scots, who held him captive for months. After his release, agents of the Muscovy Company escorted him to London.

Thanks to the ambassador's safe arrival, trade relations between Russia and England continued to thrive after Chancellor's death. However, the Muscovy Company still viewed Russia only as a step on the way to the riches of China. Two of Chancellor's crewmen, William Burrough and Arthur Pet, continued the search for a Northeast Passage.

Suggested Reading Foster Rhea Dulles, *Eastward Ho! The First English Adventurers to the Orient: Richard Chancellor, Anthony Jenkinson, James Lancaster, William Adams, Sir Thomas Roe* (Books for Libraries, 1969); Joseph Gamel, *England and Russia: Comprising the Voyages of John Tradescant the Elder, Sir Hugh Willoughby, Richard Chancellor, Nelson, and Others to the White Sea,* translated by John Leigh (reprint, Da Capo, 1968).

Chang Ch'ien. See *Zhang Qian.*

Chang K'ien. See *Zhang Qian.*

Charlevoix, Pierre François Xavier de

French
b October 24, 1682; St.-Quentin, France
d February 1, 1761; La Flèche, France
Traveled St. Lawrence River, Great Lakes, and Mississippi River

---

Jesuit member of the Society of Jesus, a Roman Catholic order founded by Ignatius of Loyola in 1534

New France French colony that included the St. Lawrence River valley, the Great Lakes region, and until 1713, Acadia (now called Nova Scotia)

Pierre François Xavier de Charlevoix was a French **Jesuit** priest who was sent to North America to search for an inland sea. This fabled "Western Sea" supposedly gave rise to rivers that emptied into the Pacific Ocean. His search led him through the Great Lakes region and down the Mississippi River. Upon his return to France, Charlevoix wrote the first detailed and reasonably accurate account of the interior of eastern North America.

The Explorer-Priest

Charlevoix was born to noble parents in France. He joined the Jesuit order as a young man and became a deacon. In 1705 he was sent to **New France** to teach at the Jesuit college in Québec, on the St. Lawrence River. He returned to France four years later, was made a priest, and took a teaching position in France. In 1719 aides to King Louis XV drew on his knowledge of the St. Lawrence River area. He was asked to recommend boundaries for Acadia (now

When Pierre François Xavier de Charlevoix's expedition arrived in New Orleans in 1722, he found a village of only "a hundred or so shacks."

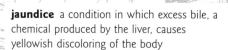

mission settlement founded by priests in a land where they hoped to convert people to Christianity

latitude distance north or south of the equator

cartographer mapmaker

voyageur expert French woodsman, boatman, and guide

jaundice a condition in which excess bile, a chemical produced by the liver, causes yellowish discoloring of the body

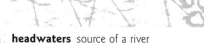

headwaters source of a river

Nova Scotia), a region claimed by both France and England. While involved in this task, he was asked to travel again to New France to research rumors about the Western Sea. This exploration was a secret, so his official reason for going was to examine the Jesuit **missions** in New France.

Charlevoix arrived in Québec on September 23, 1720, and spent the winter there. When spring arrived, he headed west. He traveled up the St. Lawrence River and then canoed through the Great Lakes. In his journal, he described the lakes' coastlines, estimated distances, and made readings of **latitudes.** His extensive notes later helped **cartographers** make more accurate maps of the Great Lakes.

Charlevoix asked everyone he met about the Western Sea. The missionaries and French officials knew nothing helpful, and the **voyageurs** and Indians made up stories. In July 1721 he decided to travel down the Mississippi River and continue his research in Louisiana. He planned to return north a year later to visit the outposts on Lake Superior, since he had not yet been there.

Travels on the Mississippi

On July 29, Charlevoix's party headed from Lake Michigan to the St. Joseph River, but bad weather and illness kept him at Fort St. Joseph for about a month. When he recovered, he continued southwest down the Kankakee and Illinois Rivers before reaching the Mississippi River. Traveling in canoes made of hollowed tree trunks, the men had a rough trip. The river was full of sandbanks and fallen trees, and the weather was unexpectedly cold. They spent Christmas Day in the settlement of Natchez, arriving in New Orleans on January 10, 1722. Charlevoix predicted that although New Orleans then consisted of only "a hundred or so shacks," it would someday be a great city.

The priest made his way to the mouth of the Mississippi River and from there traveled east to the settlement of Biloxi, on the Gulf of Mexico. There he came down with **jaundice.** He decided that in his weakened condition, he could not return up the Mississippi River to Lake Superior as planned. He attempted to return to Québec by sea but was shipwrecked on the Gulf of Mexico. All aboard survived—and spent 50 days walking back to Biloxi.

Return to France

Charlevoix tried again to sail north, but his ship took two months to get from Biloxi to the island of Hispaniola (now Haiti and the Dominican Republic). When he finally reached the island at the end of September, he decided that it was too late in the year to go north to Québec, so he sailed instead for France to make his report.

From the information he had gathered, Charlevoix concluded that the Western Sea lay between 40° and 50° north latitude, and that Indian tribes who lived west of the Sioux Indians probably knew of it. He also believed that rivers flowing west to the Pacific Ocean would be found near the **headwaters** of the Missouri River. He, therefore, offered the king's ministers two proposals for reaching the Western Sea. One was to send an expedition up the Missouri River. The other was to send missionaries to the Sioux Indians in the hope that the missionaries would also make contact with tribes to the west. Charlevoix favored the first plan, but the royal aides chose the second.

As it turned out, the Western Sea did not exist, but this fact would not be known for some time. Even so, Charlevoix's explorations were invaluable. His journal became a classic, for it combined lively stories, sharp descriptions, and scholarly records.

Suggested Reading Charles E. O'Neill, editor, *Charlevoix's Louisiana: Selections from the History and the Journal* (Louisiana State University Press, 1977).

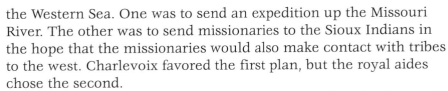

Cheng Ho. See *Zheng He.*

Ch'ien, Chang. See *Zhang Qian.*

Ching, I. See *Yi Jing.*

Chini, Eusebio Francisco. See *Kino, Eusebio Francisco.*

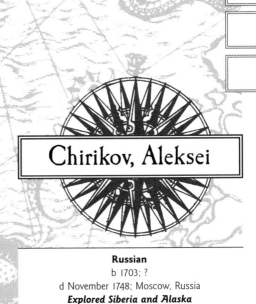

Chirikov, Aleksei

Russian
b 1703; ?
d November 1748; Moscow, Russia
Explored Siberia and Alaska

czar title of Russian monarchs from the 1200s to 1917

Captain Commander Aleksei Chirikov was second-in-command to Vitus BERING on two voyages to the Kamchatka Peninsula of eastern Russia, from 1725 to 1730 and from 1733 to 1741. On the second expedition, Chirikov was the captain of the first ship to reach Alaska from Siberia. He landed a day and a half earlier than Bering himself.

The First Kamchatka Expedition

Chirikov earned his job as Bering's chief aide by rising quickly through the ranks of the Russian navy. He graduated from the naval academy in 1721 and was immediately made a sublieutenant, skipping the rank of midshipman. After a brief tour of duty at sea, he returned to the academy to teach navigation. There he attracted the attention of the organizers of Bering's first expedition. They made Chirikov second-in-command, along with Martin Spanberg. In early 1725, Bering led the party east from the Russian capital of St. Petersburg.

The mission had been ordered by **Czar** Peter the Great to determine whether Siberia and the Americas were connected by land or separated by a strait. The plan was to travel by land across the entire width of Asia, about 12,000 miles. Along the way, the original party of 100 men picked up hundreds of laborers. When they arrived at the Siberian port of Okhotsk, they built a ship to carry men and supplies across the Sea of Okhotsk to Kamchatka. They then spent four months crossing Kamchatka, after which they built another ship, the *St. Gabriel,* for the voyage across the northern Pacific Ocean.

On July 13, 1728, the *St. Gabriel* left port and headed northeast along the coastline. Four weeks later, the explorers landed on an

island that Bering named for St. Lawrence. After sailing north for two more days, the ship was out of sight of land—with winter approaching. Chirikov argued that they should press on along the coastline, according to Czar Peter's instructions. Chirikov was willing to spend the winter in the harsh Siberian climate. Spanberg, however, suggested that they continue for only a few more days before turning back.

Bering agreed with Spanberg that it was too dangerous to spend the winter so far north. On August 16, the *St. Gabriel* turned around. Had the next day's weather been clear instead of foggy, the explorers would have seen the western edge of North America, and they would have known that they were in a narrow strait. They spent the winter in Kamchatka and then returned to St. Petersburg to make their report. Although Bering was criticized for not completing his mission, he was placed in command of a second expedition.

The Great Northern Expedition

The new plan was even more ambitious than the first. One of its purposes was to resume the search for the border of Asia and America. In addition, Bering was to investigate the route from Siberia to Japan and organize the charting of the entire Arctic coastline of Siberia. Once again the party was required to travel across Russia, a journey that took them eight years. On June 4, 1741, Bering and Chirikov were at last ready to sail from Kamchatka in search of Alaska.

Shortly after leaving the peninsula, Chirikov's and Bering's ships were separated in a storm. In mid-July, Chirikov reached Prince of Wales Island, off the Alaskan coast in what is now known as the Alexander Archipelago. A landing party went ashore, but these men failed to return. Chirikov then sent a second party, which also disappeared. He never learned their fate. Both parties were apparently taken prisoner by the island's inhabitants. The loss of 20 men with whom he had traveled for eight years seems to have broken Chirikov's spirit. Until then he had held up well under the intense pressure of the difficult journey. The disappearance of the landing parties also meant the end of any land exploration, since the lost men had taken the ship's only two boats.

The End of a Costly Mission

Chirikov was forced to return to Kamchatka, but he had little fresh water aboard his vessel. Without the boats, he could not go ashore to find food or water. Sailing through the Aleutian Islands, he received some water—but not nearly enough—from a group of cautious Aleuts, the people native to the area. By the time he reached Avatcha Bay on the Kamchatka Peninsula, 20 of his men had died from **scurvy,** and he too was suffering from that disease.

The surviving explorers spent the winter recovering. In the spring, Chirikov sailed again to search for his missing commander. He sailed close to what is now Bering Island, just east of Kamchatka. Chirikov could not have known that Bering's men had been on that island since their ship had been blown into its harbor. Bering was one of 30 men who had died on the island over the

scurvy disease caused by a lack of vitamin C and once a major cause of death among sailors; symptoms include internal bleeding, loosened teeth, and extreme fatigue

winter from scurvy and cold weather. The remaining crew members were preparing their escape at about the time Chirikov sailed past. Bad weather forced Chirikov to turn back before reaching Alaska. He settled in Moscow, but he never fully recovered from the scurvy and died at the age of 45.

Many historians, especially Russians, believe that Chirikov was a more able commander than Bering. They point to the fact that he successfully guided his crippled crew back to Siberia, while Bering failed to do so. Chirikov also made more or less the same discoveries as Bering did. Some historians argue that the Bering Strait would have been found on the first expedition if Bering had followed Chirikov's advice.

Suggested Reading Raymond H. Fisher, *Bering's Voyages: Whither and Why* (University of Washington Press, 1978); Gerhard Friedrich Müller, *Bering's Voyages: The Reports from Russia*, translated by Carol Urness (University of Alaska Press, 1986).

Chouart, Médard. See *Groseilliers, Médard Chouart des.*

Cintra, Pêro da. See *Sintra, Pedro de.*

Clapperton, Hugh

Scottish
b May 18, 1788; Annan, Scotland
d April 13, 1827; Sokoto, Nigeria
Explored western Africa

Hugh Clapperton was an outspoken opponent of the African slave trade.

sultan ruler of a Muslim nation

Hugh Clapperton, who explored much of the interior of West Africa, was a member of the first European expedition known to have reached Lake Chad. His attempts to trace the path of the Niger River were not wholly successful, but he still uncovered important information about the river's course.

Clapperton was one of 21 children of a Scottish surgeon. He left home at the age of 13 and took a job as a cabin boy on a trading ship. He joined the navy and had become a lieutenant when he was chosen for his first African expedition, led by Dr. Walter Oudney in 1820. The goal was to discover whether the Niger River ran through Bornu (in modern-day Nigeria). In Tripoli (in what is now Libya) in 1821, they were met by Dixon Denham, an army major who insisted that he had been assigned to lead the expedition.

Clapperton sided with Oudney, and the two went south to Murzuch in the Sahara without Dixon, who conducted his own explorations of villages in the area. Clapperton and Oudney reached Bornu in 1822, and within two months, they had found Lake Chad. There they learned that the Niger ran south rather than east, so they continued southwest to trace the river's path. Oudney died in early 1824, and Clapperton went west to Sokoto (in what is now northern Nigeria). Although Clapperton objected to the local slave trade, he became friendly with Sokoto's **sultan,** Bello.

Clapperton returned to London in 1825 and arranged to have his journal published. He left again for Africa later that year, but shortly after reaching Sokoto, he fell ill and died. His account of this trip was later published by his servant, Richard Lemon LANDER.

Suggested Reading Richard Lander, *Records of Captain Clapperton's Last Expedition to Africa, by Richard Lander, his Faithful Attendant and the Only Surviving Member of the Expedition; with the Subsequent Adventures of the Author* (Cass, 1967); Harry Williams, *Quest Beyond the Sahara* (R. Hale, 1965).

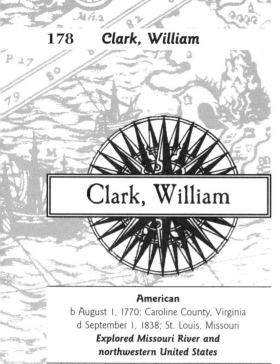

Clark, William

American
b August 1, 1770; Caroline County, Virginia
d September 1, 1838; St. Louis, Missouri
***Explored Missouri River and
northwestern United States***

The even-tempered William Clark was a perfect match for the moody Meriwether Lewis as co-commander of the Corps of Discovery.

William Clark and Meriwether Lewis were the two commanders of the Corps of Discovery, better known as the Lewis and Clark Expedition. From St. Louis, they followed the Missouri River upstream, crossed the Rocky Mountains, and followed the Columbia River to the Pacific Ocean. In crossing the North American continent, they completed what may be the most important journey of exploration ever launched by the U.S. government. Their successful expedition played a major role in the territorial expansion of the young American nation.

A Family History

William Clark was the younger brother of George Rogers Clark, a hero of the American Revolutionary War. William grew up hearing tales of his older brother's daring deeds. After the war, the Clarks, like many American families, moved west—to what is now the state of Kentucky. From 1789 to 1791, Clark took part in several skirmishes with the region's Indian tribes, who were trying to protect their lands from the settlers' claims. Clark became a lieutenant in the U.S. Army in 1792. He served for four years under General Anthony Wayne during Wayne's military and diplomatic efforts against the Indian tribes of the lower Great Lakes region. During this time, Clark met Meriwether Lewis, a fellow officer in Wayne's army. Clark began to tire of military life, however, and he resigned in 1796, one year after Wayne's final victory over the Indians. After leaving the army, Clark traveled between Indiana and Virginia for several years. In 1803 he received a letter from his former comrade Lewis, who invited Clark to join him in commanding the Corps of Discovery, which had recently been created by President Thomas Jefferson.

The Corps of Discovery

President Jefferson gave the Corps the task of exploring the enormous Louisiana Territory, which the United States had recently bought from France. This transaction, known as the Louisiana Purchase, extended the United States westward from the Mississippi River to the Rocky Mountains. Although the territory had become a part of the United States, the government in Washington, D.C., had little knowledge of the region—and even less control over it. The Corps of Discovery was asked to enter and explore these new lands on behalf of the United States and to describe their geography, natural life, and Indian tribes. Jefferson also wanted Lewis to establish a useful water route between the Mississippi River and the Pacific Ocean. The president hoped to strengthen the American claim on the Pacific Northwest that had begun with the discovery of the Columbia River by Captain Robert Gray in 1792. That region was also being claimed by Britain and Spain.

In Lewis and Clark's time, the American flag had a stripe and a star added to it for each new state. The flag they carried had 15 stars and 15 stripes.

Lewis requested that Clark be named co-commander of the expedition, and Jefferson agreed. Clark accepted the invitation, and Lewis met him at Clark's home in Kentucky. They traveled to St. Louis, and the Corps camped outside the city during the winter of 1803 to 1804. The expedition started up the Missouri River on May 14, 1804, with about 40 men, including Clark's black slave, York. By autumn they had traveled some 1,600 miles upriver to the villages of the Mandan Indians, in what is now North Dakota. There they built winter quarters and settled in to wait for spring.

Sacajawea and Pomp

During the winter, Lewis and Clark met a French-Canadian fur trader from Montréal named Toussaint Charbonneau, who asked to join the expedition. The trader's wife was a Shoshone Indian named Sacajawea, who had been captured by the Minetaree Indians and sold to Charbonneau. Sacajawea gave birth to a son while in the Corps of Discovery's winter quarters. Lewis and Clark realized that Sacajawea and her child would be valuable as a symbol of the Corps's peaceful mission, since no war party would travel with a woman and child. Sacajawea would be a great help in establishing friendly relations with western Indian tribes.

Clark took an interest in Sacajawea's child, Jean-Baptiste Charbonneau, whom he nicknamed "Pomp." In later years, Clark saw to the education of Pomp and other Charbonneau children. On April 9, 1805, the eight-week-old infant was strapped to his mother's back, and the Corps left the Mandan villages, heading west.

Lewis and Clark

During the long journey up the Missouri River, Lewis and Clark showed why they were an ideal pair of commanders. They had nearly opposite personalities, so that it was easy to divide their duties. Lewis, moody and restless, often went on long side trips off the river to explore and hunt. Meanwhile, the sociable Clark stayed with the boats. He took measurements of the land, drew maps, wrote in his journal, and enjoyed the companionship of the rest of the party.

Despite their differences as people, Lewis and Clark respected each other and worked well together. Clark was the older of the two men, and he had more experience as a frontiersman. He was also a skilled artist who drew birds, fish, and mammals with great care and accuracy. Being so even-tempered, he made the difficult journey a harmonious one.

To the Source of the Missouri River

On the way to the Mandan villages, the Corps had faced several hazards. There were minor nuisances, such as rains, strong winds, and dust storms. The party also had dangerous run-ins with grizzly bears and buffalo. One night a buffalo ran through the center of the camp, nearly crushing some of the sleeping explorers. Clark himself narrowly escaped being bitten by a rattlesnake. Yet once the group had parted from their Mandan hosts, the journey became even more uncomfortable.

portage transport of boats and supplies overland between waterways

dysentery disease that causes severe diarrhea

scurvy disease caused by a lack of vitamin C and once a major cause of death among sailors; symptoms include internal bleeding, loosened teeth, and extreme fatigue

Just below the Great Falls (in modern-day Montana), the Missouri River passed through foothills of the Rocky Mountains. The water became shallower, and the weather turned cold and wet. According to Clark, the men were often "up to their armpits in the cold water, and sometimes walk[ed] for several yards over the sharp fragments of rocks." Working with "great patience and humour," the party slowly **portaged** around 10 miles of falls. During the portage, they endured severe heat, thunderstorms, hailstorms, and even a tornado. They were attacked by mosquitoes, and the moccasins on their feet were torn by rocks and thorns, but still they marched on. By July 15, they were back on the river, but 10 days later, they reached a place now called Three Forks. There, 2,300 miles upstream from St. Louis, the river split into three streams. Lewis and Clark named the streams Jefferson, Madison, and Gallatin (after President Jefferson, Secretary of State James Madison, and Secretary of the Treasury Albert Gallatin).

Crossing the Rocky Mountains

From Three Forks, Lewis and a small group set off on foot. Clark, Sacajawea, and the rest of the expedition followed on the Jefferson River. Sacajawea was beginning to recognize landmarks from her youth, but there were still no signs of her tribe, the Shoshone. On August 17, Clark caught up with Lewis, who had made contact with the Shoshone. According to the expedition's journals, Sacajawea began to "dance and show every mark of the most extravagant joy . . . to indicate that [the Indians] were of her native tribe." Sacajawea was taken to a meeting of the tribal council and recognized the chief, Cameahwait, as her brother.

The Shoshone provided the Corps of Discovery with horses and a guide, and Lewis and Clark lost no time in moving on. The two commanders knew that they had a long way to go to reach the Pacific coast before winter. Their guide led them through the valley of the Salmon River and into the Bitterroot Range of the Rocky Mountains. The next month was the most difficult yet, as the explorers hacked their way through the wilderness. A snowfall on September 16 wiped out all signs of the trail they were following. Their troubles worsened when the party's hunters could not find enough food. Some of the explorers began to grow thin and to suffer from **dysentery** and **scurvy.**

The expedition finally reached the villages of the Nez Percé tribe. There the Shoshone guide left the explorers with two Nez Percé chiefs, who volunteered to take them to the Pacific Ocean. They started down the Clearwater River on October 7, entered the Snake River three days later, and reached the Columbia River on October 16. Thanks to Sacajawea and the Nez Percé, Lewis and Clark received a friendly welcome at all the Indian villages along the way. Around evening campfires, Lewis and Clark entertained their hosts with tobacco and with violin music.

The Pacific and Back

On October 22, the Corps came face to face with the Cascade Mountains, which stood between the explorers and the Pacific Ocean.

tributary stream or river that flows into a larger stream or river

For a map of Clark's route, see the profile of Meriwether LEWIS in Volume 2.

Although the river pass through those mountains is a difficult one, the explorers had had much experience by then and managed it easily. By November 2, they had reached tidewater, the point where salt water from the ocean meets the fresh water of a river. The party followed the river until November 15, when they caught their first sight of the Pacific. They built winter quarters, which they named Fort Clatsop, and heavy rains and snows kept them indoors for months. They spent the time eating, sleeping, and looking at the stormy ocean.

The weather cleared in March, and the Corps retraced its route to the Bitterroot River. Near the site of present-day Missoula, Montana, the group split up again. Lewis led one party through an Indian shortcut to the Missouri River and explored a northern **tributary,** the Marias River. Clark led the other group through Shoshone territory and then down the Jefferson River, to where it meets the Missouri River at Three Forks. From there Clark sent a small party down the Missouri River to Great Falls to join Lewis's men. Clark took his main group south by land to the Yellowstone River and canoed down it to where it joined the Missouri.

Lewis and Clark reunited on August 12 near the mouth of the Yellowstone River. Two days later, at the Mandan villages, they bid farewell to Sacajawea and her family. On September 23, 1806, the Corps of Discovery returned to St. Louis to the cheers of a welcoming crowd.

In the following months, Clark intended to edit the several diaries—including his own and Lewis's—that had been written by members of the party. However, he was not confident of his editing skills and decided to find a professional to complete the task. He eventually hired Nicholas Biddle of Philadelphia, but the accounts of the trip were not published until 1815. In the meantime, Clark was appointed brigadier general of militia and superintendent of Indian affairs for the Louisiana Territory. He proved to be a strong supporter of Indian causes. From 1813 on, he served as governor of the territory and lived in St. Louis until his death at the age of 68.

Although Lewis and Clark did not discover a direct water route to the Pacific, they collected a great deal of information. They gave the government a measurement of the continent's width, a new understanding of the richness of the West, and a claim to the Columbia River region. They also helped the nation to realize that the West was not merely a passageway to Asia but was also quite valuable in itself.

Suggested Reading John L. Allen, *Lewis and Clark and the Image of the American Northwest* (Dover Publications, 1991); Stephen E. Ambrose, *Undaunted Courage: Meriwether Lewis, Thomas Jefferson, and the Opening of the American West* (Simon and Schuster, 1996); Bernard DeVoto, editor, *The Journals of Lewis and Clark* (Houghton Mifflin, 1997); James P. Ronda, *Lewis and Clark Among the Indians* (University of Nebraska Press, 1984).

Claudius, Ptolemaeus. See *Ptolemy.*

Colom, Cristovão. See *Columbus, Christopher.*

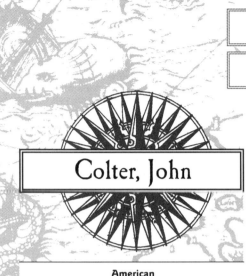

Colombo, Cristoforo. See *Columbus, Christopher.*

Colón, Cristóbal. See *Columbus, Christopher.*

Colter, John

American
b 1775?; Staunton, Virginia
d November 1813; near Missouri River
Explored Wyoming, Montana, and Idaho

John Colter was a member of the Corps of Discovery led by Meriwether LEWIS and William CLARK. He joined them on their famous expedition to the American West from 1804 to 1806. Later, Colter made one of the most remarkable journeys ever attempted in North America. He traveled alone through land that is now part of the states of Wyoming, Montana, and Idaho. He spent several months in territory that had previously been seen only by Indians. Among the many wonders he saw were the hot springs, boiling mudholes, and geysers of what is now Yellowstone National Park. Colter was the model for the type of American Mountain Man that would soon flourish in the West.

Travels with Lewis and Clark

Little is known of Colter's life before he joined the Corps of Discovery. Lewis and Clark's historic expedition traveled up the Missouri River to its source in the Rocky Mountains and then made its way to the shores of the Pacific Ocean. Both Lewis and Clark mentioned Colter frequently in their journals. They showed their confidence in him by choosing him for some especially difficult missions.

On the way back to St. Louis in the summer of 1806, the Corps of Discovery met two fur trappers named Joseph Dickson and Forrest Hancock. These two men realized that they would have an easier time finding and trapping beaver if they were guided by someone who knew the territory. They approached Colter, who was given permission by Lewis and Clark to leave the Corps early. Colter guided Dickson and Hancock around the valley of the Yellowstone River for a successful trapping season. He then started back toward St. Louis.

His journey home was interrupted yet again when he reached the mouth of the Platte River (near present-day Omaha, Nebraska). He met a businessman named Manuel Lisa, who was generally disliked but who employed many trappers. Lisa had recognized early that there was money to be made from Lewis and Clark's exploration of the West. In 1807 he hired several former members of the Corps to establish a fur-trading post on the Missouri River. He persuaded Colter to join him, and at Colter's suggestion, he built a fort and trading center where the Yellowstone River flows into the Missouri River. Lisa named it Fort Raymond after his son.

Travels Alone

Lisa's party spent the winter of 1807 to 1808 trapping beaver. Colter, meanwhile, set out on the most extraordinary solo exploration of North America ever attempted by a non-Indian. Lisa had given him two missions: to scout for new beaver territory and to encourage the Crow and other Indian tribes to the south and west to bring

their furs to Fort Raymond. From the route that Colter took, some historians have guessed that he was also looking for Spanish settlers in the southwest who could also become active in the fur trade.

Colter traveled over 500 miles in the middle of winter through the region that is now Wyoming, Montana, and Idaho. Since he left no journals, historians can only guess at the route he took, but they believe that he made a large figure eight to the south and west of Fort Raymond. After leaving the fort, he probably traveled west across the Pryor Mountains, which are part of the Bighorn Mountains. He then turned southwest and crossed the basin of the Bighorn River to the foot of the Absaroka Mountains, just east of modern-day Yellowstone National Park. After that he went southeast, following the mountains to the Shoshone River. Here he saw Yellowstone's hot springs and geysers. Still traveling south, he went around the Absaroka Mountains into the Wind River valley, turned north up the valley, and crossed into Jackson Hole. The magnificent sight of the Grand Teton Mountains stood before him.

By then it was near January, and Colter was probably running low on supplies. He was also quite far from Fort Raymond, and it was unlikely that any tribes living farther away would bring their furs to the fort. However, he decided not to turn back. He crossed the Tetons, probably on a pair of homemade snowshoes. More than a century later, in 1931, a farmer plowing near the Tetons uncovered a rock that had the name "John Colter" scratched on one side and the date "1808" on the other.

Colter turned south after crossing the Tetons, possibly still looking for Spanish settlements. He then quickly turned back north and crossed the Tetons a second time, following them into the area of Yellowstone National Park. Finally, he headed back east to Fort Raymond.

Running for His Life

Colter did not stay at the fort for long. He set out for the area in southwestern Montana where the Missouri River splits into the three lesser rivers that Lewis and Clark named the Jefferson, the Madison, and the Gallatin. He trapped beaver there in October 1808 with a man named John Potts. The two men kept a careful watch for the Blackfoot Indians. They knew that the Blackfoot were looking to avenge the death of two of their tribe who had been killed in a skirmish with Lewis in 1806. Despite their caution, Colter and Potts were surprised by Blackfoot warriors, and Potts was killed instantly when he tried to defend himself.

The Indians tormented Colter by debating what would be the most interesting way of putting him to death. At last they asked him how fast he could run. Colter understood what they were up to, and although he was a swift runner, he told them that he was slow as a turtle. Colter was then stripped naked and given a 30-second head start before the Blackfoot warriors would begin to chase him. To their surprise, Colter quickly dashed ahead and had soon outrun all but one of the Indians. With precise timing, Colter turned around, tripped the warrior, wrestled a spear away from him, and killed him.

Colter then raced for the Jefferson River. He jumped into the water and hid beneath drifting logs while the angry Blackfoot warriors searched for him. That night he swam five miles downstream in freezing waters. When he got out of river, he started running again. A week or two later, he arrived at Fort Raymond, having traveled 150 miles barefoot. His feet were badly cut, and he was naked, sunburned, and covered with insect bites. Colter took a few weeks to regain his strength. Then he set out for another season of fur trapping.

Return to Civilization

Colter had two more narrow escapes from the Blackfoot tribe. In the last encounter, his five companions fell dead around him, cut down by Blackfoot arrows. After this incident, Colter returned to Fort Raymond early in 1810 and announced his retirement with these words: "If God will only forgive me this time and let me off I will leave the country . . . and be damned if I ever come into it again." He was true to his word. A few days later, he got into his canoe and paddled the 2,000 miles to St. Louis, never again to return to the western wilderness.

Colter was well received in St. Louis by his former captain, William Clark. Clark kept a map to which he added information brought him by his former followers when they visited and discussed their travels. He added Colter's information to his map, and this was the closest Colter ever came to providing a record of his extraordinary achievements. Colter was given little credit in his time because he left neither charts nor journals of his travels. In fact, when he described to people in St. Louis some of the wonders he had seen, they found his stories of hot springs and geysers unbelievable. They gave his amazing discovery the mocking name "Colter's Hell."

Despite this early lack of recognition, John Colter has come to be known as possibly the finest example of the American mountaineer and trapper. During his journeys in the American northwest, he showed the incredible physical and mental toughness needed to survive alone for long periods. His act was a hard one to follow for later Mountain Men such as Jedediah SMITH, James BRIDGER, and Christopher CARSON.

Suggested Reading Lillian Frick, *Courageous Colter and His Companions* (L. R. Colter-Frick, 1997); Burton Harris, *John Colter: His Years in the Rockies* (Big Horn Book Company, 1977); Harriet Upton, *Trailblazers* (Rourke, 1990).

Columbus, Christopher

Italian
b August 25 to October 31, 1451?; Genoa, Italy?
d May 20, 1506; Valladolid, Spain
Discovered the Americas

On October 12, 1492, Christopher Columbus carried the flag of Spain onto a small island in the Caribbean Sea. Though he believed he had reached the shores of eastern Asia, he had in fact landed in the Americas and was probably the first European to do so since Leif ERIKSON had arrived 500 years earlier. Columbus's discovery led directly to Europe's intense long-term interest in the American continents. But historians have found it difficult to agree on the details of the voyage and of Columbus's life before it.

Some historians believe that the first European to have reached the North American coast may have been BRENDAN (later known as

Christopher Columbus earned the title "Admiral of the Ocean Sea" for his four crossings of the Atlantic.

Saint Brendan), an Irish monk of the 500s. However, it is better documented that the Norse merchant Bjarni HERJOLFSSON saw the continent in about 986, and his countryman Leif Erikson landed there around 1001. But they had little or no contact with the peoples who had inhabited the Americas for thousands of years. Other Europeans barely noticed or quickly forgot the Norse voyages. In contrast, when Columbus made his landfall in 1492 and met the Arawak and Carib Indians, Europe was ready to listen—and to act. Whether Columbus himself believed that he had found a new continent is just one of the many questions surrounding his history.

Who Was Christopher Columbus?

The questions about Columbus start with his birth. Most historians agree that he was born sometime between August 25 and October 31, 1451. But other dates have been proposed, from as early as 1435 to as late as 1460. Many suggestions have also been made about his birthplace, including the Italian city-state of Genoa, the Greek island of Khíos, the Spanish island of Majorca, and the Spanish province of Galicia. The theory that Columbus was Spanish is based on the 40 known documents and letters that bear his authentic signature. All of these are written in Spanish, as are most of the notes written in the margins of the books he owned. Columbus himself stated that he was born in Genoa, and writers of his time referred to him as Genoese.

Columbus's family background and education are also something of a mystery. Many historians describe Columbus as the eldest of five children born to a poor family of wool weavers. Others have argued that he came from a more distinguished family, perhaps even a royal one. These historians point out that his marriage to a Portuguese noblewoman would have been very unlikely had he not also been a noble.

It is widely agreed that Columbus had little formal education. His son Fernando, who wrote a biography of his famous father, claimed that Columbus had attended a university in Italy. Most scholars doubt that, but it is quite clear that Columbus understood the science and philosophy of his day, especially navigational science. He was also a student of history, a keen observer of his time, and a great reader. In particular, he was influenced by the works of the Greek philosopher Aristotle, as well as several Arab philosophers and astronomers. PTOLEMY's *Guide to Geography* and Marco POLO's *Travels* also helped form his ideas.

Columbus himself may actually have intended to cause all this confusion. Fernando wrote that his father often chose to conceal information about his birth and family. Some scholars have suggested that Columbus may have fought in a battle against Spain as a young man and may have wisely hidden that fact later in life. After all, the Spanish might not have wanted to sponsor the voyages of a former enemy.

Other scholars have recently collected evidence that Columbus was trying to hide Jewish heritage on one side of his family. In the 1490s, life in Spain was very difficult for both Jews and Muslims. In 1492, both groups were forced to convert to Christianity or leave the country. If Columbus had Jewish ancestry, he would probably have preferred to keep it secret. Whatever the truth may be, little is

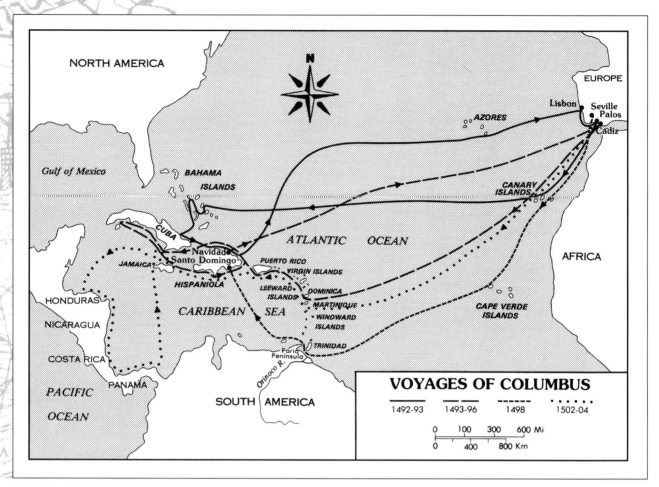

VOYAGES OF COLUMBUS

———	———	– – – –	• • • •
1492-93	1493-96	1498	1502-04

| 0 | 100 | 300 | 600 Mi |
| 0 | 400 | 800 Km |

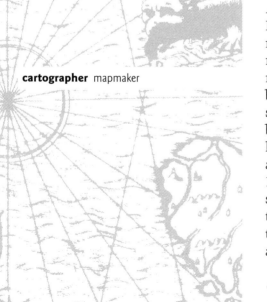

Though he believed that he had reached Asia, Columbus made important discoveries on all four of his voyages to the Caribbean.

cartographer mapmaker

known about Columbus's boyhood or early adulthood. Most historians do agree that he first went to sea at an early age with his brother Bartolomé, who was his closest friend and adviser.

An Early Career at Sea

In 1476 Columbus traveled to Lisbon, Portugal, where there was already a community of Genoese sailors who were known for their navigational skills. Bartolomé was also in Lisbon and had become a noted **cartographer.** The popular story of Columbus's arrival in Lisbon, as related by Fernando, is that he swam ashore after his ship sank during a battle off the coast. Between 1476 and 1485, Columbus sailed with the Portuguese in the Mediterranean Sea and the Atlantic Ocean, as far south as west Africa and as far north as England and Ireland. He may also have made a trip to Iceland in 1477. In 1479 he married the Portuguese noblewoman Doná Felipa Perestrello e Moriz. The couple settled in Madeira, a group of Portuguese islands off the northwest coast of Africa. The next year, they had a son, Diego. Doná Felipa died sometime between 1481 and 1485, and Columbus returned to Lisbon.

"The Enterprise of the Indies"

As early as 1483, Columbus had developed a plan to reach "the Indies," the European name for the Asian lands that were the source of valuable goods such as spices and silks. European merchants and monarchs were excited about the profits they could make by trading in the Indies. But at the time, the only known sea route was a long and dangerous voyage south and east, around Africa's Cape of Good Hope. Columbus believed that by sailing west across the Atlantic Ocean, he could make the trip more quickly and thus more inexpensively. His proposal for an "Enterprise of the Indies" was rejected in late 1483 by Portugal's King John II. Columbus then decided to take the plan to the king and queen of Spain, Ferdinand and Isabella. Meanwhile, his brother Bartolomé promoted the idea at the royal courts of England and France.

Columbus traveled to the Spanish city of Córdoba in 1485. While there, he had a mistress named Beatriz Enríque de Arana. She gave birth to Columbus's son Fernando in 1488. Columbus presented his plan to the Spanish court on two occasions, but both times a council of experts rejected the project. His ideas were ridiculed by some at the court, but he did receive the support of several powerful people. The voices in his favor included Luis de Santangel, treasurer of the royal household, and Prior Juan Perez, the queen's priest. In 1491 these men convinced Queen Isabella to approve Columbus's voyage.

The primary goal of the expedition was to find a shorter route to the Indies. Columbus was also instructed to look for gold and to convert any foreign peoples he met to Christianity. Columbus obtained a promise that he would be named governor of any lands he might discover during the voyage. He would also be given the title "Admiral of the Ocean Sea." All of these titles would pass to his sons upon his death. Columbus hoped that the wealth he would gain from these lands and titles could pay for a new **crusade** to capture Jerusalem from the Muslims who ruled it.

Unknown Waters

A crew and supplies were gathered in the town of Palos, where three ships were readied for the voyage. The flagship *Santa Maria* and two smaller **caravels,** the *Niña* and the *Pinta,* carried 90 men out of the harbor on August 3, 1492. Columbus commanded the *Santa Maria,* while the *Pinta* and the *Niña* were captained by two brothers, Martín Alonso PINZÓN and Vicente Yáñez PINZÓN. The small fleet stopped at the Canary Islands for repairs to the *Pinta* and improvements to the *Niña.* The ships finally left the Canaries on September 6 for a voyage that would test all of Columbus's skill and determination and the ability of the crews.

Columbus navigated by dead reckoning. With this method, a navigator tracks a ship's position by combining compass readings of direction with careful estimates of speed. Columbus headed west from the Canaries and let the **trade winds** carry him south and west. He believed that it would take 21 days to sail to Cipangu (the island now known as Japan), off the east coast of Asia. But it took longer to cross the Atlantic than Columbus had expected. As the days continued to pass without sight of land, he constantly had to calm the fears of his crew to prevent a **mutiny.** Columbus himself trusted his compass and had faith that the voyage was a holy

crusade Christian holy war

caravel small ship with three masts and both square and triangular sails

trade winds winds that blow from east to west in the tropics

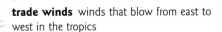

mutiny rebellion by a ship's crew against the officers

This drawing shows Christopher Columbus's first small fleet (from left to right): the *Santa Maria*, the *Pinta*, and the *Niña*.

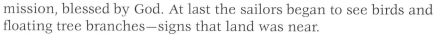

mission, blessed by God. At last the sailors began to see birds and floating tree branches—signs that land was near.

The original log of the voyage has been lost, but a crew member named Bartolomé de LAS CASAS kept a summary of it. In the log, the sharp-eyed Columbus described weather conditions, water color, cloud formations, plants, and animals. Although the 2,300-mile voyage was made during the hurricane season, Columbus found the sea "like a river and the air sweet. . . ."

Discovery of America

At two hours after midnight on October 12, Rodrigo de Triana, a sailor on the *Pinta*, peered out into the moonlight and sighted land. The voyage had taken a little over 33 days. That morning the ships anchored off an island. Columbus went ashore, named the island San Salvador, and claimed it for Spain. He met and traded with the people living on the island, who called themselves the Arawak. Columbus admired the Arawak and expressed in his journal his belief that they would make good converts to Christianity. He referred to them as Indians, mistakenly believing that he had reached the Indies of eastern Asia.

Columbus had certainly not landed in Asia, but the exact location of San Salvador remains unknown. At least nine islands have been proposed as the site of Columbus's first landfall, including what are now called Watling Island, Samana Cay, and Grand Turk Island. Many scholars today believe that it was Watling Island.

Columbus's personal banner combined the Christian cross with the initials of Ferdinand and Isabella (also spelled Ysabel), the king and queen of Spain.

Columbus left the island on October 14 after trading glass beads for parrots and "a kind of dry leaf." This plant was tobacco, which Europeans were soon to make a habit of smoking. After bringing six or seven Indians on board, Columbus sailed south to look for a king who the Indians said had much gold. He reached three more islands and named them Santa Maria de la Concepción, Fernandina, and Isabella. He then gave up the search for the king and headed west-southwest. He reached what is now Cuba on October 28 and traveled about 360 miles along the coast, observing several good harbors and making more landings. In Cuba he first encountered the fierce Carib, an Indian tribe who were known to eat human flesh. He promised to help the Arawak against this enemy and later enslaved some of the Carib.

On November 21, the captain of the *Pinta,* Martín Alonso Pinzón, took his ship to search for gold without Columbus's permission. The other ships went on, reaching a large island now called Hispaniola. On Christmas Eve, the *Santa Maria* ran aground while exploring the coast and had to be abandoned. A young Indian chief named Guacanaqari sent people to help Columbus and his crew transfer supplies to the *Niña.* The two leaders established a warm friendship. Before leaving the island, Columbus founded the first European settlement in the Americas since the time of the Vikings. He called it La Villa de La Navidad, which means Christmas Town in Spanish, and left 40 Spaniards there.

Soon Pinzón returned with the *Pinta,* and after Columbus had pardoned him for his desertion, the two remaining ships headed back to Spain. A terrible storm struck, but Columbus sailed the violent ocean with great skill. Las Casas was moved to write that "Christopher Columbus surpassed all his contemporaries in the art of navigation."

Columbus's Second Voyage

Columbus and his men received a triumphant welcome in Barcelona, Spain. He immediately began planning a second voyage. Ferdinand and Isabella showed how pleased they were by supplying a much larger fleet than before—17 ships, carrying 1,500 men. The expedition left Cadiz, Spain, on September 25, 1493, with the objectives of creating a permanent trading colony in Asia and converting the Indians to Christianity. Columbus was also ordered to explore Cuba to see whether it was an island or part of the Asian mainland.

On November 3, the island now known as Dominica was sighted. From there Columbus sailed north and west, discovering and naming the Leeward Islands. After spending six days on the large island now known as Guadeloupe, he continued northwest. After charting several other islands Columbus dropped anchor at the island now called St. Croix on November 14. Heading north, he found that St. Croix was the largest in a group of islands he named the Virgin Islands. He then sailed west to Hispaniola. There he found La Navidad in ruins. All the Spaniards left there the previous year had been killed. According to the Indians, the settlers had become violent and abusive toward the Indians, who eventually attacked the

malaria disease that is spread by mosquitoes in tropical areas

Spanish village. Columbus abandoned the site and set up a new colony called Isabella farther east, near an area where the settlers had found gold. He loaded 12 ships with gold and sent them back to Spain with a request for additional supplies.

Columbus spent the next few months exploring Hispaniola and building fortresses throughout the island. He then sailed to Cuba. After six weeks of picking his way among the small islands and dangerous shoals along the Cuban coast, he reached Cape Cruz, the island's southernmost point. Columbus was confident—but mistaken—in his belief that Cuba was not an island but a peninsula of the Asian mainland. He left off his exploration of Cuba and sailed east and south, finding the island now known as Jamaica. Already suffering from arthritis, Columbus then contracted **malaria.** He fell into a feverish daze and was forced to return to Isabella. The colony was in disorder, and the settlers had enslaved local Taino Indians in the effort to mine gold. Fortunately, his brother Bartolomé arrived from Spain with supplies and helped to restore calm. Columbus lay ill at Isabella for five months. He moved the colonists from Isabella to a new colony, Santo Domingo, and put Bartolomé in charge. Then he returned to Spain to defend himself against his enemies at court.

Columbus's Third Voyage

When he arrived in Spain, Columbus found that the king and queen still had confidence in him. They approved a third expedition to find the mainland that Columbus believed lay south of the islands he had discovered. After two years of preparation, Columbus left in 1498 with six ships. He sent three of the ships to supply Hispaniola and took the other three south to the Cape Verde Islands, off the coast of western Africa. From there he sailed west, reaching the island he named Trinidad on July 31. He followed its southern shore and then entered the Gulf of Paria. Columbus observed fresh water flowing into the gulf from northern branches of the Orinoco River and realized that he was sailing along the coast of a continent, now known as South America. He wanted to explore more of this coast, but he decided to go to Hispaniola instead. On the way, he landed on the Paria Peninsula (in present-day Venezuela), becoming the first European to set foot in South America.

When he reached Santo Domingo, Columbus had to put down a rebellion among the colonists. As a result, complaints were made against him to the royal court. The Spanish monarchs sent Francisco de Bobadilla to Hispaniola to investigate these complaints. Bobadilla had both Columbus brothers arrested and sent back to Spain for trial. Although they were found innocent of any wrongdoing, neither was allowed to return to Hispaniola for some time.

Columbus's Last Voyage

Since the time of Columbus's first discoveries in 1492, other explorers had crossed the Atlantic as well. Many people were coming to believe that Columbus had not reached Asia at all but had discovered a "new world." Columbus was eager to prove that he had indeed reached the Indies, so he asked Ferdinand and Isabella for

permission to lead another voyage. He intended to search for a water route leading to the Indian Ocean. He was allowed to sail on May 11, 1502, with four ships and 140 men. The crew included his son Fernando, and Bartolomé commanded one of the ships.

Columbus followed the route he had taken on his second voyage, sighting the island now called Martinique on June 15. He wound his way through the Leeward Islands, past what is now Puerto Rico to Hispaniola. The settlement's new governor, Nicolás de Ovando, refused him permission to land at Santo Domingo. Columbus sailed on, passing between Jamaica and Cuba and reaching the coast of (modern-day) Honduras in August. He tried to explore the coast to the east. Bad weather forced him to turn south along the coast of the area that is now Nicaragua and Costa Rica. When he reached what is now Panama, the Indians there told him that he had reached a narrow piece of land between two seas. Columbus believed that it was the Malay Peninsula in Asia. He was sure that China lay to the north, with India across the sea on the other side of the land. He was about to try to prove his theory, but he postponed his plans after finding gold in Panama.

In February 1503, Columbus attempted to found a settlement at Santa Maria de Belén in Panama, but fighting with the Indians cost him a ship and the lives of 10 men. He set sail and encountered a storm that wrecked one ship and damaged the other two badly. Unable to continue to Hispaniola, Columbus landed at St. Ann's Bay, Jamaica. Stranded, he sent two canoes carrying 12 crewmen and 20 natives to Santo Domingo for help. It took almost a year for a rescue mission to arrive. By then Columbus was completely exhausted and discouraged. He was suffering from arthritis and probably **gout** as well. He returned to Spain in November 1504 and spent the rest of his life trying to obtain the titles and awards that had been promised to him.

Passing into History

Columbus died on May 20, 1506 in Valladolid, Spain. His son Fernando wrote that the explorer's death was caused by "the gout, and by grief at seeing himself fallen from his high estate, as well as by other ills." Columbus's death went largely unnoticed at the time. His fame had been overshadowed by that of Amerigo VESPUCCI, the explorer who had declared that Columbus had discovered a "new world." Scholars still debate whether Columbus himself ever came to the same conclusion.

One final mystery hangs over the story of Columbus. To this day, no one knows where his remains are buried. They were moved from his home to Seville in 1509, to Santo Domingo in 1541, to Havana in 1796, and back to Seville in 1899. There are at least eight containers that supposedly hold his remains, in places as far apart as Rome and New York City. Though much about his life and death is uncertain, Columbus's place among the first rank of explorers is secure.

Suggested Reading Silvio A. Bedini, editor, *The Christopher Columbus Encyclopedia* (Simon and Schuster, 1992); Fernando Colón, *The Life of the Admiral Christopher Columbus* translated by Benjamin Keen (Rutgers University Press, 1959); Robert H. Fuson, translator, *The Log of Christopher Columbus* (International Marine

gout disease characterized by painful swelling of the joints

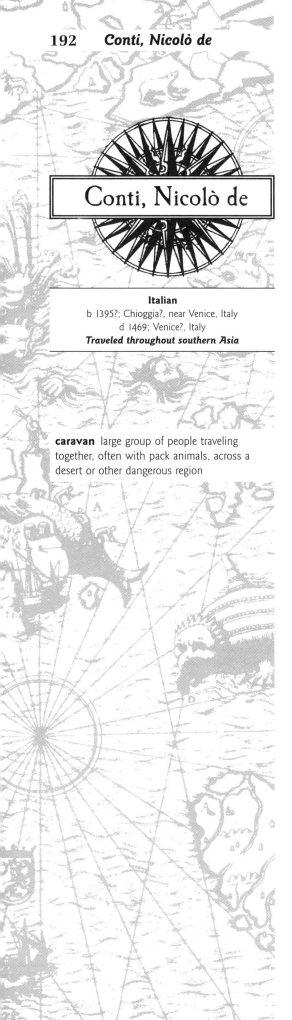

Italian
b 1395?; Chioggia?, near Venice, Italy
d 1469; Venice?, Italy
Traveled throughout southern Asia

caravan large group of people traveling together, often with pack animals, across a desert or other dangerous region

Publishing Company, 1987); Samuel Eliot Morison, *Admiral of the Ocean Sea* (Little, Brown and Company, 1942); Paolo Emilio Taviani, *Christopher Columbus: The Grand Design* (Orbis, 1985); John Boyd Thatcher, *Christopher Columbus: His Life, His Work, His Remains*, 3 volumes (AMS Press, 1967).

Religion has often played a major role in exploration and in the records left by explorers. This was true of Nicolò de Conti, although he was a merchant and not a priest. He had traveled to southern Asia and was passing through Egypt on his way home to Italy when he was forced to abandon his Christian beliefs and convert to Islam. Once back in Italy, he begged the pope to forgive him. The pope agreed—as long as Conti would give a detailed account of his travels to the pope's secretary. That account, later published in English as *India in the Fifteenth Century,* is a valuable record of life in southern Asia during the Middle Ages.

Travel to India

Conti was born in Italy but lived as a young man in the city of Damascus in Syria. There he worked as a merchant and learned to speak Arabic. In 1414 Conti and 600 other merchants set off in a **caravan** to the east. They traveled along the Euphrates River, through Baghdad (now in Iraq) to the port city of Basra. From Basra they crossed the Persian Gulf to Hormuz. Conti eventually reached Calacatia, a port on the Indian Ocean, where he stayed long enough to learn the Persian language. He next sailed with a group of merchants to the Indian state of Cambay. He married an Indian woman who traveled south with him along the coast to Goa. From there he turned inland to visit the kingdom of Deccan. Some historians believe that he was the first European to enter the Indian interior. It is not clear whether Conti crossed to India's east coast by land or water. In any case, he visited Ceylon (now Sri Lanka), remained there for a year, and became the first European to describe how cinnamon was grown there.

Sailing east across the Bay of Bengal, Conti found cannibals on the Andaman Islands. Then he landed on the coast of Burma (now Myanmar). Turning northwest, he sailed up the Ganges River, coming to what he called "cities unvisited." He arrived at a place "where aloes, gold, silver, precious stones and pearls were to be found in abundance." On this inland part of his journey, he visited many of the same places that Marco POLO had explored about 150 years earlier. Conti reported seeing tattooed men, elephant hunts, pythons, and rhinoceroses.

Lands of Spice

Conti once again returned to the sea, this time sailing to Sumatra and Java (now part of Indonesia). He and his wife now had children, and the family stayed on these islands for nine months. But Conti thought the people there were "more inhumane and cruel than any other people." During this time, he visited the Banda Islands, the only place in the world where cloves were then grown. The islands were also an important source of nutmeg and other spices.

From Java, Conti may have sailed up the eastern coast of China as far as Nanking. Some scholars, on the other hand, say that he then began his homeward journey, passing through Ciampa (now Thailand) on his way back to Ceylon. His return trip next took him across the Arabian Sea to Aden, and then up the Red Sea to Jidda (in present-day Saudi Arabia). At Jidda, Conti, his family, and his many servants began an overland trek to Cairo, Egypt.

Hardships in Cairo

Cairo is probably where Conti was forced to give up his Christian faith and adopt the Islamic religion. Conti felt that this act was a terrible sin, but he did it to protect his family. In the end, however, his wife, two of his children, and all of his servants died in Cairo from the **plague.**

In 1444 Conti finally reached Italy. The written record of his great adventure describes his return in simple words: "At last, as fortune would have it, after all his journeys by land and by sea, he arrived with his two surviving children in his native city of Venice." In 25 years, he had traveled almost as widely as Marco Polo. But unlike Polo, Conti did not have the protection of a powerful prince during his journey. It is remarkable that Conti survived his trip at all.

The record he provided helped fill in some of the blank spaces in Europe's maps of the East. Thirteen years after he returned to Venice, the great Italian mapmaker Fra Mauro began to draw his map of the world. There is no doubt that Conti's report supplied many of the details on Mauro's map.

Suggested Reading Norman Penzer, editor, *The Most Noble and Famous Travels of Marco Polo, Together with the Travels of Nicolò de' Conti* (A. and C. Black, 1937).

Cooes, Bento de. *See Goes, Bento de.*

plague contagious disease that quickly kills large numbers of people

Cook, Frederick Albert

American
b June 10 1865; Hortonville, New York
d August 5, 1940; New Rochelle, New York
Explored Arctic and Antarctica;
claimed to reach North Pole

Dr. Frederick Albert Cook was one of the world's most colorful explorers—and one of the most controversial. In the autumn of 1909, he was honored around the world as the first person to have reached the North Pole. This American physician was briefly the most famous explorer in the world. Fourteen years later, he was sitting in prison, and his claims of reaching the pole had been viciously attacked by his rival, Robert PEARY. Cook's ruined reputation was the result of a long and bizarre story.

Boyhood in Brooklyn, Adulthood in the Arctic

Growing up in New York's Catskill Mountains, Cook learned to appreciate nature's beauty and danger. He also learned to survive difficult times after his father died and his family moved to Brooklyn, New York. He worked at a vegetable stand while attending night school, then delivered milk every morning while attending medical school. The young doctor joined his first Arctic expedition in 1891,

After returning from his harrowing Arctic adventures, Frederick Cook said that he felt "exotic" in civilized society and was "native to Nowhere."

anthropologist scientist who studies human societies

Inuit people of the Canadian Arctic, sometimes known as the Eskimo

sledge heavy sled, often mounted on runners, that is pulled over snow or ice

depot place where supplies are stored

when he answered an advertisement placed by the Arctic explorer Robert Peary. Cook was hired as a medic for Peary's crossing of northern Greenland.

Two years later, Cook led his own expedition to Greenland aboard the ship *Zeta.* He returned the next year on the *Miranda.* That ship was crippled by an iceberg, ruining Cook's chance to lead an important scientific mission. For the next three years, Cook practiced medicine, but he then sailed with the Belgian Antarctic Expedition in 1898. Cook served as the surgeon, photographer, and **anthropologist,** and he was part of the first crew ever to spend a winter in Antarctica. On this voyage, Cook worked with the Norwegian explorer Roald AMUNDSEN, who thought highly of his American shipmate. After Cook and Amundsen saved the expedition from near disaster, Amundsen credited Cook with the success.

In 1901 Cook sailed north at his own expense to treat Peary, who had fallen ill during his first attempt to reach the North Pole. Cook arrived at Ellesmere Island, Canada, and found Peary in a sour and difficult mood after his failure to reach the pole. Cook swore that he would never work with his former employer again.

The First Controversy

While Peary continued his efforts in the Arctic, Cook set out on a new adventure. In 1903 he led an unsuccessful attempt to climb Alaska's Mount McKinley, the highest mountain in North America. Three years later, he tried again with Edward M. Barrill. The two men claimed to have succeeded, but recent research suggests that Cook faked a photograph showing himself at the mountain's peak.

Racing to the Pole

In 1907, while Peary was planning his final trek to the North Pole, Cook and a wealthy friend quickly made a plan of their own. They wanted the fame that would surely come to the first explorer to reach the pole. For Cook, there would also be the pleasure of robbing Peary of that great honor.

The ship *John R. Bradley* dropped off Cook and his supplies at Annoatok, 32 miles north of Etah, Greenland, on August 27, 1907. The following February, Cook began a crossing of Ellesmere Island with nine **Inuit** companions and 103 sled dogs. By March 18, he was ready to venture onto the frozen polar sea with only two of the Inuit guides. In addition to **sledges** and dogs, Cook used a folding boat made of canvas to cross the open channels of water that cut through the ice pack.

Cook claimed that on April 21, 1908, he reached the North Pole, preceding Peary's own claimed success by a year. The return trip proved even more dangerous. Cook and the two Inuit were low on supplies by the time they reached land. They were also far off course, nowhere near their supply **depot.** The three men wintered in an underground shelter near Ellesmere Island. They lived off the land, using the traditional methods of the Inuit, and returned to Annoatok in April 1909.

Claims and Questions

News of Cook's adventure did not reach Europe or the United States until September 1, 1909, just five days before Peary sent word of his own success. During that time, Cook arrived in Copenhagen, Denmark, where he was given a hero's welcome. Within days, however, Peary challenged Cook's claim, sparking a bitter and vicious controversy that continues even today.

Each explorer was backed by rival newspapers that kept the feud alive in an effort to sell papers. In fact, there were holes and contradictions in the evidence both men offered to support their claims. By the start of World War I in 1914, most scholars—and the public—thought that Cook's account was less believable than Peary's. Cook's biggest problem may have been conflicting statements made by his two Inuit companions. Peary's claim, on the other hand, was backed by the U.S. government agencies that had supported his expedition.

Continued Troubles

Cook did not give up after the controversy with Peary, even though most people now considered him a tremendous liar. In 1915 he traveled around the world, and later he made money in the Texas oil business. His dealings led to legal problems, and he was accused of selling worthless real estate. In 1923 he was found guilty of mail fraud and sentenced to a federal prison at Leavenworth, Kansas. Cook held up fairly well behind bars, considering all he had been through. He worked as a doctor in the prison hospital and edited the prison's newspaper. He also wrote about his experiences in the Arctic. Respected by his fellow inmates and the prison authorities alike, he was paroled in 1929.

Shortly before his death in 1940, Cook received a pardon from President Franklin D. Roosevelt, erasing his criminal record. No one has denied that Cook's survival in the hostile Arctic environment was an impressive feat. But nothing has erased the blemishes on his reputation as an explorer.

Suggested Reading Robert M. Bryce, *Cook and Peary: The Polar Controversy, Resolved* (Stackpole Books, 1997); Frederick Albert Cook, *My Attainment of the Pole* (Polar, 1911) and *Return from the Pole*, edited by Frederick J. Pohl (Pellegrini and Cudahy, 1951); Andrew A. Freeman, *The Case for Doctor Cook* (Coward-McCann, 1961); William R. Hunt, *To Stand at the Pole: The Dr. Cook-Admiral Peary North Pole Controversy* (Stein and Day, 1982).

Cook, James

English
b October 27, 1728; Marton-in-Cleveland, England
d February 14, 1779; Hawaii
Explored Pacific Ocean, searched for Antarctica

scurvy disease caused by a lack of vitamin C and once a major cause of death among sailors; symptoms include internal bleeding, loosened teeth, and extreme fatigue

Captain James Cook is one of the outstanding figures in the history of exploration. He made great contributions to our knowledge of the Pacific Ocean, including its islands, waters, and peoples. He also conquered **scurvy**, a disease that had long troubled sailors, and helped turn exploration into a science.

Cook may have been the greatest explorer of the 1700s, but he came from quite a humble background. He was the second of nine children born to a poor Scottish couple in a small farming village. At the age of 13, he dropped out of school to help his father in the fields and at 14 went to work for a grocer. Soon after that, the future Captain Cook went to sea.

Born in a poor English village, James Cook went on to sail around the world three times and become honored as the greatest explorer of the 1700s.

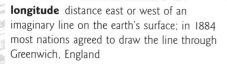

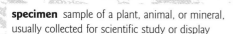

longitude distance east or west of an imaginary line on the earth's surface; in 1884 most nations agreed to draw the line through Greenwich, England

specimen sample of a plant, animal, or mineral, usually collected for scientific study or display

From Cabin Boy to Commander

Cook began his career as a cabin boy aboard the *Freelove,* a coal-hauling ship. He learned to navigate in the rough Baltic Sea and North Sea. He came to appreciate these sturdy ships as well as the seafaring life. The owner of the *Freelove* was about to promote Cook when talk spread of war against France and Germany. The young sailor then enlisted in the British Royal Navy.

Smarter and more determined than most sailors, Cook quickly worked his way up through the ranks. During the Seven Years' War against France, he was given command of the *Mercury* and sent to map the St. Lawrence River in Canada. His work helped the British capture Québec, the French city on the river.

Back in England, Cook married Elizabeth Batts in 1762. He then returned to sea. This time he went to Newfoundland, Nova Scotia, and Labrador. He drew charts of the Grand Banks that were very helpful to fishermen. While he was there, he observed a solar eclipse and used it to calculate Newfoundland's **longitude.** This achievement brought Cook to the attention of the Royal Society, an organization of British scientists.

Science on the Seas

Astronomers knew that in the summer of 1769, the planet Venus would pass across the face of the sun. This rare event could be seen from the island of Tahiti in the southern Pacific Ocean. The Royal Society wanted to send a ship to Tahiti to make observations. The government realized that such a mission would also be an ideal opportunity to search for *Terra Australis Incognita.* This Latin term means "the unknown southern continent." Many scientists of the 1700s believed that a large landmass must exist in the southern half of the earth to balance the known lands of the north.

Cook was chosen to command the *Endeavour* on a voyage to Tahiti. He was also given secret orders to search for the southern continent. The ship was a coal hauler like those which Cook had sailed as a boy, and its crew of 94 included the naturalists Joseph BANKS and Daniel Carl Solander. The expedition left Britain on August 26, 1768, crossed the Atlantic, and sailed around South America's Cape Horn. Cook stopped at Tierra del Fuego and other sites along the way so that Banks and Solander could gather plant and animal **specimens.**

Knowing how deadly disease could be on such a long journey, Cook insisted that the ship be kept clean. He also made sure that the crew ate plenty of fresh vegetables, citrus fruits, and sauerkraut. At first the sailors resisted eating the sauerkraut. But after seeing it served and eaten at the officers' dining table, the other men began to request it for themselves. For the first time in the history of naval exploration, not a single man died from scurvy.

Paradise of the South Seas

On April 13, 1769, the ship anchored at Matavai Bay, on the northwest side of Tahiti. There Cook directed the construction of Fort Venus, the crew's base for their three-month stay. During that time, Cook explored the entire island, closely observing the carefree

circumnavigation journey around the world

lifestyle of the Tahitians. He recorded details of burial ceremonies, tattooing rituals, and other aspects of the island's society.

Cook was strict but fair with his crew during their time on Tahiti, just as he was at sea. The men worked hard, but Cook also allowed them to enjoy the relaxed Tahitian social life. When it came time to leave the beautiful island, only two men thought of deserting the ship and staying behind. It is clear that Cook demanded and received the loyalty and trust of his crew. His leadership may also explain why the crew was so willing to continue the expedition, even though Cook had not yet revealed their mission.

With a Tahitian guide named Tupia, Cook sailed west to other islands near Tahiti. He claimed the entire group for England and named them the Society Islands. From there he sailed south, and in October 1769, he rediscovered the islands that Abel TASMAN had called Staaten Land in 1642. Cook spent several months circling the two main islands, proving that they were not the tip of *Terra Australis Incognita.* Today the islands are known as New Zealand, and the waterway between them is called Cook Strait. The naturalists explored the islands in great detail. Their task was difficult, since the islands' fierce Maori warriors were not as welcoming as the Tahitians.

Avoiding Disaster in Australia

Leaving New Zealand, Cook sailed west again, reaching the unexplored east coast of New Holland (now Australia). He landed at a place that Banks and Solander called Botany Bay because they collected an astonishing number of plants there. After a week, the *Endeavour* headed north as Cook guided the sturdy vessel through the maze of sea coral now known as the Great Barrier Reef. Despite his skill, the ship struck the reef and began to take on water through a gash in the hull.

The accident could have been a disaster, but Cook and his crew stayed calm and kept the ship afloat. The men patched the hole and managed to reach the Australian shore, where they made permanent repairs. The spot where they landed is today the site of Cooktown. The ship sailed again after a month of repairs. Cook headed north and charted some 2,000 miles of the Australian coastline before setting course for England. He sailed by way of New Guinea, Batavia (present-day Jakarta, Indonesia), the Indian Ocean, and Africa's Cape of Good Hope. This route completed Cook's first **circumnavigation.**

The Southern Continent

Cook came home on July 12, 1771. A year and a day later, he set sail once again. Some people, especially the scientist Alexander DALRYMPLE, still believed that *Terra Australis Incognita* existed somewhere in the south seas. Dalrymple, a wealthy Scottish nobleman, wanted to lead the search expedition. But thanks to reforms of the navy initiated by Admiral George ANSON, the more qualified Cook was given command.

This time his ship was the *Resolution,* and he was joined by a second ship, the *Adventure.* The two vessels sailed down the African

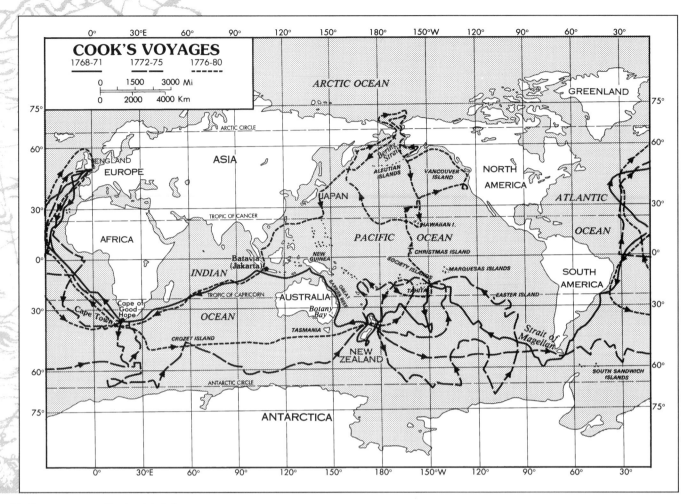

COOK'S VOYAGES

1768-71	1772-75	1776-80

0   1500   3000 Mi

0   2000   4000 Km

On his three voyages, Cook added dozens of new islands to European maps of the world.

coast. Instead of rounding the Cape of Good Hope into the Indian Ocean, they continued south, becoming the first crews to sail into Antarctic waters. Cook led the ships south through bitter cold and icebergs, but the broken ice soon turned solid, and Cook was forced to return north—much to the crews' relief. In a dense fog, the two ships became separated, but they met as planned in New Zealand three months later. In New Zealand, a landing party from the *Adventure* disappeared, probably killed by Maori warriors.

Cook spent the following months sailing the unknown waters between Australia and South America. He hoped to find *Terra Australis Incognita,* but all he saw was endless ocean and a few small islands. In August 1773, he returned to Tahiti for a month. He then visited other Society Islands, the Friendly (or Tonga) Islands, and New Zealand. In the meantime, the ships became separated and failed to meet again. The *Adventure* returned to England.

In November 1774, Cook turned the *Resolution* to the south once again. By December the ship was surrounded by icebergs, and Cook was suffering from a problem with his gallbladder, a gland near the liver. One of the naturalists on board, Johann Reinhold FORSTER, sacrificed his pet dog so that Cook would have the meat he needed to regain his strength.

When he recovered, Cook sailed for warmer waters. The crew hoped that they were finally heading home, but Cook made another turn southward. By the end of the voyage, he had sailed around the world at a **latitude** very far to the south. Although he could not get past the floating polar ice, he was able to rule out the existence of a major southern continent. Even so, he correctly suspected that a polar landmass could exist. In his journal, he wrote: "That there may be a continent or large tract of land near the Pole I will not deny; on the contrary I am of the opinion that there is, and it is probable that we have seen a part of it."

From Ice to Fire

At that point, Cook could have turned the *Resolution* back toward England, but he thought that he could still learn more about the Pacific. In early March 1775, the *Resolution* reached Easter Island and made its first landfall in four months. Cook was the first European to visit the island since the Dutchman Jacob ROGGEVEEN had discovered it 53 years before. Cook found about 700 people living on this island of fiery volcanoes. The people were friendly, but they had a practice of stealing from the Europeans nearly anything they could carry. Cook noted with interest that the islanders could easily communicate with Oddidy, a Tahitian whom he was taking to England. This led Cook to believe that the many island peoples of the southern Pacific were related.

After three days on Easter Island, Cook sailed north to the Marquesas, another group of islands that Europeans had already discovered but had not yet charted. He then sailed to Tahiti, where he and his crew received a warm welcome. Continuing west, he charted and named the New Hebrides, New Caledonia, and Norfolk Island. Next, he sailed east to return home by way of Cape Horn, the tip of South America, just in case he had missed something in his search for *Terra Australis Incognita.* He did not find the continent, but he did find and name South Georgia Island and the South Sandwich Islands.

The Third Voyage Begins

Three years and 18 days after leaving England, the *Resolution* returned to its harbor, having sailed more than 70,000 miles. Cook had lost only four men, none from scurvy. He received many honors and was promoted to captain, but he did not take much time to enjoy his increasing fame. He began recruiting for yet another voyage. Since Cook had just answered one of his day's greatest geographical questions, the British navy asked him to answer another. His new mission was to search for a **Northwest Passage.**

The navy sent two expeditions to search for the passage's Atlantic entrance. Meanwhile, Cook was to explore the Pacific north of the Bering Strait, which separated Asia and North America. He once again commanded the *Resolution,* leaving Plymouth, England, along with the *Discovery* on July 12, 1776.

The two ships sailed south to Cape Town (in present-day South Africa) and then headed into the southern Indian Ocean, where they found a group of rocky islands. Cook named them the Crozet Islands after the French explorer who had first sighted them four years earlier. He continued eastward, sailing for nearly a month through thick fog, until he reached Tasmania, an island south of

latitude distance north or south of the equator

Northwest Passage water route connecting the Atlantic Ocean and Pacific Ocean through the Arctic islands of northern Canada

This 1902 oil painting by the Australian artist E. Phillips Fox (1865–1915) is titled *The Landing of Captain Cook at Botany Bay 1770.*

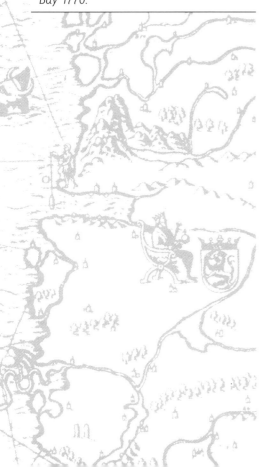

Australia, in January 1777. He anchored for four days at Adventure Bay and observed what he called the "wretched" lives of the islanders.

Lands Familiar and Unknown

Cook made several stops in the South Seas: at New Zealand, Tahiti, the Friendly Islands, and a group now known as the Cook Islands. Tensions ran high during the few weeks he spent on New Zealand. The Maori believed that Cook had come to take revenge for the deaths of the *Adventure*'s landing party. Fortunately, there were no major incidents on this visit.

Cook spent most of the summer and fall as an honored guest throughout Polynesia, the vast island region of the southern Pacific. He offered the islanders gifts of livestock from England, and again he took the opportunity to study the peoples' customs. He was the first European to note the islanders' idea of taboo, meaning something forbidden by culture or religion. He also recorded his disgust with the human sacrifices and cannibalism he saw even in Tahiti. He left the Society Islands in early December and sailed north.

On December 25, the British landed on a deserted island just above the equator and named it Christmas Island (now called Kiritimati). On January 20, 1778, they reached a group of islands that Cook named after the earl of Sandwich. These islands are now the American state of Hawaii. Cook was probably the first European to see them.

On this visit to the Sandwich Islands, Cook stayed less than two weeks. He noted the similarities between the people who lived there and those on other Polynesian islands, and he wondered how they had come to inhabit such a vast expanse of ocean. During their short stay, the British sailors also made a strong impression on the islanders, who included the pale-skinned strangers in their spoken histories.

The Arctic Ocean

The expedition spent the spring and summer of 1778 charting the North American coast from what is now Oregon to the Bering Strait, searching for the Northwest Passage. Cook anchored his ships in what is now called Nootka Sound, where he and his men were greeted by Nootka Indians in elaborate costumes—headdresses, masks, and painted faces.

Continuing north and west, the *Resolution* and the *Discovery* sailed past the Pacific coasts of Canada and southern Alaska. The farther west they sailed, the less convinced Cook was that he would find a clear passage to the Atlantic Ocean. He sailed along the Aleutian Islands and on into the Bering Sea, heading north until ice blocked his path. With the ships taking a beating from the surrounding ice, Cook decided to head for the safety and warmth of the south to make repairs. He set course for the Sandwich Islands, planning to renew his search for the Northwest Passage the following summer.

Trouble in Hawaii

When he anchored in Kealakekua Bay, he was greeted by crowds of islanders bearing gifts. On that day, January 17, 1779, Cook made the last entry in his journal. The events of the next few weeks, up to the captain's death, were recorded only by his crew.

At first the visit went well. To the Hawaiians, Cook was a god who had come to earth by sailing into their sacred bay. The island chiefs feasted with him and called him "Orono" or "Lorono," the name of their god of peace and prosperity. After two weeks or so, Cook tried to leave Hawaii, but bad weather forced him to return the ships to the bay.

Although the Hawaiians thought that Cook was a god, they did not hesitate to steal from the crew. At his many stops in the Pacific islands, Cook had grown accustomed to the islanders' habit of thievery. They simply did not think of objects as property that someone owned. Cook usually punished offenders to prevent further thefts, but he was never harsh, and he avoided the use of real force. But on Hawaii, the islanders overran the *Resolution* and *Discovery,* practically trying to take the ships apart. Frustrated, Cook allowed his men to display their weapons. The Hawaiians seemed more surprised than frightened by this threat, and the number of thefts increased. On the morning of February 14, 1779, one of the ship's small boats was missing, and Cook decided that things had gone too far.

The Death of Captain Cook

Cook decided to bring a Hawaiian chief on board and hold him until the boat was returned. When Cook went ashore, a great crowd of

Captain Cook carried this version of the British Union Jack around the world.

islanders gathered. Offshore, crewmen waited in boats, holding their guns. Tensions rose on both sides. When some of the islanders advanced toward the British landing party, a crewman fired, killing an important chief. Cook turned around to tell his men to hold their fire, but at that moment, the Hawaiians fell on him in a fury. They stabbed him in the back and then hacked his body to pieces. Four of Cook's crewmen died with him.

The captain's death left the British in a state of shock. After the islanders dispersed, some of the crew went ashore and gathered as much of Cook's body as they could, then gave him a burial at sea. The captain was 50 when he died, leaving behind his widow and three children.

Charles Clerke, commander of the *Discovery,* then took charge of the expedition, but he died soon after of **tuberculosis.** Command then fell to Lieutenant John Gore. The two ships sailed to eastern Russia, where they sent word of Cook's death back to England. They then attempted to complete their mission, heading north once again to search for the Northwest Passage. They failed, just as Cook had the year before. After a stop in Russia to repair damage caused by the ice, the two ships sailed west to England and arrived on August 22, 1780.

tuberculosis infection of the lungs

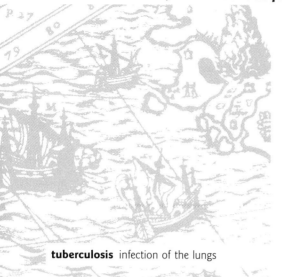

The Work of an Explorer

Cook once wrote that his ambition was "to go as far as it was possible for a man to go, and to make an exact recording of all that I saw." He succeeded, and in the process, he helped turn exploration into a modern science.

Cook opened possibilities for trade on the northwest coast of North America and throughout the Pacific. But his main accomplishments were scientific. His journals from his voyages contained detailed observations of the peoples and customs of the Pacific island cultures. He mapped thousands of miles of coastlines, and his experiments with shipboard diet virtually ended death at sea from scurvy. In his searches for *Terra Australis Incognita* and the Northwest Passage, he devoted his life to answering questions about the world.

Suggested Reading J. C. Beaglehole, *The Life of Captain James Cook* (Stanford University Press, 1974); James Cook, *Seventy North to Fifty South,* edited by Paul W. Dale (Prentice Hall, 1969); Robin Fisher and Hugh Johnson, editors, *Captain James Cook and His Times* (University of Washington Press, 1979); A. Grenfell Price, editor, *The Explorations of Captain James Cook in the Pacific as Told by Selections of His Own Journals, 1768-1779* (Heritage, 1976); Alan Villiers, *Captain James Cook: A Definitive Biography* (Scribners, 1970).

Coronado, Francisco Vásquez de

Spanish
b 1510?; Salamanca, Spain
d 1554; Mexico City, Mexico
Explored southwestern North America

In 1540 Francisco Vásquez de Coronado was the wealthy, respected governor of New Galicia, a province of **New Spain.** But he left his comfortable position to make an extraordinary search for lands of great riches. He never found those legendary places, but he did explore the land that became the states of Arizona, New Mexico, Texas, and Oklahoma. This **conquistador** traveled as far as central Kansas—farther north than anyone had gone from New Spain. Coronado's travels, along with those of Hernando de Soto, helped reveal the size and diversity of the North American continent.

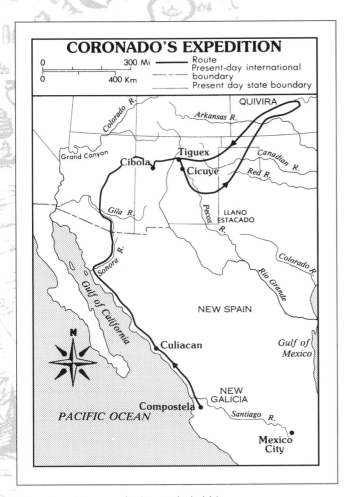

CORONADO'S EXPEDITION

0	300 Mi	──── Route
0	400 Km	- - - - Present-day international boundary
		Present day state boundary

QUIVIRA

Colorado R.

Arkansas R.

Grand Canyon

Tiguex

Cibola

Canadian R.

Cicuye

Red R.

Gila R.

Pecos R.

LLANO ESTACADO

Sonora R.

Colorado R.

Rio Grande

NEW SPAIN

Gulf of California

Culiacan

Gulf of Mexico

NEW GALICIA

Compostela

Santiago R.

PACIFIC OCEAN

Mexico City

Francisco Vásquez de Coronado led his exhausted Spanish troops on a futile search for gold in the dusty plains of the American Southwest.

New Spain region of Spanish colonial empire that included the areas now occupied by Mexico, Florida, Texas, New Mexico, Arizona, California, and various Caribbean islands

conquistador Spanish or Portuguese explorer and military leader in the Americas

viceroy governor of a Spanish colony in the Americas

pueblo Indian village or dwelling in the American Southwest, often built of sun-dried bricks

Privilege and Power

Coronado came from a noble Spanish family. Little is known of his life before he came to New Spain in 1535 with the new **viceroy,** Antonio de Mendoza. Two years later, Coronado gained fame for ending a revolt by miners in Amatepeque (near modern-day Taxco, Mexico). He also advanced his position when he married Beatriz de Estrada, a wealthy cousin of the Spanish king Charles I.

Thanks to his skills and status, Coronado was named the governor of New Galicia in 1538. In that role, he helped prepare the expedition of Father MARCOS DE NIZA, who had been assigned by Viceroy Mendoza to explore the lands north of New Spain. Marcos returned from his journey with tales of a realm called Cíbola that consisted of seven fabulously wealthy cities. Marcos claimed to have seen the cities from a distance, and Mendoza immediately made plans to find and conquer them. He chose Coronado for the task, with Marcos to serve as a guide.

Slow Progress

During the first few weeks of 1540, Coronado assembled his expedition in Compostela, a city on the Pacific coast of central Mexico. He gathered about 340 Spaniards, 300 Mexican Indian allies, and 1,000 Indian and black slaves. For food he took herds of cattle, sheep, pigs, and goats. On February 23, this enormous group left Compostela and marched along the coast of the Gulf of California to Culiacán. At that time, Culiacán was farther northwest than any other European settlement in North America.

Coronado was frustrated by the slow pace of his large expedition. There were too many causes for delay, such as the need to carry the cattle one at a time across rivers. Coronado decided to move ahead with 100 lightly equipped Spaniards and some of the Indians. He sent a soldier named Melchior Diaz to scout a route. The main body of the expedition would follow Coronado at a slower pace.

The conquistador proceeded into northern Arizona. Crossing the Gila River, he and his men headed northeast across the area that is now the Fort Apache Indian Reservation. Many of the men became ill from eating berries they found there. Then Diaz reappeared with disappointing news. He had seen what was thought to be the first city of Cíbola—merely an overcrowded village of huts.

The Great Plains and the Grand Canyon

Despite the bad news, Coronado traveled on. He crossed into what is now New Mexico and reached the Zuñi Indian **pueblo** of Hawikuh about July 4, 1540. What Father Marcos had described as a fabulous city was in fact a collection of huts made of stone and sun-dried clay. Marcos was sent back to Mexico City in disgrace. With food and morale both running low, Coronado attacked and conquered the pueblo. He made it his headquarters, allowing

Coronado's travels took him to the Texas prairie. There, he and his men were amazed to see bison, which they called "humpback oxen."

his men to rest and sending Diaz to retrieve the rest of the expeditionary force. He then sent small parties to explore other Zuñi pueblos in the area.

Next, Coronado sent a scouting party to the northwest, where his men found seven Hopi Indian villages and learned of a great river farther west. Intrigued, Coronado sent a soldier named Garcia López de Cárdenas to search for this river. That journey ended abruptly when Cárdenas reached the Grand Canyon. It was impossible to descend the steep canyon walls to the Colorado River below. Cárdenas and his men were the first Europeans to find the Grand Canyon and the first to record a sighting of the Colorado River.

Coronado also sent scouting parties to the east. One party found villages along the Rio Grande that were larger and could provide more food than the Zuñi pueblos. Coronado moved his headquarters to Tiguex, the largest of these villages. During the winter of 1540 to 1541, the Spanish endured severe weather and constant Indian attacks. Coronado brought an end to the attacks by burning several Indian prisoners to death.

The Search for Quivira

On one of his many trips away from Tiguex, Coronado met a Plains Indian whom he called "the Turk." This Indian told Coronado of a rich land to the northeast, known as Quivira. The Indian described fish as large as horses, gold jugs and bowls used for eating, and gold bells hanging from a tree. Coronado was impressed by these stories, and not wanting to return to New Spain empty-handed, he decided to seek the riches of Quivira.

On April 23, 1541, Coronado's expedition left Tiguex with "the Turk" as its guide. Heading east to Cicuye (present-day Pecos, New Mexico) and crossing the Pecos River, the men marched across what they called the Llano Estacado (the modern-day Staked Plain in Texas). Though the Indians they met gave them food, pottery, cloth, and some turquoise, the Spanish were disappointed not to find any gold or silver. Often the Indians simply fled in fear of the Spaniards' horses, a type of animal that they had never seen before.

After five weeks of wandering eastward across Texas, Coronado began to mistrust his guide. Coronado became convinced that "the Turk" was lying in an effort to get the Spaniards lost in the wilderness. When the guide confessed that this was true, Coronado executed him. Food was by then running low, so Coronado sent most of his soldiers back to Tiguex. He and 30 horsemen headed north, where the local Tejas Indians had suggested that he might find Quivira.

Disappointment in the North

The Spaniards traveled north for 42 days. They crossed the Canadian River and rode through the western part of Oklahoma before turning northeast. Reaching the Arkansas River, they crossed it and followed it downstream. At last they met some Quivira Indians (later referred to as the Wichita), who guided the Spanish to their village.

The Quivira settlement was a small group of thatched huts, not the wealthy civilization described by "the Turk." But Coronado could not bring himself to give up his search for treasure. He made several journeys into the surrounding area. He never found gold, and he did not consider the region suitable for Spanish settlements. At last he decided to rejoin his men in Tiguex.

A few Quivira Indians guided the Spanish back to Tiguex, following a shorter route than the party had originally taken. This route later became part of the Santa Fe Trail, famous for the wagons that traveled it between New Mexico and Missouri in the 1800s. Coronado spent the winter of 1541 to 1542 in Tiguex. During that time, he was seriously injured when he fell off a horse.

A Beaten Conquistador

In April 1542, the Spanish began the long march back to New Spain. It was a terrible journey. The exhausted soldiers complained constantly, and they began deserting the group as soon as they saw Spanish settlements. By the time Coronado reached Mexico City to report to Viceroy Mendoza, he had fewer than 100 men left. One soldier wrote that Coronado was "very sad and very weary, completely worn out and shame-faced."

Although he had failed to meet his goals, Coronado was allowed to continue to serve as governor of New Galicia until 1544. He then retired to Mexico City. Spanish officials questioned him for executing "the Turk" and for leaving the northern lands without setting up permanent Spanish control. A royal court found him innocent of misconduct, and he returned to his quiet retirement. But he never fully recovered from his fall, and his health remained poor until he died 10 years later.

Coronado may have considered his mission a failure, but historians see it as a remarkable feat of exploration. He opened up a vast region to the Spanish and greatly expanded the boundaries of New Spain. The names of Coronado Mountain in Arizona, the Coronado State Monument in New Mexico, and Coronado City in Kansas are reminders of his lasting importance.

Suggested Reading Herbert E. Bolton, *Coronado on the Turquoise Trail: Knight of Pueblos and Plains* (University of New Mexico, 1949); Pedro de Castañeda, *The Journey of Coronado, 1540-1542*, translated by George Parker Winship (Readex Microprint, 1966); Arthur Grove Day, *Coronado's Quest: The Discovery of the Southwestern States* (Greenwood, 1982); George Parker Winship, *The Coronado Expedition, 1540-1542* (Rio Grande Press, 1964).

Cortés, Hernán

Spanish
b 1485; Medellín, Spain
d December 2, 1547; near Seville, Spain
Explored Mexico; conquered Aztec Empire

New Spain region of Spanish colonial empire that included the areas now occupied by Mexico, Florida, Texas, New Mexico, Arizona, California, and various Caribbean islands

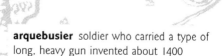

arquebusier soldier who carried a type of long, heavy gun invented about 1400

Hernán Cortés invaded Central America in 1519 with a small force of Spanish soldiers. He conquered the empire of the Aztec Indians through a combination of trickery, military skill, diplomacy, and cruelty. He then quickly brought a huge area which he named **New Spain** under Spanish control. His efforts on behalf of Spain made him a controversial figure both in his own time and today.

Choosing a Life of Danger

At the age of 14, Cortés left the Spanish town in which he grew up. He went to college to study law but left after two years for unknown reasons. The academic life may not have suited him. After a couple of aimless years, he decided to pursue a life of adventure.

In 1504 Cortés sailed on a merchant ship headed for Spanish colonies in the Caribbean Sea. He settled on Hispaniola (the island now occupied by Haiti and the Dominican Republic) and became a minor public official in the town of Azua. During the Spanish conquest of Cuba from 1511 to 1518, he served under Diego Velásquez, who became Cuba's governor.

At first Cortés had a good relationship with Velásquez. The governor appreciated Cortés's military skills, lively personality, and talent as a writer. Velásquez named Cortés mayor of the Spanish settlement at Santiago de Cuba. But trouble soon arose between the two men. Cortés was a free spirit who resisted anyone else's authority. He was accused of trying to overthrow Velásquez. Although he was pardoned, he and the governor had a strained relationship from then on.

Despite the tension, Velásquez named Cortés commander of an expedition to Mexico in 1518. Velásquez was eager to investigate the reports of two Spanish explorers that gold and fabulous temples could be found on the Yucatán Peninsula. While preparing for his new mission, Cortés learned that the governor had decided to remove him from command. On November 18, 1518, before the order could be delivered, Cortés quietly sailed out of the harbor. He got the rest of the supplies he needed at the ports of Trinidad and Havana. His final count of men and supplies included 780 soldiers, 100 sailors, 32 crossbowmen, 13 **arquebusiers,** 16 horses, and 10 canoes.

The First Encounters

Cortés first landed on the island of Cozumel, off the coast of the Yucatán Peninsula. He conquered the local Indians, pulled down their

Hernán Cortés's independent spirit helped him conquer Mexico, but as governor of a new colony, he had trouble controlling his political enemies.

conquistador Spanish or Portuguese explorer and military leader in the Americas

cacique Indian chief in Central America and South America

plateau high, flat area of land

religious statues, and began converting them to Christianity. Like all **conquistadors,** Cortés explored in the name of "God and King." If the Indians refused to convert, they were killed for being in league with the devil. On Cozumel, Cortés also found Jerónimo de Aguilar, a Spaniard who had been captured during an expedition eight years earlier. Aguilar joined Cortés as an interpreter, having learned the Mayan language from his captors.

Cortés then sailed to the coast of the mainland. He won his battle with the Indians there when they fled at the sight of horses, which had never before been seen in the Americas. Later, a group of **caciques** brought food, gold, and women to win Cortés's favor. One of the women, named Malinche (also known as Malintzin), was a noble of the Aztecs, the most powerful tribe in Central America. Malinche became Cortés's interpreter and mistress. Her skill with languages and diplomacy made her a very important member of the Spanish expedition. The Spaniards baptized her, naming her Doña Marina.

Contact with the Aztec Empire

Cortés sailed again, heading north along the eastern coast of Mexico. He landed at the harbor called San Juan de Ulúa. There he met with an ambassador sent by Montezuma, the emperor of the Aztecs. The ambassador had been instructed to find out whether the Spaniards were human invaders or messengers of the Aztec god Quetzalcoatl. The ambassador reported that the newcomers were humans, not gods, but Montezuma was still uncertain. He wondered if Cortés was Quetzalcoatl himself. The emperor sent more representatives bearing gifts of gold, hoping that the Spanish would leave.

Realizing just how wealthy the Aztec Empire was, Cortés began planning a military attack. However, he knew that he did not have permission to conquer Mexico. He solved this problem by creating his own colony, Villa Rica de Vera Cruz (now Veracruz), and named himself its leader. Having built this settlement, Cortés had all his ships destroyed so that his men would not be tempted to return to Cuba. Then he made detailed plans for the attack. He would march inland, defeat the local Indian tribes, and persuade them to fight with him against the Aztecs. During his battles with the Aztecs, he would put his Indian allies in the front lines.

On August 16, 1519, Cortés left Vera Cruz, marching his men from the hot, swampy coastal lands to the bleak **plateau** where the Tlaxcala Indians lived. The Spanish defeated the Tlaxcala, who then became Cortés's most loyal allies. Next the invasion force moved south to the city of Cholula and then headed west to a high point overlooking the Valley of Mexico. Cortés could see the center of the fabulous Aztec Empire, with its great cities and acres of farmland surrounded by lakes and volcanoes.

A Royal Prisoner

Cortés and his men marched through the valley, passing lakes and irrigated fields before crossing a drawbridge into the Aztec capital

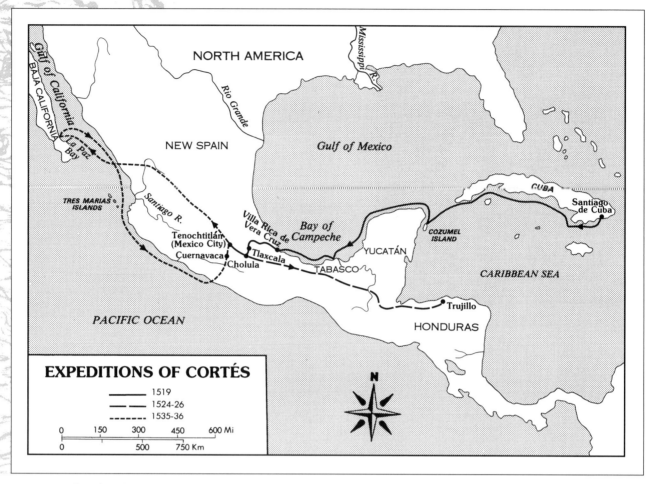

EXPEDITIONS OF CORTÉS

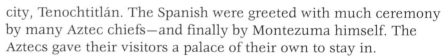

————	1519
— — —	1524-26
- - - -	1535-36

0	150	300	450	600 Mi
0		500	750 Km	

Cortés's conquests and explorations helped extend Spanish influence throughout Central America.

city, Tenochtitlán. The Spanish were greeted with much ceremony by many Aztec chiefs—and finally by Montezuma himself. The Aztecs gave their visitors a palace of their own to stay in.

Cortés realized that he could not attack as he had planned. Since the drawbridge was the only way out of the city, the Spaniards could easily be trapped there. He decided instead to take Montezuma prisoner. At a meeting with the emperor, Cortés first threatened Montezuma but then promised to treat him well if he cooperated. The Aztec leader reluctantly agreed to live with the Spaniards at their palace. By controlling Montezuma, Cortés now controlled the empire—but much fighting was yet to come.

Trouble on All Sides

Cortés received word that a new enemy was on the way. Governor Velásquez had sent Pánfilo de NARVÁEZ with a Spanish army to relieve Cortés of his command. But Cortés launched a surprise attack. He captured Narváez and won the support of Narváez's troops.

When Cortés returned to Tenochtitlán with his new army, he found the city on the verge of warfare. Pedro de ALVARADO, in command during Cortés's absence, had tried to stop the Aztec religious practice of human sacrifice. Alvarado had executed some 200 nobles, and the Aztecs were furious. Trying to restore calm, Cortés released some Aztec prisoners and asked Montezuma to talk to his

This Aztec drawing shows messengers bringing gifts to Cortés at the Spanish camp.

brigantine two-masted sailing ship with both square and triangular sails

Setting out for Tenochtitlán, one of Cortés's men wrote, "We left the camp with our banner unfurled and four of our company guarding its bearer. . . ."

angry people. They responded by pelting their emperor with rocks, and he later died from his wounds.

Cortés was forced to abandon Tenochtitlán. He fought his way out of the city on the night of June 30, 1520, which the Spanish later called the "Sorrowful Night." In the battle, Cortés lost half his men, all of his horses, and most of his captured treasure. He retreated to the plateau of the Tlaxcala, the only Indian tribe that did not desert him.

A Hard Conquest

Cortés was not ready to give up. With his usual quick thinking, he planned a naval attack on Tenochtitlán. Juan Rodriguez CABRILLO, an expert shipbuilder who had arrived with Narváez, oversaw the construction of 13 **brigantines.** The ships were then taken apart and carried to lakes and rivers around Tenochtitlán, where they were put back together. Meanwhile, smallpox, a highly contagious and fatal disease, was sweeping through Mexico, killing many thousands of Indians. The Spanish attacked the weakened Aztecs and took the city on August 13, 1521, after three months of heavy fighting.

Back in Spain, Cortés's actions in Mexico were being investigated. Velásquez and other enemies worked hard to stir up trouble, but a royal committee decided that Cortés had not done anything wrong. He received honors for his conquests, and in 1522 he was named the political and military leader of the colony of New Spain.

Cortés began to build a new capital city, which he called Mexico City, on the site of Tenochtitlán. He also sent out many expeditions to explore the surrounding area. One of these missions was led by Cristóbal de Olid to what is now Honduras. When Olid reached Honduras, he decided to set up his own colony. In 1524 Cortés was forced to travel to Honduras to arrest him, but Olid had died by the time Cortés arrived.

Less Success in Later Life

While Cortés was dealing with the problem of Olid, his enemies in Mexico City spread rumors that he was dead. When he returned, he had been replaced as governor. Cortés sailed to Spain in 1528 to try to correct this situation. The Spanish people gave him a thunderous welcome, and he was honored by the king, but he was not restored to his position as governor.

Cortés returned to Mexico and financed several explorations in search of treasure. In 1535 he led an expedition himself and tried to start a colony on the peninsula called Baja California. The mission was a failure. Cortés eventually returned to Spain, where he fell ill and died in 1547.

Throughout his career as a conquistador, Cortés was determined and brilliant—but also brutal. His conquest of the Aztec Empire was an impressive military feat. It was also a political act that helped the Spanish take control of all the lands and peoples of Central America.

Suggested Reading Francisco Lopez de Gomara, *Cortés: The Life of the Conqueror by His Secretary*, translated and edited by Byrd Simpson (University of California Press, 1964); Salvador de Madariaga, *Hernan*

Cortés, Conqueror of Mexico (University of Miami Press, 1967); Albert Marrin, *Aztecs and Spaniards: Cortés and the Conquest of Mexico* (Atheneum, 1986).

Cosa, Juan de La.   *See La Cosa, Juan de.*

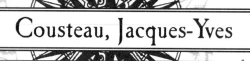

Cousteau, Jacques-Yves

French
b June 11, 1910; St. André-de-Cubzac, France
d June 25, 1997; Paris, France
Explored oceans underwater

oceanographer scientist who studies the ocean and underwater life

scuba equipment that allows a diver to carry oxygen underwater; letters stand for "self-contained underwater breathing apparatus"

Many explorers have sailed on the oceans, but few have taken the time to look beneath the waves. Captain Jacques-Yves Cousteau explored the earth's underwater world and shared the wonders he saw through films, books, and television programs. His global audience probably made him the most famous **oceanographer** in history.

Above and Below the Oceans

Cousteau had an early interest in the water. He grew up in France, but it was at a summer camp in Vermont that he learned to swim at the age of 10. During the early 1930s, as a young officer in the French navy, he obtained a pair of underwater goggles. He wore them in the Mediterranean Sea, where he saw "a jungle of fish. That was like an electric shock. . . ." His lifelong interest in the oceans had begun.

In 1943 Cousteau and an engineer named Émile Gagnan introduced the Aqua-Lung, the first **scuba** gear. With the Aqua-Lung, divers could stay underwater for long periods without using air hoses or bulky diving suits. Scuba gear is now widely used for both scientific and recreational purposes.

After World War II, Cousteau organized a research company, and in 1950 he acquired the ship *Calypso*. With his entire family, he sailed the world's oceans, taking cameras underwater and capturing marine life on film. In 1956 his motion picture *The Silent World* won an Academy Award.

Later Research Projects

In the early 1960s, Cousteau was intrigued by the idea that humans could live under the water. His *Conshelf* project proved that this was possible. He and four others lived in an underwater structure for a month in 1963. The experiment was filmed and shown on television.

At the age of 75, Cousteau began his most ambitious project ever. "Rediscovery of the World" was a years-long study of the health of the earth's waters. In 1996 the famous *Calypso* was hit by another ship, and it sank in the harbor of Singapore. Not one to give up, Cousteau was planning to build a new research vessel at the time of his death in 1997.

Suggested Reading Jacques-Yves Cousteau, Frédéric Dumas, and James Dugan, *Silent World* (Harper and Row, 1953); James Dugan, *Man Under the Sea* (Harper and Row, 1956); Richard Munson, *Cousteau: The Captain and His World* (Paragon House, 1991).

Audiences around the world were fascinated by the underwater explorations of Jacques-Yves Cousteau.

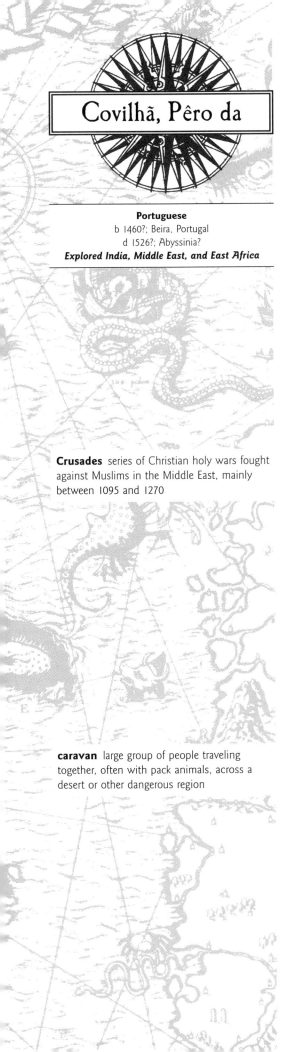

Covilhã, Pêro da

Portuguese
b 1460?; Beira, Portugal
d 1526?; Abyssinia?
Explored India, Middle East, and East Africa

Crusades series of Christian holy wars fought against Muslims in the Middle East, mainly between 1095 and 1270

caravan large group of people traveling together, often with pack animals, across a desert or other dangerous region

Pêro da Covilhã was a Portuguese explorer who traveled to India, Arabia, and Africa. His goals were to identify trade routes to Asia and to find a Christian king named Prester John. Covilhã explored the trade centers of India and visited the Islamic holy cities of Mecca and Medina. When he traveled to Abyssinia (now Ethiopia), he was welcomed and given an official position. He was also forbidden to leave the country, and he never again returned to Portugal.

As a young man, Covilhã served King Alfonso V of Portugal. When Alfonso died, Covilhã served the next Portuguese king, John II, carrying messages to Spain and perhaps also spying in North Africa. On one mission, he disguised himself as a merchant in order to befriend the ruler of Tlemcen (in present-day Algeria). In 1487 King John chose Covilhã to travel to the kingdom of Abyssinia in eastern Africa. The Portuguese believed that this region was the land of Prester John.

The Legend of Prester John

The idea that a fabulously wealthy Christian kingdom existed somewhere in the east had been popular in Europe for centuries. This land's ruler, Prester John, was believed to be immortal, thanks to a nearby "fountain of youth." Rumors of Christians in Africa or Asia may well have been based in fact. Christian missionaries may have reached those continents during the time of the **Crusades** or before. In 1165 a letter from Prester John to European rulers stirred much interest. The letter described a kingdom where beds were made of sapphires and tables were made of emeralds. The letter also called Prester John and his powerful armies the protectors of Christians everywhere.

Although the letter turned out to be a fake, it fueled Europeans' desire to find such a strong ally against the Islamic empire. By Covilhã's time, no one imagined that Prester John was quite so wealthy and powerful. But most people still believed in the existence of a kingdom ruled by Prester John's descendants. This belief encouraged many voyages of exploration and discovery.

Traveling in Disguise

Covilhã left Portugal in 1487. At that time, Prester John's kingdom was thought to be in Abyssinia. Covilhã passed through Spain and Italy on his way to Alexandria, Egypt. To protect himself where Christians were unwelcome, Covilhã disguised himself as a Muslim merchant and joined a **caravan** headed for Cairo. He traveled south from Cairo, crossing the Red Sea to Aden (in present-day Yemen). He accompanied Arab traders to the Malabar Coast of India and then turned back west through the Persian Gulf and Arabia. Still disguised, Covilhã entered the Islamic holy cities of Mecca and Medina, which were strictly closed to Christians. Covilhã then returned to Cairo in about 1493, having visited many of the leading trade centers of the east. The reports he sent to King John became very useful to later explorers such as Vasco da GAMA.

Prisoner in Abyssinia

Covilhã then went to Abyssinia to search for Prester John. When he got there, Emperor Eskender offered him a friendly welcome. The emperor gave him a house, servants, and a prestigious post as governor of one of the empire's districts. Eskender then forbade Covilhã ever to leave Abyssinia.

While Covilhã was gone, King John sent other explorers in search of Prester John. They often started on Africa's west coast and traveled inland. African slaves who had been converted to Christianity were also sent to various locations with gifts for Prester John. Thirty years passed before Europe learned of Covilhã's fate. The Portuguese king sent Francisco ALVARES as an ambassador to Abyssinia. Alvares arrived to find Covilhã, who was now an elderly man, a healthy and happy captive. Covilhã did not want to leave his African home, but he permitted his 23-year-old son to return to Portugal to be educated. As late as 1526, Covilhã was reported to be alive and well in Abyssinia.

Suggested Reading Francisco Alvares, *The Prester John of the Indies: A True Relation of the Lands of the Prester John, Being the Narrative of the Portuguese Embassy to Ethiopia in 1520*, translated by Lord Stanley of Alderley (Hakluyt Society, 1961); Eric Axelson, *Congo to Cape: Early Portuguese Explorers* (Faber, 1973).

---

da Gama, Vasco. See *Gama, Vasco de*.

Dalrymple, Alexander

Scottish
b July 24, 1737; New Hailes, Scotland
d June 19, 1808; London, England
Promoted search for southern continent

hydrographer scientist who studies bodies of water to make navigation easier

Alexander Dalrymple was certain of the existence of a legendary southern continent, but he was passed over for command of a mission to find it.

Alexander Dalrymple was a Scottish scholar, seaman, and geographer. He considered himself an expert on a mythical southern land called *Terra Australis Incognita*. His book on the subject sparked Britain's interest in a complete exploration of the Pacific Ocean. Dalrymple was also the first to hold the post of **hydrographer** to the British Royal Navy.

Dalrymple was born in 1737 into an ancient and noble Scottish family. When he was a young man, his heroes were the great explorers Christopher COLUMBUS and Ferdinand MAGELLAN. He later went to work for the British East India Company in the Pacific and eventually became its staff hydrographer. However, when Dalrymple boldly told his employers that they should change their way of working, move the company's headquarters, and put him in charge, they sent him back to England.

The Invisible Continent

Dalrymple had studied the writings of the ancient Greek geographer and astronomer PTOLEMY, who had been the first to suggest that a great southern continent existed. Ptolemy believed that landmasses, not oceans, covered most of the earth's surface. He pictured an enormous continent stretching from Africa to Asia, with the Indian Ocean an inland sea. His book *Geography* greatly influenced the European geographers who followed him.

Explorers such as Bartolomeu DIAS, Ferdinand Magellan, and Abel TASMAN had proved that Africa, South America, and Australia were not parts of one great southern continent. But geographers, including Dalrymple, refused to rule out the unknown land's existence, believing that earlier explorers had simply missed it. Dalrymple wrote a book in which he used various scientific theories to support his claims. In 1768 the British navy planned an expedition to find and claim the continent. Dalrymple offered his services as the perfect commander for the mission.

Stubborn to the End

Because Dalrymple was a member of the Royal Society, an organization of British scientists, he was asked to take part as an observer. James Cook, a highly skilled navy officer, was chosen to command the voyage. Dalrymple was so angry that he refused to go at all. Cook's expedition proved that *Terra Australis Incognita* did not exist. Dalrymple alone did not accept Cook's findings. Despite this conflict, Dalrymple remained a respected scientist. He was an expert in charting winds and currents, and in 1795 he was the first to be named hydrographer to the Royal Navy. He died 13 years later at the age of 70.

Suggested Reading Howard Tyrell Fry, *Alexander Dalrymple (1737-1808) and the Expansion of British Trade* (University of Toronto Press, 1970).

Dampier, William Cecil

English
b 1652?; Yoevil, England
d March 1715; England
Discovered New Britain; explored Australia

buccaneer pirate, especially one who attacked Spanish colonies and ships in the 1600s

William Cecil Dampier may have been the most famous **buccaneer** of the 1600s. His sharp eye and talent for observation helped him to write popular books that turned Europe's attention to the Pacific. He circled the world three times and explored the west coasts of Central and South America as well as Australia and New Zealand. Dampier kept a careful journal in which he documented winds, currents, and plant and animal life.

Dampier was born around 1652 in a small village in southwestern England. He went to sea as a youth and worked in Newfoundland and the Caribbean. In 1674 Dampier signed on at a log-cutting camp on the Gulf of Mexico. He worked there for four years, until a hurricane destroyed most of the area's timber. This disaster left him penniless.

A Pirate's Journal

Despite his problems, Dampier did not lose his adventurous spirit. He joined a band of over 300 buccaneers led by John Coxon and Bartholomew Sharp. They crossed Panama to the Pacific Ocean and sailed down the west coast of South America, raiding villages along the way. In the spring of 1681, Dampier and nearly 50 of the others set out to seek their own fortunes. Dampier started keeping a journal and wrote in it faithfully until he returned to England. He protected the journal in a hollow bamboo case sealed with wax. For 10 years, Dampier moved from ship to ship and from adventure to adventure. He wrote that he was a pirate "more to indulge my curiosity than to get wealth." His travels from South America's Cape Horn took him north to Mexico and west to the Galápagos Islands. Dampier was not a typical pirate. He drank little and stayed away from the rough men who worked alongside him.

In 1686 Dampier guided Captain Charles Swan's buccaneer ship *Cygnet* and another vessel from Mexico to Guam, an island in the Pacific Ocean. They traveled 7,300 miles in 51 days, fortunately reaching land before their supplies ran out. The *Cygnet* sailed on to the Philippines and New Holland (present-day Australia). Dampier left the *Cygnet* at the Nicobar Islands in the Indian Ocean. He spent the next three years working aboard merchant ships in Southeast Asian waters.

NIEUWE REYSTOGT
RONDOM DE
WERRELD,

waarin omſtandiglyk beſchꝛeeven woꝛden

De Land-engte van Amerika , verſcheydene Kuſten en Eylanden in Weſtindie , de eylanden van Kabo Verde , de door-togt van de Straat Le Maire na de Zuydzee , de kuſten van Chili , Peru , Mexiko ; 't eyland Guam een van de Ladrones, 't eyland Min-danao een van de Filippines; en de Ooſtindiſche eylanden ontrent Kam-bodia , Cina , Formoſa , Lukonia , Celebes, enz. voorts Nieuw Holland, Sumatra , de eylanden van Nikobar , de Kaap van Goede Hoop , en 't eyland Sante Helena.

MITSGADERS

Derzelver Landsdouw / Rivieren / Havens / Gewaſſen / Vꝛuchten / Gebierten / en Inwooners / beneffens hunne Gewoonten / Godsdienſt / Regeering / Handel / enz.

In 't Engelſch beſchꝛeeven door

WILLIAM DAMPIER,

en daarupt vertaald dooꝛ

W. SEWEL.

Met naauwkeurige Landkaarten , en kopere Plaaten vercierd.

In 's G R A V E N H A G E,

By A B R A H A M D E H O N D T , Boekverkooper op de Zaal van 't Hof / in de Foꝛtupn 1698.

Above is the title page in Dutch of William Dampier's *A New Voyage Around the World,* which may have inspired parts of Jonathan Swift's *Gulliver's Travels.*

privateer privately owned ship hired by a government to attack enemy ships

Darwin, Charles Robert

English
b February 12, 1809; Shrewsbury, England
d April 19, 1882; Down, England
Explored South America and Pacific;
developed theory of evolution

Dampier returned to England in 1691 with his journal, which is now kept in the British Library. Six years later, he published his first book, *A New Voyage Round the World.* It quickly became a best-seller. Dampier's later books included geographical information and charts, which James COOK and other explorers used on their own voyages.

Troubles at the Top

Dampier's reputation as a navigator spread. In 1698 he was chosen to command the H.M.S. *Roebuck* on an expedition to search for *Terra Australis Incognita,* the unknown southern continent. The *Roebuck* was barely seaworthy, and Dampier was not well liked by his crew, who resented taking orders from a former pirate.

Dampier explored New Holland's west and northwest coast and the island chain that now bears his name. He also discovered New Britain Island off the coast of New Guinea. On the way back to England, the *Roebuck* went down off Ascension Island in the southern Atlantic Ocean. Some weeks later, passing English merchant ships rescued both captain and crew.

Dampier was brought to trial in 1699 for his actions as commander of the sunken ship. A military court decided that he was "not a fit person to command any of Her Majesty's ships." But three years later, he was back on the high seas. He obtained a license to sail as a **privateer** off the coast of South America. But by that time, he had lost his buccaneering touch. His license was stolen, and he was thrown into jail in the Dutch East Indies for being a pirate.

A Quiet Conclusion

Dampier was eventually released, and he returned to England in 1707. A year later, another privateer hired him as ship's pilot. He roamed the Pacific for three very profitable years, but he had to sue his employer in order to get his share of the riches. After several years of legal battles, he received a large sum of money. But by then his fame had faded, and when he died a few years later, he was an unknown man.

Suggested Reading Christopher Lloyd, *William Dampier* (Faber, 1966); Leslie R. Marchant, *An Island unto Itself: William Dampier and New Holland* (Hesperian, 1988); Joseph C. Shipman, *William Dampier, Seaman-Scientist* (University of Kansas Press, 1962).

Charles Darwin was a naturalist who spent five years on a scientific expedition to South America and the Pacific Ocean. Sailing aboard the British research ship *Beagle,* Darwin studied the natural history and plant and animal life of the regions he visited. What he saw led him to develop the theory of evolution, in which he suggested that plant and animal **species** change over long spans of time to fit their environments. This theory caused a great public debate when he first described it in his book *The Origin of Species,* published in 1859.

Charles Darwin's theory of evolution is now the basis of modern biology, but it continues to cause religious and scientific debates.

species type of plant or animal

specimen sample of a plant, animal, or mineral, usually collected for scientific study or display

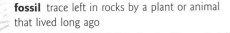

fossil trace left in rocks by a plant or animal that lived long ago

A Hobby Becomes a Career

Darwin's family taught him a love of science. His grandfather was a poet and a naturalist, and his father was a doctor. As a boy of eight, Darwin also showed an interest in science. He began collecting flowers, insects, birds, rocks, and butterflies. But he was only an average student in school, and it seemed that he could never have a career as a scientist. He tried attending medical school in Scotland but left because he disliked the sight of blood.

When he was 19, he entered Cambridge University to study to become a minister. Three years later, just weeks away from completing his studies, Darwin received an exciting offer. His friend and professor John Stevens Henslow had recommended him for an unpaid post as naturalist aboard the *Beagle*. The ship's mission was to chart the coasts of South America. Darwin accepted, and this decision was a turning point for him. He later wrote: "The voyage of the *Beagle* has been by far the most important event in my life."

Science Across the Ocean

The *Beagle*'s commander was Captain Robert FITZROY. Fitzroy's view of science was typical of the time. He believed that the goal of science was to prove that the Bible was literally true. Like most Christians of that period, he thought that the earth and all of the species on it were created together about 6,000 years ago and had stayed the same ever since. Although Fitzroy and Darwin came to disagree on such questions, they became good friends during the voyage.

The *Beagle* set sail in the winter of 1831. Darwin collected **specimens** at sea by towing a net through the water behind the boat. He continued working even when he was terribly seasick. He also went ashore whenever he could and often made long journeys on foot. He would arrange for the *Beagle* to drop him off and pick him up days or even weeks later. He explored the high mountains and the wide grasslands of South America. He also traveled up rivers to places that no European had ever seen before.

Darwin was struck by the way in which even the smallest animals struggled for survival in the natural world. He carefully studied the way different animals lived together in the same area. He also observed how they were affected by their natural environment. Darwin and an assistant collected and preserved many plants, animals, and rocks. The cabin he shared with Captain Fitzroy started to look like a museum.

The Secrets of Fossils

In 1832, on the Atlantic coast of Argentina, Darwin made an important discovery. He found **fossils** of giant prehistoric mammals. These extinct creatures resembled animals that existed in his own time. Darwin began to doubt the biblical idea that certain species had become extinct because they had not boarded Noah's ark in time to be saved from the flood. Darwin thought that too many species had disappeared for that story to be true. The fossils that he found set his new ideas in motion. He began to believe that the earth and the creatures on it do not stay the same but are constantly changing.

barnacle small, hard-shelled sea animal that often attaches itself to the bottoms of boats

In 1834 Darwin spent six weeks high in the Andes Mountains. He was 12,000 feet above sea level and about 700 miles from the Atlantic Ocean. In that place so far from water, he found fossils of seashells. Beneath a layer of seashell fossils, he found fossils of pine forests. These discoveries led him to a revolutionary idea. He came to think that the area had been a forest that was later submerged, remained underwater until it was covered in seashells, and then was thrust back out of the water in the form of mountains. He believed that these incredible changes must have taken millions of years, not just 6,000.

In 1835, three Andean volcanoes that were thousands of miles apart erupted at the same time. A month later, there was a major earthquake farther south, in Chile. Darwin noticed that the earthquake lifted the land in some areas by two or three feet. He was now more convinced than ever that the earth is highly unstable.

Evidence for Evolution

Darwin was not the first scientist to suggest that animal species evolve and change over time. In fact, his own grandfather had hinted at this possibility. But no one had figured out how evolution actually took place. Darwin found evidence to explain such a process on the Galápagos Islands. These islands are in the Pacific Ocean, about 600 miles west of South America.

While in the Galápagos, Darwin studied more than 12 different species of finches in different areas of the islands. All of these birds looked alike, but each species had a different beak. Each finch's beak matched the kind of food it ate. Those with strong beaks ate large, hard seeds that were difficult to crush. Those with more delicate beaks ate smaller seeds. Darwin realized that the finches' beaks were suited to eat the food that they could find nearby. He suggested that in an area where most of the seeds were hard, birds with strong beaks would have an easier time surviving than birds with smaller beaks. The surviving birds would reproduce, and after some time, most of the birds in the area would have large beaks. Darwin referred to this process of survival and evolution as "natural selection."

Troubling Questions and Answers

A year later, the expedition returned to Britain. After 5 years aboard the *Beagle,* Darwin was homesick, and he never again went out to sea. He spent 10 years making a catalog of all the specimens he had collected. He spent another 8 years studying one species of **barnacle** that he had found during the voyage. In 1839 he married a cousin, Emma Wedgewood. Three years later, the couple moved to the village of Down, outside London, where the family grew to include 10 children. Darwin continued his research, studying sheep, pigs, goldfish, bees, and pigeons.

He came to some shocking conclusions. He probably realized that many people would refuse to accept his theory of evolution because it went against the accepted Christian beliefs about nature. In fact, his own religious beliefs were deeply shaken. He waited until 1858 to present his ideas, in a paper written with another naturalist,

Alfred Russel WALLACE. A year later, he published *The Origin of Species.* At first the book was attacked angrily, but later it was praised and translated into almost every European language. Darwin went on to publish eight more major works.

Though he had been a healthy man during the *Beagle* expedition, Darwin never enjoyed good health after returning to Britain. His long illness may have been the result of mosquito bites that he suffered in South America. He died in Downs at the age of 73 and is buried alongside other British heroes in London's Westminster Abbey.

Suggested Reading Nora Barlow, editor, *Charles Darwin and the Voyage of the* Beagle (Philosophical Library, 1946); Charles Darwin, *The Origin of Species* (New American Library, 1986); Robert S. Hopkins, *Darwin's South America* (John Day, 1969); Alan Moorehead, *Darwin and the* Beagle, revised edition (Penguin, 1979).

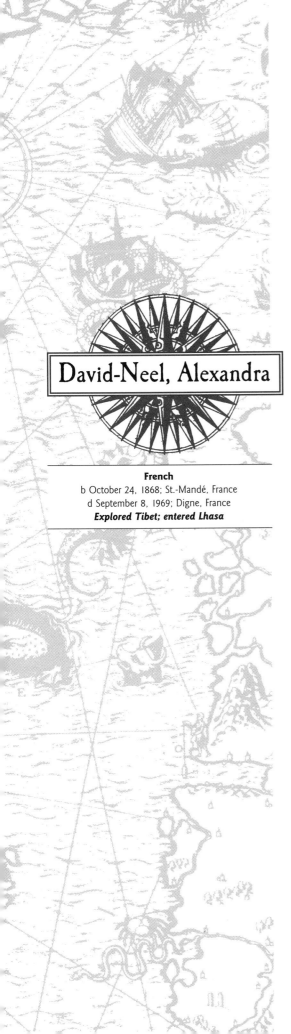

David-Neel, Alexandra

French
b October 24, 1868; St.-Mandé, France
d September 8, 1969; Digne, France
Explored Tibet; entered Lhasa

Alexandra David-Neel became famous as the first European woman to enter the forbidden city of Lhasa, Tibet. Lhasa was the home of Tibet's spiritual leader, the Dalai Lama. At the time, Tibetans considered Lhasa sacred and off-limits to foreigners. Many famous travelers, such as the great Swedish explorer Sven Anders HEDIN, had tried and failed to enter the holy city. In 1924, at the age of 55, David-Neel made the dangerous trek from China to Tibet. Disguised as a Mongolian peasant, she was able to enter Lhasa. This journey captured the imagination of the world. Her sudden fame rewarded long years of dedicated study and travel in Asia.

An Outrageous Young Woman
David-Neel was born into a wealthy French family. Her father, Louis David, was the nephew of the French painter Jacques-Louis David. He was also a friend of the novelist Victor Hugo. Political trouble in France forced Louis David to move to Belgium, where he met and married Alexandrine Borghmans. The couple returned to France in 1867, and their daughter Alexandra was born a year later.

Alexandra was a good student with an interest in religion. She also had an independent spirit. As a teenager, she often traveled alone to far-off places without telling anyone where she was going. She went to Italy by train and to Spain by bicycle. In those days, such behavior was thought to be outrageous for a young woman from a respected family. During a trip to London, Alexandra David became interested in Eastern religions. At the age of 21, she spent all the money she had inherited from her family so that she could visit India and Ceylon (now Sri Lanka).

From the Opera House to a Cave
When she returned to Europe, David studied music in Belgium and France. In 1893 she began working as an opera singer and pianist in eastern Asia, the Mediterranean, and North Africa. She also wrote essays on a wide range of topics, including women's rights and Buddhism.

In 1900 she met Philippe Neel, a passionate man who was the chief engineer of a French railroad company. These two free spirits married

A recognized authority on Tibetan Buddhism, Alexandra David-Neel gave Europeans a wider insight into the spiritual world of Asia.

maharaja king or prince in India

lama Buddhist priest or monk of high rank in Tibet and Mongolia

prilgrimage journey to a sacred place

in Tunisia in 1904. Philippe preferred to live in Europe, but he did not mind his wife traveling as much as she wished. In fact, he funded many of her trips to the East. Alexandra wrote to her husband whenever she could. When he died in 1941, she said that she had lost her greatest friend.

David-Neel became a successful writer, and she gave lectures across Europe. In 1910 she finished a book on Buddhism. A year later, she sailed to India, where she studied Eastern religions and continued to write. She also learned to speak many Asian languages.

In 1912 she traveled to the kingdom of Sikkim in the Himalaya Mountains, on India's northeastern border. She befriended the **maharaja,** who introduced her to the Dalai Lama. The Dalai Lama had fled to Sikkim to escape a Chinese invasion of Tibet. David-Neel lived for several months in a mountain cave. She then entered a Buddhist monastery, where she met a 15-year-old boy named Aphur Yongden, who later became her adopted son. Some people in the region believed that she was a goddess who had died and returned to earth.

Daring Journeys

The British were furious when they learned that David-Neel, who was French, had been crossing the border into Tibet. They wanted to keep other Europeans out of Tibet because it bordered on British territory in India. David-Neel was ordered to leave the area. She decided to return to Tibet by way of China, but first she and Yongden traveled to Burma (now Myanmar), Vietnam, Korea, and Japan. In October 1917, they arrived in Beijing, China. That winter they began a 2,000-mile trek westward across China. It was a difficult and dangerous journey. China was in the midst of a civil war, and bandits often attacked travelers on the roads.

After six months, David-Neel and Yongden reached Kumbum, on the border between China and Tibet. They stayed there for more than three years. They studied Buddhism, translated sacred texts, and made occasional trips into Mongolia and Tibet. Meanwhile, the situation in Asia grew worse. A civil war in Russia spread to Mongolia. Fighting increased in China and along the border between China and Tibet. In February 1921, David-Neel and Yongden left Kumbum.

They wandered for nearly three years. In the fall of 1923, they entered Tibet, determined to reach Lhasa. David-Neel spoke Tibetan almost perfectly. She dyed her skin and her hair with ink and dressed in ragged peasant clothes. Yongden posed as a **lama,** and David-Neel pretended to be his mother. They told anyone who asked that they were making a **pilgrimage** to Lhasa. They traveled by night and slept by day. The mountain passes were lonely, cold, and dangerous. Thieves tried to rob them, but David-Neel scared them off by firing her pistol. She and Yongden used an Eastern method to fight the cold weather—they raised their body temperatures through intense concentration. On Christmas Day, they rested in a cave.

They had nothing to eat but soup made from boiling water and pieces of leather which they had cut from their shoes.

Disguised in a Holy City

After four months of travel, they caught sight of the highest point in Lhasa—the golden roof of the Dalai Lama's palace, the Potala. David-Neel's disguise was successful, and she and Yongden entered the city safely. They wandered in Lhasa for the next two months. They even visited the Potala, which was open to pilgrims for a New Year festival. Then they happened to witness a domestic quarrel. The Tibetan police asked them to attend a court hearing. David-Neel was afraid that if she went to court, the Tibetans would discover that she was a European, so she and Yongden left the city and returned to India. In 1925 David-Neel came home to France, after 14 years in the East.

Fame and Honors

David-Neel was not the first European to enter Lhasa. But this fact did not stop the French from making her a national hero. France named her a **chevalier** of the Legion of Honor. The geographic societies of France and Belgium awarded her gold medals. Audiences packed the halls where she gave lectures, and her books became best-sellers.

In 1937 she received money from the French government to return to China and continue her studies. As World War II spread in the East, she moved to southeastern Tibet and then again to China. After the war, she returned to her home in Digne, a mountain town in the French Alps. Yongden lived with her until he died in 1955. David-Neel continued to write, and when she died at the age of 100, she was working on four major books.

Suggested Reading Tiziana Baldizzone, *Tibet: Journey to the Forbidden City: Retracing the Steps of Alexandra David-Neel* (Stewart, Tabori and Chang, 1996); Alexandra David-Neel, *My Journey to Lhasa* (Beacon, 1993); Barbara Foster, *Forbidden Journey: The Life of Alexandra David-Neel* (Overlook, 1997).

chevalier member of the French knighthood

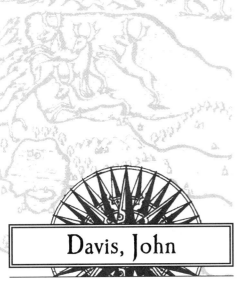

Davis, John

English
b 1550?; Sandridge, England
d December 29 or 30, 1605;
Bintan Island, near Singapore
Explored Canadian Arctic

quadrant navigational instrument used since the Middle Ages to determine distance north or south of the equator

longitude distance east or west of an imaginary line on the earth's surface; in 1884 most nations agreed to draw the line through Greenwich, England

Northwest Passage water route connecting the Atlantic Ocean and Pacific Ocean through the Arctic islands of northern Canada

John Davis was an expert navigator who invented a version of the **quadrant.** He was also a first-rate explorer. In 1587 he sailed into the waters west of Greenland and traveled farther north than Sir Martin FROBISHER had traveled 10 years earlier. But neither Frobisher nor Davis had an accurate instrument to measure **longitude,** and both were confused by faulty maps made by Nicolo Zeno. They did not realize that they had both "discovered" the same region. They both thought that Frobisher had been on the east coast of Greenland, when in fact he was on the east coast of what is now called Baffin Island. Davis was the first to chart that coast, and he left the area believing that a **Northwest Passage** might begin there. It would be up to William BAFFIN to test that theory about 30 years later.

Ready for the Land of Desolation

Davis grew up in southwestern England. As a youth, he was friends with Walter RALEIGH and Humphrey GILBERT. Gilbert was excited about the possibility of a Northwest Passage, and his enthusiasm eventually inspired Davis to undertake his own explorations. Davis

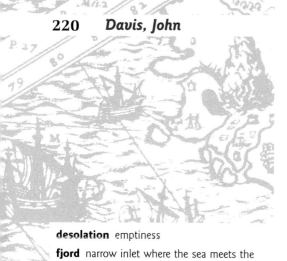

desolation emptiness

fjord narrow inlet where the sea meets the shore between steep cliffs

Inuit people of the Canadian Arctic, sometimes known as the Eskimo

kayak small canoe, usually made of sealskin stretched over a light frame of bone or wood

pinnace small boat that can sail in shallow waters

latitude distance north or south of the equator

spent 14 years at sea, becoming a trusted and skilled captain. He decided that he was ready for the Arctic Ocean.

In the 1580s, Davis, Raleigh, and Adrian Gilbert (Humphrey's brother) formed a company to carry out the adventure. They planned it with the help of John Dee, a mathematician and geographer. They also consulted Sir Francis Walsingham, an advisor to Queen Elizabeth I. A wealthy merchant named William Sanderson directed the preparations and handled the money.

In June 1585, Davis headed out to sea with two small vessels, the *Sunshine* and the *Moonshine.* On July 20 he sighted the east coast of Greenland, which he called "the Land of **Desolation.**" He rounded its southern tip and anchored in a **fjord** that he named Gilbert Sound (now known as Godthaab Fjord). When he came across a group of **Inuit,** he enchanted them with music played by four crewmen. Soon the fjord was full of Inuit in **kayaks.** The English and the Inuit traded, and Davis acquired five of the kayaks.

He then took his ships into the sea west of Greenland, in what is now called Davis Strait. He made careful notes about the local plant and animal life. Eventually the winds changed, and signs of bad weather appeared. Davis had to return to England, but he was optimistic about finding a sea route to Asia in those waters.

A Second Chance at Success

The next year, Davis led a second expedition back to Davis Strait. His two ships were joined by a larger ship, the *Mermaid,* and a **pinnace,** the *North Star.* At that time, most scientists and navigators believed that there was an open Arctic sea beyond the wall of ice near Greenland. Two of the ships were sent to try to break through this ice, but it was impossible. Those two ships returned to England. Meanwhile, Davis took the *Mermaid* and the *Moonshine* back to Godthaab Fjord, where his crew again befriended the Inuit. The English and the Inuit traded briskly and even held soccer and wrestling matches. Curious about the area's natural history, Davis took time to explore some coastal and inland areas of Greenland before heading back to sea.

When the ships encountered dangerous pack ice, most of the crewmen were frightened and wanted to turn back. Davis talked some of the men into continuing the mission aboard the *Moonshine.* He allowed the rest of the crew to return to England aboard the *Mermaid.* Although the *Moonshine* made little progress, its crew caught a large number of fish in Davis Strait. Profits from the catch helped to pay some of the voyage's costs. Davis's investors were encouraged enough to fund yet another journey to the Arctic Ocean.

Fighting Ice, Wind, and the Spanish Fleet

The third expedition began in 1587 with three ships. Soon it was just Davis and a few sailors aboard the small pinnace *Ellen.* As before, most of the men had turned back, and Davis had inspired a few volunteers to push on. He made sure that he would make a profit by setting up a fishery off Godthaab Fjord before he took the *Ellen* up the coast of Greenland to a high northern **latitude.** Ice and winds kept Davis from sailing farther north and forced him back to the south. The *Ellen* barely escaped being frozen in the ice. Davis then explored the coast of Baffin Island, where both he and Frobisher had been before. Encouraged by strong winds at the opening of Frobisher's "Mistaken Strait" (present-day Hudson Strait), Davis hoped that he had found the beginning of the Northwest Passage.

After the *Ellen* returned home, war broke out between England and Spain. Davis commanded the *Black Dog* against the Spanish Armada in 1588. The English won the battle, and as the ruined Spanish fleet drifted helplessly north to Scotland, Davis took the *Drake* to attack what was left.

Bad Luck on the High Seas

With the money he had made from his efforts against the Spanish, Davis hoped to search for the Northwest Passage from the Pacific coast of North America. He sailed to the south of Africa with Thomas CAVENDISH's expedition of 1592. But that venture failed badly, and Davis lost most of his fortune. On his way back to England, he discovered what are now the Falkland Islands (also known as the Malvinas).

Though no longer wealthy, Davis still had an estate in England. He retired there and wrote two books that summed up his experiences as a navigator and explorer. He also provided information for a globe that was designed in 1592. This globe was of great interest to those who saw it, because the outlines of the earth's continents were beginning to be known.

Davis's retirement did not last long. In 1596 and 1597, he served in the English navy. The next year, he was hired by the Dutch to pilot their first voyage to the East Indies. Davis wrote the only known account of this difficult voyage, in which the mission's commander was killed in a battle on the Malay Peninsula. Because of his experience, Davis was hired by the English East India Company for its own first voyage to the Indies, from 1601 to 1603.

A rival company hired him to sail the same route two years later. His ship was attacked by Japanese pirates off the coast of the Malay Peninsula. The pirates had boarded the ship peacefully and were having dinner with their English hosts when they suddenly drew their swords. John Davis was one of the first to be killed.

Suggested Reading Albert Hastings Markam, editor, *The Voyages and Works of John Davis, the Navigator* (reprint, Burt Franklin, 1970).

For more information about Nicolo Zeno, see the profile of Antonio ZENO in Volume 3.

---

del Cano, Juan Sebastián. See *Elcano, Juan Sebastián de.*

De Long, George Washington

American
b August 22, 1844; New York City, New York
d October 30, 1881; Lena River, Russia
Explored Russian and Alaskan Arctic

Lieutenant Commander George Washington De Long of the U.S. Navy led a daring and dangerous expedition into the Arctic Ocean. He was testing a theory that the warm summer waters of the Pacific Ocean might melt a passage through the polar ice pack. He hoped to follow such a waterway as far as possible, perhaps even to the pole itself. The voyage was financed by Gordon Bennett, a New York newspaper publisher.

George Washington De Long searched for the missing Arctic explorer Charles Francis HALL. In later years, rescuers would search the Arctic for De Long.

Bennett knew that if the theory was correct, the results would be spectacular. In exchange for Bennett's support, De Long promised to let Bennett's newspaper publish the mission's daily log. De Long made entries in the log right up to the day he died from starvation and severe cold weather.

Frozen in the Ice

In the summer of 1879, De Long entered the Arctic Ocean through the Bering Strait, which separates Siberia and Alaska. His ship, the *Jeannette,* was caught by rapidly freezing ice near Herald Island on September 5. The ship drifted northwest, trapped in the ice pack, for almost two years. In the summer of 1881, a sudden shift of the ice crushed the *Jeannette* to pieces. De Long and 32 crew members managed to escape the wreck in three small boats. They turned the boats into sleds and dragged their supplies over the frozen sea, hoping to reach Russian settlements.

After a long and difficult haul, the explorers reached the New Siberian Islands at the end of July. They sailed the boats on the open waters of the Laptev Sea but were separated in a storm. One boat was never heard from again, but the other two landed successfully at the mouth of the Lena River, on the coast of Siberia. Tragically, the survivors were separated again. A party led by George Melville, the expedition's chief engineer, made it to Yakutsk in December 1881. Melville immediately set out to save De Long's group. He found only two survivors. De Long had died over two months earlier, at the age of 37.

The *Jeannette's* Surprising Journey

Though many expeditions had met with disaster in the course of Arctic exploration, De Long's voyage was set apart from the rest by a strange event. Three years after the sinking of the *Jeannette,* the ship's wrecked remains washed up on the shores of Greenland, having floated halfway around the world. Scientists realized that the polar ice pack drifts clockwise around the North Pole. A few years later, this knowledge inspired the Norwegian explorer Fridtjof NANSEN to repeat the *Jeannette's* drift in a specially designed research vessel called the *Fram.*

Suggested Reading Emma Wotton De Long, *Explorer's Wife* (Dodd, Mead and Company, 1938); Leonard F. Guttridge, *Icebound: The* Jeannette *Expedition's Quest for the North Pole* (Paragon House, 1988); A. A. Hoehling, *The* Jeannette *Expedition: An Ill-Fated Journey to the Arctic* (Abelard-Schuman, 1969).

---

de Novaes, Bartolomeu. See *Dias, Bartolomeu.*

D'Entrecasteaux, Antoine Raymond Joseph de Bruni.
See *Entrecasteaux, Antoine Raymond Joseph de Bruni d'.*

---

de Soto, Hernando. See *Soto, Hernando de.*

Dezhnev, Semyon Ivanov

Russian
b 1605; Veliki Ustyug, Russia
d 1672; Moscow, Russia
Sailed through Bering Strait; explored Siberia

czar title of Russian monarchs from the 1200s to 1917

sable mammal of northern Europe and Asia, related to the mink and the weasel

Semyon Dezhnev made a major discovery in 1648, but he failed to report it properly, and his feats were almost forgotten. He was the first European known to have sailed through what is now called the Bering Strait. This narrow northern waterway separates Siberia and Alaska. By sailing through it, Dezhnev discovered that Asia and North America are not connected by land. But because he could neither read nor write, Dezhnev kept no written records of his voyage. The news of his discovery did not make it back to Europe from the distant outposts of Siberia. Vitus BERING sailed into the same strait 80 years later and announced his own success right away. Bering is now well known to history, and the strait is named after him. Dezhnev's achievement was finally recognized many years later.

Not much is known about Dezhnev's early years. He probably grew up in the European part of Russia. Somehow he gained experience as a sailor and then signed on to work for the Russian **czar.** He was sent to Siberia to collect tribute from the people. Siberian villages were forced to pay tribute as a sign that the czar was their ruler. In this way, Russia extended its influence all the way from the Ural Mountains to the Pacific Ocean.

The Sea of Ice

Records show that Dezhnev was sent to work in northeastern Siberia, where he helped build the first Russian outpost on the Kolyma River. Many Russian traders were drawn to this area, attracted by reports of rivers farther to the east. They had heard that the region was a rich source of **sable** furs, walrus tusks, and silver. There was soon great interest in exploring that area east of the Kolyma River. The terrain was rough, and great risk and hardship would be involved. But adventurers dreamed of great fortunes and were willing to face the challenge.

In 1648 Dezhnev was selected to lead an expedition to the east. He was told to find villages along the way that had not yet paid tribute to the czar. Dezhnev and about 90 explorers and traders sailed north on the Kolyma River and into the Arctic Ocean. They traveled east along the Arctic coast in seven ships called *koches.* These ships had strong hulls designed to survive the pounding they would take in the ice-filled waters of the Arctic Ocean. Even so, four ships were lost by the time the small fleet sailed out of the Arctic. Explorers who braved the Arctic seas later on were amazed that any of the ships had made it through at all. Dezhnev then led the three remaining koches south through what is now called the Bering Strait and into the sea beyond, which was later named the Bering Sea. With Siberia on the west side of the strait and Alaska to the east, Dezhnev could see that Asia and North America were separate continents.

Little else is known about the actual voyage. The next time Dezhnev's party was sighted was in September 1648. The Russians fought with the Chukchi people who lived on the nearby Chukotski Peninsula (also called the Chukchi Peninsula). By then they had lost another ship, and before long the last two ships were also wrecked.

Dias, Bartolomeu

Portuguese
b 1450?; Portugal
d May 24, 1500; at sea, off South Africa
*Explored African Congo;
discovered Cape of Good Hope*

In the Service of the Czar

It took Dezhnev and his men about 10 weeks to walk from the site of their last shipwreck to the mouth of the Anadyr River. They built new boats and continued up the river to the region of the Anual people. There Dezhnev began to carry out his task of collecting tribute. His usual method was simply to take control of a village—by force if necessary. Then he would take hostages and hold them until the proper amount of tribute was presented. Dezhnev also used his position to build his personal fortune. He often collected furs and ivory tusks for himself in addition to what he collected for the czar.

Dezhnev spent the next 12 years exploring the uncharted areas of Siberia and gathering tribute from the people he encountered. His work took him to regions along the Lena and the Yana Rivers. In 1654 he asked to be taken off the job, but another five years passed before his replacement arrived.

In 1661 Dezhnev traveled to the Russian city of Irkutsk with furs, silver, and more than two tons of walrus tusks. He gave a full report of his mission, describing in detail his hardships, wounds, debts, and costs. He then requested that he be paid the salary owed to him for his 19 years of service.

In the end, Dezhnev had to go all the way to Moscow, the Russian capital. He presented his case to the czar's agency in charge of Siberia and finally received his pay. He then returned to eastern Siberia with his nephew. There he served as an officer on the Olenek River for several years. After a short time on the Vilyui River, he took a job protecting a shipment of furs to Moscow. The trip took two years. He arrived in Moscow safely and died there two years later.

Suggested Reading Raymond H. Fisher, *The Voyage of Semen Dezhnev in 1648: Bering's Precursor* (Hakluyt Society, 1981).

Bartolomeu Dias commanded the first European expedition to sail past the Cape of Good Hope, the southernmost tip of Africa. He found that point almost by accident. But his discovery opened the sea route to Asia that Europeans had been hoping to find for decades. On his historic voyage, Dias added some 1,260 miles to maps of the African coast. In later years, he took part in the Portuguese discovery of Brazil.

The Unknown South

Dias was born in Portugal sometime around 1450. Some historians believe that several of his older relatives were also sailors. In 1481 he joined an expedition to the part of Africa's west coast that was known as the Gold Coast. Six years later, Portugal's King John II gave Dias command of three ships and sent him to find the southern tip of Africa. Since the early 1400s, the Portuguese had sent sea captains such as Gil EANNES and Diogo CÃO south along Africa's west coast. The missions had made steady progress, but no one had found the end of the coastline. It seemed to stretch on forever. Dias was instructed to continue his countrymen's work, find the southern

Bartolomeu Dias was honored by his country with this stamp, issued by Portugal in 1945.

cape, and sail around it. On the other side of Africa, he was to search for the legendary land of Prester John, a Christian king who was said to rule a land of great riches in the east. King John of Portugal was also eager to find a sea route to the Indies because trouble in eastern Europe and central Asia had closed overland trade routes between western Europe and eastern Asia.

Dias left Lisbon in the summer of 1487. Of his three ships, he used one—commanded by his brother Pedro—only to carry supplies. That way he and his men would have enough food and water to stay at sea for many months. He also brought several Africans who had lived in Europe and so could help communicate with any African peoples the explorers might meet. Dias sailed south for four months, stopping along the way to trade, and soon passed the stone pillar left by Cão in what is now Namibia. The stone marked the southernmost point yet reached by the Portuguese. As he continued south, Dias left pillars of his own along the coast.

A Stormy Discovery

By the end of December, Dias's ships had passed the Orange River, just to the north of present-day South Africa. The ships then sailed into a terrible storm. Fierce winds blew them southward for the next 13 days. When the storm finally ended, Dias sailed east, expecting to spot Africa's west coast once again. When he did not find any land, he headed north, reaching Bahia dos Vaquieros (present-day Mossel Bay) on February 3, 1488. The coast certainly looked like part of Africa, but Dias did not yet realize that he had rounded the cape. He was on the southern shores of Africa, about 200 miles east of the Cape of Good Hope.

Dias did not stay long at Bahia dos Vaquieros. Warriors of the Hottentot tribe that lived there greeted the Portuguese by throwing stones, and Dias killed one of these attackers. He then sailed east and landed on an island in Algoa Bay, which he named Santa Cruz. This was probably the first ground past the cape ever walked on by a European. Dias continued sailing east for a few more days until he reached a river, which he named Rio de Infante in honor of the commander of his second ship.

Dias would have sailed on in search of the Indies, but his frightened crew begged him to turn around. He did so only after they signed letters that said that he was a brave and skilled navigator. Dias hoped that these documents would support him if the king demanded to know why he had turned back before reaching Asia.

Return to Portugal

As he sailed west on his way home, Dias finally spotted the cape he had been sent to find. He did not know that the Cape of Good Hope was actually not the southernmost point in Africa. That honor belongs to Cape Agulhas, about 160 miles to the east. The rest of the return voyage was uneventful—with one exception. Dias had left the supply ship behind at Guinea, and when he found it, six of its nine crewmen were dead, and all of the supplies on board had been stolen.

Dias brought his expedition back to the port of Lisbon in December 1488, 16 months and 17 days after leaving. His success frustrated the hopes of a little-known Italian navigator named Christopher COLUMBUS. At that time, Columbus was trying to convince King John II to finance a voyage to the Indies that would sail west, not east as Dias had done. The king might have been interested had Dias not found the cape. But now it looked as if Portugal's route to Asia was open, so Columbus had to look to Spain for support.

A Little Fame and an Early Death

World maps based on the ideas of the Greek scientist PTOLEMY showed land connecting southern Africa with Asia, making the Indian Ocean an inland sea. Dias's voyage, and that of Vasco da GAMA nine years later, showed that the tip of Africa was not connected to land to the east. Dias began the long process by which Europeans abandoned their faith in Ptolemy's writings and began to form their own opinions about the world.

But Portugal could not follow up on Dias's discoveries right away. The country had a tense relationship with Spain as well as other problems within Portugal. In those difficult times, Dias did not receive the honors he deserved as a hero of exploration. Even so, in 1494 he was named to prepare a fleet of ships to be led by Gama. Three years later, the ships sailed for India by way of the Cape of Good Hope. Dias made the trip as far as the Cape Verde Islands, off Africa's west coast. The new Portuguese king, Manuel I, had ordered him to leave Gama and set up a trading post on the islands. The post was a success, and Dias then started another one on the continent's east coast.

In March 1500, Dias sailed on his last voyage. He commanded a **caravel** headed for India with the fleet of Pedro Álvares CABRAL. The ships sailed south from the Cape Verde Islands and crossed the equator. When they encountered the **trade winds,** Cabral was forced to the west. As a result, the explorers landed on the coast of Brazil at what is now Pôrto Seguro. After about a month, the fleet left Brazil to return to its original route south of Africa. Somewhere near the Cape of Good Hope, a tremendous storm sank four of the ships, including the one commanded by Dias.

Suggested Reading Eric Victor Axelson, *Congo to Cape: Early Portuguese Explorers* (Barnes and Noble, 1973).

> For a map of Dias's route, see the profile of Vasco da GAMA in Volume 2.

caravel small ship with three masts and both square and triangular sails

trade winds winds that blow from east to west in the tropics

---

d' Iberville, Pierre Le Moyne. See *Iberville, Pierre Le Moyne d'.*

Doughty, Charles Montagu

English
b August 19, 1843; Leiston, England
d January 20, 1926; Sissinghurst, England
Wrote about his travels in Arabia

geology the scientific study of the earth's natural history

Charles Doughty lived for two years among the bedouin, the wandering tribes of the Arabian desert. He wrote a detailed account of the region and its people. This volume, *Travels in Arabia Deserta,* attracted little attention when it was published in 1888. But since then it has been recognized as a masterpiece of travel writing.

A Passion for the Desert

Doughty studied **geology** and literature at Cambridge University. A trip he had made as a young man to the Middle East inspired his

caravan large group of people traveling together, often with pack animals, across a desert or other dangerous region

plateau high, flat area of land

Charles Doughty was a serious, quiet scholar whose greatest passion was the history and daily life of Arabia.

life-long interest in Arabia. When his studies were completed, he spent a year in Damascus (in present-day Syria) learning Arabic. He then disguised himself as a Syrian Christian and joined a **caravan** bound for Mecca (in what is now Saudi Arabia). Doughty traveled with the caravan as far as Madayin Salah (now in eastern Syria). He stayed there for several months, studying tombs and monuments in the region. He made copies of their engravings by placing paper against hard surfaces and rubbing the paper with a special crayon. Doughty sent his rubbings to British officials in Damascus. He then spent the next few months living with a bedouin family in the Arabian wilderness.

Doughty shared many adventures and hardships with his Muslim hosts. He moved with them as they sought fresh pasture for their camels. Each day he recorded details of bedouin household activities and daily life. Doughty and the bedouins wandered south through the hills and deserts of Arabia. Then he decided to join a party headed for the Harra **Plateau,** which is made of black lava. Doughty described this region as an "iron wilderness" where he found a "bare and black shining beach of heated volcanic stones."

Seeing and Learning

Doughty also spent some time with the Moahib tribe and the Bishr tribe as they traveled to Hail (now in Saudi Arabia). Along the way, he saw many strange animals, including antelope with straight horns. The weary scholar pushed on, making his way to several other cities that are now in Saudi Arabia and studying the area's Jewish history. Finally, Doughty returned to Damascus to collect his rubbings. He then traveled to Naples, Italy, where he wrote his account of his travels. His work is a classic description of the land and people of the Arabian desert.

Suggested Reading Charles Doughty, *Travels in Arabia Deserta,* edited by H. L. MacRitchie (Bloomsbury, 1989); Stephen E. Tabachnik, editor, *Explorations in Doughty's Arabia Deserta* (University of Georgia Press, 1987).